THE CARIBBEAN WRITER

Volume 18
2004

Editor
Marvin E. Williams

Editorial Board
David Edgecombe   Patricia Harkins-Pierre
David Gould   Kim Dismont Robinson

Managing Editor
Quilin B. Mars

Advisory Editorial Board
Opal Palmer Adisa   George Lamming
Kamau Brathwaite   Laurence Lieberman
Alwin Bully   Earl Lovelace
Edwidge Danticat   E. A. Markham
Zee Edgell   Caryl Phillips
Merle Hodge   Olive Senior
           Derek Walcott

Front Cover Art   "Hauling the Catch" Kathy Carlson
Reproduced from an originial painting
by Mango Tango Art Gallery

Distributed by Lexicon Ltd. (Trinidad), Novelty Trading
Company (Jamaica) and Ubiquity (U.S.)

Indexed by the Index of American Periodical Verse and Book
Review Index

THE CARIBBEAN WRITER

The Caribbean Writer is an international literary anthology with a Caribbean focus, published in the summer of each year by the University of the Virgin Islands.

President
LaVerne E. Ragster

Provost
Gwen-Marie Moolenaar

Vice Provost for Research and Public Service
Henry H. Smith

The Caribbean Writer, University of the Virgin Islands, RR 02, Box 10,000, Kingshill, St. Croix, USVI 00850; Phone: (340) 692-4152; Fax: (340) 692-4026; Email: qmars@uvi.edu

Visit our website
www.TheCaribbeanWriter.com

and see contributors' biographies, poetry, short fiction, essays, translations, interviews and book reviews from past and current editions, prize winners, submission guidelines, ordering information and a searchable index to all previous volumes. Volumes may be purchased on-line now.

Madeline Meehan

CONTENTS

POETRY

SHORT FICTION

SPECIAL SECTION: Edwidge Danticat

SPECIAL SECTION:
Virgin Islands - Two Cultural Icons

BOOK REVIEWS

IN MEMORIAM
Errol Gaston Hill
August 5, 1921 - September 15, 2003

POETRY

"Bomba"   Hilda Lewis Joyce

The Rhythm of it All

Sue William Silverman

Standing on a wood stool ironing my Pluto hankie, drizzling
water stored in Father's old wicker-weave St. John's Bay Rum
bottle, the way we dampened cotton back then, tropical rain
showering ashore, pinging corrugated tin roofs, curling hair
at my nape, lizards skittering verandahs, termites riddling
books, furniture, me in red madras, buffalo-hide sandals,
sucking sugar cane for lunch, the way it tasted

climbing 99 Steps, Dronningens Gade up Government Hill,
hibiscus, flamboyants, cerise bougainvillea weeping over
whitewashed *chevaux-de-frise* spiked with shards of glass,
the way they kept us separate back then, higher up volcanic
sweep, Caribair arcing mountain peak, *S. S. Morro Castle*
cruising white past Hassel Island, Charlotte Amalie, tourists
in Bermudas, sun burns, straw hats thinking paradise

smelling Nile-green moscovado canebrake, thwack of cutlass,
    machete,
saying *meddle, bobbinet, for true, calabash, catch trouble,*
    listening
Sylvanita's Anancy stories back then, *a wealthy black king of*
    Guinea,
must be, morning banana boats knocking docks, stores selling
roasted breadfruit, stewed cashew—fields of fever grass trilling
bananaquits, fading in noon heat, swimming Magens Bay,
    garlands
of seaweed in my hair, tart salt-crusted sea grapes, days
    lingering

dancing Carnival merenge *all night Mary Ann*, moko-jumbies
    swaying tall
on stilts and mirrors, guava ice, snake weed tea, coconut fritter,
    what we lived
on back then, women topped in headties, laden baskets, men in
    Calypso
shirts, bim-bams, maraca gourds rattling beans, parading skull
    and crossbone

floats—Blackbeard and Bluebeard sailing Main to Emancipation
       Park, fortune
tellers, spells and voodoo, palm-frond booths, games of chance,
       scarlet tanager
feathers, sequined masks, believing in invisible spirits

touching rubies and emeralds, Beretta Center, cuckoo clocks,
Little Switzerland, bells of All-Saints Parish tolling colonial
time back then, mahogany barreled rum in Riise's, the way
       white
parents drank *cuba libres*, men in linen, women draped silk
       guipure
dancing, children leading goats and donkeys, Market Square,
sliced Bombay mangoes, orange leaves burn for luck, opening
hurricane shutters, marooned in circular summer

waving at the *Danmark* anchoring beside mounds of bauxite,
square-rigged sails billowing sunlit sailors starched white
suits and caps, island girls awaiting dance at the Grand back
then, hair curled, braided, tropical dresses, steel drums
pong-ponging "Coconut Woman," "Gimme de Dark Kimono,"
up mountain, home later, ship below aglow with flambeaux,
dreaming of bijous, foreign sailors

staring out paneless windows from school desk, Antilles,
       ignoring
French verbs, math exacting, back then, trade winds skimming
       seas
and shore, rustling royal palmed verandahs, trailing mimosa,
       frangipani
across savannahs, red-streaked limestone dusk. Nights, in
       mahogany
four-poster, gauzy marquisette netting, tasting rain forests,
       hearing
the breath of lignum vitae, scenting coral reefed azure water,
       touching
the tail of the mongoose, seeing the heart of the island, with all
of our only senses.

Island

Mary Kate Azcuy

The little propeller plane takes off on a sand bar,
dredged, pounded down chalky, white sand,
mixed with skeletons, shells hardened to cement;
this is our graveyard ascent.

The azure, seafoam, keyhole waters migrate—
in a blue-green-pale-white ballet, a ceaseless swaying
that is in harmony with the sea's dependable moon.

Red and green firecracker plants, proboscis tubes,
and yellow flaming tongues of life hang onto the flowered
shrubs at the sandy exit from the sea.

Palms sit centered on this stage,
where brown jumping spiders live without webs,
freelancers who devour their prey,
below them cunning sand mounds hide biting,
red fire ants.

The seashell-filled waters have been picked over.
As the sun descends off the ledge of the world
and closes its orange/pink eye in tears—
the shadows swim, tails directing
baby lemon sharks, six-foot tigers, hammer heads.

Screw pines' crooked trunks grow like giraffe necks,
enormous palm leaves and giant pine cone fruits, bend
in orchestration with the hiding light.

The sapphire sea combs across the sandy beach
leaving little trademark ripples of seeded beds.
Slowly like the arms of a sun-warmed lover
each wave moves back and forth;
the air moves lightly and the breath of all is.

The sun rests, life clatters, and the sinking eye
closes into its sea of tears.
Descending, a lost immigrant,
I hold to the image for a brief moment
awaiting.

Havana Morning

James Plath

Not too far from the government
stores, before dawn assembles
block-long lines for bread and
milk and gasoline coupons,

Near the opera house, where ballet
dancers arced last night like lightning
across Midwestern skies, Cervantes
nodding in approval somewhere,

Across from the Parque Central,
its streets both repair shop and
showroom for high-sheen
Edsels, Studebakers, Chevys,

Inside the great hotel, with its gold
trimmed chíc and deco statues,
the two of us sipping respite
in a café full of empty chairs,

Two roosters so close they could be
parrots on our shoulders announce
no eggs, and no chickens, in a
voice so haltering it begs that
the messenger not be shot.

Keeper of the Bells

Toodesh Ramesar

1

5 am, and the cocks are all asleep or else eaten,
or more sensibly, just saving that last guttural hurrah
for Christmas; why scream out like a crazed alarm clock,
like a schoolmaster, like bad news in the morning paper?
The day will come all gift-wrapped with its load of burden,
and the only sound stirring is the soul-buzzing silence
steaming in its mist-laden cauldron of darkness;
that moment of contemplation, have I done this,
have I done that, and to what end, pray darkness, tell.
That's before the bell-beaten, bell-trodden morning
hurriedly emerges with its sharp array of glinting knives.
Leaves wave their usual, imperceptible, dew-wet goodbyes,
almost on the sly, as if knowing what you'll never know,
what the day portends or maybe it's just your conscience.
While dogs slowly crawl into the shade to be their own masters,
where the only signature they scrawl is their homely smells.

2

You brace your ear in the crisp morning air
scanning the momentary calm of the jagged breadline
of the horizon, broken like the jerk and stop of the maxi,
avoiding that local delicacy, breakfast news of murder and robbery,
and in the lines, orderly as a prison's, the children's roar
drown what's left of the warbling tune of nesting birds,
and as a jail's orderly, you belt out the rules in subdued clues,
a benevolent smiling monster preaching law and order,
drowning out whatever music was the early morning—
the still music of the dew, the lush green wet with lust,
the sunlight peeping out like desire as the wind ruffles
skirts and heels; but these you deny in the mournful coil
of anthem and prayer, as you deny the world for the father,
a world wicked and cruel, a snare and trap for the innocent,
news that the young greet with a deserved glum and ear indifferent.

3

I'm keeper of the bells, clockwatcher of creeping sunrise
and the fading purple of sunsets. I'm that fly
darting about in the sweatbox of midday,
in the midden of papers, files of mystery,
invigilator of sudden noises, curses, knives,
smeller of toilets, dustbins, drains and bric-a-brac.
I'm the one with beams of chalkdust in my eyes
making a fuss about the hazy-lazy-laid-back glimmers in others.
I'm your usual aggressor, your knot-headed problem-solver,
a problem by itself since I'm usually made out to be
the first worst example of human error,
how I'm not made, my tone, my character, etcetera.
Every problem brings me face to face again with my mirror.
In defense I blurt and shout about duty, respect, earning your meal,
trying to plug all the holes that are breached in that torn fishnet
called authority. Our torn fishnets of schools don't easily heal.
I, keeper of the bells, with all the noises in my head.
I, disoriented with familiar smells, flitting hither thither,
a fly trapped in the maelstrom of chalkdust, voices, heat.
Just trying desperately to earn my keep, and a very late meal.

The Hardest Love Poem

Lauren K. Alleyne

I will speak of you   my islands

seal your fiery sun in my words   bolt your wildness down
   in Time's New Roman, size 12 font, one-and-a-half inch
     margins, single spaced.

I want to crack your heart open   ma patrie   catch the rhythm
   of your limbo, the beat of your calypso your steel your soca.

I will make this poem your poem   madre mia   burn:

  hot   like kutchela like anchar like chow, like asphalt
    steamed in sun, like Carnival like the twitch of broad hips;

     red as cherries as hibiscus blooms, as the balisier,
       as the wing of the Ibis in flight;

        white as the break of Las Cuevas waves, as Maracas sands &

         black   as the land's blood deep drilled and plenty,
           as the fields of earth at the root of your sweetness.

I want your spirit to haunt this house with your magic
   your melody   La Trinité   with your music that drives
                      my singing.

The Twelve Foot Neon Woman on Top of Marla's Exotik Pleasure Palace Speaks of Papayas, Hurricanes, and Wakes

Loretta Collins

Look, with that scaffold up my back,
I was feeling Christ-like, like the stone Xavior
on the rock pinnacles of Río de Janeiro.
Felt like conducting the bloody symphony
of carnaval in Río's Sambodrome, or stalking
through the streets like Oya, orisha of whirlwinds
and cemeteries. Felt like flying to Guadeloupe,
Point-á-Pitre, where Kweyol rap booms through
the graveyards. Felt like landing on the black and white
checkerboard crypts of Morne-á-l'Eau.
Felt like it would free me from mourning you.
Felt like tasting of salt, and reggae, and rude boys.
Felt like sunning myself on the walls of the Fortaleza.
Felt like stretching my electric legs.
Felt like having daughters, big round brown
ones, who dance bomba in green skirts
and splash away from the crystalline jellyfish
and darting diamond angels of Aguadilla and Luquillo.
Felt like never cooking again, especially for you.
Felt like eating salty alcapurias con yucca y guineo.
Felt like banishing the tired crone in me, the one
begging Obatala for healing, patience, and wisdom.
Felt like riding a Shango train song all the way home,
letting the blues of it, and the R&B of it, and the funk
of it, and the beguine of it, and the mento of it,
and the quadrille of it rattle my hip bones to heaven.
Felt like starting a fire. Felt like starting a really big
conflagration to burn the urban plantation.
Felt like dressing in glass beads and silver.
Felt like tracking hurricanes, felt like drinking
tea of anise and lime peels. Felt like taking a bush bath

to cure the you in me. Felt like playing the cuatro
at a wake. Felt the Chupacabra in me rising—
Puerto Rican, blood-sucking soucriant.
Check it out. Nine thousand websites
have reported sightings of me, a creature
who terrifies Paso Finos in the fields, drains
the blood of fowls, ram goats, and pigs without
tearing flesh. The spines ridging my back
are raised. See the warning?
So I got down from the scaffold, baby,
and I switched off my neon tits, blink, blink. . .
When you call, I'm not home. I'm listening
to Stevie Wonder. I'm listening to my daughter
listen to Sister Carol who chats, singjay stylee,
about the natural jacuzzi I have in my rainforest backyard.
The flamboyant flames, the papayas are lush,
and neighbors give me star fruit and poma rosa by the bag.
Why did I let you bring me down, Papi?
Mamma and daddy only taught me how to sing
the blues; you taught me how to write them.
My only tears are for history, now.
Felt like wearing a cornflower blue dress, hem
trailing the water I walk on, tossing stars
into sea foam. Felt like weaving
Pennyroyale into my hair. Felt like writing
my son and daughter all my love songs—
each one ending with the words "fyah burn."

Different Moons

Susan Broili

"We don't make our short meetings more frequent,
thus our fate looks after our peace of mind."
Anna Akhmatova

We will not wake to the same birdsong,
or make lazy, morning love.
We will not share mangoes at a daily table,
or sit on the veranda,
after the dishes are done,
and watch the sun set,
and have no need to talk,
our conversation of years
wrapped around us,
like a soft, warm blanket,
edged in satin.

Over the miles, I speak
of wanting to see you sooner.
You say you can wait.
I think: forever, if necessary.
Dreams of love make no demands.
Yet, I recall the wail,
like a child wrenched from his mother,
when you asked me under the same sun:
"When are you coming back?"
And, I replied: "But I'm still here."

I cannot see the Southern Cross,
nor you the North Star.
Even our full moons seem different.
Yours shines like a florin,
glazes palm fronds,
spills a trace of liquid silver onto the waves.
Mine's caught by purple clouds,
clenched like the hunter's hand,
around the pure, white throat of Atemis.

Ode to Fruits

Cassandra Ward-Shah

There is a certain sleep of oranges
and the stoic natures of pears
that neither a still-life painting
nor a sculpted fruit bowl
with glazed fruits can capture.

The death of fruits is never so sudden.

Even half-cut and sliced lemons
with their acrid smell curdling the air
dream of a slower death
like the rotting of apples
or the silent blackening of bananas.

And there is a certain sadness of avocadoes
or a rebelliousness within
armored pineapples
that transforms them into metaphors
for dispossessed individuals.

The locked senses within
the flesh of pomegranates
and papayas
are fragments of another life,
of a different home,
now lost.

I yearn for the lands
these fruits remind me of;
I want to feel again
those warm summer hands
that gave birth to these fruits.

Here, in the unbearable
pain of winter,
naked trees shiver on the road
and raise their branches,
like arms,
towards a god
who has refused them more fruit.

Land & Home

Berkley Wendell Semple

The cliff's face blames the surgical
wind for a scarred visage
and angry juts and angled
pike thrown out into space

trees' choir sues the trades
in absentia, long fled to other shores
of our island hosts
where no rooted thing can track.

But these are burdens of mountain
and molehill and trees with lips
of dust, sharing the inertia of
day's infinite light and day's darkness.

They die in the bloom of their rising
from limb-fisted seed dropped
when ax whistles, mountain
under miner's truncheon, molehill my hoe

and empty space is memory
of what was there. Today I care
that the cricket ground keeps its boundary
briarwood, not knowing why,

no connoisseur of plimpla and razor
tendrils, sylphs groaning history
wearing ages for a waist. Green is color
new or renewing with rain.

Thoughts of barren desert
with olive behind ears
on a bald pate despair me; oasis is
accident, home is stay and come

home when snow countries
or desert demesne binds me;
a stand of cedars is my consolation
saying come home and cricket ground.

A Man Gone

William Hudson

In Memory of Raymond Roche

"Listen, Creole seemed to be saying, listen. Now these are Sonny's blues."
—James Baldwin

Raymond, I know denying
what happened
won't bring you
back.

You, whiplean, dry as some
shrew but with not one
mean bone.

Who bore, sweetly,
my stumbles in
French.

Who called my wife,
with a lilt,
Little Mama.

Who, welcoming,
escorted my family
to the *Chante Noelle*
and introduced us
then stood back
and let us,
simply,
be part of
the gathering.

(And I remember
you there: like Matisse had
cut you in blue, dancing
on a sunstruck page. . .)

Third generation Islander,
third also at the *Lycee*,

and the last man
alive you'd think
would be found

dead, battered,
hammered in his
own bed.

(What kind of fury
brings this tremble
to hand?)

Dominican Born Woman

Alba Cruz-Hacker

Bound in slip, bra and girdle under a cotton dress,
she hails each horizon by a stove,
readying the *greka* for demi-cups of thick coffee.
Her fingers know the best way to strip
the waxy skin from yucca, scoop oil over brown
eggs, keep the edges crisp, a soft core.
They come. She serves and stands,
plate in hand, anticipating needs.

Armed with brillo and lye soap, she scrubs
until *calderos* gleam; then partnered with a cornhusk
broom, she sways to Merengue over cement,
switches lead to shine by towel and stick.
Sweat chases trails across her covered chest
when *Arroz con pollo's* smell escapes the kitchen
through the wood-slab window. There's a place,
flatware for everyone, every dish: rice with meat
does not touch black beans or the vinegary cabbage.
And they come. She serves and stands,
her plate in hand, anticipating needs.

She's intimate with the cold dish-bucket and the one
for cloth mounds: those her hands pound and hang
on ropes where warm beams and breezes do their share.
She folds, irons the spectrum of color, of texture;
mops her fine tanned face, bathes
another time in steam from pots and pans, spaces
the mountain of dishes, glasses, silverware,
white rice and beans, adobo-spiced meat.
They come again. She serves and stands,
her own plate between her hands.

Universal Gestures

Marci Sellers

While searching for the Bridgetown bus depot,
we take a left rather than a right,
walking past tourist map perimeters,
and onto an uncharted side street.
A border without fences is crossed.
No artsy-craftsy, dust-collecting doodads in sight;
no endless displays of rainbow-tinted tee-shirts arc from store to store.
It's us, unadorned shop windows that stare black in the sun,
and silence—until a slight breeze carries
toward us the acrid taste of seaweed
along with disembodied scatterings of conversation.
We follow this unwritten signpost
to the clatter and clutter of a tin-roofed dock.

You approach the clump of men
who are focused on mending a tangle of fishnets.
Intrusion of a lost tourist is welcome.
I hear good-natured bickering
as to the best route back.
I wait in a slant of shade.

There is something comfortable
about the surrounding strangeness.
For on a tall, four-legged stool, a Bajan woman sits.
Minus dusky skin, she could be my grandmother sitting
on a tall, four-legged stool
next to the gray formica counter
in her Brooklyn kitchen.
The resemblance is astonishing.

I recognize the grandmother's universal
come-close-watch-and-learn gesture.
A sense of duty draws me to her side.
With economy born of repetition, she cuts
through blue-green scales of a flying fish.
Displayed for me upon a granite slab is the lesson:
a white-boned bracelet of delicate spine.

Like a sculptress—
knowing what to keep, knowing what to take away—
the woman edges her blade under thin fish ribs,
slicing out the superfluous.

She holds out the handle of the knife to me.
Worn finger-grooves curve along its length.
I decline, deferring to her artistry.

Memories of my mangled attempts
to bone whitefish under grandmother's stern gaze
come rushing back.
Am I hearing this Bajan woman lilt?
"It's fine, mammeleh, I'll show you again."

Nine Night

Rohan Preston

James Sylvester Folkes (11 February 1909 - 6 March 1994)

1.   Bearing Pall

When we shouldered you out of the creaky church,
buckling under the heft and heave of an oak
casket so burnished it reddened and wetted
our shiny eyes, we knew that it was you
who wanted to go, only we, here, dragging
you back.   You carried us through hurricanes
that lifted roofs like easy skirts, billowing
carefree intimacies through our district—
led us when we cast off the teeth-marked, ripped-
leaf zinc remaining after those winds bit.
And the velour wattle-and-daub we used
for firewood as you laid concrete into grilles
that will be here after us. You carried
our drink when drought made the ground a road-map
of cracked, criss-crossed parchment crumbling in hand.

You carried us through and through—conveyed, supported,
drove and loved. Now, for once, we carried you,
heavy, yes, but only the sky's hanging,
not on anyone—a no slip we slip,
nor slide, and the gravel crunching underfoot,
just a gnawing in the craw, a chewing
up of grief, this day, the only time folks
threw stones your way, your face erased
and bedded in a scratch of dry dirt.

2.   Ballplate & Coconut Rice

His Winchester bucking up one
shoulder and ballplates on a sash
down the other, Conka strides home
with birds splayed like fish-lures, their wing

feathers in frozen surprise, necks
still oily and iridescent,

26

their eyes bearing Grandmother's grief
but feet tomato ripe—all bouncing

for the hot bathing pot. He had lain
in ambush over Old Walk
and Bunko Way, still-life host
to ticks and mosquitoes. And when he

eased down on the metal bird-tongue,
the roar had made them bloom in the crown
of raw moon, blossom in the hair
of the same breadnut tree we feed

to cows to make milk rich. Birds that
never fly low lilted like black
crucifixes to the trunk of
cottonwood and blue mahoe,

prayer-shrouding at the base of
palmetto berry and guango tree.
Later, over coconut rice
and the rainbow riot of

festival, Conka would tell us
how a hawk came after him once when
he bagged a white belly partridge—
cutting for him like a sharp shard.

And as we drank up his gestures,
our mouths gave up coconut rice
with sweet jerk sauce and pimento
grains, our teeth crunched on scattershot.

3.   *Apiary*

To most eyes he was just a man
out back—weightless in a bubble suit—
floating through multi-citrus plants
he had made bear sundry fruit

(orange, lemon and tangerine);
far out past other grafted trees—
see him feeling in the smoke,
slow hands in the passion of bees,

fingering for his honey pot
like some slow-motion lunar ace—
yes, he could have been an astronaut
signing on from an edge of space.

But common eyes may not see
how Papa cued that astral tune—
he was no Neil Armstrong, but he
brought us manna from the moon.

4.   Revising Icarus

Up over Tumble Hill, he's still sending
large kites that test the strength of ten-pound
test, with twins Peter and Pauline
screaming higher than their hopes.

The Greeks got it all wrong—with mere wax
and feathers in the stratosphere;
Papa's teaching them true flight,
to be true—to soar and be sincere.

5.   Excuse Me, People

"If you have need to throw some water
into the dew-damp dusk,
clear your throat as if with laughter
and beg for pardon thus:

'Excuse me, people—to you, my
great and greater grands,
thank you for your safe home keeping
on Papa's captured land.

Thank you for swearing off evil
ghosts rustling near our yard,
keep shuffling those craven devils
like some old playing cards.'

That way our blood-spirit friends
will look kindly on your cup,
and will only take small offense
if you should splash them up.

28

They will keep the duppy headman
away from our sandalwood,
and keep our sleeping steady,
and keep our dreaming good.

So, say this grace like hearty prayers,
and be upful and glad.
And never mind what nitwit call you
stark and raving mad."

6.   Rolling Calf

When Papa heard the moonless din,
the clickety-clackety rin-tin-tin,
he grabbed his shotgun in a fright
to find wha' warra a tear up the night,

tear up rock-stone and churn it soft,
slurp up the road like marmalade,
chase the moon over Boeing Park
and make the croaking lizards 'fraid.

Yes, even the gnarly mawga dog
just a whimper like a tight-tail puppy,
but Papa know say if gun no do i'
then one growl haffe run the duppy.

So you could imagine the right surprise
when Papa buck up on the rolling calf,
iron tripe a catch up inna him eyes
and frighten just a make him laugh,

"ka-ka ka-ka ke-ke keng-keng
whoi! Burnside, come look whey me find,
dog a hitch up with goat and pig
and patu deh out ya a rukumbine."

But the rolling calf was a duppy for true,
a no patu nor goat—no, not a pig,
whey Papa see, him never did see
though him eyes deh open big.

So one rahtid shadow rail up quick
to take set 'pon me old man head
and when Papa eyes roll up them lids
him see himself a float 'way dead.

The man drop him gun and dash a yard
fly in through the shut-closed door,
him breathe so hard and tremble so
him belly just a mop up the floor.

When dawn wipe ol' Tukuma 'way
and dull the duppy metal load,
Papa tiptoe inna broad day to find
his prized Winchester no out a road,

but another panic take him now
for the night-time calf turn morning cow:
Papa buck up on a big black bull who
look square at him and schmile say, boo.

Ol' man dashed back a yard and stay
inna him house to this very day:
No, gun can't fire, and ugly won't do it
when duppy decide fe dance a street.

7.   *Deacon Folkes lick duppy under the sermon:*

"The shadow-trappers will wait like spiders—
like spit-fire tongues in spit-wipe ambush,
to draw their spells in sibilant wells
to coil and roil and push

their way through your consciousness,
turning all colors silver foam
and burning your vision into a twilight
mist. The shadow-trappers roam

the creaks of front doors and backrooms,
transparent and rightly see-through,
for when you have no shadow, friend,
and the air passes clear through you,

then they have taken your color,
making you the shock of film negatives,
they have fuzzed and fudged up your likeness
and you can still live

but only as wind and gossamer shreds,
here all right, but barely holding
light or casting an image—walking
upright but upright dead."

8.   *Wet Words*

Strung out and hanging heavy
like clothes drooping on a yard line,
every wet word runs into a dirge
of wrung and twisting grooves, blue
dripping and the chafe of soap,
into fading stains and holes
big enough for children to peer
through—every wet word in strains
which beat down on patient grass,
coursing bleached, washed-out garments
barely holding color, or spirit.

Every bruised wailing soaked through,
refrains sag in cold moonlight as
we sing that you take the candle-
lit shadows of your favored things—
the double-barrel gun for hunting
berry-bunches of ball-plates,
the organ leaking Sunday mass
and kette drum for revival runs.
Take castings of trees grafted
with orange, grapefruit, tangerine,
and the repair box you used often
for strangers on the road—take these
and other sweet things, so that you
may rest as you lived, in peace.

We sing to set your spirit free
not roving like fire-borne rags
which sometimes tear through our sleep
still seeking some cool home,

or patu bawling in the night
for people who never answer.
We sing to rock you into the bosom,
rock-a-by now, this long-long night.

9.   *Every thing*

Every thing remains: in air, in
water, water as air condensed
for rain, every drooping drop
still here, every striking drip—
remains.

Feelers finger bones, push up buds
and fruits, fall leaf-burn enable trees
to root in earth turning for spring,
metaplasia for every now and not-now
thing.

Every inched gain, every pinched loss,
every rupture and stitch, every
river or ditch crossed, every
tomorrow yesterday coming—
again.

Every living thing's breath draws in
the dust of every not thing, every
death here in every spirit thing,
every dead, living: here in birth,
here after.

Every baby cry renews souls,
every forgotten remembered,
clued in split nuclei, traced
in mist, every cloud, spirit-tissue,
every mysticism.

Every perfection, every fault,
every confection, every salt,
every here, there, and there, here,
everywhere: every thing a
everything.

In the not looking

Rohan Preston

We found God in the slingshot swoosh
that peeled hummingbirds from the bells
of star-gazer lilies, picked them out
of hibiscus calyxes in

the oiled wattle-and-weave of schoolgirls'
plaits. And in thread-thin strings dangling
chameleons that have forgotten
how to channel colors, turning all

damson-purple in the bounce of boys
at recess. And in the metal-
retching of croaking lizards who snake-spat
from under zinc coils at night—God.

And when we were found out to be
braiding twigs into calabans
for white belly partridges and pea
doves, found to be spinning gigs

atop tombstones and running down balls
cracked from coconut bats into the
grave yard (of all places, since patus
still hoot for spirit relations),

when we were found out—we found
silence black as any moonless sea,
and breathless shame. And in that deep-
blue hush, with whips and switches

and bruised canes dripping over us like
the tongues of dogs in the hot time—
like monitor lizards' tasting of air—
in such mum quivering, God found us.

Finding Paradise

Marvin E. Williams

The lyrical dream of return
to where memory, an indulgent lover,
massages needs, feeds each whim
before its birth, scratches dandruff
from a sun-oiled head made dry
by snow and the scruff
winter shovels unto souls—this dream
dissolves into a drought
that cultures churches and bars
to which numbed parishioners
seek ablution from the doubt
that chews upon itself.

Yet you pursue
the myopic wish of license plates
that declare home Eden; the aesthete
in you believes that the pure
green of the hills painted by rain,
the pristine white of the sand, the fugue
of sky and sea that belies the pain
that gives them color—you believe they embrace
a parcel of the Edenic you celebrate
in your deepest journeys inland.

You pursue
the evocative conch shell
if not the conch who skipped shore
having heard the death knell
sounded in the ravenous need
of farmers displaced from the hell
of their island farms to feed
their families from the Yankee
creed that nurses their hunger.

You pursue
the you you've locked from the vault
of the expanding you.

But you come to discover
those blue pigeons and grand doves,
those herons and the droves
of pelicans and gaulins that wing above
habitats of fish and worms, lending,
you imagined, energy to the air
were but the gentle flapping of desire
that return to roost when the fire
burning after fortune and fame
grows colder than the hearths that name
you before the cultural blending.

You come to discover
the finicky graveyard which held
verdant youth
(and was soon to hold your father)
within its manicured walls, devours
infants whose epitaphs are forged hours
after the umbilical cords are severed.

You discover
that vaunted paradise
is the idyll within your eyes.

Geoffrey Wondered

Marvin E. Williams

Strolling around the University of the Virgin
Islands, eyes pulled to the hills that signature
home, Geoffrey stumbled upon a poem—the tomb

of Peter Rist, six red cinder block columns
linked by iron chains. *Who was this man?*
Geoffrey wondered to me. I did not know

so I decided to speak to Peter across the years,
braced for the laughter or the tears, for
an accounting that would satisfy our questions.

Below the great house (yellow bricked with
ships' ballast and coral which continue
to hear the drowning howls in ocean and holes)

in a grove of mahogany trees lies your tomb,
Peter Rist, undated and unknown to generations
that would not inquire of you—whether you were

mere privileged visitor stricken by a new world
before the immunization of sea, sun, forest
each bearing its bounty and its bile; or were you

master of all you surveyed—the green horizon
of cane wafting between a golden grove of palms,
tethered mules and the fettered dark-skinned

laborers whose bodies sapped the sun, whose
greedy gulping of breath drained the air
to forestall the whip? From your hillside balcony

did you contemplate the intriguing beauty
of emancipation or did you count your cargo
and, like Shylock, hanker after more, already

grinning as you visualized the sacrifice of greater
slave quarters, another shrewd investment in wattle,
claub and cane leaf thatch; in quick-lime and cow dung?

Were you missionary, mariner to the soul or
butcher grown fat on the flesh of Kamina folk—
Fante, Amina, Fula, Arrada, the coast of a continent

still reeling from centuries' blood-letting, still
letting blood brown the savannas? Peter Rist,
were you advocate of education for the Africans

or apologist for the darky's darkness which procured
wealth and its whiteness? You need not answer,
but let me tell you something that might raise your ire:

A university of ex-slaves has confiscated your plantation; your
great house has been renamed Student Affairs, your
cane fields have expanded into a dorm, your

slave quarters have been gentrified into classrooms, your
kitchen heats and feeds The Caribbean Writer, your
slaves' progeny, avoiding books, are now students; your

embalmers call me bitter, insulting, cruel;
you are more honest than your ancestors who to exonerate
themselves exonerate you; so, I wonder, how do you feel?

George Seaman Remembers Drought on St. Croix

Anne McCrary Sullivan

—a found poem

I have known years when deer stomped cactus leaves
in feverish search of moisture; years when small things
burrowed deep, and a few bedraggled butterflies
clustered at a weeping rock. Pastures were bare.
The land turned grey. Cattle, hairless and moaning,
waited death under blue hides.

In times of drought, skies grow pale with sun-dogs.
Tin cans scraping empty cisterns, the devout
question their prayers. Crotolaria rattle
their seeds—dirge castanets.

And in this same time
the silk cotton's bare limbs
break open, deliver pinkish flowers.
Buzzing insect masses come
and chirping yellow-breasts, a pandemonium.
At night descends a different fluttering horde, ravenous
fruit bats squeaking and quivering, tremulous bodies
snipping and chewing, pulsing in ecstatic frenzy.

A Woman, an Island

Rachel Davis McVearry

Mazes of coral and sea foam, amazed
to be alone inside this green and blue
absolute tunnel of wonderful you

on a slope of water I slip into the bottom
of dark caves, to ripe volcanic beginnings,
shimmy like striped wahoo to the open sea
away from lagoons splayed with nurse sharks

then up again to bathe in the shine of
white rays, cloaked in wind of brine and
skimming wide crests of wild-eyed,
yellow-bikinied tides rich with brown people

who grin like the sun's first upside-down
appearance at tropical dawn; even a frown is
a smile with light bursting from its seams
in sugar-cane dreams, stripped down

life like you never knew it could be, just
free as the moon that hangs itself high when
the sky is still the color of aquamarine.

Ah Write!

Joanne C. Hillhouse

Ah write
'Cause it in me
Ah write
'Cause my spirit
Banging on it cage
Yearning to be free
Ah write because
Tings does vex me
An' people does irk me
An ah write
'Cause ah worry
An' 'bout more than me
But 'bout country
An' dis hot ass reality
'Bout where we be
We woman
We neaga people
Still under man
Foot
Still laka de day
Ah massa
An' massa minions
Ah write 'cause
Is so ah cut
Is so ah wound
Is so ah let loose
An' when mah words
Come good good
Is true true
Utopia.
Ah write for me people
An' me
Ah write cause is dat what set
Me free

Ah write
Bout innocence
Jadedness
Peace
Turmoil
Lack of relief
How we grieve
How we laugh
An' music
We music
We culture
We pride
An' we shame
An' we politicians
An' dem game
An' hear wha
Ah write celebration
And tears
'Bout Ivena elevation
An' poor people degradation
Ah write cause is
So ah sing an'
Dance an' bring mah
Art
Man, ah tell you ah
Write cause like
Sometimes dey
Forget we bleed
An' have needs
Like burdensome tax
Relief
An' fuh people do
We right
An' fuh sit comftable
Roun' dis table
Call life

When ah write
Ah don' waan'
You smile an'
Say nice nice
Ah waan' you
Vex and rage

And let loose
Fix on your battle face
Sound de conch
Beat de drum
Remember
We heritage
Embrace um
Ah write cause
All de people
Dat was
Come to me
Waan' come to
Be
An' ah gi dem
Power
De power o'
De words widdin me

Ah write
Cause sometimes
Ah waan' cry
Ah write cause sometimes
My spirit like it waan'
Die
Ah write
Cause the hurt
Bitter
Like cyakkle tongue
Ah write cause ah de
Memory o' he an' he
She an' she
Dis an' dat, de trials an'
De su su
Ah write
So ah can let it go
Ah don' write for you
Ah write cause my
Muse direc' me to
An' she tell me
Write true
An' all de people
Will feel it
Too.

Diego Martin Valley

Nigel Assam

I   Crystal Stream

That years-old landscape: a valley,
hills, houses on both sides, slanted
walls of stone descending to

the very shallow river's flow.
Then, when it rained, the flash floods came,
filling its track with brown water

channeling garbage. In its surge,
its force held parts of cars, and more—
an old fridge, trees' limbs. . .I never

knew where it came from. Behind
my father's fence, I watched its rush,
or, standing on the wall's lip on

the other side of his fence.
Sometimes the river would fill to
overflow in his yard. Thoughts brimmed

of me being caught in that flow,
where I would go, would I be saved,
or drowned into the sea.

I watched until it would die
into its calm, shallow pass in
which we would walk, yet, always

it was there, the fear: rushing to
us unaware, downstream, from somewhere,
unimpeded in the headlands.

II   My Father's Yard

Beneath the citrus in his yard, croaking
frogs that scared a child's play. We dug up

his grass in games of football, the goal's net
marked by two posts in his fence on one side;

for the other, we made markings. For sidelines
there were none, but the whole yard, from the porch

to the fence above the river's wall. Teams
like Liverpool, Everton, Manchester

United, the English greats! Barefoot we
kicked, tripped, slipped, scored, or almost.

Through to dusk we played, not stopping for food,
until, dirt-covered, we sank to the grass.

III   The Look-out

I never reciprocated its love,
the landscape's, or its inhabitants'.
Looking through my telescope to the moon,
then beyond, to Saturn. The sky much more
alluring to my young eyes. And just as
appealing was the television. I
thought elsewhere, as those cannons sea-faced
atop Fort George, their barrels belonging
to history, muted, painted and rusted.
What did I care, except to pretend
among the barrels as a colonial
soldier, or to sit with my young eyes fixed
seaward. Diego Martin sank behind me.

Divali

Nigel Assam

Soon again,
those lights that tongue the night
sitting on every conceivable ledge, rooftop,
house, wall and sidewalk will be lit, guiding
the god's path back to his home along
the knitted thread.

Something in these flames
that, like the constellation illuminating
this island, ties us to India, that other
and more ancient house hidden behind
the horizon, whose inhabitants speak a language
only my great grandfather

knew, its syllables
incomprehensible, as unsettled as the fires
in these deyas. He translated the reasons
for these rituals from epics as mythical
as any of those in history, saying
what the oil means,

that the fires mean this,
the deyas are for that; but they are dead
now. I have never been to India,
and what I know is only through his
stories. My eyes know this horizon
and what India looks like

as it hangs
like an ornament in my bedroom where I
would practice to learn the names of towns.
But I would stammer to say Bhopal, Jobalpur,
Sholapur, even something as easy as Assam.
Our ocean is not the Indian

but the Gulf of Paria.
I would try to tell over the stories if

my children would ask, but they don't!
And they are now so fragmented
that I burn my mind to remember
the next stanza,

and why the god
is returning, and to where? And why it
can't be our mountains he wanders? They are
just as humid as any in India, and our villages
are just as dire as any over there! Maybe because
these limited ranges

are diminished
by India's, and he needs something
bigger for his god's stature! Maybe he too
big for us? Or maybe he can't cross over
the water? My grandfather dead, my
parents too. All his books gone.

And the Elders too.
My children and wife outside with the fireworks
that are too loud for ears, frightening
deyas, shaking them. The streets continue
their constellation that wants to be as grand as anything
I imagine, but in sections this thread is snipped.

These damn lamps are a nuisance to keep lit!

I might never get to India.
I will never see my grandfather again, but in a boy's
face in red in some magazine. So I sit on
the porch then, watching the children, slapping the mosquitoes
from my skin—these damn lamps!—and wiping up the oil
seeping through the deyas,

keeping a watch for the god's passing.

Stop Here to Never Forget

Thomas Reiter

Lettered in Day-Glo on a lava boulder,
STOP HERE TO NEVER FORGET drew us
To pull over in our rental minimoke.
A man stepped out from shade behind that sign,
wearing a T-shirt that read "Picture Man."
One U.S. dollar per Polaroid. Where?
That churchyard across the road. "My studio,"
Mr. Levery said. "I call it Kingdom Stone."
As exposures developed from a grayness
like the pre-dawn sea's, he talked,
moving us among the colonizers, vaults
pitted by salt, walls out of true.
He posed us by all that remains
Of St. Thomas's, a chancel wall half-
collapsed, and noted a bonus view
of the volcano on whose upper slopes
Carib Indians lie buried, unmarked,
in pale blue light of the cloud forest.
At the center of the cemetery, a tomb
with remnants or iron palings around it,
a pitched roof on walls of lava stone.
Thomas Warner, Englishman, Mr. Levery
told us, the first governor of St. Kitts.
"In 1626 he massacre Caribs here."
Some lettering remained:
much lamented. . .thou art therefore taught.
Posing there, we understood
one spin on STOP HERE TO NEVER FORGET.
He peeled away the Polaroid's skin and gave
a sharp laugh: In the corner above our heads
a hummingbird flared its violet crest.
The doctorbird's destination? That very plot.
From a rosette of broadsword leaves,
its time come, a stalk had sprung,
"tall as three graves make long," and bearing
a candelabrum of yellow flowers:
century plant. "How things go change," he began

as we looked up at that hoverer after nectar,
"from when the gods make hummingbirds
for Carib souls to survive in."
Warner's cross fashioned from coral lay
at our feet, intact on consecrated ground
that a termite tunnel climbing his tomb
connected to the darkness within.
"No money for restoration," Mr. Levery said,
"and everywhere the dead be broken so."

Ark of Bones

Virgil Suárez

after the welded metal sculpture by Ed Love

We can say the obvious here: we are a ship
    Of bones, that's true, a wide-open vessel taking
In water. Our ribs catch the susurrus of wind,
    Sing this song-riddle of places we have seen,

Touched. What is the taste of metal on our lips?
    Knowing bitterness is the way of the warrior.
Poet-soldiers, warrior-artists. In the fighting
    Stance, we dance around in this dangerous room,

One leg down as pivot. Turn, turn, the images
    Change from this welded metal that you coaxed
To speak of pain and beauty to art as battle.
    Blowtorch in hand, you are a super hero, blaster

Of words into pieces of scrap iron. In the good ship,
    Jesus doesn't look like Jesus. He looks like you,
The tall man who's been down in the hold too long.
    His big hands cramp up from this constant welding.

His body a receptacle for luminous, strong bones.
    When this god rises, he walks among his people
In pursuit of humanity. In his chest he makes
    His heart rattle, sounding like a bell—this sweet

Sound of beckoning. This ship hurries on home
    Now through turbulent waters. Those left behind,
We are on to something, call it this magic of art,
    One piece of metal shaking hands with another,

Delivering us finally into this amalgam of purity.

Anguilla Cemetery

Clemens Schoenebeck

The tide folds and unfolds
its turquoise drumming,
silvers a glistening lace
on the sands of Mead Bay.

Its rhythm inhales and exhales
a kind of moving breath,
rustles a ghost of lavender
in this place of interrupted dreams.

Scattered like pickup sticks,
bleached coffins lie in repose,
as if tranquilized
by Caribbean light.

Clouds billow like wedding gowns,
blush into marriage with the setting sun.
The tiniest grave, a dollhouse cathedral,
faces east in search of a new day.

Her epitaph glows, bronzed
by the low angle of falling light.
Mary is advised,
Sleep on, Beloved. . .

Chair

Cecil Gray

The circling curves of the bentwood rocker still
draw the heart's genuflections where it is stored now
with all the sparseness of the room, shining dark brown
and silken smooth for a child's sliding hand to glide
on. The trellised cane seat and back were pale yellow
and too large for a small boy. So when the chair rocked
small pangs of panic sweet as a roller-coaster's
shot thrill after thrill through him. Though times when the seat
was frayed and a large hole opened under the weight
of his grandmother he could not manage to keep
his bottom from sinking, ending up hunchbacked.

She would sit in it heavy with troubles the days
came loaded with, going forward and back with smooth
even changes, telling him what had to be faced.
But the chair was her cradle of solace. As she
ironed the floor with its tread and gazed to the ground
the motion that always consoles, the lullaby
the body responds to, sedated the prickles
of pain, with its easy remedy for ailments
without any cure. But so strong was the power
the chair had, all it has left in his memory
is varnished and polished to gleam like a relic
from that room of love. No injuries could tarnish
that. He was cossetted in its tenderness then.
In his picture the chair is repaired. It's glossy
and curved everywhere. His finger slips on its glass.

Practice

Cecil Gray

For Peter

There's a spot in that yard which was worn.
It's all grassy now though.
It had served as the crease of a wicket
once when a father inveigled his son
to come bravely out to learn cricket,
to hold a straight bat, to drive through
the covers, pat the ball past the slips.

The boundary, of course, was the hedge
with magenta hibiscus flowers.
The glass louvres shone in the house
solvent in soft saffron sun
so hooks and sixes were out.

It was a makeshift scramble at dreams.
In late afternoon light two teams
took the field, one the father never played on,
and one that he wanted his son
to fit into at school. In that yard then
the past was entreating the future
to make good on a promise time seemed
to have made then deserted the picture.

There, taking his stance at the patch,
a devoted boy, tense and nervous,
gave all that he could to the task
as if knowing his was the innings
counted on for winning a match,
that he had to defy any risk
to dip into time's fictions and snatch
for his father a refracted glow of success.

It's Dark that Frightens Us

Patricia Harkins-Pierre

(dedicated to Merle DeFreitas on the occasion of the November 2003 VI floods)

It's dark that frightens us. So far from dawn
The gift of light seems lost. Imagined song
Is not enough to still our brooding hearts.
We need to hear the sound of winged words start
And gather force to soar above all sad
And sordid dreams to make us glad
Enough to wake and beat back fear
With laughter loud as thunderclaps. So near
Are we to God at that brave sound we fly
In reason's face. All shame, all terror dies.
We're free to rest. And graced with joy, alight
So close to God we hear His heart all night.
We know the Son who rose will come again
To wipe away all tears and banish pain.

Magus with Reverse Bananas

Laurence Lieberman

                                    Are they freaks, pranks
                    played by nature on the poorest small-scale
                                banana farmer? Or did
                        his sly attempts
                            to cross-fertilize
        new hybrid banana forms backfire? He holds up a tall
                                stalk to the light
                            as if he's proud
                    to display his handiwork. And no regrets!
                        His dreamy smile is proof.
                    We wonder how those
                                five bananas could grow

backwards on the clumps, stem ends
    flaring outwards, pointy banana tips queerly joined
    to that cluster rim. The Magus, no mere carnival trickster,
        blithely harvests
            his banana crops and sells to the public.
He still earns his keep, sustains a modest living for his family,
        but loss of export
    sales eats into his profits—of late betrayed

                                by America's new crunch
                on island quotas. Since most U.S. buyers now
                            favor his Latin rivals,
                        he turns his hand
                            to magic—to win back
        fair trade. *Reverse Bananas* may hypnotize the middle men,
                        as new games often lure
                        wayward children
                back to the play yard. . .His velvety black skin
                        seems ashimmer with purple
                    glaze, while the gold
                            bananas, too, are bathed

in purplish light. It could be
glows of late sunset, pre-dusk maroons swirling
across the strings of fruit and man limbs alike, marrying
grower to his crops
in a new-birth caul of second skin luster.
The colorist, himself a conjuror of arcane states, had come upon
unique shades of purple
in Britain last year. They partook of both earth

and big sky, a mix of sea-
sky and land-sky, colors that lurk and hover
upon horizons. He filed
away that gift
of new tints in memory
journal of novel hues, and waited to bequeath them a mimic's
afterglow life within
his painted forms.
Others would carry home new shirts, cloaks, scarfs,
belts—high fad or fashion
garb—from their trips
abroad. But he, charged

with a slant of fresh eyescape,
returned from his travels bearing new color power,
armed with a stockpile of pigments to dress up and costume,
afresh, his paint kit. . .
Stanley's Guyana roots, his childhood and youth
in Georgetown, are transferred to his Magus. Those early daybreak
offerings on the sea wall—
gifts to the Gods, the Holy Spirits—engendered

his belief in wide horizon
as linear springboard for the happy display
of marvels. The clothesline,
here, is best
recurrent magic locus.
Wherever humans reside, from city to farm settings, our laundry
twines stretch across yards:
constant turnover
of hanging garments and motley blend of other rope
danglers make this *horizon*
quiver and flutter

with human accoutrements—

a favorite site for shaman's
  rituals. The Magus simply extends his right arm
    toward the line, and his palm print or fingerprint whorls
      launch the topsy-
        turvy realignment of things in motion. It's
a highwire dance act. A tightrope walk of objects that commences
      horizontal side-to-side
struts across the canvas. An airborne ballet

                    of acrylics. . .That wide-ribbed
  expanded umbrella, capacious as a small parachute,
                stands erect on its curved
          handle—stationed
            in mid line. It cannot
fall. A strong wind and darting rain or pelted hail can shake it,
        make its silks flap in tumult,
          but never dislodge
    or unsettle it from secure handle placement, true
        footing on the rope. We sense
      this deep aerial
          anchorage in taut symmetry

and poise of stance. The fall-proof
  mode. . .A wave movement flows outward from that hand's
    least shake, its minimal tremblings, and the cool succession
      of balancing feats
        resumes. Two candles teeter on the line, one far
to each side of blonde wood of umbrella grip—both upright candles
      sporting long wicks curled
    like a woman's sexy eye lash. A sapphire-colored

                    butterfly with crimson wing
      margins and pink stripes lolls on one candle's
              tall wick, it's wings half-opened
          on verge of takeoff
              or landing, you can't say
  which, but in-between state reveals it must be one or the other.
          Flux, not stasis. . .A single
        banana is placed
    upon the dome of umbrella nylon, its pointy ends
      curving upwards—in reverse

of the black fabric's
   concave swell (*the Magus*

wants to make us laugh, he can do
   funny things without limit: sadly, he cannot win
      those banana wars—but lifts our hearts). Like a scattering
         of smiles, the lovely
            curves feed into each other: candle wicks,
      umbrella handle, butterfly wings and phallic arch of long bananas.
         All half-hidden smile lines
      seem to flicker, in happy interplay, up and down

                  length of clothesline. . .Maestro
      Stanley, twin of the Magus, hums his ardor
               for this motif as he traces
            invisible curves
               over the painting's frame
   with his left index finger wand. And so it is we discover—to my
            delight—we are both Southpaws,
            he and I, our wrong
      curves mirror images to everyone else's. I may as well
         team up with the morning's
         passion—surprise line
            swoops and misturned bananas.

   (after the painting by Stanley Greaves)

SHORT FICTION

"Miss Rosita de Fish Lady"   Hilda Lewis Joyce

Counting Conch

Richard James Byrne

Underwater, he can calculate almost anything. Brilliant. Gifted. Prodigy is the word they used after the IQ evaluation in London when he was seven. "Intended for greatness." "Greatness." The word hissed sharply through the square white lab coat's square white teeth. He could still hear it 4,128 miles, 21.795840 million feet, 261.550080 million inches away, through thirty-three feet, 10.05842 meters, of undulating Aqua-Velva blue. Skimming across the pastel palette—the emerald reef, the violet sea fans, the infinite pale sand—he suffers, a lifetime from greatness. Counting conch: one, two, three.

When he counts ten and the yellow mesh bag is full, he slides the ring down the cord and heads for the surface. Reginald J. Johnson, "Whizmon" to his friends, is brilliant. His IQ measures 169, fourteen points above genius. He released his first word when he was just three months and read his first at just eighteen months. By the time he was four he had swallowed every book in his parents' house and then gulped them down house by house through the town.

By the time he was seven, he had devoured every paperback and hardcover; every volume, every manuscript, every abstract and index card in the town library, possibly every book on the island. Probably more books than anyone else he knew, which isn't saying much. He lives on Anegada, an inconsequential coral island in the British Virgins that rises just twenty-eight feet, 861.53846 centimeters, at its highest point, above the Caribbean Sea. It has under 200 permanent residents descended from a few families who live in a dusty area called the Settlement. Reginald counts sixty-two as his direct relations.

He works, as most every man on the island does, as a fisherman—he free dives for conch. At night, he's a bartender at the Anegada Reef Hotel, which caters to the wealthy yacht captains that moor the scrubbed-white chartered sailboats in the bay each afternoon. Mostly Americans, but some French and Swedes, they come to experience the wonder of remote island life. Reginald has become proficient in those languages, yet he never speaks them, hiding instead behind the sing-songy pigeon tongue he was born with.

He knows a lot about the world. Which is remarkable since other than short boat rides to Cooper or Virgin Gorda (73,920 feet, 887,040 inches away) he never leaves the island. He has learned some from books and some from crossword puzzles in the *New York Times*, the airline magazines, and other newspapers which are left behind at the bar. All of the other bartender cousins know to save them for Whizmon, stacking them up next to the sticky chrome blender and corrugated cans of Cocoa Lopez. He does them religiously, completing them in ink often in less than twenty minutes, just 1.38% of his day, each box filled, each answer correct. 1 Across: Jazz town. "N-E-W-O-R-L-E-A-N-S," he writes. 53 Down: Chez Everest. "N-E-P-A-L" is quickly penned in.

Reginald is cemented in place by a deep swirling inertia of self-doubt. He was made to hide his talent. From the very beginning his father disheartened him, told him books "are far dem sissies and girls, deep divin', conch divin', and bone fish is far the mens." It was his mother that convinced a researcher to bring him to London for tests. When the results arrived, his father burned the papers in a coffee can and spread the black pieces and ash in the sand next to a pungent pile of conch shells behind their tin roof house. But she hid a letter from the agency behind an old black and white framed photograph of Queen Elizabeth that hung on the wall. "Reginald has extraordinary intelligence," it said. "His IQ, at 169, is among the highest in the Empire."

Both are dead now, and he is forty-two—15,342 days, 367,920 hours, 22,075,200 minutes, 1,324,512,000 seconds, and counting.

He hasn't read the letter in years. In fact, in almost everything but the crosswords, Reginald conceals his ability. He views his intelligence as a burden, as if his brain were an overloaded bag of conch, too heavy to surface. But it is the real him, floating inside a big-lipped, brown paper island doll like they sell at the hotel shop—trapped energy, never diminished, never transferred.

Like the conch he counts, he retreats deep into the loneliness of a hard spiny shell, burying the ache of lost promise in the silky gray sand, in the soundless reef, in the swaying green sea grass. To keep the swell of brain inactivity, like the tide, from pushing through his ears and drowning him, he calculates the angles of geometric shapes between the pink shell waypoints. Or he recites passages from books to the fish: *Great Expectations, Middlemarch, Living Language's Conversational French*, TimeLife's *Small Engine Repair*. He's absorbed them all.

There is solace below the surface.

And so he has given up that he will ever see the crossword places for himself, that he will ever be anything but a conch diver—a conch diver on Anegada.

Until this Saturday. This Saturday, he breaks the surface and there is something else. The water sheets off his mask to reveal a sparkling blue sailboat, rising high above the thin coral atoll behind it. *Serena.* A yawl. He recalls the sail configuration from *Chapman Piloting, Seamanship and Small Boat Handling. A rig for two-masted sailboats, in which there is a main mast and a smaller mizzen mast, stepped aft of the rudder post* flashes through his mind's eye. On deck he sees a man, a flat straw hat balanced above a wrinkled face.

"You there," the voice, British, is crowded with age, "I've fouled the prop, can you get it loose?"

"Ya-mon." Reginald responds, sets his mask, and slips below. As he works the line slack from the shaft, he can see the man hanging over the transom. Distorted in the carnival mirror surface, his skin is like the leather purse made from stingray hide Reginald once saw in a tourist shop on Cooper, dark and textured. Deep lines stream down from the corners of his eyes and mouth. Too severe to be only from sun and age, they are lifeless rivers in scorched earth, a millennium in the making. A bony silver barracuda hovers nearby; its black doll's eye fixed on the situation, wondering, no doubt, why such a small fish would endeavor to harass such a large one. *Master, I marvel how the fishes live in the sea. Why as men do a-land, the great ones eat up the little ones.* Shakespeare.

"Ya free, mon." He spits out water and breath and arches his back to dive.

"Wait a minute there, permission granted to come aboard." The man flips a rope-and-wood ladder over the gunwale, before disappearing below deck.

Reginald pulls himself onto the gray teak. Hot wood on cool feet. He has never been aboard a boat this magnificent and immaculate. He was hired as a guide a few times on charter boats—white, molded-plastic giants—but the private yachts navigated the reef themselves. And *Serena* is among the best he's seen. He admires the knots in the rigging—bowlines, clove hitches, reef knots, and monkey fists are sketches in the *Sailor's Handbook, Updated Edition.* The varnished bulwark caps catch sun in beaded-water diamonds, and the halyards tinkle against the aluminum masts. But the man is gone.

A few silent minutes. Then he squeezes in front the chrome wheel in the cockpit, wondering what it would be like to command her, to glide past the reef one final time, past Cooper, and Virgin Gorda, and Tortola, and Beef Island, to make the sprint to Puerto Rico, and the passage to Bermuda, the Carolinas, Norfolk, New York, Boston. *To sail beyond the sunset, and the baths of all the western stars, until I die.* Tennyson.

He steps down the companionway, leaning his head under the sliding hatch. Nothing. Two more steps and he is standing in *Serena's* saloon. Like the inside of a jewelry box, it is almost entirely varnished mahogany highlighted by polished brass and chrome fixtures reflecting blue, green, and red-tinted spots of light as they swing in their gimbals. He senses the distinct quality of loneliness here, like in the bottomless blue pockets around the reef. Completely devoid of the idiosyncratic touches of identity and life, it's as if humans didn't inhabit the place at all. And he is an expert.

Then, there *they* are. Along the port side is a long expanse of bookshelves, stacked, piled, and heaving with hundreds of books, enough books to occupy him for years. Reginald recognizes most of the authors: Coover, Wolfe, Casey, Michener, Irving. So mesmerized by the vibrant spines and covers, he involuntarily tips sideways as he walks, and he's completely forgotten his brown paper self. It's as if he's underwater again soaring over the reef and plunging into a limitless valley.

At the end of the shelves is a fold-down table suspended by a brass chain. On it is a pile of six books all by the same author, James R. Henry. He picks up the first on the pile and forces his mind to stop thinking in pigeon: "With his sixth book, *Desperate Valley*, James R. Henry takes his readers on another roller coaster journey deep into the human psyche, beyond the barrier of sanity and into the endless blue-black expanse of a complicated mind." On the back of the dust jacket is a black and white photograph of the author, which he recognizes as a younger version of the wrinkled man, the lines less pronounced. The smile is forced and not radiating past the lips and mouth. "James R. Henry, an avid yachtsman and world traveler, has written six books and is a regular guest at Buckingham Palace. He lives alone aboard the sixty-six foot yawl *Serena* berthed in London, Naples, Lisbon, and New York."

Next to the pile is the *New York Times Crossword Omnibus.*
The spine is broken and the book lays open to "The Bard's
Follies." He can see only one answer hasn't been filled in. In that
moment, *Serena* is like heaven to him, and he contemplates the
possibility that the water finally pushed its way into his ears, that
he drowned. Then there are steps behind him.

"Who said you could come below?" It is James R. Henry
standing in the companionway, straw hat removed, the face lines
opening and closing with anger.

"One sixteen," Reginald releases in his best English, annunci-
ating every syllable.

"What. . .what are you—"

"'Blank minds,' twenty-three across, four letters. . .it's from
Sonnet 116, 'Let me not to the marriage of *true* minds admit
impediments.' The answer is true." It is the first time he's quot-
ed anything out loud in years. The entirety of the sonnet remains
in his mind's eye.

"Yes. . .well. . .yes. . .true, of course." The man angles a dis-
believing glance at the open crossword book. "Well that may be,
but you take this and go. Nobody comes below." The buzz of a
small engine—an outburst of mechanical sound—grows and the
wake spanks the boat abeam and rolls under. There is a dance
of light spots across the books, mahogany, and wrinkles. When
the man steadies himself, an American five-dollar bill is shoved
forward, and Reginald is the paper doll again. The burden and
blood move into his cheeks and ears.

"Ya, mon." And then Whizmon is back below the surface,
fully silenced, as if he had never left. But his mind is full of the
books and full of the man James R. Henry, "world traveler."

For a week, *Serena* is anchored in front of the hotel, the
beach bar where he bartends, inside the reef. During the days he
dives below her, slipping effortlessly through her shadow on the
rippled sand, and looks up at the fat red keel suspended mysti-
cally in the surface tension, where the dogfish have taken up residence. *The volume of a floating body displaces an equal amount
of fluid. Intro to Elementary Physics I.*

In the last few days he's visited the library in the Settlement,
which he hasn't been to in years, not since his mother died. He
still knows most of the books there, as they have not been
replaced, but he manages to gather an armful new material. He's

ravenous. He transports the precious haul back to the baked cinder block cottage on the edge of the Settlement where he lives alone. His heart gallops as he jams them under the mattress like a child. *A Man in Full, Spartina, Five Frogs on a Log, Merriam Webster's Guide to Business Correspondence*, and the fourth edition of *Desperate Valley*. *Desperate Valley* by James R. Henry. He takes it first, the thin blue-striped polyester sheet pulled up over his head. He peels back the foreword, his lips move with the words: "*Desperate Valley* is James R. Henry's last book. Soon after its release and the deaths of his wife and son, he never published another word and withdrew completely from public life, a great loss to the genre."

As the days pass, he does not see him on deck, but he is aware of life on *Serena*. He hears the report of her various expulsions which pour into the water and create foam. At night from his perch at the bar he sees the dull orange glow of the port lights. He finishes the day's crosswords with 54 Across: Dante's Burden. "C-I-R-C-L-E-O-F-H-E-L-L." Under the sun, he swims close, hoping to be noticed by James R. Henry, eager and terrified to engage him about *Desperate Valley*, about the Queen, about the condition of the larger world. "Why would he want to talk to me about anything?" he thinks. "I'm sho day no conch divin' in dem books o his, mon." He dives.

It is six days before he encounters him again. Reginald finishes his catch from the library and his mind is bursting with fresh quotes and the world. He is under *Serena*, the empty mesh bag attached to his waist flutters behind him. A small school of goatfish follows, their yellow stripes and silver bellies discharging sunlight like flashbulb pops. His audience.

He surfaces. As *Serena* swings into the wind on her anchor chain, the transom with its shining gold-leaf letters is only a few feet away. His eyes adjust in the sunlight to see James R. Henry at the life rail, his hands cupped around his mouth: "You there. . .I need you to come aboard."

He nods, mask on his forehead, delighted at the invitation. He glides to the rope ladder and pulls himself up, rushing with excitement into his greeting. "I'm Reginald Johnson," he says, one foot on the deck, extending his hand. "My friends call me Whiz—" He stops himself as suddenly with the sound of his own voice; he's embarrassed. He wants to blurt out: "I have a 169 IQ, among the highest in the empire. I know Shakespeare,

Hemingway, and Keats, and physics, and every element in the periodic table, and calculus. I've read *Desperate Valley*. I am a genius." He wants to blurt this out before he is asked the price for some conch, or lobster, or to scrape the growth off the bottom, or to point out the best snorkeling or bone fishing spot. Before he slips below the surface again. But he doesn't, and he feels the blood and disappointment move into his face.

"Whiz?" the pebbly British voice claims all of its octave. "I'm J.R. Henry." His hand moves into Reginald's, liberates a burst, one short shake, and retreats. "You're a diver."

"Yes, the solitude. . .it's what keeps me sane," he says. He can't believe he said it. It's the first truly honest thing he's said to anyone in a long time. His brain, like his pupils dilating below the surface, swells with the possibility of true engagement, of a dialogue, and suddenly with a quiver, the din of quotes drains from his mind. "*Serena* must be your solitude." No recognition. His eyes follow the teak seams forward to occupy the silence, and he rolls his neck back and explores the rigging before settling back on J. R.'s over-ripened face. He is a tall man, but faintly stooped with age. His hair is perfectly white, absent any color, and is pushed back from his forehead. A few strands like bundled wire slip over one side and bounce in the wind. He is severe, Reginald thinks, like *Serena*, somehow antiseptic, somehow lifeless. Magnificent and immaculate. He too is a paper doll.

"I need the bottom scraped." The words hiss and hang cold in the breeze. "How much?" Green American bills in his hand.

Reginald drains. He can't even slip below to drown the sound, to drown. *In the deepest recess of the human mind there is something more than regular darkness. It is blue black.* J. R. Henry. He shuffles weight from one foot to the other, and some trapped salt water slips out from under the mask and stings his eyes. He is flat like Anegada, perilously suspended above the surface, barely existing until the next hurricane or tectonic shift. "Ya, mon, fifty."

There is silence while J. R. produces a plastic bucket and a bottle of liquid soap from under a hatch in the deck.

Reginald retreats to the opening in the life rail and then something bursts inside him: "Why no seventh?" It came out in perfectly annunciated English. For the first time in years, his mind is operating without its governor. "No seventh book. . .no more books at all?" His heart flutters with the release.

J.R. stiffens, his white eyebrows clenched, his face parched from the absence of human charity. "I don't need a review from some island boy who thinks he's qualified because he's good at the crosswords." He moves the bucket forward across the deck with his foot. "I don't know what you want from me, but I'm not interested." J.R. is done with the human race, his patience with it exhausted long ago. "So take the bucket and get to work, or go."

Reginald knows J.R.'s face. It is a creation of the deep loneliness that results from an existence of isolation, from years—even more years than *he* has dedicated—of struggling to keep the water out. "I'm sorry," he blurts a reflex. Like the blinding white surface light, he is suddenly in possession of the truth: he is expert in only one subject. He has devoted his life to it. To J.R., people are like barracuda, staring with black doll's eyes, lifeless eyes. Reginald feels himself in his skin for the first time since he was a child. "I'm sorry. I thought you might want a friend on the island." He is sincere, and honest, and sad. "Someone to bounce the crosswords off of." He picks up the bucket by its crusty rope handle and drops a foot over the side to the first rung of the ladder. His other foot hangs out over the vast blue liquid canyon. He knows what it looks like from below—to the angels, and the goatfish, and the conch—but all he thinks of is the pressure of the water pushing him further down until the sunlight is flimsy and *Serena* is gone. But before he steps, he senses acknowledgment. There is an almost inaudible human sound. A confession of gratitude reveals itself in J.R.'s expression. There is something in Reginald that disarms J.R. It's as if he were not part of the human race at all, but living coral of the Anegada reef—alive, but benign. "Well," he says, "I suppose there's no harm in working on a few puzzles together, you might learn something. When you're done with the boat."

A broad smile swells on Reginald's mouth and remains even as he disappears below the gunwale and into the canyon with a slap and a splash. Along the curved white boot stripe, *Serena* is endless, the vertical edge of a newborn universe. He scrapes, and brushes, and dives along the keel until the water is coated with delicate pink diamonds—a gift of the Caribbean twilight. On the beach, flames from the oil-drum barbeques are furious, soaking the air black with kerosene and wood ash. Tonight Anegada is at rest, motionless. It is a night for the sand fleas. A night when the breeze comes sluggishly in chunks like the first drops of island rain.

He wonders, for the first time, about the library in Road Town on Tortola, lying behind him in the distance, and he can't think of why he hasn't visited. He imagines the university on St. Thomas. He allows the pale images of London to invade his mind's eye.

Reginald works on *Serena* everyday for a week, scrubbing the bottom, the bright work, the brass and chrome. J.R. recounts the life of a celebrated novelist as Reginald sands and polishes. The places he's seen: Sydney, Johannesburg, New York, Miami, and others; and the people he's known: the Hollywood starlets, intellectuals, Nobel scientists, and politicians. Reginald quotes from memory and sketches reef fish on a pad. He writes the genus and phylum below in block letters and shows him. And they finish the crosswords in the *Omnibus* and the magazines that he brings from the bar. J.R. gives him his collection of signed books. "I wrote them, and I never read them."

The days pass and *Serena's* perfection is maintained, a Ceylon sapphire on a platinum band. And for the first time in an eternity, Reginald's curiosity and talent is unbridled. And for the first time in an eternity, J.R.'s bitterness is relieved. Their loneliness is a common bond, and like aging prizefighters, or men who have been to war, the experience is a communal meal portioned and swallowed like a sacred right. It is a sacrament for a lifetime of isolation. It is atonement, and fulfillment, and nourishment.

He dives. The purple sea fans salute in unison as he soars above them. He wonders how long it's been since he's appreciated their loveliness, the fragility of their life. And there *is* sound. Shifting sand and rocks tinkle with each invisible surge, and the ocean, rhythmic and pounding, thunders in its ceaseless struggle to claim the island. He slips sideways between towering formations past a wary female leatherback. *Then beauty is its own excuse for being.* Emerson.

One late pink afternoon as *Serena* strains in creeks and pops on her galvanized chain, Reginald and J.R. are in the cockpit. Reginald produces a Tupperware container. "It's conch stew," he says, "my mother's recipe." And by the time he emerges from the galley, the thick brown gravy and conch chunks spooned onto paper plates, the sun has retired into a glass harbor.

J.R. lays out across the white vinyl cushion, one knee up, his wire hair spilling out from under the straw hat, the horizon burning behind him. "If I were you, I'd never leave this island. . .I'd stay exactly as you are." He deposits a hot conch piece between his lips, rolling it around in his mouth to keep it from burning. "You've never asked me why," he says with a nod and a hard swallow. Reginald sees his face distorted and misshaped in the chrome compass binnacle, but he knows what he means: why no life off *Serena*; why suppress an incredible talent; why no seventh book. He realizes these are *his* questions, and he already knows the answer. "The world is too cruel." J.R.'s hands shake with age and the weight of it. As the final slivers of light retreat into the horizon, J.R. tells him of the death of his wife and son. How he was in New York promoting *Desperate Valley*, and they were in London. How his wife was mentally ill. How she drowned their son in a warm bath and slit her wrists, the blood dripping through the ceiling to the servants' quarters below. How he dined at the Waldorf on shrimp cocktail, porterhouse, and Stoli that night. How he left on *Serena* and never returned to the world.

"When I stopped writing. . .stopped producing, my so-called friendships dried up. In this world, people who want something from you, *they* are your friends. All the intellect in the universe can't change that." Reginald passes another steaming scoop of stew onto J.R.'s plate. J.R. is pale to him.

"But there are so many opportunities when you have a talent like yours," Reginald says. But it is hollow, not for lack of sincerity but because, like the lines in J.R.'s face, the sourness is deep; the damage too severe. J.R. dips his head and releases a long forced breath through his nose. With it, Reginald's calloused envy of the outside world begins to dissipate. In J.R.'s world, too, Reginald is a man; Whizmon is a paper doll.

At night, Reginald is back at the beach bar, among the cousins, friends, and pigeon English. They talk about tourist girls and fishing. One of his cousins has gotten a job with an airline on Beef Island and will be traveling daily to Puerto Rico and Florida. They share a drink in celebration. He decides to walk home, his head singing with Pusser's and the hum and crackle of the blender and ice. The moon is bright and casts long tree shadows across the sandy road in front of him. Through the breaks in the trees, he sees the harbor, the white mastheads are strung in a line like Christmas tree lights and the whine of the rubber Avons—their drunk crews returning from shore—fades in and out.

His living room is stale with trapped air. Kneeling on the worn sofa, he lifts the black and white photograph of Queen Elizabeth and turns it over revealing a folded piece of typing paper, yellowed with age. He reads:

Dear Mrs. Johnson,

After completing the standard battery of intelligence quotient examinations on your son, Reginald Johnson, we've determined that he is a very special young man. Reginald has extraordinary intelligence, and his IQ, at 169, is among the highest in the Empire. We recommend that he be placed in special school in London, where his talent and intelligence can be properly addressed and nurtured. We have no doubt that with the proper education, Reginald will have a significant contribution to make in his chosen field of endeavor.

Reginald pinches the paper back along the original folds and drops it into a plastic kitchen garbage can next to the sink, before shutting off the light.

The next day, the sun comes in the open window, across the blue pinstripes and his face. He rolls over, chin on the concrete sill, and looks out across the dusty yard through a small grove of scraggly palm trees to the infinite expanse of blue and white. There is a flamingo poking through some standing rainwater by the road's edge, the spindle legs and snake neck an unkind gag of evolution, he thinks. It's Sunday. By ten o'clock he is in the flat-roofed, cinder block chapel next to the library under the hand-carved crucifix, fluorescent lights, and ceiling fans. Whizmon is enveloped by his family, the aunts and cousins, the infants and the teenagers, round and slim brown faces and bright floral shirts. There is singing, and swaying, and crying. After, there are handshakes and lunch of curried fish roti and cold Carib served from the bed of a thick-wheeled Toyota pick-up.

The next day he calls the university on St. Thomas and requests some materials about their programs: Business Management, Computer Science, Language Arts, Literature, and Creative Writing. He can't decide which one; maybe he'll study them all. He slides a paperback out from under the mattress and reads until the daylight is gone.

The next day, he dives again. In the afternoon, he swims out toward the radiant *Serena*. He's proud. Behind her, a fresh flotilla of chartered sailboats and crosswords motors around the reef. Their eager crews lean on forestays and assemble on gunwales for their first glimpse.

As he comes up for air, he sees J.R. on the bow. He's under again. With the next breath, he recognizes *Serena* is prepared to leave. There is a small octopus below him changing color with the sand as he passes over. *Of the wide world I stand alone, and think Till love and fame to nothingness sink.* Keats.

Serena's anchor breaks the surface and drips, and he realizes that he won't make it to her before she slips forward, beyond the reef. He thinks of the acidity of J.R.'s deep bitterness, of his loneliness, of his choice to let it consume him wholly. Maybe it's not a choice, he thinks, but like the swollen Caribbean grinding away at Anegada, it's a relentless, throbbing, involuntary motion. When *Serena* grows thin and transparent, he feels alone. It's the loneliness he felt when his mother died, the loneliness he felt in London, the unique loneliness of being Whizmon.

He dives, and there is silence. The chartered boats have found their moorings in the harbor in front of the hotel. Below, he skims across the edge of the green reef out over a deep gorge, plotting a course through a squadron of emperor angels toward a glowing nebula of pink conch.

Queen of Heaven

Anesa Miller

There was nothing in the ringing of the phone to warn of bad news. It was late afternoon, a time when friends often called or occasionally Emilio's family from Spain, always careful not to bother the young people later in the evening. So Marga felt no dread as she stepped away from diapering her infant daughter and reached for the receiver.

Static was the first clue—a bad international connection. Then Marga recognized the voice. Dolores Pilar, calling from Nicaragua. From home. It occurred to Marga that the two of them had never spoken by phone before.

Dolores Pilar's first words were formal, offering good wishes for Margarita Luisa's health and for the baby. Then emotion overwhelmed the polite phrases.

"It's about Hector, your dear papa," she said. "This morning at the garage he was inspecting a truck—the head mechanic told me. He leaned in to listen to the motor, and next thing they knew—he had fallen on the ground."

Between sobs, the woman explained that Marga's father had suffered a heart attack. By the time Dolores Pilar arrived, an ambulance had taken him to the nearest clinic. From there she was obliged to dash to the hospital, asking every medic and orderly she could find if he was all right and where exactly he had been transferred.

"It took all day," she said. "I just got home."

Her voice gave in to a moment's relief on the word "home."

"Did they take him to San Miguel?" Marga asked. "I can call from here. I still know some people on the staff—"

She glanced at Felisa, naked on the couch waving her tiny feet in the air, and stretched the phone cord to its limit, reaching to cover her against the draft that seeped from the windows.

"No, my child, my poor orphan!" Dolores Pilar exclaimed, clearly dismayed at her failure to say what she must. "He is not at the hospital now—he is already in heaven! I had them take him to Guillermoprieto's funeral parlor."

The baby grew still, and the wind stopped rattling bushes outside the apartment. Marga wanted to look in all the places Dolores Pilar had named, to see if what she said could possibly be true: Managua trembled in the heat rising from its streets, as her mind raced from the garage to the neighborhood clinic and then the Hospital of San Miguel. There Marga pictured the patient roster on a clipboard at the same desk where she had worked as a medical student eight years before.

But she couldn't remember where Guillermoprieto's was located and so could not continue her search there.

Dolores Pilar had moved on to practical matters.

"I'll have the deacon take photos for you at the funeral. Don't worry yourself—we'll see that it's done properly. Just one thing I must ask, my dear, please call your brothers and sister in Florida to give them the sad news. You have their numbers, right?"

These were Marga's half-siblings in Miami, the town where she, too, had lived before venturing into America's heartland.

Their conversation at an end, the two women said a formal good-bye. Marga lifted the baby to her shoulder and whispered, "You will never meet your grandfather."

But she said it in English so the child wouldn't understand, being too small for the burden of sorrow.

After zipping Felisa into a warm sleeper, Marga tried calling Emilio at the university. He wasn't at the grad students' office, the Philosophy Department or the Language Lab. She left messages everywhere.

"Where is your papa when I need him?" she asked—also in English.

Gathering the baby under a blanket, she walked to the campus chapel. It would have been enough to sit in a pew alone with her thoughts, but a vesper service was beginning when she slipped in among a dozen worshippers. Phrases like "our heavenly father" served to swell the lump of feelings in her chest, while Felisa's warm breaths puffed against her neck.

"Like the barnacle on a rock—no storm can dislodge me!"

That was how her father used to reassure the denizens of the kitchen at the narrow house near central Managua where Marga spent her early years.

Calling that afternoon, Dolores Pilar had played a familiar role as disrupter of ideal memories. Childless herself, the resident housekeeper and paramour routinely voiced her respect for Marga as nominal mistress of the home, while filling the downstairs rooms with her own numerous relatives.

When Marga returned from boarding school to attend the medical institute, she was surprised to find herself sharing suppers with some half-dozen elderly peasant women—her father had neglected to mention the growing domestic population in his letters. They all made a point of saying nice things about Señor Hector—such a kind man, so hard-working, untiring in support of the people's rights.

Dolores Pilar praised Hector's devotion to his children. How he'd spared no expense to protect Marga's half-brothers—born to lesser mistresses around the city—from conscription and probable death in the Contra War. So far he had sent four of them to the United States. Marga was lucky, she said, to have such a wise and generous father.

Now, with Felisa pressed to her shoulder, Marga pictured her father in a white suit on the square outside the cathedral, beaming at her as she came down the steps to meet him for their Sunday stroll; or laughing on the curb by his garage, when a man from the docks brought him a decrepit car, claiming all it needed was a new carburetor.

At the altar rail she took a wafer from the priest's hand onto her tongue. She thought of staying behind to ask for a memorial mass but decided instead to hurry home, hoping Emilio might have come in during her absence.

At nine o'clock, Marga began calling all her friends until someone told her that Emilio had gone to Jean-Claude's apartment with the usual crowd of foreign students. Since there was no phone, Marga asked a neighbor to stay with the baby while she went looking for her boyfriend.

Jean-Claude was struggling to explain a theory, which taught that greed no longer functioned as a prime cause of world poverty. A research assistant in the Institute for Ethics and Social Policy, Jean-Claude had averaged the wage gap in numerous countries, counterbalanced against prevailing rates of unemployment and standard of living.

"Poverty is still a problem," he conceded when his friends scoffed at the idea. "Disease, natural disasters—all kinds of things make people poor. But in the postmodern world, greed increases universal wealth rather than creating new cases of poverty."

Objections came from all sides. The Latin American students argued that trickle-down economics never reached the bottom, where the masses were left with nothing.

Emilio spoke up.

"But I think there's something to it. The face of evil is changing. We used to say, 'The dictator is evil,' or 'The upper class is greedy.' But in the global economy good and bad are harder to distinguish."

Marga could hear all the talk as she climbed the stairs. Before the baby came she used to join these gatherings, although her contribution tended to be in the area of making sangria, rather than discussing abstract topics. Despite her years in America, speaking English remained a challenge.

By custom, Marga opened the door without knocking. When she stepped into the room, her eye caught Emilio's sudden movement away from a European girl at the table, dropping his arm from the back of her chair.

An embarrassed pause settled over the gathering, except for Emilio himself, who looked up and said brightly, "Ah, *mi amor!* What's up? Where's the baby?"

I should ask you what's up, Marga thought darkly. But she kept her face composed, unwilling to stoop to domestic bickering in front of everyone.

"The baby's at home asleep," she said in Spanish. "She's doing fine. But my father's friend called this afternoon." Marga glanced at the clock. "She called six hours ago. My father died today. He had a heart attack."

The guests who spoke Spanish gasped and offered condolences. They explained the situation to the English-speakers. Emilio rushed to embrace Marga, while the girl who'd been at his side moved to another chair.

Anger falling away, Marga gave in to her first tears since she'd learned the news. She sank into the chair and tried to answer her friends' questions.

"He was never sick in all his life," she said. "We talked on the phone often, but I hadn't seen him since I came to the U.S. He was so happy when Felisa was born. . ."

Of course she didn't mention that when they talked, her father always promised to send Dolores Pilar's family packing. With the war over, they could safely return to the countryside. He would take an apartment, sell the house, and send Marga the money for her baby. Unless she still wanted to come live in that old house herself—? But he didn't recommend it. No one in Managua earned enough to make ends meet, least of all the average doctor.

One of the North Americans asked if she'd be going home for the funeral. Emilio explained that an immigrant's life was complicated. If Marga returned to Nicaragua, she could lose her refugee status and would not be allowed back into the United States.

Then Marga whispered to her boyfriend, "Dolores Pilar wants me to call Miami and tell the brothers what happened. Unless someone else thought to phone them, they still haven't heard."

Emilio nodded. "Let's go home. I'll take care of it."

Later that night Marga spoke to her aunt, Hector's sister, who had raised her from birth to the age of ten. Tia Pureza said that Dolores Pilar had already filed for survivorship on all the property: house, garage and business assets—a flattering term for the battered fleet of taxis and trucks that had sustained Hector's toehold in the middle-class for over 30 years. Common-law wives enjoyed such rights under the new statutes, but so did children born out of wedlock. Several of Hector's still lived in Managua, so they all faced a messy battle for inheritance.

Tia Pureza offered to file a claim on Marga's behalf—after all, she was the firstborn and sole legitimate child.

"I'm ready to defend your interests, mi hija. We'll get a lawyer and take back your mother's house. Hector always intended it to go to you. What do you say?"

Again Marga pictured her father. This time sitting at a table on the plaza in the sun of a tropical winter. He tossed a cracker to the ever-present flock of sparrows that proceeded to fight for pecking rights on the broken bits. When two ladies at the next table laughed at their struggle, Hector flashed his flirtatious grin and pointed significantly toward the sky, saying, "That's what they do to us—keep us scrambling over the crumbs!"

Turning from the women to twelve-year-old Marga, he said more sternly, "Don't ever waste your strength fighting for crumbs, mi hija. Only fight for what's worth having."

With a sigh Marga told her aunt, "I will file no claim."

She felt drained, as if she'd renounced a royal crown.

But Tia Pureza said, "I understand, mi hija. After all, you're in America now. What do you need with an old house in the slums? If you ever do come home, you can always stay with me."

Over the next days, Emilio spent more time around the apartment, although Marga sent him out on errands whenever he offered to help. Alone, she would lie with the baby at her side and gaze at grief like an ocean around her, not something that could possibly pass through the narrow ducts of her eyes. Like two oceans, in fact, forever advancing on either side of a small country that only wanted peace and safety enough to remember its own name.

One evening, Emilio came home to find her staring at an old hinged frame with two black-and-white photos—Marga's parents posing on their wedding day. One was a portrait of her mother, lovely with a white mantilla draped over dark ringlets. She didn't smile, but her eyes reflected a restrained excitement.

"She was so glad to be moving to the city," Marga said. "And to think that he'd bought a house just for her!"

Emilio knew that Marga had no memory of the mother who died at her birth, but still carried a tiny copy of the wedding portrait in the locket she wore around her neck.

In the second photo the young couple stood side by side, their hands joined around a bouquet of lilies. Hector's face shone with a solemn pride.

Emilio took the frame and placed it on the windowsill.

"They're looking down on us from heaven," Marga whispered.

"But can they see us in the dark?" Emilio asked.

He switched off the light and pulled her close, kissing her neck, jaw, cheeks, temples. . .

Marga had always liked to think that her mother kept watch on the child for whom she'd given her life, glad to see her daughter overcoming dangers and difficulties. Surely she wouldn't mind if Marga took a break from grief long enough to taste the consolation of Emilio's love.

As for her father—let him be the one to look the other way for once.

Marga joined Emilio's kisses, and when the tears flowed from her eyes he licked out the tiny pools they made in the cups of her ears. Next morning, she felt happier, especially when Emilio stayed at home to work on his thesis. To her disappointment, after a few weeks of such attentive behavior, he went back to spending evenings at the library or out with friends.

Marga found that memories of her father clustered around the times he had sent her away. Tia Pureza stayed with them after Marga's mother died but when she received an offer of marriage, Hector dispatched his daughter to board at the convent dormitory.

In those years anger at the government was growing all over the city, coming to a furious boil. With it, a new courage spread like wildfire throughout the layers of society.

At age fourteen, Marga told her father that schoolwork was keeping her too busy to visit home on weekends. A fine story, but she knew he suspected the truth: Like other children she spent her time going door to door throughout the shantytowns. There they spread word of the latest demonstrations, urging the people to show support for the Sandinistas.

Thinking back, Marga still tightened her arms across her chest, where she used to carry literacy booklets—the holy sisters had told her to show these to the police, if they asked what she was doing so far from her own neighborhood. Children as young as eight and nine had been "disappeared" for political activity, sometimes to be found dead on the edge of the city, sometimes not to be found at all.

Marga's father finally sent one of his taxis to fetch her from the convent. On entering the house, she saw a trunk ready and waiting at the foot of the stairs. Hector announced that she was going to Costa Rica—to a secluded school, far from the distraction of riots in the streets.

She refused, resorting to revolutionary jargon—her duty to fight for country and people. So what if the schools might be closed for a while? She wouldn't fall behind when all her classmates faced the same delays.

In the chill tone of authority Hector replied that children could not decide for themselves, much less for their country. These were adult affairs.

For the first time in her life, Marga answered back.

"Oh yes, 'adult affairs.' Like moving your new woman right in here. She'll be mistress of the house with me out of the way."

Her father's eyes betrayed the shock of these words. Of course Marga knew that Dolores Pilar had been living in the room behind the kitchen for over a year already, but up till now she'd gone along with ignoring the obvious. Seeing her father's stricken face, she relished the power of opposition, even as she realized her reasoning was flawed: She should have stuck with dedication to the cause, not made a lower-class woman like Dolores Pilar into a scapegoat. But in the heat of the moment she couldn't think what other weapon to use against the wishes of her father, who had never been wrong before.

He turned the tables by naming the person most sacred to them both.

"Your mother will always be mistress of this house. It's in honor of her memory that I want what is best for you."

Then, speaking as if to a fellow adult, he said there was no doubt that the revolution would triumph—he could tell from the mood of drivers, mechanics and clients he talked to each day. The ground swell would sweep the dictatorship aside like dust from a doorway.

"Afterward," he said, "when you're an educated person— that's when you can help your country."

Marga was struck by his serious tone. And she had to admit, he was right about her mother—she would want Marga to finish school and develop a profession.

The following afternoon she departed for Costa Rica, waving to her father and Dolores Pilar from the train. She did not go home again until she was ready to start medical training.

One month after the news of Hector's death, it came time for Felisa's well-baby visit. At the clinic that offered free check-ups they sat in the crowded waiting room, and Marga watched the doctor sorting through a stack of folders behind the desk. She hadn't seen this woman on previous visits, but it was easy to tell that she was the doctor because she wore a crisp white coat over a red dress, and the receptionist spoke to her with obvious deference.

How nice it must be to work in a respected field. Since coming to the U.S., Marga had held all sorts of jobs while she scrimped and saved, trying to take the classes she'd missed in the medical curriculum back home. But as the years passed, her return seemed ever more remote. She no longer knew if her goal of practicing medicine in Nicaragua was a good idea or a nostalgic dream.

How Emilio might fit into the picture remained a troubling question. And now Felisa had taken over as Priority Number One.

Hearing her name called, Marga carried the baby to the examination room. She did her best to answer the nurse's questions about appetite and sleep habits. Her accent made this slow going, with the nurse asking her to repeat several times.

After a moment the doctor breezed in, white coat rustling as she removed Felisa's diaper to check her joints. She was an attractive woman, only a few years older than Marga.

Marga could not resist asking, "Did you always dream to be a doctor?"

The woman looked puzzled.

"Did I dream about it? You mean, is it what I always wanted? Actually, I started out in engineering, but calc and physics weren't my forte. Medicine was the perfect compromise."

Marga didn't know what calquan physics was. Maybe it had to do with a new technology, unknown at the medical institute in Managua. Still, she was glad to hear that the doctor had served at a fort—some kind of military assignment. This meant they had something in common, after all.

"Many students quit my institute when our country went to fight the soldiers from Honduras," Marga said.

She phrased it this way so the woman wouldn't feel that she blamed the American people for their government's awful role in the Contra War. She tried to explain that, as the fighting wore on, her classmates had joined army medical units or agricultural brigades.

"Myself—I volunteer on the state farm, picking coffee, because we need trade income."

The doctor looked up from measuring Felisa's head.

She said, "Our office manager is trained as a social worker. I'm sure she could help you with the supplemental income program."

Marga shook her head.

"In my country doctors also give social service, but it is hard for students—we can't finish our training. Picking coffee is no good. Two girls in my camp are raped by soldiers. Then my father won't let me stay there. He sent me to Miami."

"Oh my!" the doctor said, "I'm sorry to hear that."

She handed Marga a disposable diaper for Felisa and plotted the child's length and weight on her chart. Leading the way back to the reception desk, she asked Marga to wait while she riffled through a drawer and whispered something to the nurse.

After a moment, they found a small card that the doctor pressed into Marga's hand.

She said, "These are good people. They can help, if you'll let them."

The words "Rape Crisis Hotline" were not unfamiliar to Marga, but she didn't know how they could help anyone to finish medical school. She grasped the doctor's arm and tried one more time.

"It's hard for women to get to be doctors. And you, too? Do you ever think you must give up your dream?"

"Oh yes," the doctor said, "bad dreams are a common reaction." She pointed at the card. "They can refer you to a woman doctor, but I'm not on their list myself." She shrugged and smiled, a little sadly. "I'm a pediatrician."

She pulled away and turned back to the examining room.

"Good luck," the nurse said softly, as a bewildered Marga turned to leave under the eyes of all the waiting mothers.

"—And there's a beautiful church in my city, in my neighborhood," Emilio was saying. "It's called Our Lady, Queen of Heaven. It has ancient mosaics. Carved stone. That's where I was baptized. We can baptize Felisa there, too."

With his final semester in the United States drawing to a close, Emilio was keeping later hours than ever before, but the growing stack of printed pages on his desk showed that he was spending his evenings finishing his master's thesis.

Several times he had brought up the question of what would become of them when he had to depart for Spain. Now he repeated the litany of inducements for Marga to come along: Everyone would welcome them with open arms, and he would earn a good living in the family business. They would have a nice apartment, close enough so his parents could help with the baby, but not so close that they would breathe down Marga's neck.

"We can get married at the Queen of Heaven, if that's what you want. It would make my family very happy."

"How romantic," Marga said dryly, continuing to fold a basket of laundry. "It would make your family happy."

"What am I supposed to say?" Emilio demanded. "I don't know what you want. You won't talk about our future. Are you coming with me to Spain or not?"

"So you would go without us if it comes to that? Without your daughter and me?"

"You know that's not what I want."

"I need time to think," Marga insisted.

Emilio took the computer files from his desk and stalked out of the apartment.

How nice. A lovely wedding, Marga thought bitterly, as she watched him walk away. But how will the groom behave afterwards? If he's going to run around, then I'll run faster.

That same afternoon, Marga was baking pastries for a local coffeehouse—her latest scheme for making money at home. While Felisa shook a set of nested spoons on the floor, she pulled the last batch of scones from the oven and set them to cool on the stovetop.

An old-fashioned ballad came on the Spanish-language radio. As Marga turned to grab her spatula, the corner of her eye caught sight of a rubber glove she used for cleaning, tossed on the counter by the sink.

In a flash she imagined her father reaching out his hand for a sweet in the kitchen back at home. Almost involuntarily, she cried an admonitory "Aaaa!"—her voice sounding like Dolores Pilar, of all people—as she gave the glove an impulsive slap with her fingertips.

Then she conjured his image in her mind's eye, the way he'd looked when they were together for the last time at the Managuan airport. He wore a gray suit over a new white shirt left open at the neck. Marga knew he had little to spare after buying her ticket and visa. Still he insisted on stopping for a sit-down lunch before her departure.

She muttered out loud, "You've been dead for more than 40 days. So what are you doing, appearing here now?"

In her mind his voice teased, just as he would have done in real life.

"Funny, I want to ask you the same thing."

"What do you mean? I'm living in America like you told me to. You're the one who sent me here, remember?"

"Sure, I know," he laughed. "And who do you think sent me?"

Marga's hand went to her throat. Did he really mean—?

He nodded, suddenly serious. "She wants you to know that we're watching over you and your family. Both of us are."

Marga had hoped her parents might be reunited in the spiritual realm, but at the moment she was in no mood to indulge her father with tender sentiments.

"What else did she say?" Marga asked. "Has she forgiven you for giving me a dozen half-siblings? Or was it two dozen—who could keep track?"

There came the look of shock, horror at his little girl's precocious accusation. The conjured Hector protested.

"There was nothing of the sort in her day! How can you even imagine it?"

"How can I not imagine? Aren't you men all alike when it comes to that?"

"Well—" he dropped his eyes humbly, but she could see them shifting irresistibly toward the pastries. "—it's true, men can be prodigal where women are concerned. But you must put a stop to it. Rein him in! Be his equal and lay down the law."

So—Marga reasoned, as the ballad came to an end and left the radio abruptly silent—Hector would have wanted me to stick with Emilio and go to Spain. Is that what this is all about?

"We want what is best for you, like always," the voice went on, "but you have to decide what that will be. Go to Spain, see if you like it. You can travel from there to Nicaragua, and Uncle Sam never needs to know. Keep your options open."

"As if it was so simple," Marga said, unable to let go of her scowl.

"Look, mi hija, sometimes we have to use other people just a little bit. God himself understands that—when he needs to get rid of a tyrant, he uses the oppressed poor. When he needs stability, he uses the middle class—"

"And if a young mother needs help arranging her life—" Marga whispered, a new idea emerging from her father's fading image, "she can always use the grandparents."

She glanced down to see Felisa staring at her with a look of wide-eyed attention. Lifting the child onto her hip, she crossed to the telephone, pressed the international code and rang up Emilio's mother.

Guests milled around at the Bon Voyage party, shoulder-to-shoulder in the kitchen and living room, two-deep on the couch and perched on top of Emilio's desk. The table had been moved to the center of the room, where it stood laden with cake, champagne and other refreshments.

Emilio held Felisa on his shoulder with her ruffled skirt covering half his face and her feet in satin slippers drumming on his chest. He let her stand on the kitchen counter, gripping both his hands, so she could demonstrate how she was almost ready to walk. Everyone cheered and applauded and took turns holding her in their arms.

Marga had also dressed up—in a maroon suit with flared skirt, purchased from the engagement money sent by her future family-in-law. She had kicked off the high-heels that went with the outfit to dance sporadic tangos with one friend after another. They all remarked that she hadn't looked so happy in quite some time.

Emilio's mother had also purchased tickets for the couple's honeymoon—Madrid to Managua. Round-trip, since she made no secret of her hope that they would settle down close to home with her first grandchild. Still, she understood that Marga needed to visit her homeland.

Felisa was fast asleep in the bassinet and the party was winding down, when Emilio and Jean-Claude settled on the couch with one of their professors to polish off a bottle of wine. One arm around Emilio's shoulder, the professor spoke of his envy for young people and their passions.

"—To create your life in the freedom of youth," he declared, his speech beginning to slur, eyes inspired, "that's something truly godlike! Follow the energy of desire, and it leads to your destiny."

"But there is no such perfect freedom," Jean-Claude objected, "except, maybe, in the mind. . ."

Emilio spoke as if each word were dear to him, mementos of his last philosophical discussion in the adopted country he was leaving behind.

With a glance at his sleeping daughter, he said, "To be truly godlike, I think you must create something that has a mind of its own, with the freedom to flout your will and your desire."

As the men considered this, Marga crossed the room towards them, gathering paper plates as she came.

She chimed in, speaking Spanish, "But creating life is not a question of will or freedom. It's something deeper that happens whether you want it or not. Like the ground swell of a revolution or a biological process."

Emilio looked up, as if seeing her for the first time after a long absence. He translated what she had said for his friends.

Jean-Claude smirked, but the professor seemed deeply moved. A look mingling joy and pain came over his face, and he saluted Marga with a clenched fist. Using the young men's knees for leverage, he rose to his feet, took the plates from her hands and dropped them by the overflowing trash can.

With surprising energy, he pulled her close in a passable version of tango stance. He began to sing.

"Good-bye to my Juan, good-bye Rosalita! Adios, mis amigos, Jesús y Maria—"

Marga arched her back and spun out to the extent of the old man's arm. Whirling into his embrace again, she tossed her head and looked over at Emilio. Seeing his eyes drawn to her in a smoldering gaze, she laughed with all the power of her heart.

The Artist's Wife

Patti M. Marxsen

Everyone likes to paint, but everyone is not an artist. In Port-au-Prince they sell pictures on street corners, in the airport shops, at hotels, and door-to-door in places where tourists and missionaries go. Some artists have apprentices, groups of boys who help them finish their paintings faster, making more to sell. Gallery owners, websites, even cab drivers sell paintings. It is always the same subject, the deep green countryside where Black Madonnas carry fruit in round baskets balanced on their heads, fruit that echoes the curves of their bodies. Leaves and flowers, fruit and smooth-skinned women. It is the artists who find beauty in this place, hunting it down, capturing it, no matter how elusive. The best artists find customers in America so Americans believe they have the best collections of Haitian art. But that is a lie because the best art is always hidden, never leaving the realm of its creation.

A few people whispered as Lilliane Hippolyte crossed the hot tarmac in Port-au-Prince and swayed into the crowded aisle of the plane. She was a large and dignified Haitian woman, like an African Queen with hair arranged upward and earrings made of fake gold dangling the length of her thick neck. She wore a cotton jacket and a long floral dress. Isn't she someone famous? they whispered as she lumbered forward. Is it her, the mother of the president or maybe the wife of that artist who died last year, dropped dead in broad daylight, didn't he? That's it. She is the wife of Max Hippolyte. They remembered seeing her photograph at his funeral in *Le Nouvelliste*.

Lilliane felt conspicuous in such a small place. She pushed her cross-tied bundle under the seat and squeezed in next to the window. She had never been on an airplane before and never traveled to America. Already it felt like a bad idea, even though the cost was covered by the university in Boston where eight of Max's paintings would be on exhibit for a month. A young woman with a coconut-colored baby stood in the aisle studying seat numbers then moved on. A white man in a tee-shirt that said NO PAIN, NO GAIN moved in quickly and dropped into the seat next to her. *"Bonjour,"* he said grudgingly. His eyes were pulled forward, pensive and frowning.

Lilliane stared out the window at the concrete buildings and hazy sky. It was a hot day and she had been awake since 5 a.m. The house was locked, the plants were watered, Monsieur Jo-Jo would come and feed the birds tomorrow, two old parrots, named Lola and Maurice after Max's grandparents, who lived in a cage in front of the kitchen window. Everything was done so she might as well go, she told herself as she walked down the hill at dawn to catch a tap-tap. But now that she had gotten this far, she wanted to turn back. Her lungs filled slowly as she looked toward the door. A white girl in a neat, navy blue suit was pulling the latch, smiling at the wall with painted lips. "Prepare for take-off," a voice said as another girl with a bright smile leaned across the white man and asked Lilliane to fasten her seatbelt. The belt was too tight but she obliged. The young man put a headset over his ears and closed his eyes as the plane began to move.

Ever since the young American professor had contacted her and come all the way to Haiti last January, Lilliane had lived behind a veil of dread and excitement. They wanted to honor Max Hippolyte with a special exhibition of Haitian art, he said, sitting in the yard with a fine leather satchel leaning against his foot. There would also be work by Haitian-American artists living and working in Boston and a special wall devoted to Max Hippolyte. "The *diaspora*, you know," he said, enunciating the word *diaspora* as if it were a secret. Many people in Boston owned paintings by Max Hippolyte. Did she have any others that she might loan to this exhibition?

Lilliane laughed aloud as she recalled that question in his first letter. Did she have any others? Only every inch of every wall, she wanted to say, though she knew that every picture she owned was not his best work. But so what? She was not a critic or a dealer or a collector. She was the artist's wife and she loved each painting because each one held a memory, a moment, a vivid image of Max working in the garden or in the studio. She remembered his paint-stained hands and the little bits of speckled cloth that used to pile up in the studio. She remembered the smell of paint and the stark excitement of prepared canvas—stretched taut and carefully primed—before he went to work on it. Do you have any others? *Mon Seigneur!* She had a few hundred and most of them had been photographed and made into slides. Would that interest the young American professor? She wrote back with a proud heart.

Dr. Gabriel Jones came quickly, flying to Port-au-Prince from Boston with a leather satchel, a tape recorder, a digital camera, and an envelope filled with letters of introduction, including one from the Haitian Consulate and another from a dean at the famous university. This young man was well-prepared, she thought, as they sat for an hour in the small garden drinking limeade before she let him into the house. His eyes told her that he was sincere, that he respected art. He followed her room to room, looking up and down, admiring the paintings that hung in the shadows from floor to ceiling in wooden frames Max made himself. "This is beautiful," he said with a broad smile. "Beautiful." She noticed that he wasn't looking at any particular painting when he said that.

Later he asked, "How did he work? Inside the studio from memory? Or *en plein air*, in the country?" He spoke good French and wanted to know everything. He asked if he could turn on the tape recorder and she nodded. Could he take a few photos? When did Max begin to paint? How did he work? Which series was his own personal favorite? He asked a lot of questions but they were all easy to answer. Then he asked her if she would like to come to America and attend the reception for the exhibition in September. He thought he could get funds to cover her travel and her stay in Boston. Would she like to stay at his house for three days, or would she prefer a hotel? Lilliane shrugged her shoulders as she straightened a painting in the tiny hallway. "You have been to my home. I would like to come to your home," she said. Dr. Jones smiled at that and said he would take care of everything.

After he left, she stood in the main room of the house and watched the golden light as it danced on Max's paintings, turning his greens and purples into sparkling jewels. She loved the way the house came to life at this hour of the day, the dance of light and shade on the polished wood furniture, the scuttle of Lola and Maurice in their cage in the kitchen. She walked into the bedroom where the flickering light continued to dart through wooden slats. Her favorite paintings were here, in this small space protected with mahogany shutters Max had made so they could sleep or make love any hour of the day. His only self-portrait hung next to the bureau on a narrow slice of wall.

"You coming to be a famous man," she said quietly to the self-portrait. "I'll do for you what I said I would. I'll help you out, you know I will." She smiled at the deep-set eyes that stared back at her with the ribbon-like curl of green leaves behind him; the silvery light made his head look hard and shiny like a bed post. "I'll always do it," she said, "til God takes me someplace else."

Soon after his visit, Dr. Jones sent her a plane ticket with a typed letter that told her how to get a visa to travel outside of Haiti. She didn't like the forms she had to fill out or the waiting rooms filled with young people and small children. It seemed that everyone wanted to travel outside of Haiti but no one looked happy about it. Besides, it was hard work finding the right office and getting the forms to the right person before the office closed for the day. Dr. Jones also sent her money to reproduce a careful selection of her slides and to cover the cost of mailing them to America. Then, a week before her departure, he sent forty American dollars in cash wrapped in several sheets of paper so she would have some money to use when she got to Miami.

"Everyone is very happy that you can come," he wrote. "I will introduce you at the reception as the artist's wife and you will be proud."

That was the first thing Dr. Jones said that she didn't like. Didn't he understand she was already proud to be the wife of Max Hippolyte? She had been proud to ride on his bicycle handlebars when they were still in school and she had been proud to be his lover under the trees along the beaches and be his bride and have his children and cook his food and keep his home. She didn't need any trip to America to be proud of her life as the wife of Max Hippolyte.

"Why do you do so much for him?" her sister asked a long time ago.

"He is a great artist," she replied. "You don't expect Michelangelo to take out the garbage, do you?"

Her sister shrieked with laughter at that remark and afterwards she always called her brother-in-law "Michelangelo." She found a picture of the Sistine Chapel in a magazine and gave it to Lilliane. It was a joke, but it was also a sign of respect.

* * * * *

The plane landed in Miami and everyone had to get out and walk a long way down two empty corridors and up steep flights of steps to a little booth where a man with a silver badge stamped her travel documents. Then there was another long corridor with swinging aluminum doors and light fixtures floating on the low ceiling that gave out a flat, greenish light. Lilliane had never seen such a big building. After a long walk she came to a vast open area with food counters all around and electric signs that spelled out words like TACOS and PIZZA. People were sitting at round tables eating food out Styrofoam containers that most of them left on the table when they got up. She wanted to sit down and drink some coffee but she was afraid she would miss the next plane from Miami to Boston if she stopped moving. It wasn't clear where the plane was or how long it would take to get there.

She kept walking past the food counters and found herself in another long hallway that led to a pavilion with tall glass windows. There were shops, carts, and crowds of people in the pavilion and more round tables and Styrofoam cups and boxes. Everyone seemed busy and in a hurry, so she tried to walk faster, hoping to feel more like them. She put her bundle on her head to balance the weight and free up her arms. Then she found an airline desk and a place to sit until it was time for her flight. Her watch said two o'clock. The plane would leave at two thirty. She sighed and decided to sit right where she was until they told her to get on the plane.

When the plane landed in Boston there was a loud bump and a whoosh of cold air. Lilliane was glad to see Dr. Jones when she came out into the waiting room. "A familiar face is a good thing," she said as they shook hands.

He was surprised she had made the journey with a single bundle and no checked baggage but seemed glad too. "That will save us some time," he said. "Friday traffic is always pretty bad here." They drove into the mouth of the city, through a dark tunnel and along a four-lane highway streaming with fast cars. The drive seemed to last a long while and Lilliane held her breath most of the way. Everything she saw was gray or blurred by speed. Finally, they left the highway and pulled into the driveway of a brick house surrounded by a dark green hedge.

Inside, Leslie Jones stood smiling as her husband introduced "the esteemed Lilliane Hippolyte, the artist's wife." Leslie was pale and flat-faced with thick black hair that she tucked behind her ears. She led Lilliane toward the back of the house to a private room with its own bathroom and a window that looked out on the back yard. It was a small yard, a square of dull grass with a neat hedge growing along one side. There were no birds or flowers or children in the yard. Lilliane wrinkled her nose and wondered why.

"You must be tired," Leslie said, "and we really should leave for the reception in an hour. So maybe you'd like to lie down. Or maybe you'd like to have some coffee, or a glass of juice." Lilliane looked at the young woman, not knowing what to say. Was it polite to arrive at someone's house and lie down before you even had a chance to talk? She didn't know.

"Well, why don't you freshen up and let me know," Leslie said, closing the door to the room. Lilliane did not know what it meant to "freshen up" so she stood at the window for a while, then went out and asked for a glass of water, still clutching her bundle. She decided to keep it with her, even though Leslie Jones tried to convince her to leave it behind.

* * * * *

The reception for the Haitian Art Exhibit Featuring the Work of Max Hippolyte took place in a spacious gallery at a university near the center of the city. The crowd was humming like a hive when they entered and turned to watch as Leslie and Gabriel Jones guided Lilliane to the special green wall with large red letters: Max Hippolyte 1934-1998. There were five other walls in the L-shaped gallery hung with tropical landscapes and close-up portraits of black faces, but this wall was for Max alone. Lilliane stood in front of the wall and studied the pictures with blank eyes. This is not his best work, she thought, as she remembered the waterfalls and banana fields where he had sketched these scenes. There were dark women with baskets balanced on their heads, donkeys and houses, children in the forests, but the eight paintings presented here seemed too small on this big wall and the room was too noisy to see them with a clear head. It is better to look at his work in the quiet of our house, she thought, as Dr. Jones led her to a machine that looked like a television set. The machine stood on a tall table and made clicking sounds as images of Max's paintings flashed before her eyes. This is better work, she said, but there was no texture to the surface of the machine so the pictures looked faraway and the colors seemed to melt in the hot light. Lilliane felt sad and turned away. It was as if Max's paintings had been chopped up and sent to America and fed to the machine. The leaves and flowers were in the wrong place, like rooster feathers on a goat, she thought.

"I'd like to sit down," she said softly, but she could see there was nowhere to sit. Dr. Jones gave his wife a worried look and sent someone out for a chair. The room was cold and everyone spoke in rapid English, a sound that reminded Lilliane of hands clapping. The women were thin and dressed in dark, short dresses. Most of the men were pale and scrubbed with pink, spongy faces. Others had beards and prickly moustaches and one, a student, wore his hair in long braids.

A chair appeared and Lilliane sat down across from the green wall with Max's name on it, the central picture reminding her of the mountains she knew as a child. Her feet hurt but she was afraid to remove her shoes. Leslie Jones vanished and returned with a cup of punch that tasted sour. Lilliane wanted to spit it out but there was nowhere to spit so she swallowed it quickly and coughed. Leslie came back again with a glass of water and a plate of food, small, hard triangles covered with salt. A few people stopped and said hello, but the Black people she met seemed uncomfortable and the white people seemed to laugh at her behind sharp features. A young man with silver rings in his nose and eyebrows shook her hand and said he admired her husband's work. He said he was an artist too so she smiled at him.

After a while, no one seemed to notice her anymore. Gabriel and Leslie Jones were at the other end of the room surrounded with white people wearing expensive clothes. Lilliane was glad to be invisible for awhile, though she was still hungry and wondered if anyone would be bringing out rice or meat. She remembered the avocados at home on the kitchen table and the half melon still in the refrigerator. She wondered if Monsieur Jo-Jo would help himself to a slice of that when he came to feed the old parrots. She hoped he would because otherwise the melon would spoil. It was hard to shop for one person after having a man around for years who was willing to eat everything in sight.

A new group of people arrived like a flock of birds. Lilliane watched Leslie grab their hands then stop to chat with a tall man in a suit. Suddenly, Lilliane couldn't stand it anymore. She stood up and hurried through the crowd, down the steps, and out into the street, cradling her round bundle. They would think she had gone off to find a toilette. That would give her some time. From the sidewalk, she could see the gallery glowing behind her and the green wall at one end of it. She walked briskly until she came to a busy intersection where she stood for a long time until a taxi cab stopped at the light and opened the door.

"I must get to the airport," she said. "I'm late."

The cab driver flipped a lever on his dash board and drove fast so Lilliane bounced up and down, like riding a horse down a path. She held tight to the vinyl arm rest and smiled broadly, glad to be going home. She would get back on the next plane and be home in time for sunrise in the garden.

* * * * *

After waiting a while in a long room with seats welded to the floor, a Black man in a uniform told her she was in the wrong terminal. She followed him around a curved wall of mirrored glass that multiplied their images two hundred times. She removed her shoes and stuffed them into the bundle which she carried on her head until she found a sign she recognized.

"You can't change this ticket without an extra charge." It was another American girl in a navy blue suit.

"How much?"

"Seventy-five dollars. If you have a visa I can charge it for you."

Lilliane smiled, relieved, and reached into the pocket of her cloth coat for her travel documents. She placed her visa on the counter with a smile.

"No, I'm sorry, not that kind of visa. I mean a credit card. A VISA. Do you have a credit card?"

Lilliane looked puzzled.

"Anyway, there's no flight tonight. You'd have to wait until six o'clock in the morning. But I'd need a way to pay for the change."

"I have no way to pay," Lilliane said, staring passively at the girl.

"I see." The girl looked away, as if to search for help. "I'm sorry. You see, we have to go by the ticket you have. And it's for Monday at six o'clock in the morning."

"Monday morning," Lilliane echoed the words. "That will be fine."

She walked away from the girl without saying anything else. It was Friday night. Monday morning was a long way off, but the buildings had electricity and heat and there were plenty of toilettes and food, it seemed, to eat. The chairs were wide and padded and if she looked around, she figured she could find a bench to stretch out on. The rest of the time she would just walk around or look at American newspapers. It wouldn't be so bad. These airports are like towns, she told herself. People were walking to and from as if they were going to work. What was the difference?

Once when they were young, she and Max lived at the beach for a week without a hotel room. Two days of living in a big modern airport didn't seem so bad. She settled into a chair and began to wait.

* * * * *

When Lilliane Hippolyte landed in Port-au-Prince on Monday evening, she took a cab to her house and paid the driver ten American dollars, the last of the money from Dr. Jones. The house was quiet on the outside, half-hidden in evening shadows, but inside Lola and Maurice scrambled and cawed as she unlocked the door. Her hand reached for a familiar light and she dropped her bundle on the table. She turned a light on in each room and greeted Max's paintings like old friends as she moved toward the bedroom. On the far wall, next to the window, his self-portrait glared at her. She glared back, as if they were having words. Was he angry at her for coming back so suddenly or for going to America in the first place? She couldn't tell. There was a glint in his eye that she had not noticed before, a thin splinter of humor that wanted to laugh but took life too seriously to laugh just now. Maybe a moment from now, but not now.

"Maybe if you lived your life somewhere else, maybe you would be a happier man," she said aloud. "But you would not be happier in America." He looked back, almost ready to smile, absorbing every word.

Then, slowly, she removed her cloth jacket, her long dress, her shiny black slip and stockings, her earrings, her white bra, and panties. The odor of her body filled the room like dusk as she stood defiantly in front of the self-portrait, showing herself with pride, thinking how she had now lived longer and gone farther out in the world than he had, all the way to America and back. Then she unpinned her hair and let it hang in matted clumps around her head. She stood there like that for a while, exposed, immodest, letting the self-portrait look her over. "Listen to me," she said. "No one in that place is happier than we were here. I am your wife and I know what I'm saying." She met his eyes for a moment, then added, "You just gotta trust me on that. And you know you can trust me because I know you." Then she shook her head a little to free the hair that needed combing out, crawled under the sheet with a groan, and slept for a long time.

Ángel Moreno

Jeff Percifield

I was making *mojitos* when I first got in on the Plan. I had just negotiated a profit with a fat German tourist who'd tried to give me Euros. "No Euros," I declared, "only dollars." He grunted, and slipped me a twenty. I crushed the mint in the bottom of the glass with a fork, added brown sugar and lemon, ice, rum, and soda, handed him the glass, then me and my friends Luis and Jacobo watched through a broken window while the German porked Marisela, the skinny negrita *jinetera*[1] , on the back seat of a 1947 Impala.

"He jumps like a frog," Luis said.

It was entertaining, and besides, we couldn't watch TV as the power was out in town again. I was seven years old, a black-market entrepreneur in Cuba, a socialist paradise with an OUT OF ORDER sign on it.

"Ángel Moreno!"

I turned and blinked: it was Senorita Montes, my mutton-faced teacher.

"What filthy children!" she snapped. What was *she* doing here? She carried a stick with which she swiped at the others, who scrambled out of the way, although she clipped Luis.

"Look at you!" she said. "What will become of such a child?"

I tipped my chin up defiantly. "I'm going to be a *jinetero!* " I declared. She *smacked* me across the face. I hit her back but she grabbed my wrist.

"You must come with me, Ángel," she said firmly. "You have a scholarship."

"Que?" I paled. In Cuba, to win a scholarship means an appointment with State Security. What had I done? Or rather, what hadn't I done?

I lived with my Aunt Trina, at least I think she was my aunt. But I didn't stay there much because of my hated cousins. Aunt Trina worked at the Department of Revolutionary Metaphors and her boyfriend was a "tour guide," meaning he slept with European tourists for hard currency. I wanted to be a *jinetero* too when I was a little bigger—say, ten—but right now I hung out with the unemployed, AKA the Defenders of the Revolution. (That is, if the Revolution failed, they would have to go to work.) I mixed drinks, ran bribes, informed, stole dogs for the butcher, and hustled tourists for Marisela, although I hoped to increase my staff.

"I didn't do anything," I insisted, as Senorita Montes hustled me along.

"That's the problem, Ángel," she said. Poor thing, she was too ugly to be a *jinetera*, so she had to work for pesos. You can't eat pesos.

We came to the school and I froze. Out front was a 1959 black Chevy—it really was State Security, with two beefy *mulatos* beside it. But what really worried me was what was next to them—my father.

"Hello, my shame," he said.

My mother I hadn't seen in over two years. I heard she lived in Santiago with her new baby and boyfriend. I was left alone when my brother Jesús set off for the States on a slab of Styrofoam.

"Take me with you!" I'd begged him.

"You're too little," he said, even though he was only twelve at the time. Now he lived in America where he would be a baseball star like El Duque, and as soon as I could, I would follow. My father showed up once or twice a year and Aunt Trina would tell him horror stories about me. He'd beat me, give her some money, and vanish. But he'd never come to school.

"*Gracias, Senorita,*" he said with a leer—always the playboy— then *yanked* me into the car.

"Where are we going?" I said as the *mulatos* drove us away.

"Listen to me," my father said, "you are not going to ruin this for me, *escucha?* " He took out a handkerchief and wiped his brow, as it was humid. "You will do exactly as you are told, you little shit. Or I will break you into pieces."

We bounced along the steaming asphalt, ruts sprouting weeds and cornflowers, past the sepia countryside, a snapshot frozen since 1959: shanties and naked children, burros, bicycles, listing telephone poles. In Cuba, the modern world had passed us by; if Columbus had pulled up in his caravel, he would have felt right at home. It was a stucco of socialism smeared on a colonial frame, flaking away in the Caribbean torpor. We had healthcare but no medicine, education but no books, housing but no roofs, a glorious past but no tomorrow.

And now, it seemed, I was in big trouble. "I didn't do anything," I announced.

"You're just like your mother," my father sneered, "completely worthless."

I looked at him. "My mother is beautiful," I said. He looked at me and turned away. Actually I didn't even have a picture of my mother, and, sadly, could not recall what she'd looked like, only that she was beautiful. Every time I saw a pretty soft-drink model, or a lovely tourist from Madrid or Buenos Aires, I'd think, she looks just like my mother!

With some excitement, I watched as we turned towards Havana. Havana, city of ruins, tumbling into the sea! She was a stained etching in charcoal and faded glory, empty plazas, walls canting every which way as if they did not know that Modern Art was subversive. She was a tropical beauty who cast off her dour Soviet babushka and now tarted it up in hot pants and pumps, trolling for dollars, but she didn't pay her bills so they turned off the electricity.

Across the rooftops, as far as the eye could see, an armada of waving laundry, dirty white flags of underwear: we surrender! I leaned out the window, smelled frying fish and plantains, whistled at a *jinetera* with a nose like a toucan, and my father pulled me roughly back. His hair was sweating; I had never seen him this nervous, but then I saw why. We were going up the hill to the mysterious and much-feared Directorate of Democracy.

They waved us through the triple-guarded gates, we drew up in front of a crumbling staircase embroidered with moss, and the *mulato* goons ushered us out. Inside, guards marched us through a maze of shadows and obfuscations, past pillars of lies upholding a framework of failure, iron ramparts of suffering and oppression reared into a tottering tower of ego, corruption, and ruin. We passed wheezing generators laboring in the heat, an empty swimming pool shaped like an alligator, shuttered Departments and Compartments and Retrenchments, and finally swept into a grand chamber wallpapered with armed soldiers. There sat the Council of Ministers, looking darkly at us. My father held my hand tight in his. No one spoke. Then in strode the Maximum Leader.

The Ministers all jumped to their feet. I couldn't believe it, it was our Supreme Leader himself, AKA El Comandante, El Presidente-for-Life, the Beard, El Loco Supremo, and You-Know-Who, in trademark rumpled fatigues and bristle-brush beard. He saluted listlessly, motioned for the Council to sit, then turned.

"Behold!" he bellowed, with a sweep of his long arm, "here is the future of Cuba!" He was pointing to me.

My father could not suppress a spasm.

"There are those who say Cuba is falling behind," the Beard said. The Ministers all became preoccupied with their buttons. "But I tell you, we are forging ahead along the path to Socialism!"

I could think of a great many Russians who would say the path led right off a cliff, but kept it to myself.

"You see," said the Beard, "it is all part of *the Plan*. Tell me Ángel," he said, swiveling to face me, "why do you think there is no opposition press in Cuba, *hmmm*? Because there is no paper! Brilliant, no?!"

He grinned hugely, then glowered under his bushy brows until his Ministers applauded tepidly. He lit a cigar and blew a wraith of blue smoke; it looked vaguely like the Virgin de la Caridad, and he frowned.

"You see, Ángel," he continued, "we *could* be rich, if we wanted to. We *could* be Miami."

I must have looked skeptical.

"Well, we could be Tampa," he said. "We could be *Vegas*, for Christ's sake!"

"We could?" I said, and my father *whapped* me on the head.

"We could," the Beard repeated, "but we don't want to. And why? Because of the Mafia," he said. "It took the Revolution to drive the Mafia out of Cuba, and do you know what it would take to bring it back? *The Disney Channel.* That's all it would take."

He blew another cloud of smoke, this time Christ on the cross, and angrily waved it away.

"Comrades!" he thundered, spreading his arms. "We aim for another record in sugar production!" (Meaning, the crop sucked again.)

"The children of Cuba will have new school uniforms this year!" (Meaning, shorter pants to save fabric; if mine got any shorter, I'd be wearing a bib.)

"I am unveiling a new, streamlined, Five Year Plan!" He pulled out a scroll, one end of which dropped to the floor, rolled down the center of the hall, down the steps, and out the door. The Beard began to recite.

Several hours later, he was still going strong. "Point nine hundred and ninety-nine," he read, "in order to increase production, we will set the clocks back every night, thus adding additional days to the month. Socialism triumphs over time!"

The Ministers had all fallen asleep. The soldiers, too, were dozing, some snoring. My father had dozed off, too, right where he stood, weaving slightly. I was sitting on the floor, drawing a dinosaur with a bit of chalk. Even the flies were sleepy; one of them buzzed lazily, then dropped onto my drawing with a tiny snore. I brushed it aside.

"*. . .pass what may pass, fall who may fall, die who may DIE!*"

I looked up. The Beard was posed like a statue, one arm raised, staring defiantly into eternity. His beetling eyes slid sideways, aware for the first time that the room was not quite rapt. I quickly raised my hand.

"Question? Yes?"

"*Por favor,*" I said, "when are we going to crush the Yanqi dogs?"

He smiled like a cat. "Soon, Ángel," he purred, "but we need a little help." (Aside from food, shelter, and electricity, we seemed to be doing just fine.) "We need a teensy weensy bit of assistance, Ángel," he continued, "and *you* can help us."

"Me?"

He raised an eyebrow. "You do recall Elián?"

Elián. That little shit, of course I remembered him. Elián, in the land of milk and Pepsi, we all envied the brat, who could believe he'd want to return to this roofless, decaying No-Fun Zone. Elián! It was all we heard for months. El Loco would close the schools and we'd have to march in the heat chanting *Devuelvan a Elián!* Send him home! (But we didn't, we made up our own chants, such as *Elián, amigo, mandame un abrigo!* Elián, buddy, send me a coat!)

"Elián was the best thing to happen to me since Khrushchev," the Beard sighed. "Too bad about the mother, though." He *swatted* at a pesky fly, then turned to me. "But that's where you come in."

He reached behind his chair, swept up an inner tube (!) and threw it down in front of me, *whap* like a gauntlet. Everyone jumped.

"You're going to Florida, my boy!" he grinned, and lit a cigar.

"Oh boy!" I said.

His face darkened like blood pudding. He took several enormous strides towards me and leaned forwards, the awful history of his face just inches from mine.

"*Only—for—a while,*" he said. He clicked his heels together, spun round, and painted us all a vision of the Plan. "You will be plucked from the sea by Brothers to the Rescue! You will tell them your mother and the rest of your sorry *balseros*[2] drowned! The exiles will try to keep you, and play right into my hands! Your anguished father will appear on TV, begging for your return!"

I looked up at my father; he curled his lip.

"And in the end," the Beard finished, "you come home, and I get the kind of publicity you just can't buy. It's a win/win thing: you get a trip to Disney World, I get a puff piece with Barbara Walters."

It all was too amazing! But something confused me. "Where is my mother?" I said. "Is she coming with me?"

My father looked away. The Beard knelt down in front of me. "Don't worry, Angelito," he said, "your mother will be waiting for you when you return. She's in on *the Plan*."

And then, just in case I didn't understand, he leaned forward and whispered what he would do to me if I failed at any point.

"*Comprendes?*" he growled. I gulped, and nodded. "*Bueno!*" he said. He snapped his fingers at us and strode out, my father dragging me in tow, all the Ministers scurrying in our wake.

"Our Navy will take you out to sea," Our Leader waved.

"We have a Navy??" I gushed. *Whap* went my father.

El Comandante stopped short, so that we all ran into him, and frowned down at me. "You do know how to swim?" he said.

I nodded furiously, and his beard split into a wicked grin.

Unfortunately, he wasn't kidding about the inner tube. "That's *all* ?" I said, when we were rolling at sea on the deck of a marked-down Soviet trawler; even Jésus' piece of Styrofoam was bigger.

"You're a *balsero*," the Beard said, dropping a compass round my neck, "this is coach. Any last words?" he called to my father.

Seasick, sprawled on a bench with a paper sack at his gorge, my father waved carelessly without looking up.

"*O-kay*," the Beard shrugged. And with that he picked me up and *threw me overboard.*

I came up gasping, spluttering in the foamy sea. I kicked my way to the inner tube and clung to the side like a drowned cat.

"Don't drink the water!" the Beard barked. "That's a joke," he added, and all the Ministers laughed. And then they left.

The Plan immediately fell apart; in that respect, it was quintessentially Cuban.

For one thing, the Brothers to the Fucking Rescue never showed up. Every plane that flew over flew away. I shouted myself hoarse, I waved my arms, I paddled due north. Alone in that blue immensity. I peered down at the fish beneath, the sun refracting into the deeps. Far below were galleons, sunken dreams, the waving arms of lost *balseros*. The sea, she is immense. I clung to my inner tube as it whirled into troughs so deep it was night at the bottom, then up, up, up, Himalayas of swells, so high it was snowing on top, or maybe it was mist. There were sharks too, sawing through the water, back and forth, as if waiting for the dinner bell. Salt, sun, and rainbows. Rimed, blinded, dazzled, I huddled on my inner tube, shivering and excited. *My name is Ángel Moreno,* I whispered, *I am a balsero. . .*I thought about my mother, waiting for me in Santiago; she must have been very worried, although I couldn't believe she'd known they were going to throw me out here like bait.

I saw a school of marlins, leaping north, and I leapt too, and fell off the inner tube. "I am coming!" I spluttered. "Jésus! I am coming!" Then I burst into tears.

I woke in a becalmed night. Overhead, a black sky shot full of stars. Around me, the dark sea was dappled with a flotilla of phosphorescent jellyfish. A shark *bumped* my inner tube. *"Coño!"* I swore, kicking at it. Well, it was only a small shark; perhaps it just wanted to play. Then I saw a blinking light, and paddled towards it.

I heard voices, Russian and Spanish. A dark ship squatted on the sea. I heard the slapping of the water against the hull, saw flashlights winking on and off. There was a snatch of *cumbia* music, abruptly cut short. "Quiet, you idiots!" a voice hissed. I steered towards it.

"Hello!" I called. Instantly a bullet seared the night and grazed my inner tube, which began to keen.

"Who's there?" boomed a voice. A searchlight blinded me.

"It's a fucking kid."

"It's me," I gasped, "Ángel Moreno, from Cuba. My mother, she is dead. Please, where is CNN?"

Silence. "Fucking *balsero*."

"Sorry, kid, this ain't no orphanage. Keep paddling."

"But you shot my inner tube!"

"Life is tough."

With a whine, my inner tube turned into a puddle of rubber. I swallowed salt, and came up gasping. "Please!" I called. "I will drown."

"Vait a minute," said a Russian voice, "how tall is he?"

"One hundred thirty centimeters!" I called, gargling seawater.

"Perfect!" A rope uncoiled out of the darkness and I pulled myself forwards, until I *banged* against a metal hull.

"Hey!" I said. The searchlight blinked off, and I found myself next to a *submarine*, floating on the night. A hairy paw hauled me onto a deck.

"Sorry, kid," said a pot-bellied Latino in stained underwear. "We thought you were DEA."

A boat, silent and dark, was moored alongside the sub, and men were transferring bales wrapped in black plastic from the boat and lowering them through an open hatchway painted with a spray of yellow stars on a red flag. "What's in those?" I asked.

"Unicef," the Latino said, and the others laughed.

"Are we going to Miami?" I said. "I really need to get there."

"Never mind," said another voice, a Russian. "Vaht do you know about torpedoes?"

"Everything!" I said. "A torpedo is rum, vodka, cognac, crème de menthe, cucumber, and propane!"

The Russian smiled at me. "I like zis kid," he said, and then peed over the side.

And so I found myself on a Chinese surplus sub, purchased by the Cartel to ship cocaine across the Caribbean, thus avoiding the Cuban navy, which would stop the boats and extort a cut. Inside, it was like a sewer, dark and sweating, which, because it was Chinese, was two sizes too small for everyone but me. The ship swarmed with Colombian mobsters but was manned by Russians; the Colombians wore pistols strapped to their hips, the Russians wore military caps. Everyone squeezed through the sub's tropical innards in their underwear, like pale termites in a nest.

The Colombians were led by a barrel-chested bullfrog named Ulíses; he had a right arm, a brooding Mestizo, lean and angular, as if carved from spite with a sharp knife. The Russian crew was led by General Zam-something, who drank vodka out of a canteen. General Z was puffy-eyed and red-nosed and had once commanded a Soviet Typhoon submarine in the Far East.

"Two hundred men and twenty-four Sturgeon missiles," he said proudly, offering me a Vienna sausage in the dank nook of the bridge. "Now look at me. Goddamn Gorbachev. Russia, she is za bargain basement of za whole vorld."

An oily rat darted boldly out and snatched a sausage. One of the Colombians took a shot at it, and the bullet *zinged* and ricocheted through the maze of pipes and ladders and everyone ducked.

"Goddamit, no firing on board!" General Z shouted. He shook his head. "Vaht a scurvy lot."

My job was to clean the torpedo tubes, some loaded, and some of which, according to the General, "zose idiot Colombians" had packed with hashish on a previous run. I squirreled my way inside a metal tube, and the heady resin went straight to my head, making me dizzy. General Z was impressed.

"How old you say you are?" he said, squinting in the opening.

"Seven!"

He shook his head. "If Cuba stays Communist," he said, "ze Cubans vill soon be smaller zan za Chinese."

We were supposed to be quiet on board, so the DEA wouldn't blow us all to smithereens, but the rusting pipes *pinged* and knocked like a percussionist. Also, the Colombians kept forgetting and playing *cumbias*.

"Zis piece of crap is noisier zan a whore vis za clap," the General sighed.

In the whispery dark, I swung through that sinister jungle gym like a monkey, exploring, sneaking, stealing, although the tension made me nervous. I caught predatory glances, felt fingers brush against me in the dark, and every time I turned around, it seemed, I saw the Mestizo, staring balefully at me.

Dizzy, a bit seasick, I slid down a manhole into a foul and close tube lined with narrow berths like coffins, towels draped over them for privacy. I poked my way along, over and under pipes, to see what I could filch. Under an empty bunk, I found an envelope and lifted it; inside, however, was neither drugs nor money, only snapshots of naked children. Suddenly I felt a grip on my shoulder and turned: it was the Mestizo. His face wore a mandala of black blemishes, like burn marks. He grabbed me roughly.

"Angelito!" came a voice behind us.

It was Orestes, the pot-bellied Colombian who'd fished me out of the sea. He and the Mestizo stared at each other. "What's the matter?" he said.

"My tummy hurts," I said.

Orestes took my hand. "Come," he said.

We lay in his bunk together and he gave me a little white pill. "Is this for my tummy?" I said.

"It's for your heart," he winked, and popped one in his mouth.

I chewed mine, but it tasted terrible. He showed me pictures of his wife and daughters in Barranquilla. "No sons," he sighed, and lit a cigarette. Suddenly I sat up.

"I feel funny, Orestes."

"Relax," he said, and wiped my brow. I felt shaky, and then nauseous, but then my heart opened just like a flower, and I burned with love for my mother.

"*Quiero a mi mamá,*" I whispered.

"Of course you do, Angelito."

"My mother, she is so beautiful!" I said. "But I am such a bad boy!"

"Hush, Angelito."

"It's true!" I said. "That's why she left. But I'm going to see her soon! I'm going to be very very good, and we're going to be together!"

I lay there, blinded with love for my mother.

When I woke up, Orestes was gone. I felt clear as an empty bottle, resolved to be very good. I went to find General Z.

"I need to get to Miami right away," I said.

"Tut," he said, "make me a *mojito*." At a little bar of clinking bottles, I crushed the mint carefully between my fingers, and shook it up as quietly as I could. "You are very lucky boy," he slurred, tousling my hair. "I vill show you Vladivostok and St. Petersburg, vee'll trade coca for black market varheads—"

BOOM!

The sub juddered so hard I saw double, and there was a terrible noise, as if every screw slipped a notch.

"Attack!" the General bellowed. "All hands on deck!"

Everyone ran this way and that and I was knocked about like a pinball. *BOOM!* Terrified, I jumped down a manhole, and ran to find Orestes, but barreled right into the Mestizo. His sunken eyes unpeeled me like a banana, and then he pulled me into a latrine.

"Orestes!" I screamed. The Mestizo put his hand over my mouth, his maroon *pinga* saluting up out of his damp boxers. I bit down hard, tasting blood, and he gawped in an eerie, ululating yowl: he had no tongue. Steam shot out from pipes, alarms chittering; from somewhere overheard a stream of water poured down on me as I skittered through that labyrinth, the Mestizo right on my ass.

He cornered me in the torpedo room, and I dove into a tube.

His prehistoric face, purple with rage and desire, filled the opening, his long arm clawing at me. I scrabbled away, watched as he jerked off, shot a foam of jism at me, then *slammed* the hatch shut.

BOOM BOOM BOOM! The walls of the tube played a tom-tom on my head as the sub shook from side to side. In total darkness, I felt a great rushing roar through the wall: they had just fired an adjacent torpedo! Then with a whoosh! I was ejected into the blue and bottomless sea.

I came up gasping in a whirl of bubbles just as the sub surfaced. It was night. There was a huge ship full of soldiers and— happy day!—an American flag. A searchlight picked me out.

"Is that a kid?"

"Please," I gurgled, "I am Ángel Moreno, from Cuba. Which way is Disney World?" Then I passed out.

* * * * *

And so I found myself in DEA custody in Florida. For General Z it meant arrest and deportation, but Orestes told them my story and the agents were sympathetic. That is, until my uncle Porfi from Miami showed up. He took one look at me, like the leftover trash, and spat.

"Send his sorry ass back to Cuba," he said. It was a little setback to the Plan.

See, I hadn't told El Loco that my uncle Porfi had always said he would strangle me with his bare hands if I ever set foot in Florida. Apparently, my mother had filled him in on the many ways I'd broken her heart. He was my father's uncle or something, but they didn't get along, or so I gathered as I sat in his 1979 Coupe on the way to his house in Little Havana, dazzled by the gajillion neon signs of America.

"Useless piece of shit, just like your father," he said, *yanking* me down into my seat. "Don't think you're not on the next boat to Cuba."

I remembered what the Beard said he would do to me if I screwed this up.

"Oh please, Uncle Porfi," I said, "don't you want me to grow up in the land of freedom and cable TV?"

"Shut up, you little delinquent," he snapped. "This ain't no garbage dump."

"The poor thing," my Aunt Naty said when I got there late at night, "he's lost his mother."

"He probably killed her," Uncle Porfi said, shrugging off his suspenders. He threw me a blanket and I curled up on the living room couch.

I am here, Jésus, I whispered, *I made it!*

I woke up smelling America. It had a delicious aroma: bacon, tobacco, old carpet, hope, endless opportunities. I turned on the TV and helped myself to a cigarette. Aunt Naty almost had an attack.

"What a filthy habit," she tsk'd, *yanking* the cigarette away and setting down a huge plate of breakfast, enough to feed a whole province. Poor Aunt Naty had a forgotten look, like a package that was never delivered, and Uncle Porfi was in a very bad mood that morning.

"Have you looked outside?" she whispered to him.

"Goddamit, how did they find out?" he hissed.

I peeped out the window and gasped: outside the picket fence of their neat and tiny yard was a huge crowd of reporters with TV cameras. Uncle Porfi jerked the curtains shut. Then my cousin America came out.

America! With her red lips and blue lenses and purple nails, she wore earrings like cherries and sunglasses with daisies on them and hats like parasols so that she looked like a tropical drink. She was named for the Western Hemisphere, she said, and Panama was her navel. She showed me on a map and it was true; she did look like it: big boobs, big butt, tiny waist. She was glamorous, like a well-fed *jinetera*, and her bulletproof hair, always a different shade of blonde, was whipped into a frothing confection and sticky with hair spray, like spun sugar.

Uncle Porfi told her to keep me out of sight, but as soon as she saw the cameras, she ran to her room, colored her face, starched her hair, squeezed herself into a too-small top and too-short skirt, *snapped* on a flashing Orion of cut-glass jewelry and marched me outside.

FLASH! The cameras all crowded forward.

America beamed like a VACANCY sign. "This child's MOTH-ER," she announced—(*"What was her name?"* she whispered. *"María,"* I prompted.)—"MARÍA, sacrificed her life to bring this child to FREEDOM!"

Everyone applauded. FLASH!

"We will raise him as she wanted!" America gushed.

"What about the child's father in Cuba?" a reporter said.

Twenty microphones pressed forward and America whispered to me my first line as an American. "My father is Jorge Washington!" I said, and the street burst into applause.

And so I came to live with my new, improved family in Miami, headed by Uncle Porfi and Aunt Naty, who were like worn down pencil stubs. In Cuba, the people were tired, starved for hope and protein, but in America it was because they had to work, work, work. Uncle Porfi lifted crates at the docks, with his bad back, bad knees, and bad breath; Aunt Naty was a cashier at Super Cake, her feet swollen and knotted like yucca roots. In Havana, they could have sat around all day playing cards with the Defenders of the Revolution, but Uncle Porfi said that was not a life for a man but a dog. I wanted to be a good American too, and offered to open a *mojito* stand—always popular—but Aunt Naty said *"Dios mío!"*

America worked as a dental assistant, which suited her because she said she was naturally personable and liked to converse without interruptions. I shared her party-colored room and followed her around and couldn't wash off the smell of her vanilla perfume, but I didn't care because she was so pretty!

The Moreno bungalow filled up with scores of relatives, people I'd never heard of. There was a roast pig in the backyard and a band and congressmen and lawyers and reporters and famous people like La Vieja, the hundred-year-old salsa singer in blonde wig and platforms who pinched my cheek when I made her a Zombie. *"Azúcar!"* she said. A state senator brought me a puppy.

"I hate dogs," I said, and the senator gave me a slippery smile. It was a great party, at least until my Uncle Amado showed up. He was my mother's half-brother. Thin-framed, with his dimples and eyeglasses, I imagined he looked like a sad version of my mother. He put his arms around me and sobbed.

"Poor María," he wept, "she was so good, and now she's dead."

"Oh but she's not dead, Uncle Amado" I said, feeling terrible, and everyone looked at me. "I mean, she's in Heaven," I added.

"That's right," America said, peeling off a long thin strip of barbecued ribs, "Ángel's mother is in Heaven, waiting for Cuba to be free."

Uncle Porfi gave me a long, thin look, but America squeezed my cheek. "Make me another drink, *papito.*"

That night, as we prepared for bed, America made me kneel down beside her. "Time to say your prayers, Ángel."

Prayers? "I say mine in my head," I told her.

"Well, here we say them out loud," she said.

"You first," I said.

"Okay," she said. "Blessed Mother, thank you for sending Ángel to us. Thank you for my good hair and my parents even though they make me crazy. Thank you for the embargo and for Jesse Helms and please give You-Know-Who a coronary. Grant us everlasting peace. And maybe a little bit smaller ass. Your turn, Ángel."

I looked up past the glowing candles at the calm and peaceful Virgin. "Please take care of my mother," I whispered, and when I looked at America, she had tears in her eyes.

"America," I said, as we got into bed, "is it wrong to lie?"

"Oh, it's a *sin*, Ángel," she said. "Only bad people lie, but you're a good good boy!" And she covered my head with kisses.

The crowds outside my uncle's house grew bigger and bigger, especially after the Blessed Virgin appeared in an oil stain in the driveway. I would stand by the window, scanning the faces, while America and Aunt Naty watched *Mi Vida Desdichada*, their favorite *novela*.

"I can't understand why my brother Jésus hasn't come," I said.

America looked at me gravely. "I'm sure he'll come soon, Ángel," she said. Aunt Naty gave me a cookie. Even Uncle Porfi came round when he heard that El Gordo Appliance was giving me a jumbo-screen TV to console me for my loss.

We drove to a strip mall where apparently word had gotten round; crowds were jammed out front yelling *Ángel! Ángel!* and waving signs. (It was only many years later that I realized that every place in America was not populated by hordes of cameramen.) El Gordo, a sweaty man as big as a billboard, led me into a store with wall to wall TV screens, and me on every one. TV crews filmed El Gordo shaking my hand.

"Of course it can't make up for the loss of your mother," he wheezed, "but maybe two hundred and fifty channels can make a dent."

"Look!" America gasped, for there was my father on a hundred TV screens.

"Ángel-I-miss-you-so-much-I-am-doing-everything-I-can-please-do-not-worry," he said, reading woodenly from a piece of paper. Great, Pops, don't quit your day job. The image cut to the Beard himself, who appeared to be angling for a putt on a golf course. America crossed herself.

"A boy needs to be with his father," the Beard said, without looking up. "This is about family values." He made the shot, two under par.

Maybe it was because I was a little tipsy, having sneaked half of America's chili margarita, but I suddenly ran to the wall of TV screens and *kicked* it.

"*Abajo!*" I shouted. "*Abajo el Barbón!* Down with the Beard!"

A great cheer went up and suddenly everyone, the whole store, the whole street, was chanting along with me. I spun round and round, joyous, dizzy, watching a hundred little Ángels shaking their fists, shouting *Abajo el Barbón!* Everyone was laughing and crying and chanting, the voices beating around me like voodoo drums, but then I stopped: a man was standing outside, looking in at me through the glass. Alone in that delirious congregation—*Abajo! Abajo!*—he was silent and unsmiling, and my voice faltered in my throat.

After that, Uncle Porfi announced he was going to raise me as his own. "For the United States of America," he proclaimed to the cameras, in case anyone thought it was for the new appliances and the fact that he was on paid leave from the docks so he could run the Save Ángel fund, a job that seemed to consist of sitting in front of his new wall-to-wall TV in his T-shirt. Letters stuffed with real dollars poured in for my legal fees, although I noticed the bungalow got a new paint job.

In Cuba, the kids all had to march around yelling *Devuelvan a Ángel*, which confirmed that I was the most hated boy on the island.

America, she was like a dream! (I mean the country, not the dental assistant.) I wanted to stay there forever, and wished I could send for my mother. Of course, there was the little matter I'd told everyone she was dead, but, still, there could be a way. It was dangerous, double-crossing the Beard, but day by day I feared him less. I watched *novelas* with America, studied the labyrinthine plots, the incredible coincidences, the double and triple-crosses. And then it came to me.

"My mother," I announced one morning at breakfast, "she has a twin sister."

"Que?" they all said.

"That's right," I nodded. "Her name is. . .Epifania. They look *exactly alike.*"

They all looked nervously at each other, like I was cuckoo, but I knew what I was doing.

I heard that the State Supreme Court had ruled against us and Uncle Porfi became very upset when it looked like his little cash *vaca* was going to be shipped home. "We'll never surrender him!" he declared, stringing barbed wire across the porch. He ran practice drills, and when he blew a whistle, we all had to scramble into the crawlspace under the floor, except that America didn't fit.

"Lay off the *pasteles*," he grumbled.

One night, when America's snoring kept me awake, I slipped out to sneak a cigarette in the bathroom. As I was making my way back to bed, I heard voices. It was Uncle Porfi, having another late-night conference.

"We know they're going to try to snatch him," a voice said.

"We can't let that happen!" said another voice.

"Screw them!" Uncle Porfi said; he'd obviously been drinking.

"Of course," said another voice, an unfamiliar one, "the most important thing is that the Beard doesn't win." Everyone agreed. "If there's a raid, there could be. . .a little accident."

"What do you mean?" Uncle Porfi slurred.

"It would be. . .unfortunate. But it would be *their fault. Comprendes?*"

Then there was a heavy *clunk* as someone set something on the table.

"You know what they say," the voice said, "better dead than Red."

"Dios mío," Uncle Porfi whispered.

"We're all counting on you, Porfi."

I hurried back to bed.

And so it happened that early one morning, America and I were woken from sleep by Aunt Naty screaming bloody murder and Uncle Porfi telling her to shut the fuck up. "Where's the goddamn whistle?" he barked. Suddenly the door *burst* open and a soldier in a ski mask pointed a submachine gun at us.

"Here he is!" he yelled.

America tried to protect us with a curling iron—she wasn't much of a fighter—but the commandos were upon us. One of them swiftly disarmed America.

"She looks fatter on TV," he noted, before stuffing me into a burlap bag.

And then screams and darkness and tear gas. In the black night of the bag, I whispered, *Quiero a mi mamá.* And I heard her, then, very close: *Estoy aqui, mi Angelito.* . .

Later, I heard tinkling music and came to, blinking; I looked around for my father, and El Presidente For Life. But I didn't seem to be in the Plaza de la Revolucion, unless they had recently added animatronic Eskimos and dancing yaks. *It's a world of laughter, a world of tears.* . .

"Where am I?" I said.

"Fantasyland," said a voice—it was America! For we had been kidnapped not by Immigration, but by exile commandos. Tipped off that the INS was going to snatch me, they'd beat them to the punch, smuggled me to Orlando, then barricaded themselves inside "It's a Small World."

"They'd never take a kid away from the Magic Kingdom," one of my ski-masked saviors winked.

The whole world is watching! they began to chant. I looked out between the clog-dancing Matterhorn girls and the chirruping goats: I was a prisoner of Disney World.

Well, it wasn't so bad. The vendors gave us free hot dogs and supplicants lit a field of *velas* out front, swaying, holding pictures of me and the Virgin de la Caridad as though it were a shrine. The Disney Corporation said they would like the situation resolved and Miami announced a boycott and Disney Corp shut up. I could hardly sleep for that accursed song—*There's so much that we share, that it's time we're aware*—which it seemed would go on and on and on, world without end, and for the crowds out front chanting *Ángel, Ángel.* . .

People came from all over to have their picture taken with me, and America said we should charge money, so for five dollars a shot I smiled until I was green.

"Cheetohs!" America said, and everybody laughed. FLASH! I noticed Mickey Mouse, looking at me askance.

In fact, every time I turned around, that Mouse seemed to be skulking around, giving me the Evil Eye. "I'm afraid of him," I told America, but she just laughed.

"Oh, Ángel, it's just a mouse," she teased, but I hadn't grown up in the belly of State Security for nothing. And I was right.

And so we were riding Pirates of the Caribbean for the thousandth time—*Yo ho, yo ho, a pirate's life for me!*—and as we surged up a waterfall, something reached down out of the darkness and pulled me right out of my seat.

"Ángel!" America shrieked, but it was too late, there was a blanket over me, muffling my cries, and then I was rushing, rushing through the dark underbelly of that make-believe Kingdom. . .

When they pulled the blanket off, I was in a bare room, at a bare table, a bare light bulb buzzing overhead. Across from me sat Mickey Mouse, and behind him, snout lowered, was Goofy.

"We know about the Plan, Ángel," said Mickey Mouse.

Gulp. "My name is Ángel Moreno," I said in a thin voice, "My mother and everyone else drowned—"

"LIAR!" Goofy screamed. He leapt at me and shook me like a maracas, until Mickey Mouse pulled him off.

"Easy, *easy*," said the Mouse. "Sorry kid. My buddy, he gets kinda out of control. You don't want him out of control, do you?"

I shook my head, terrified.

"Why don't you tell Mickey what's really going on?"

"What do you mean?" I whispered.

"For starters, we know you didn't come here with your mother."

Gulp. "My mother," I admitted, "she is waiting for me in Santiago."

"LIAR!" Goofy screamed, but Mickey held up his hand.

"Ángel, Ángel," he tsk'd, "don't you know it's a sin to tell a lie?"

"It's true!" I cried. "They made me do it! My father and El Loco! My mother had nothing to do with it! I want my Mommy!"

The Mouse tsk'd, and laid a necklace on the table. I looked at it. "Take it," he said.

I picked it up.

"Do you recognize it?"

"It's my mother's," I nodded. I popped it open, and there was a picture of me and Jésus, two very little boys. "Is she here?" I said.

"Ángel, you know very well your mother died of AIDS six months ago."

I looked at the Mouse. "That's not true," I said. Goofy growled at me.

"IT'S NOT TRUE!" I screamed, and charged, sending Goofy sprawling. "Liar! Liar!" I screamed, beating at him with my fists, until Mickey pulled me off.

"Calm down!" said a disturbed Mouse. Goofy feinted at me, but Mickey slapped him. "Both of you!" He straightened his bow tie. "Okay, Ángel, you win," he said. "You want to go back to Cuba?"

"I want my Mommy!" I said.

"Okay," the Mouse said. "On one condition—you work for us."

"What do you mean?" I sniffed.

"We'll be in touch," he said. He leaned over and pinned a tiny Mickey Mouse face to my shirt. "Once you're in Cuba," he whispered, "your code name will be Pedro Pan. Our agents will get in touch with you."

"I just want my Mommy," I said.

They helicoptered me out of Disney World due to the throngs of chanting Cubans that ringed the park. I sat hunched by the door, deafened by the propellers. A burst of light exploded off starboard. "Fireworks!" I whispered, but the Mouse pulled me back: it was the exiles, shelling us with mortar and anti-aircraft fire to block our escape. And then darkness, and the rushing sea, and I pulled at my mother's necklace around my throat. . .

A story is always subversive, because it is not true, and, once begun, does not end with its telling.

. . .and then the Plaza de la Revolucion, which swarmed with more throngs, only thinner, shabbier, waving their arms, holding aloft candles in red cups, *Ángel, Ángel.* What could I mean to them? Maddened parakeets wheeled like blue and yellow furies over their heads. High above, a billboard with my picture on it (!) loured over the Ministry of Shortages. Soldiers marched me through a gauntlet of waving, seething hysterics, then up up up a dizzying platform, to a podium that teetered over that cauldron of human souls like a scaffold. There was the Maximum Leader, and behind him, my father, and I even saw the Nobel Prize-winning writer, that grizzled Colombian always handy for a hundred years' worth of solicitude; whenever El Loco Supremo needed a friendly photo op, he'd fly him in on his private jet and trot him out like a dog on a leash.

There was no sign of my mother.

The Beard did not smile as he taped a ribbon to me, Hero of the Revolution. The crowd convulsed, but then the Supreme Leader raised his hands and that vast electric went quiet, as if he'd pulled the plug.

"Comrades!" he thundered, his voice echoing to the ends of the earth, "today we have seen the triumph of Socialism!" Cheers, pandemonium, and again he stilled that fury with one upraised hand. And then a strange thing happened. A green parrot, picking at nits on the rail in front of us, swiveled its tufted head, cocked its eye, and squawked, *"AWK! Abajo el Barbón! Down with the Beard!"*

A million souls gasped at once. Had that bird seen my antics on TV? Was it a CIA rogue? The Maximum Leader fixed that parrot with a fierce glare, and the toadying Nobel Prize-winner shooed the counterrevolutionary avian away. But then from somewhere far, far back in the crowd, a thin weary voice, flattened, beaten into the ground for fifty years, emboldened at last by the bravery of a bird, rose up and croaked *"Abajo el Barbón!"*

And then it came at us, like a hurricane pulling itself together from the tropical torpor, and that whole innumerable mass of humanity surged forward, crying *Abajo! Abajo! Abajo!* And the Maximum Traitor, for the first time ever, took a step back.

And it spread: up and down the streets and alleys, windows *popped* open, voices crying *Abajo! Abajo!*, and across the Plaza de la Revolucion, the stone lions stood up on their legs and growled *Abajo!* and at the Memorial José Marti the old buzzard raised his fist and croaked *Abajo!* and General Gomez reared on his bronze horse and his anti-socialist equine whinnied *Abajo!* and in the Cristóbal de Colón cemetery, the weary cadavers rose up on their catafalques and turned thumbs down, the Black Madonna swore *Coño!*, gave the finger, and shouted *Abajo!* and still it spread, across the ruined and weeping countryside where the roosters pecking the yellow dirt crowed *Abajo!*, the mangroves lifted their muddy skirts and shook their mantillas of moss, *Abajo!*, an infinity of parrots exploded like subversive confetti shrieking *Abajo!* until finally that terrible reverberating prayer resounded down the length and breadth of that whole sad and suffering island *Abajo! Abajo! Abajo!*

And then the gunfire.

The troops began to fire over the heads of that surging delirium, and it was blood and history right at our feet. The podium began to tremble. . .

My father *slapped* my face. "This is all your fault, you little shit!" I backed away, slipped, tripped, then fell over the precipice, but the crowd caught me and then I was bouncing across the heads of that rapturous fury as they shouted *Abajo! Abajo!* Or was it *Ángel! Ángel!*

A *merengue* of machine-gun fire. I landed on the hard and bloodied pavement with a *thud*, was kicked sideways like a broken doll, and scrambled into a sewer grate.

Thunder raged as I huddled in the dark, screams, gunfire, pounding feet, and then a man fell right in the grate, eyes bloodied and unseeing, and I screamed and ran. I dove down a manhole, and then another, zigzagging through the dark tunnels, down and away, down and away, I ran as far into the safe and silent earth as I could go. . .

What had I done?

And at last I came to a forgotten tunnel, deep beneath Havana, wide, silent, and dim, most of the ancient, buzzing light bulbs long-blown. All along that endless tunnel sat squat crates on broken wooden blocks, draped with dusty tarpaulin, and through the years of grime one could barely read the stenciling, **CCCP**: supplies, delivered from the Soviet Union, moldering down here for who knows how long since the days of the Cold War, postcards from a lost empire. All still, all quiet, except for the skittering rats.

And then I heard a voice.

It was a woman, old and stooped, muttering to herself as she dragged a rickety ladder through eternity, laboriously changing the burnt-out bulbs, but it was a losing battle, and sooner or later that underworld would go dark. I watched as she made her arthritic way down the ladder.

"Hola, doña."

"Eh?" she started. She squinted at me through watery lenses, all but blind. "Who is there?"

"Ángel Moreno," I said. "What are you doing?"

"Defending the Revolution," she croaked. "The Yanqi dogs are going to attack us because of the U.S. missiles."

"The U.S. missiles?"

"The Union Soviet."

I gasped; had she really been down here for fifty years, mobilizing for a crisis that had long since faded into myth?

"Lo siento, doña," I said. "The Soviet Union, she is gone."

"Que?"

I nodded sadly. "Communism, she is gone too. The Yanqi dogs, they won. We are all alone."

"Alone?"

"*Sí,*" I said, wiping a tear. "Cuba, she is all alone; she is a *balsero*, floating in the ocean."

"*Dios mío,*" she whispered.

I couldn't believe she'd been down there all those years. "What did you eat?" I said, as we walked along.

"Communist chicken," she chuckled. She led me to a tidy nest she'd made for herself where a little fire burned, roasting a fat rat. Of course; one could grow fat, eating the rats of Cuba. She gave me some, and I tasted; too salty.

"*Hijito,*" she said, "can it really be that the world has left us behind?"

"*Sí, mamá,*" I said, "the world, she is changed." I opened my mother's locket and looked at Jésus and me, but it was all blurry.

"*Ay,*" she whistled, "I can't even remember the world. Is it lovely?"

"*Yes,*" I whispered. And then I took her by the hand and led her—slowly, for she was old and stooped—through those forgotten catacombs, relics of a lost world, until by and by we began to smell the sea. We hobbled down a long tunnel through which a stream of sewage trickled. I saw a distant circle of light, and finally the tunnel opened up, onto a desolate and empty beach where the blue waves rolled and the white light dazzled.

We stood there, hand in hand in the yawning opening, and the old woman blinked back fifty years of shadows. A ruined pier ran out into the water and collapsed. There was only the white sky and the blue sea and the cries of gulls.

"I can't see, *hijito,*" she said, shading her eyes. "Is it beautiful?"

"*Sí,*" I whispered, "it's as beautiful as my mother. Cuba, she is the most beautiful mother in the world."

End Notes

[1] A carnal entrepreneur
[2] One who leaves Cuba on a raft, or *balsa*

Stretch, Smooth, Fold, Tuck

Donna Hemans

Stretch, smooth, fold, tuck. Stretch, smooth, fold, tuck. I hearing the lady's smooth, smooth voice. Not like the voice of them teachers from primary school days. They was always fussing, fussing, "Speak better than that, girl." Asking, "Can't you speak better?" as if my mother and father and the people I grow up roun' speak any other way. Them teacher ladies with accent like any British woman.

But I wasn' really thinking on what I doing, not the sheets pulled tight and smooth. I was moving and it was relaxing me, sort of like the hairdresser washing my hair, her fingers moving in circles over my scalp and my eyes closing down, just waiting for sleep. Two towels folded. Two towels hanging. One small rag folded. Another small rag hanging by the sink. One bath soap. One little facial soap. One roll o' tissue, loose end folded like a triangle, like I making a paper plane. I was moving, thinking 'bout that girl giving me problems, standing out on the road at all hours o' night talking to that useless boy. I was thinking 'bout my boy, already acking like he father, just chatting up everybody he see—man, woman, chile—as if somebody appoint him mayor. In everybody business. Talking politics with everybody on the road. And I was thinking 'bout the meat man who took my goats and two pig and my father two pig, and who still can't give me my money though the goat long turn curry and the pork jerk long time now. Every time I see him, he say next week, next week. He sell the meat but he can't pay me till he collec' the money. The hotel don' always pay same time he deliver. So wait. And is long time I waiting now. *Stretch, smooth, fold, tuck.* I see him here sometimes. Come empty handed and walk round pass the bougainvillea curving over the wrought iron like a flowering gate, pass the pool and the children screaming and splashing, and round to the office in the back. Same way he come in, same way he leave. Long hands empty. All the tourist they bringing inside this place and still they telling him check not ready. Come back next week. This tourist thing is a funny business, you know. Same way he can't get his money, same way they won't buy nothing from me. I tell the office I have plenty callaloo and tomato and sweet pepper. I tell the neighbors, I'll buy from them, put it all together and supply the big business—the hotels, the schools—any place that buy in bulk. But all the lady in the office say is *No. They buy from big supplier already.* Big supplier buy NAFTA tomato that don't spoil so easy, big tomato with a sticker that say "No refrigeration necessary." Big American tomato that shiny and stiff because it force ripe and full up o' pesticide. All those things I thinking 'bout. Exam fee for the big girl due and still I can't get the goat and pig money from the meat man.

All that I thinking when in Miss Lady walks telling me 'bout some child Game Boy that missing.

"What Game Boy?" I ask, though I know what she talking. That little thing the children walk roun' with, head down, like the thing directing their feet, opening doors. At the pool, in the tour bus, standing outside, beep, beep, fingers pressing, eyes barely blinking. But I'm the new girl. Something missing and they come see me first.

I tell she to check my bag at the end of the day. Right now I have nine more rooms to clean, plus one back there, the honeymoon suite with the sign on the door. I could tell her 'bout the safes the people don' always use, the rings they leave on the bathroom counter so they don't get lost in the pool. I could tell her 'bout the factory at the free trade zone where I used to work before this. Morning they check to see what you bringing in. Evening they check to see what you tekin' out. Place set up like any prison, grill round the place, guards searching people things like we're prisoner. But I push my cart, dirty towels on top, mop and broom in front, and move to the nex' room.

Stretch, smooth, fold, tuck.

Afternoon come, and this tourist lady come up to me. "What's the real Jamaica like?" she ask.

And I want to ask her what the real America is like, if she live like the soap opera people, if she stand in her kitchen in spike heel when she cleaning chicken and peeling carrot, if she live like this when she home, black people cleaning her room and bringing her food.

"The real Jamaica is what you see." And I open my arms wide and point to the sea, the coconut trees and the palm trees, their bottoms painted white.

"No. No. All this seems so, so, plastic. Everything just seems so perfect. I want to see the real Jamaica." Her face light up and her head bend down like she talking to a little girl whose head she about to pat.

"Where've you been?"

"Ocho Rios. Went up the falls and rode through Fern Gully. Went rafting. That was nice. And horseback riding out by. . .can't remember the name. . .something with a cove. I've been on the tours. But on the tours, it's as if everything's set up for us, people in costumes. A stage show. You know what I mean."

I tell her I've never been on one of those tourist buses, air conditioning blowing all the time, the windows shut tight against the sea breeze and the natural heat and the seats shampoo clean. I tell her I've never rafted down a river, or been in one of those jeeps they paint up with zebra stripes. And the closest I come to riding a horse is the donkey my father used to have when I was little. And that donkey was stubborn, bwoy. But is like she not hearing me. I could tell her I haven't ever slept in a hotel bed, or had dinner in a restaurant like the one they have set up downstairs. No waiter ever bring me food and stand back waiting to take my plate. That's for the tourist them and the people here who live like they're Americans. Restaurant? Not even the jerk chicken and pork they sell by the roadside I ever eat. My mother used to ask, whey they wash them han'? And is the same thing I ask. So I cook my food my own way, boil banana and yam and cornmeal dumpling and rice, and stew the chicken or the pork or beef when I have it.

The real Jamaica, I tell you. I wan' laugh. But she look serious. And I look serious too. *Stretch, smooth, fold, tuck.* I have another room to clean so I lef' she standing there wondering where the real Jamaica is.

The big girl put a pot on the stove. She curry the chicken I wanted to stew down after church Sunday. Home Ec she studying now. Practicing for the exam practical. Want to work in the hotel industry when she graduate. One day she make callaloo fritters. Never hear 'bout that before. But it did taste good anyhow. I try telling her to do something else. The computer thing big now. Or nursing cause people always sick. I tell her the tourist business not always so good, cause when the planes come in half empty and the hotel rooms not full there's no work. Remember after September 11? Everybody stop fly. The hotels empty and no room to clean. But is that she say she wan' do. So who to stop her. She cook the chicken and all that's lef' is the rice. I peel a piece o' yellow yam and put two plantain on to boil.

The little girl mix some syrup and water with a little bit o' lime and the big girl shred some cabbage and carrot for a salad.

Husband come with the four chairs and the table he make for Smitty dining room. Later he go drop it off when Smitty come home. He get the goats, and look 'bout the pigs because the boy on the evening shift. And after he eat the dinner, he leave for Smitty house. He come back after nine with the money from Smitty. He count out eight thousand for the big girl exam fee, and he breathe real hard because his mother eye drops finish and she going next week to see the specialis' in Kingston 'bout the catarac' covering up her eye.

"How much the operation goin' cost?"

"Don' know yet."

He don't tell me how much left. And I don't ask. Payday coming Friday anyhow. He leave and go sit outside because the night still cool and I don' like the cigarette smoke inside the house. Grayson out there and I can hear the two o' them running joke.

In bed, just before I sleep, I laugh when I remember the tourist lady asking me what the real Jamaica is like. It right there before her eyes, me working, working and still can't get no where. The driver o' the bus she traveling in, who driving all day and can't even buy a car of his own. Not even one o' the used Japanese imports everybody start call *deportee*. And she looking and still can't find it.

On Saturday, I take the big girl to work with me so she can see what the tourist industry is really all about. *Stretch, smooth, fold, tuck*, I tell her. *And don't touch anything. Not even the pile o' coins that the tourists don't know how to count.* After the third room, she ask if that is all I do. I send her to the laundry room with the pile o' towels from the three rooms. And after that she go to the kitchen to help little bit prepare the food. In the afternoon she sit by the front desk watching the girls greet the visitors, the voices all sing-songy and sweet for the foreigners.

"What else people do here?"

"Well you could play nanny and watch the children when the parents want to go off by themselves," I tell her. "Or you could play tour guide and ride roun' in them buses pointing out things. Escorting. Or you could dress up like them women I see sometimes in the folk costume, the plaid skirts and head tie up with the same cloth." Native woman dolly I call them for they face, with all the makeup and lipstick, make them look like a dolly.

I can tell she rethinking her plans. And I glad though she only taking Home Ec, and Sewing and Social Studies and Maths and English. I wanted her to take biology and computer studies too. But she didn't want to take biology and she say the computer thing look hard. She young still, anyhow.

We leaving early Saturday afternoon and I see the same tourist lady from early in the week, the one looking for the real Jamaica.

"Is she your daughter?" she ask, eyes squinting in the sun.

"Yes."

"Are you still in school?"

"Yes, Miss. Grade 11, Miss."

"Oh, she's so polite."

And I smile because I hear the American children barking at their parents like they're the adults and the parents are the children.

"Do you work here too?" the lady ask.

"No, Miss. Just came with Mama because she wanted me to see what working here was like."

"Is that what you want to do?"

And I can hear in her voice that she want to tell the girl to aspire to something more.

"I'm still thinking," Sheryl says.

"I'm a guidance counselor at a high school," she says and looks at me. "And I'll tell you what I would tell any of my students. Don't give up on college. Your education is one thing nobody can ever take away from you. And make sure you don't have a baby too soon."

That's the one time I truly thankful for a tourist. She tell the girl what I been wanting to tell her. Make sure you educated.

Tourist lady waves at a man in a taxi and I think that she found someone to show her the real Jamaica. "I'm off she says," and runs to the taxi, hair bouncing like a donkey tail.

Sheryl is quiet the entire bus ride home and I don't bother her because I know she thinking 'bout what she want to do. She tired o' seeing we struggle, tired o' seeing her father go beg the people that owe him money for even part of the payment. She went with me already to the meat man. Thirty-four thousand dollars he owe me now for the pigs and goat. I cry that evening in front the man and his wife because we were going the day after to hear the eye doctor tell us one more time that without surgery Mama, my husband mother, would go blind. She stan' up behind me all the time I bawling. And she walk quiet, quiet all the way home.

Tuesday morning I go to the bank in MoBay and pay the money for Sheryl exam fee. Line long, long and the two people behind the counter moving slow, slow like fat croaking lizard. And all the other clerks back there just looking out as if other people business mean nothing at all. When I finally reach the counter, I don't care anymore 'bout the air conditioning inside the bank, or how clean the inside look. The air comfortable yes, but it don' mean nothing when you have to stan' up so long.

I step back outside and it raining hard, hard. Water running down the street like a little river, carrying the box drink boxes and rolled-up patty paper bags, drinking straws floating like cylinder boats, and I can't step down off the piazza without water covering up my ankles. When I walk down the corner, I see somebody come before and clean the drain. But they only leave the dirt pile up beside the hole and the drain left open so all the dirt and the papers and everything can wash back in.

This is Montego Bay, inside the city where the tourists don't always come. When I reach back to Gloucester Avenue, where the tourist shops are and the restaurants that look expensive even from the outside, is a whole different thing. Water flowing clean, clean. Not a paper, not a box drink box, not a straw.

Back inside the hotel a big man come ask me to answer a questionnaire. He asking all the hotel staff which people make the best visitors—Americans, Canadians, English people, Chinese, Japanese? He want to know which people treat we nicest, but nobody wan' know how much money I take home and whether the job conditions fair. The men that work security here all hours o' the night and can' even get a taxi or a bus to take them home. Same with the cook and the wait staff. Nobody wan' know how I fret everyday that the planes goin' stop fly here and the job soon gone. Nobody wan' know that the little money just can' stretch. Anyhow, I tell him Germans, though most times I can' understan' they English and they can' understan' mine. I should have told him Canadians 'cause they don't ask for too much. Not like the Americans who want and want and want.

One time I wanted was to sell crafts in the Craft Market. I tell Sonny to make the things, carve some fish and bird and wall plaques seeing as how sometimes he make the furniture and the people won't pay. Sometimes he make the furniture and it sit there long time until somebody else come with cash in them pocket and buy another man piece. I used to tell him to make the things and I would sell them. That was when the factory out at Freeport close and they lef' we here with no job and no severance benefits. Not even one o' the little T-shirt them that I know they carry a foreign and sell for more than it worth. And this after the gov'ment make them come and don't pay no taxes. But what to do? We have the children them and I tell him to make the things and I would rent a stall, sell little bit every day. But he say no. He see how the tourist business work. He see the people them sitting there all day long, the crafts collec'ing dus' and everyone o' them trying to sell the same little thing to every tourist that walk through. So I went and learn how to stretch, smooth, fold, and tuck the sheets on the bed.

This touris' business funny though. The gov'ment spen' all the money building roads and hotels to bring the tourist them here. But for all the touris' coming we still owe the IMF and the World Bank money and the children them to go to school can't even get a little free lunch or books. But is not that I thinkin' on.

Things with Mama worse now. Is not jus' the eye problem. She have diabetes too and the medicine done but she don't tell nobody. Her sugar gone up high, high and the doctor say he going have to cut off four toes. Mama don't want to lose no part o' her body because she say same way she come, same way she wan' to go. Whole. And I understand though I think she shouldn't worry too much 'bout four toes. She still can walk on the one good foot. The diabetes, the medications and the catarac'. All o' this coming now.

Saturday morning before I wake up good, good, I hear the people out in Flankers demonstrating against police brutality. Police shoot up a car and kill two men little older than me. I coulda been in that car cause sometimes when I late I take the taxi out to the hotel past the airport. And sometimes when I shopping in MoBay I take a taxi back out here. Before the day finish, the people burn two trucks in the roadway, and police and soldier come now quick, quick not because two men dead without reason but because the people burning fire right next to the airport runway, down by the bottom part where the planes come down and turn before rolling back up to the terminal. And this is Montego Bay, the tourist capital and we sen'ing this bad image a foreign and the tourist them might stop come. The people on the radio worrying already 'bout the damage to the tourist industry, whether the traffic going fall off again.

Still and all, I have to go to work. *Stretch, smooth, fold, tuck.* So I walk since no car not passing through. I don't even know how much miles. Three. Four. Panic, panic at the hotel. One woman at the desk asking if she goin' miss her flight. But the airport in between she and the protests and she can travel on all right. I see again the same tourist lady from early in the week, her bags at her side and her hair braid up with beads on the end.

"Oh, Jamaica is so beautiful," she says and she hugs me tight as if is I is the goddess that make the country. "I extended my stay. Should have gone back Wednesday but I just had to stay a little longer. It's so beautiful, I just wish I could stay longer."

I want to tell her we thankful for the little tourist dollars. But the hotel owned by foreigners and it's hard to know how much o' that extra money goin' stay here in the country, pay off some o' that debt we owe, build a health clinic closer to home. She wearing a ten dollar T-shirt and a woman make a little money braiding her hair. She might have bought other souvenirs. So I smile because I work in the tourist industry and we always supposed to be welcoming. She run down the stairs and I see her when she climb into the air condition bus and look back and wave at the staff working reception. And she don't know what it take for me to get here to get the rooms ready for another bus load of tourists who goin' come.

Twelve rooms today. If the roadblock don' clear up by evening I goin' have to walk again. Another three, four miles. So I push the cart to begin the day. Clean towels folded on the bottom. Clean sheets next to the towels. Rolls of tissue and wrapped soap in the middle. *Stretch, smooth, fold, tuck.*

A Change of Heart

Tonya Haynes

Jack Sprat was a drunkard. Mind you, there wasn't a man in the village who didn't spend a little time in the rum-shop. Every Friday Sleepy and crew would drink flask after flask until their wives come down to take what money was left from them. But Jack Sprat was another story. One Christmas time Jack Sprat drink the rum-shop dry and come Boxing Day there wasn't a rum left for anybody else. Big men sitting down sipping cokes and cursing Jack Sprat who passed out in the doorway gurgling his own vomit.

After years of being more drunk than a fish, all of a sudden it seemed like Jack Sprat had a change of heart. He still drank, but he started to build a wall at the back of the house. When Jack Sprat pass on his way to the rum-shop people stopping him and hailing him up and asking if it is water-toilet and bath he building or if he repairing the house or what. Jack Sprat feel proud with the attention because for years now people were just stepping over him to enter the rum-shop and muttering about how he good-for-nothing. Jack Sprat's wife happy too. She used to be shame shame when she had to pick him up out of the gutter and bring him home, but now even though she ain't sure exactly what he building and even though most nights she still has to go and bring him home at least she sure that it was a wall he building. She walking about the district with her head high because she know that everybody buzzing about her new water-toilet and bath.

Most people didn't have water toilet and bath and nobody had a wall-house, so in everybody's eyes Jack Sprat was some kind of king. When Jack Sprat wasn't out working or drinking he was working on the wall at the back of the house. He laying all the bricks himself. Sometimes the men come and help him in an effort to find what exactly it is he building. Even though they have new respect for Jack Sprat they all hope that he ain't building water-toilet and bath in truth. What would that say about them? Jack Sprat drink out all he money but still he could afford a water-toilet and bath, and them saving and saving and still struggling.

Soon it look like Jack Sprat building a little room and even though his wife very proud she a little suspicious. One day he was

124

in a good mood, smiling and laughing and singing to himself, so she decide to ask him exactly what he doing, because he spending so much time building that she begin to wonder if he going mad or something. Truth be told, she was blue-vex that he wasn't building a water-toilet and bath.

"I buildin' a wall-house. See it now, three bedrooms, a verandah. I might even make it upstairs-and-downstairs. I buildin' slow, you see, but in time it will all be finish. It gine even got water-toilet and bath. You got to start small, you know. But I buildin' a wall house for you and the children."

Jack Sprat's wife never felt so happy in her life; she flit from house to house bragging, leaving all her neighbours jealous. Now Jack Sprat getting even more respect. Especially from his children. They start arguing about who going to get which bedroom and who will share a bedroom with who.

"I want the upstairs bedroom," they all say.

Every time Jack Sprat stumble home his children shout "Daddy," and even the older ones sit on his lap and all of them plead with him to let them have the upstairs bedroom. They ain't ashamed of he no more and beg he to come to PTA meetings and take them to the school fair and take them kite-flying and every moment they have alone with him they bargain with him to let them have the upstairs bedroom. And Jack Sprat promise each child the upstairs bedroom.

One day the children sitting at home, getting along real good like a real family for the first time. Jack Sprat in the rum shop sipping some Mount Gay Eclipse rum and enjoying its burning warmth. His wife sitting on a neighbour's doorstep and telling her that she will be going to America to work and send back some money so that Jack Sprat would finish the house faster.

"You hear something? Wunna ain't hear something?"

The children look outside. Men with hammers picking apart the old wooden house from around them. They start to panic because the upstairs-and-downstairs house is only a very small room made crudely out of bricks with two holes for windows.

"Go and call Mummy!"

"Call Daddy too!"

Jack Sprat never had much furniture, and pretty soon the chattel house gone—just a stack of boards on the back of a truck. Jack Sprat's wife ran home to an open-air living room. She was too embarrassed to confront Jack Sprat. She took up the few possessions she had and went to stay with one of her relatives.

Tonya Haynes

When Jack Sprat stumbled home that night he curled up alone on the cold hard floor of the little room he had built—the money from the sale of his house making an uncomfortable bulge in his pocket.

The Night Stevie Died

Garfield Ellis

Skin came to get me close to six o'clock curfew.

When he did, I was still washing dishes. He dropped into the old chair at the back of the house near the pig pen, placed the long silver cutlass on the ground beside him and asked me how come I wasn't ready yet.

I told him I had gotten home late from school.

"Mr. Hozzy goin' vex," he said, "Him like when we come on time."

"I stopped to watch a gunfight," I told him. "You never hear 'bout the war out on the main road?"

"You was out there?" He rose from the chair and came to the door of the kitchen so his face was inches from where I was packing the wet dishes to dry.

"You hear 'bout it?" I asked him.

"Yes," he told me. "When me come back from cow bush, everybody in the house talking 'bout how Patrick and some of the boys from the hill come down to fight with Spragga and the outer lane boy them—stopped traffic pon the road. So you see it?" He pointed his nose at me.

"See it and hear it," I boasted. "As I step off the bus, I hear gunshot like dirt. Gunshots everywhere. I had to run straight inside Miss Rose shop."

"So how you see it if you in the shop?" he asked, testing me.

"Mi come back out. Once we see that the war was on the road on the other side, we just come out and watch. It was just like T.V. Just like a cowboy show."

His eyes widened in wonder. "A lie! Tell me how it go."

"Make me finish wash the plate them," I told him.

"Tell me, man! Who come down off the hill with Patrick? You see Don Dunda? Mi hear say Spragga and Cow did come up from the lane, and Dadda Dog too. Specialist was out there?"

"Cho!" I told him, my excitement returning. "Cho! You should a out there, man. Cowboy show, mi tell you. . .like cowboy show. But make mi done wash the plate them."

"Then the plate them no done wash?"

"Make mi wipe off the table. And make me get mi 'lass."

I finished the dishes, collected my cutlas from behind the

127

door and yelled to tell my mother I was going on watch. From inside, sewing a dress for my sister, she called to tell me be careful.

My father was not yet home.

"So what happen after you come off the bus?" Skin was getting impatient as we headed for the front of the yard.

"Me no tell you that already, man?" I was deliberately toying with him.

"So what happen?"

"Make we wait on Colin. Him suppose to meet us here."

So we left my yard and sat on the curb with our cutlasses beside us to wait on Colin. Then I told him the story of how I walked off the bus from school and stepped into the middle of a war.

It wasn't a big war as war goes. But it was so exciting my skin still tingled as I told him and my heart still beat like thunder in my throat.

As soon as I stepped off the *Pen Overland* bus, a barrage of gunshot filled the evening.

There was a mad rush for cover and I ran directly into Miss Rose shop.

A minute into the shop and I realised that the gunshots were coming from somewhere in the space between the highways where four men were lying on their bellies with guns pointing toward the Kingston bound stretch of road. Another was chasing and shooting at a bike that was going at medium pace toward Kingston.

"Spragga brave eehh," someone whispered in the shop. "Him a run down the bike go right inna the PNP area."

As he ran, and shot, the bike turned quickly and began to speed down the highway against the flow of traffic toward him. The rider hunched over and the pillion rider stood, brandished two guns and began firing at Spragga like a cowboy upright in his stirrups. Spragga turned quickly and began to run back toward his colleagues who were lying in the dirt of the divide. And as he ran, low and weaving, his friends opened covering fire at the bike coming toward them.

It was like a scene from a cowboy movie—with two cowboys on a horse bearing down on another group bunkered down in a thicket.

Suddenly Spragga dove into the dirt and the bike flashed by him. Then as it passed, the pillion rider flipped around in a flash so that he was now sitting back to back with the rider and facing the men in the divide. A cacophony of gunshots erupted. The man on the bike firing his two guns and the five in the divide opening up at him.

In a second they had passed toward Zion Hill lane. The firing stopped, the bike turned around and the men in the divide waited for him to pass again. *And he had to pass again, for the entrance to the hill was on the other side.*

The bike revved high, the front wheel lifted from the ground and they were off again toward Kingston, oblivious of the traffic scattering to all sides and the people diving away. As they passed, the men opened up at them again and Spragga chased them again, firing his gun and hitting nothing.

As soon as the bike reached a safe range from Spragga, it stopped and both riders disembarked, sprawled behind it like cowboys behind a fallen horse and began firing their guns.

I was mesmerised. Not afraid, but mesmerised and fascinated.

Then suddenly from behind a corner near where the bike was parked, a black open-back land rover emerged, reversing at top speed down the thoroughfare—against the traffic. In the back of it, three men sat, lifting and aiming a heavy gun at Spragga now trapped between the roads. The gun seemed so heavy that it took three men to operate it in the speeding land rover.

Faced with the prospect of a bigger gun and a bigger, faster vehicle, Spragga's men broke ranks and sprinted across the road toward outer lane. But Spragga was trapped further up the road.

Spragga turned and began to run. The men with the big gun began to fire. The shot was so loud it was as if all the other shots had rolled into one and slammed the air against us, *Bladaam*. And the gun was so powerful that I literally saw the dust kick up where the bullet entered the ground at the feet of the gunman running toward us.

Another shot rang out and shattered the glass of an approaching car and caused the driver to lose control. He skidded into the large tree inside the divide.

By now Spragga was dashing across the road toward us. The crowd scattered as he came. He dived over the concrete side walk as if there was water there. He rose quickly as the big gun roared behind him and vaulted the fence into the yard adjoining Miss Rose shop. The bullet slammed into the upper right hand corner of the shop and concrete and dust filled the air.

As Spragga, disappeared the men in the vehicle stood, discarded their gun, pumped their fists in the air and gesticulated rudely as the vehicle began to make its way slowly toward wherever it had come from.

After a while, I joined the excited crowd as they stared and pointed at the large hole the bullet had made in the upper left-hand corner of Miss Rose shop.

Skin's eyes widen as I finished the story. "Blouse and skirt, a big hole."

"When you go out there, you will see it," I told him, nodding my head.

He slammed his cutlass on the ground. "Who you see from Hillside? You see Patrick?"

"A think so. I think Patrick was riding the bike."

"And Specialist, with The Two Gun Kid style?"

"Maybe or maybe with the big gun."

"And who from Laneside? You see Punta?"

"A think so."

"And who else?"

"How me mus' know. I don't know all of them. Plus when the big gun came, everybody disappear."

"What kind a gun them did have?"

"You mean the big gun? Mi no know."

"No, man! What kinda gun them did have inna the shoot-out part?"

"I don' know, Skin!"

"How you so idiot, man?" He looked at me and shook his head. "How you so fool, fool? You can inna the middle of a shootout and don' know what kinda gun the man them did have? Bet you, if it was me, I would a tell you what kind a gun every single gunman out there have. You don' have no information inna you story."

"You was out there?" I enquired. "A you did out there? I was out there! And that is what I see."

"But you don' see nothing!"

"I see shoot-out. You ever see a shoot-out yet, Skin?"

"Rahtid, look how much time me see shoot-out. Me never out there the Sunday evening when them shoot Hog inna the Pentecostal church?"

"You too lie!" I challenged "You wasn't out there. Plus them never shoot him inna the church. Is down the road them shoot him and him stagger into the churchyard and dead. You too lie!"

"How you mean if me was out there?"

"You never see it. Plus wasn't shoot-out: that was a killing. . .that was assassination."

"Go way, 'bout *'sassination.*"

"Come, man," I picked up my cutlass. "See Colin coming deh."

Colin came from around the corner with a *billy* in his hand. Not a long firm sword-like bladed cutlass that Skin and I had, but his weapon was made of a thinner flat steel that flared away from the handle like a baseball bat flattened to the thinness of skillet and sharpened like a barber's blade; when he flexed his wrist it bent and snapped like an angry twig.

As soon as he got to the curb, Skin began to tell him my story as if he had seen the shoot-out himself. And I knew immediately that the only credit I would get would be somewhere at the end when he wanted to say how I had been there for the whole thing and never even found out what gun was used.

But halfway through the story Colin yelled that he had heard about the whole thing. "You was out there, Skin?"

"No! No the one Wesley," he pointed to me. "And him not even know one o' the gun them that the man them used."

"Is set them set up Spragga, though," Collin quipped as we started up the road. "Is so me hear. Because them know that him well wan' kill Patrick, them bait him and try kill him with the big gun."

"Is not so it mus' go," Skin said. "Patrick mus' come down come face Spragga himself if him bad."

I laughed at that. "You think Patrick 'fraid a Spragga. I was out there. Him never look afraid to me."

"It was a plan," Collin offered.

"Cho," Skin said, "A man mus' face a man. Is so you know who *badder.*"

"You think is chevy chase this." I quipped.

"But even if is chevy chase, the one Patrick would 'fraid a Spragga," Skin said.

"You a joker!" I said, "Eh, Colin, Spragga could play chevey chase better than Patrick though?"

"The two o' them a' the same," Colin said. "And it depend on whose side them on."

"Ahh," Skin said.

"Ahh?" I laughed. "You know who bad pon chevy chase, boy."

"Who?" Skin asked.

"Stevie," Colin said, "Stevie. Nobody can' bruck like Stevie. Nobody can' cover base like Stevie."

"Depend on whose side him deh pon," Skin said.

"No, no!" Colin and I came out. "Stevie play good pon any side. And you well an' know that, Skin. You too lie."

"You remember the time," Colin said, "when we play chevy chase till late, and then we go show, and come back and play chevy chase again. . ."

"And Stevie mother lock him out," Skin laughed.

"Yes," I said. "And Patrick chase Spragga right round the housing scheme."

"Yeah."

"And it take three man fi corner Spragga inna Miss Blossom shop."

"Yeah."

"Same thing me tell you say Spragga better than Patrick," Skin re-enforced.

"Yeah, but the same thing happen to Patrick too, man; them couldn't catch him that night. Is because we stop play and go catch Larry van why the game did stop," I said.

"Is not that night," Colin reminded me. "I mean the night when Stevie mother lock him out and we decide to bleach with him and run a boat inna Patrick father hog pen. You remember. And Spragga tell pure Big Boy story. You no remember who and who was there?"

"Me remember," said Skin.

"Me too. Make me tell you who. Three of us did deh deh," I said.

"Yes. And Stevie, and Spragga, and Patrick. Yes and Patrick cousin Michael."

"And Tony Blues, but him couldn't bleach so him go home as the food done."

"Yeah," said Skin. "But the food never cook good."

"True, the dumpling them too tight."

"Boy, Spragga could kneed some tight dumpling, bwai. And Patrick too."

"And then all a we leave early with Skin, go cow bush, you remember?"

"Yes, and Stevie still get beaten the next day."

"All you too, man." Skin laughed at me.

"Yeah. We used to have some nice time."

"Couldn't tell when we play little chevy chase," Colin said.
"Everybody jus' split up," Skin said.

"Couldn't tell when we play little chevy chase," I repeated
sombrely.

Mr. Hozzy lived five minutes from my house but it took us ten
minutes to get there. All because of the excitement about the
gunfight, and Skin's jumping up and down and slapping his cutlass on the asphalt with every joke he cracked. When we got
there Mr. Hozzy, his wife, Ms. Bev, Mr. Lloyd and Clive were sitting
around a ludo board. Mr. Hozzy was shaking the cup flamboy-
antly as he surveyed the board and the placement of the pieces
on it. He threw a three and an ace. Clive laughed and challenged
him to make his move.

"How onoo just a come?" Mr. Hozzy said to us, making to rise
from the board. He was obviously losing and wanted an excuse
to leave the game.

"Move, man!" his wife screamed at him, "Stevie don't come
yet."

"Well, if him don't come in the next five minutes we leaving
him." Mr. Hozzy reviewed the pieces on the board and made a
half-hearted move. He had to place his man on his wife's gate.
A six from her dice and it would be dead.

"So how onoo jus' coming?" Mr. Lloyd regarded us with a
smile.

"The one Wesley a watch gunfight," Skin said, as he sat on
the low verandah wall.

"You did come early?" I countered.

Ms. Bev screamed as she threw a six. She rose and picked
up her husband's piece, squeezed it hard then threw it aside with
a laugh. "You dead this evening," she bellowed as she got ready
to throw again.

I sat beside Skin on the concrete wall of the verandah as the
game progressed. I wondered where Stevie could be. Well not
wonder, just thought of him a bit, for I knew where he was and
what he was doing. He was at his house doing his homework. His
mother insisted on that, beat him for it too. Homework was a part
of Stevie as cow bush was a part of Skin and washing the dishes

was a part of me. We never leave home without doing it. But this was our watch night. And Stevie knew that curfew started at six. So he should have completed his homework by now.

Missing watch night would be worse than missing a cricket match. It was the one night in two weeks when we would don our cutlasses and patrol the perimeter of our housing scheme from six to six. We lived in a little scheme of about three hundred houses that was bordered on both sides by warring political factions. The JLP called us a Socialist Scheme and the PNP called us a Laborite Scheme. We had no gunmen, and we tried to have friends from all sides. So many times the gunmen from both sides would trample through the scheme to fight or scout around the edges, molest us and threaten us. At times they would break into our houses or fire gunshot at the homes they felt supported the party they hated.

So we formed our own patrol and established a six to six curfew.

Now to venture through our scheme after six o'clock would be to take one's life into one's own hands. Every family was involved, and every yard must volunteer someone at least one night per month. Some were too afraid to go, some refused on the grounds that they were not policemen. Some like Mr. Hozzy took it seriously as his civic duty. Others like Mass Lloyd came because he had nothing else to do, and us boys went for the adventure and fun of it.

The last time we were on duty we had a chance to chase two people from one end of the scheme to the other. Skin accosted a man twice his size and slapped him so hard with his cutlass that he fell to the ground. We would have beaten him senseless had Mr. Hozzy not held us back. It turned out the man was just a stranger from Clarendon who was foolish enough to try and cut through to the main road after six.

When Stevie finally arrived, Mr. Hozzy was three rounds from losing the game of ludo. He got up quickly from the board much to the chagrin of his hot tempered wife who insisted that he returned to the game.

"Woman, you don't see we late?" he yelled back at her as he walked into his house to retrieve a little black bag. "You don't see we late?"

"Is Daylight Saving Time," she yelled "and ten minutes not going make much difference."

But Mr. Hozzy had already vacated the board and Mr. Lloyd and Clive had already begun to retrieve their cutlasses.

Stevie came with his school bag that evening. He hailed us, placed it at the foot of the ludo table and asked Ms. Bev if he could study a bit before he left. There was no light at his house that day.

Ms. Bev shouted for Mr. Hozzy to return because Stevie wanted to study before he went.

"Is a long homework Stevie?" She eyed Stevie with sympathy.

"No, Ms. Bev, me almost finished."

"Of course you can do you homework, Stevie. You hear, Hozzy? Stevie can do him homework."

Mr. Hozzy returned to the door in his black jeans jacket and black floppy hat and gave the stern business-like look he must have used in his post as supervisor at the Guinness factory.

"Stevie can study at ten o'clock break," he said. "If the homework not long him can do it ten o'clock. We have work to do. And time a go. Leave you bag right under the table there so, Stevie," he said. "We late already."

Skin slid over to me, "Mr. Hozzy have a gun. Tell you say him have a gun."

I shrugged him off, but I was already tingling with excitement. He had told me the day before but I had not believed him.

Now as Mr. Hozzy left his veranda with only a little black bag in his hand, while the rest of us sported sharpened machetes, I had my confirmation. Suddenly our little group was filled with a sudden importance. We had a gun in our midst. Let any other patrol, any other night top that.

So there were seven of us on duty that night that Stevie died. Three men, four boys, six cutlasses, and a gun. Mr. Hozzy was a supervisor at Guinness; he was married with three children, one of whom was Patrick, the gunman on the hill. His daughter attended St. Jago High School, his other son was in primary school and his wife worked at a store in Spanish Town. Mr. Lloyd was his neighbour, a twitching, bespectacled older man who had retired from his job at the post office. His wife worked at a factory in Spanish Town, his son had grown and left the village and his only daughter was attending primary school. Clive was a groom at Caymanas Park. Skin was fifteen and attended Spanish Town Primary, Colin was sixteen and learning trade at a mechanic shop in Kingston. I was in Third Form at Kingston College and Stevie, fourteen, attended St. Georges High School. Three men, four boys, six cutlasses, and a gun.

When we got to the first crossroads, Mr. Hozzy stopped and split the group in two. Much to Skin's protest, he placed him in a group with Colin, Mr. Lloyd and Clive. They would patrol from one end. Mr. Hozzy, Stevie and I would patrol from the other. We would meet again in about two hours under the large guango tree on the playing field near the gully.

It was Daylight Savings Time, on the edge of summer and the day had plenty light in it. People were going about their businesses, families were having dinner. Women were on their verandahs, leaning against their fences, strolling with their children down the streets—boys were playing football on the road, teenagers were checking each other out, men were playing dominoes and ludo, people were watering their lawns.

As we walked the streets, everyone would know we were on watch that night.

People would call us over, talk with us for a while, point out where they had seen a suspicious character, volunteer information on where to double back at what time of the night, ask about our families and wished us well. Patrolling was a stroll in the evening, but everyone knew that later when they went to bed, we would still be there walking the streets, sitting on the corners, patrolling the dark lanes, accosting strangers. . .protecting ourselves from election time.

The closest police station was five miles away. There was no telephone in the housing scheme. But there was an election coming. There were gunmen at war on either side of us that used our community as a tramping ground and an arena for battles. They preyed on us, molested us, stoned our houses and harassed our families.

Them ketch one!

The shout brought terror to me. I looked around at Mr. Hozzy and he too had momentarily frozen. There was nothing but fear in Stevie's eyes.

"Mr. Hozzy, them catch one man up there so," the little girl squealed. "Wesley," she turned to me, "him say him know you. Skin say you mus' run come before them kill him."

At the sound of Skin's name we broke into a run. As I ran, I tried to remember the names and faces of all the people I could know on either side of the political divide, all those I grew up with, met by chance or through friendships; all those who were gunmen, killers or thieves. All those who were PNP and JLP and those who would be desperate enough to invoke my name to ward off the wrath of a mob.

My heart was in my throat.

We got to the angry crowd at the corner near the south border of the scheme a few paces down from Dove's shop. Even before we stopped, I could hear a voce shouting: *Don' wait pon no body, man. Come we kill him now!* But Skin and the rest of the group were keeping things in order. The crowd parted for us as we got to it, but just barely, and we still had to press our way through bodies to get to where someone lay cowering in the dirt. Skin and the guard team were standing around him with their cutlasses at the ready, and Clive had him draped by the collar.

He had already suffered some sort of beating, for there was a spattering of blood on his shirt. A small black bag and two books were strewn in the dirt off to the side.

"Wesley, you know this man?"

This was Mr. Lloyd.

"Wesley don' know him!" Skin screamed. He lifted the cutlass and shaped at the cowering figure.

At the sound of my name the man lifted his head from the curl of the fetal position he held. And the terrified face of one of my best friends looked up at me. "Henry!" The word was out of my mouth before I realised it. "Henry, whe' you doing here?"

"You know him?" Skin asked. "How me no know him?"

"Whe' you know him from?" Mr. Hozzy asked sternly. The questions were coming from all sides. They were making me nervous.

"We go the same school," I said. "What you doing here?" I asked Henry again.

Colin shoved him to his feet. The crowd held its ground. They still wanted to know, if he was a spy, or how could I tell he was not a bad man even though he attended my school. "Nuff a them go school and still walk and kill people." One woman shouted. "Kill him, kill all a them."

"He is a Christian," I shouted. "Him is a Christian!"

"That don' say," the voice in the crowd defended. "You no hear how much parson them ketch a thief!"

"Alright, go on now," Mr. Hozzy said to Henry who was drawing close to me. "You can' stay here." Then to me he said, "You don't tell you friend them that they can' come in here after six o'clock?"

"But me tell you that," I shouted at Henry. "Me never tell you?"

"But you say we could swap book this evening."

"I said that?" Yes I had; I remembered telling him that he could come for some books that evening. "But before six o'clock," I shouted at him again. "Before six o'clock."

"But is not six o'clock yet!" poor Henry shouted as Skin stuffed his empty bag into his arms.

"Is nearly seven; is Daylight Saving Time."

"Run boy!" Colin shouted. "Run!"

That was the last we saw of Henry that night. At Colin's shout and Skin's menace he darted away with his empty bag leaving his two books still on the ground. Then I heard him scream and saw him stumble as someone threw a stone that hit him square in the back of his head. But he did not stop. He covered his head with his hands and disappeared across the border.

After that, the evening became a strange place to me and the idea of being on watch filled me with a certain anxiety. Suddenly it wasn't so exciting to be there anymore. I began to fear the sharpened cutlass in my hand and the real circumstances that an actual confrontation could bring. I could not lose the pain that sat in my stomach from the minute I pressed through the crowd and saw Henry lying on the ground—nor the fear I felt when he drew close to me and the terror of the recognition and admission that I knew him. Nor the menace and anger of the mob, or the sight of the stone bursting his head.

How could someone die for forgetting it was Daylight Saving Time? How could someone have to die for forgetting what time of the day it is.

"That is how onoo young people stay," Mr. Hozzy offered. "Onoo don't know time. Same thing with Adrian," he referred to his son, "same thing with him—big ol' boy and I have to wake him every morning. Not one morning him can wake himself. If I sick one day him never reach school. Young people don' know time."

"Maybe we should allow students to pass through," Stevie volunteered, "people who want books and so. My mother was saying we should make church people pass through."

"Rule is rule," Mr. Hozzy said. "And Wesley said him did tell him. Bet you him never forget Daylight Saving Time again."

"Them never have to lick him with no stone," I said.

"So them things go," Mr. Hozzy said. "Next time him stay over him side. Onoo tell onoo friend them that is Daylight Saving Time now. And six o'clock is six o'clock. Is different time now."

"Is true," Stevie said.

"I not saying onoo no right but they did not have to hit him with the stone."

"You right, Wesley, but is so life go."

We walked slowly on. Covering the scheme piece by piece. My mood had fallen, but Mr. Hozzy's walk seemed to have solidified into a strut of greater importance as he tightened his hold on the pouch with the gun from his son. Stevie fell beside me and began quizzing me on some theories of Geometry and after a while we began to recite them as a sort of game. Mr. Hozzy hushed us sternly with a warning that this was serious business. We should not be making noise while we were on duty—the lives of our neighbours were in our hands. So we stopped reciting and walked quietly beside him.

Night did not come till eight o'clock or so, and it brought with it a slight drizzle.

As the rain came down we ran to shelter in Miss Winsome's shop. Stevie whipped an exercise book out of nowhere. He wanted to continue with Geometry.

Mr. Hozzy told him there was a time for everything.

I commented that I thought he had left all his books in his bag on Mr. Hozzy's veranda.

He said he needed to study for an exam.

"So who going watch the pass?" Mr. Hozzy said drawing up in his own importance.

Stevie was having problems with the Pythagorus theory and I began to help him. Mr. Hozzy ignored us, found a cigarette, pulled a chair off to the side, blew smoke into the rain, and wondered where Mr. Lloyd and the rest were.

As I helped Stevie, I began to think of my own homework that I had left so eagerly to come on watch. Why wasn't I more like Stevie? That was a question my mother asked me several times per week since as long as I could remember. I could never find an answer for that. Stevie was Stevie and I was me. We were different people, but I always wondered why I was not like him.

He was small, not as stocky as I was nor as lithe as Skin, but small and firm and fast like a jet—and tough. You couldn't get a ball around him on a football field nor dare to tag him in chevy chase-catch at a hundred metre run. He was the only one of us who made a school team playing centre forward for St. Georges. He did not have the freedom that we had, Skin and I. He had to have permission to play on the streets. When we wanted him for a game we had to troop up to his house and ask his mother. And he had to do his homework first. When we wanted to go to the river or cane piece—we had to solicit his father's support.

But he always did his homework, always did well at his exams. And now I was helping him with his homework while mine was laying somewhere in the bottom of my bag at home.

"Lloyd them mus' wet up," I heard Mr. Hozzy muse. "Either that or them 'round the gully long time. I think we should go roun' there as soon as the rain ease up."

The housing scheme was built on a large square of land about a mile on each side. One side bordered Big Lane. A large bushy ravine with large trees and tangled weeds, Gully Side, ran along the east side and wrapped away to the south of it where a large playing field we called the Common is. East of the ravine the houses and shacks of Outer Lane rimmed the playing field.

The thieves and badmen from Outer Lane would lurk along the length of the ravine. Most scheme houses on that side had very high concrete fences with barbed wire or bottles cemented into the concrete to make them hard to scale. Every now and then both Big and Outer Lane would square off on the Common. Sometimes their war would spill over into the housing scheme.

After the rain, we went through the alley onto the playing field and around by the gully to see what was happening there. The grass was wet. As we hugged to the fence and approached the bushes of the ravine, the water fell from the hibiscus leaves as we brushed them. We stopped at the edge of Miss Rena's back fence where it made a corner with the gully and the playing field.

There was no sign of Skin and their group. We made to sit under the large quango tree, but the root was wet and the grass around it slick with water. So we stood round. Mr. Hozzy mused as to whether or not the other group had come and gone or not come at all. It seemed to me he was hitching to go on the gully bank. But I did not remember that as part of the plan. This had been my third time at watch and we had never gone beyond the gully bank. Our job was to make sure no one came through there into the scheme.

"A wonder if the one Lloyd them gone 'round the Gully?" Mr. Hozzy said again. But this time he whispered.

"Them don' reach yet, man," I told him. "Them no reach yet. I bet you them stop 'round a Jumbo in the rain."

"Look so." Stevie agreed.

Mr. Hozzy felt the tree trunk and declared that it wasn't so wet; he leaned against it and looked around cautiously. "All right, we will wait little," he said.

After fifteen minutes or so, there was a sound from the gully. Not a loud sound, just a rustling, the kind of noise a cow makes when it grazes through thick bush. A long rustle, a stumping sound, then a quietness. . .then the sound of bush rattling, then a silence.

"Hear that?" Stevie whispered.

"Hear that long time," Mr. Hozzy said.

I cocked my ear for the sound again. Then we heard it clearly, moving away from us.

"Look like a some cow," I said calmly.

"Cow nothing," Mr. Hozzy clutched his bag, "Is somebody that."

"Maybe Skin them coming from the other side," Stevie said.

"And I tell the one Lloyd that is this side we going enter from," Mr. Hozzy seemed irritated. "I tell him is this side."

"We going in the gully?" I was surprised; we had never gone into the gully before.

"Well patrol is patrol," Mr. Hozzy whispered sternly. "Patrol is patrol. Is either you patrollin' or you not patrollin'. Remember that some o' them boys from down the lane jump people fence at nights. We checking the back fence them tonight."

For another ten minutes no further noises came from the gully. Then suddenly we heard the definite sound of bodies hitting the ground and voices whispering hurriedly.

"A wonder if is Skin them playing the fool. You know how that Skin love to play the fool," Mr. Hozzy said.

"Suppose is bad man?" Stevie asked, sounding just a bit nervous.

My heart had begun to beat a little faster. And I had drawn into the trunk of the tree. We were all three of us drawn to the trunk of the tree and peeping cautiously around it toward the gully as we whispered among ourselves.

Not that there was much to see. The night was not too dark but one could still not see too far beyond. I could, however, see across the clearing to the small rise where the gully turned away from the fence to form the eastern edge of the playing field. And with the sound playing in my head, the small distance of a few metres seemed a large open space.

"Maybe we should wait on Skin and Mr. Lloyd them," Stevie said.

"For what?" I asked angrily. "Why we going 'round there."

"You too coward." Suddenly, Stevie was getting excited.

"Coward man keep sound bone," Mr. Hozzy remarked, and made me smile in the darkness, "but death in delay," he continued. "Death in delay."

"Suppose Skin them round there?" Stevie asked me.

"Suppose bad man round there?" I asked.

Stevie was dying to go and I would have wanted to also, but not when there were only three of us.

After a while, Mr. Hozzy shrugged, opened his pouch, checked his gun inside without taking it out, held it halfway in from of him and stood with the demeanor of a man with much responsibilities on his shoulders. "Might as well we go take a look."

So we went to check it out, slipped across the space and slithered along the wall like commandos; Mr. Hozzy in the front with his gun, Stevie behind him and I bringing up the rear, crouched half-way my cutlass ready, resting on my shoulders like a Samurai. Behind us the night seemed suddenly empty, ahead the wall stretched for ten houses before it broke at Mrs. Mable's wire fence. To our right, the gully, running parallel, sloped steeply toward its center with patches of empty space braking the mass of cherry trees, broom weed and casha maca trees.

Then from some yards ahead in the gully where the bush was densest for the longest stretch, we heard the rustling again, but a bit louder and with the distinct sound of subdued voices.

We stopped as one and froze against the wall. Mr. Hozzy, holding his hands high like a platoon leader from the movies and Stevie and I laying low, listening keenly like obedient troops. And all the time my heart was beating hard in my breast because the urgency of the moment was beginning to frighten me. No matter what we thought or believed we could do, no one could guarantee what was making that sound up ahead in the gully. What would we do if some bad men began shooting at us?

And then Mr. Hozzy did the most stupid thing: He shouted ahead with a hoarse whisper, "Is who that out there?" One would think the rustling had been in his own back yard. And by the time

I could get over my shock to tell him not to, that there may have been killers out there, he whispered loudly again, "Is who out there? Lloyd, Skin, is onoo out there?"

What would Skin and Mr. Lloyd be doing in the heart of the gully!

Mr. Hozzy was losing his nerve. I could see him in the darkness fussing with his pouch, reaching inside for the gun. He held the gun awkwardly in his hands and began to rise slightly. His hands were trembling as he passed the empty pouch back to Stevie.

More and more I began to sense that our lives were in danger.

"Don't shout again, Mr. Hozzy," I managed to whisper. "Don't shout again!"

"Make we turn back." Stevie was not excited anymore. "Suppose bad man out there, Mr. Hozzy?"

"I have to warn them that I may shoot. . .make them turn back." Mr. Hozzy was again not making sense.

"Don't shout again!" I whispered urgently. "Don't shout again, Mr. Hozzy. Make we watch little. Maybe is just a cow."

The night dragged slowly and the silence hung around us like the sudden ending of rain.

Suddenly Spragga materialised from the darkness into a little piece of clearing, like a piece of the shadow of the bushes had suddenly fallen away, to stand by itself. Out of nowhere, he just stood there, holding a gun against his leg.

I had never seen him like that before—so close, looking so dangerous. We had grown up together, had known each other from before we could lift a real cricket bat. We had travelled every corner of Central Village, attended the same primary school, hunted fish, shot bird. . .and I had never been afraid of him. . .felt his danger. Even though I heard people talk of it—how cold-blooded he had become, how many people he had killed. . .how easy it was for him to pull a trigger. . .I had never feared him. For he had been my friend. Was my friend. And I never understood the danger he was, until I felt it that night across the gully, thick and dark and harsh.

"Spragga, is me," I said hastily before Mr. Hozzy could say or do anything stupid. For he was trembling and nervous and I could see him holding the gun uncertainly and dangerously against his belly.

"Spragga, is me, Wesley."

"Me know is you," he said lightly across the space. "That's why you no dead yet."

"Is me and Mr. Hozzy and Stevie."

"So me see. What onoo doing on gully bank this time a night?"

"Neighbourhood watch," Mr. Hozzy said, "We on neighbour-hood watch. Nothing not wrong with that."

"This is not you neighbourhood. This a gully bank."

"We just take a shortcut back to the Scheme," I offered.

"Then wha' happen to the short cut whe onoo just pass. Onoo stay in the scheme and we wi' watch here so."

"Behind the fence is our scheme and we free to walk any-where!" Mr. Hozzy blurted as he began to straighten himself.

The last thing I wanted Spragga to see was the gun in Mr. Hozzy's hand. For Mr. Hozzy did not seem to appreciate just how dangerous Spragga had become. He had known all of us as boys and somewhere in the back of his mind, I knew, he felt we were still children. . .his children. . .just like my mother would feel about us or Spragga. Our adults felt they could talk us down at any time.

But the Spragga standing casually across the space could not be talked down by anyone, least of all Mr. Hozzy.

"Old Boy, Hozzy, you should be in you bed now, man. Better you go on home now. And watch the one Stevie, whe' you doin' wid cutlass a night, Stevie? You and Wesley stop go school now. Onoo stop have homework?"

"We just a take the short cut, Spragga," I said calmly, feign-ing a smile, trying a light laugh. "Everything allright with you?"

"Things cool, yes. Better onoo go on home now, place might soon get hot. Next thing old boy Hozzy go get heart attack."

"Old boy no! You think me 'fraid a you!" And then Mr. Hozzy made a step forward. He lifted the gun, innocuously, not point-ing at anything in particular. I saw Spragga lean slightly, but before he could do anything, Mr. Hozzy slipped on the wet grass, his hands flayed in the air, and he began to slide down into the gully. The gun dropped, bounced against the wall and fell at Stevie's feet.

"Hold," I heard Spragga say in a quick low voice, motioning to the bush at his right.

There must have been others down there and there were other guns pointing at us.

Mr. Hozzy's slide came to a halt in a thicket of broom weed.

Stevie picked up the gun and held it against himself in the dark.

Spragga hardly even moved. "Same thing me tell you," he said to Mr. Hozzy. "Same thing me tell you. A better you go home before you hurt yourself."

"A slide me slide," was all an embarrassed Mr. Hozzy could say.

"Whe' you bad boy son deh?" Spragga asked. "Whe you bad boy deh? You have him a hide 'round a you house inna the scheme?"

"Spragga, no bother bring my boy into this. I am on neighbourhood watch. You just tell your friend them to keep out o' where decent people live."

Spragga stepped toward him till there was just a yard between them. He lifted the gun and pointed it at Mr. Hozzy's head.

"A soon just shoot you. You don' hear say you son a swear fi kill me. You never hear say if you can' catch quakoo you mus' catch him shirt. You wan' me just' shoot you now. . .shoot you fi you son!"

"That no call for, Spragga," I said, cautiously. "How Mr. Hozzy must know what Patrick say or what him up to."

"But the boy Hozzy have too much mouth, man. You wan' me make him have fi run lef' him scheme house?"

To hear of it and see it are two different things. I could remember any given time, a year or two before, when all four of us would be standing in any of our yards talking with the same passion about any other given subject. And Mr. Hozzy would have been the centre of respect and Stevie, Spragga and I would be just boys looking up to him. But tonight Spragga was holding a gun at Mr. Hozzy's head and was threatening to kill him. And we all knew that Spragga not only could, but would, if he had a mind to. And that there was nothing we could do to stop it.

Spragga scared me as I had never been scared in my life. There was a coldness in him, a deliberate, casual coldness that even Mr. Hozzy began to finally get the message.

His voice trembled, "I don't business with you and Patrick, Spragga," he said, "I don' business wid onoo."

"Then you mus' business if you a go walk pon canal bank them time a night yah."

"Is little neighbourhood watch!"

"Just thank God say Stevie and Wesley with you. Alright! Go on, run! Run up the hill. Onoo go home now."

"Mr. Hozzy began to race up the slippery incline. I did not need a second telling. I pulled Stevie's shirt and we turned to go.

"Stevie!" Spragga shouted, "Stevie, where you goin' wid the gun? You take me fi fool?"

Stevie paused, and turned with the gun lifted up. Mr. Hozzy had just cleared the rim of the gully. As Stevie turned, they collided and fell on the path against the wet wall. Before Spragga or I could react, the gun exploded loudly. For a moment everything seemed to stop. Then Mr. Hozzy rolled away from Stevie to slide halfway down the gully once more, clutching the wound in his breast, as his heart beat his life from him in blood that soaked his clothing.

And Stevie, backed away, walking backwards on his bottom-not rising, just sliding backwards and away—his feet pumping and slipping in the wet grass, till his back hit the wall, and even when it did and he could not move farther, he kept moving his feet, sliding and slipping in the wet grass—his hands on his face, his features contorted in a strange, ugly, childish helplessness. Mucus trailed down his chin, tears and horror were in his eyes, his mouth was agape with a silent ugly scream.

And the rain began to fall again. And I did not know what to do. Spragga had disappeared into the bush as if the shadow had sucked him back in. And I began to pull Stevie's shirt for him to come. And he would not come. He just kept backing into the wall with the silent scream in his mouth and the look of horror frozen on his face. I pulled him, "Come, Stevie, come," and I pulled him and he would not move. Then I slapped him hard on his face like I see them do on T.V and he snapped his face around at me.

"Come, Stevie," I said.

And he rose and we began to run back along the gully bank, till we got to the cricket field. And then he was not beside me anymore and I looked around and he was leaning against the wall, holding his belly and sliding to the ground. And I returned and picked him up and dragged him along into the field. And then he screamed a loud and terrible scream as if all the horror that was in his heart was finally letting out. And then he began to run—ran so fast I could not catch him. I ran after Stevie that night but I could not catch him. We ran through the field, through Big Lane and through the back bushes of Central Village. We ran till my lungs were bursting. We ran past people sitting at fences talking, men leaving the last of their domino games to shelter from the rain. We ran past cars parked. We ran past curious people wondering what was the matter. But we never stopped until we got to the river and Stevie fell as he tried to dive into it. And when I caught him on the edge of the river, it was still raining, but I could see his face and it was filled with the same horror and his eyes had the blank, desperate look of a lost child.

He fell against me and his body rocked with sobs and trembled with fear, emotions that mixed and mirrored my own. And we never moved from there even when the rains stopped; we never moved till morning began to peep and we heard the loud voices of people calling our names.

Stevie came alert with the wild look in his eyes. And I knew he was looking to run. And I was looking to run too. But it was too late. Skin, our parents and a large group of people were coming through the bushes. A policeman was also there. They cut off the route ahead and the river was to our backs. And when they saw us they began to run and we backed into the water as they came, backed into the water till it touched our knees. But they ran to us and dragged us to shore.

Everybody was filled with concern. Everyone spoke at once. Skin was the loudest of all and the closest.

"Whole night we a look for onoo," he said, whole night. People say them see onoo a run all over the place after Spragga shot Mr. Hozzy. We a look fi onoo the whole night. We think onoo get shot too."

"Spragga shoot Mr. Hozzy?" I muttered eying Stevie, whose face was blank and focussed on the ground. "Spragga don' shoot Mr. Hozzy!"

"Me couldn't believe neither," Skin wailed. "But police kill him back; them was looking for him from the shootout in the evening. Them kill the four a them last night. Big shootout. All now people no gone back to sleep yet. Big shootout in the gully."

"Big shootout in the gully."

"Spragga don' kill Mr. Hozzy!" My voice was weaker now.

"Them inna shock!" somebody yelled. By that time my father was by my side and Stevie's parents had him, and the crowd had us and we were engulfed in love and concern.

Stevie never spoke another word after that, except twice with me when we were alone; once at my house when I swore to him that "till I died, I would never tell a soul." And he had stared at me with wide open eyes and asked me if the police would kill him if I told them. The other time was when he tried to kill himself and I went to his house to find him laying in the backyard under the plum tree from which his father had cut him down. And he had looked at me with the same wild stare and shouted roughly: "Wesley, mi a go hell, don't it? Me a go a hell!"

I tried to tell my mother once but halfway through, she hushed me violently and told me "the matter done, it done; no make me hear you talk one more word like that again. Shut you damn mouth."

Sometimes I tell myself that if we had confessed that morning when they pulled us from the river, it would have all been different. And I would have been able to save him; that he would have returned to Mr. Hozzy's house for his books, that he would not have left his home to wander the streets never to return to school again.

I would have saved him.

But I hold this lump inside me and he has closed his lips forever.

And he walks the streets, like a piece of shadow. His face is set ahead and blank, his eyes are wild and unblinking and there is no light there. Any given day you will see him under the overhead bridge, lying in his waste and the filth that has gathered there. . .and if you called him he wouldn't even know his name.

Rhythms

Joanne C. Hillhouse

When I get home, it's about six. The sun is doing a lazy stretch and yawn into another day. It is Saturday, my day off.

I am on the late shift again at work, 10:30 p.m. to 5:30 a.m. This is compounded by the fact that I am stationed clean at Liberta.

Moses doesn't like it, is constantly behind me to quit. I tell him I like being a police officer, I'm not about to give up my years, and I am not about to cave to somebody's victimisation. And we both know it's victimisation, for me being too outspoken. But I tell Moses if I could manage nearly a whole day of labour with our big-head-big-foot-long-body boy, I can more than put up with the police commissioner and his petty politics.

The house is still sleeping when I get in. They are alike that way. The only time they ever got up early is when I am here behind them. This morning, though, my bed is calling me.

When I ease in next to him, he reaches for me.

It has always been like this with us. As reserved and serious as most people say he is, Moses is still the warmest man I know. Still so affectionate after. . .Hm, another year makes 17 years.

I get wi chile for him when I was about 18. He was already a big man then. I tell you, Mammy kick up, kick up, put on a lick-ing on me, push me out her door, tell me if I want to waste all the money she spending on me for the Commercial programme at the College over man, then go live with man.

I was scared that night when I went to his house. Yes, I'd been drawn to him. I'd been the aggressor, not him. He is tall, attractive. . .serious yes, but I could see something of his spirit in his eyes, and I could see that he was a good person. And I was drawn to him.

Even so, I didn't have any reason to believe that he was up for anything as serious as having me set up house in his home. But he didn't even blink, and I've been sleeping next to him ever since.

No regrets.

Next thing I hear is a loud knocking, a chair scraping on the hard wood floor, a door opening, and Moses, "Boy, where you think you going?"

Joanne C. Hillhouse

The "Boy" is our son, 16-year-old Ashe. Yes, Ashe. You see, my husband is a tennis instructor. He was an athlete in his day. Travelled all over the place playing for Antigua. Now, he work at one of them four star, five star hotel. Been doing that for years. He love tennis more than he love cricket, which is saying a lot in Antigua. He named our only child Ashe for his favourite tennis player Arthur Ashe. Arthur, he said, was a true gentleman.

Of course, Ashe's favourite sport is basketball. His favourite athlete is Allen Iverson, a vagabond, as far as Moses is concerned. Ashe is on the basketball team at his school. He is almost as tall as his father, which is saying a lot, because his father's a big man.

Our boy plays quite a few sports. Cricket, with his school team. He likes kicking around the football with the other boys on the field across from our home. He's not as good at that, though. Too much legs and arms.

I look forward to the day when he grows into himself. But right now, he is an awkward looking thing. But then again, all those boys look funny. Hair tall, tall, and never combed. Clothes rumpled, inside out, pants all down round their knees.

Listen to me, I sounding like Moses. Oh, he hates to see it. Always behind Ashe to tuck in his shirt, pull up his pants, tighten his belt. As if the boy not going to just take it all out again once he reach where he going. When they had that problem with security and gangs at the school not too long ago, he was one they had to pull up. No, no, no, he wasn't involved in any of that vandalism and threatening the principal and all of that. But much as he left here looking presentable, security had to stop him at the gate, get him to pull up his pants, take off the skull cap. Last licking he get from Moses was for that. They didn't talk for weeks.

If I remember correctly, Ashe was the one who caved on that one. He had some sound clash he wanted to go to. I tell him ask his father.

I hear the rumble of their voices now. Both irritated as is too common lately.

"Remember the yard waan' cut."

"I'll do it later."

"Where you going?"

"Just outside."

"When you going go barber to cut that hair? I tell you I don't want your hair tall, tall like that, you know."

150

"Mammy say I can keep it like this."

Oh, dear.

Well, sue me. I don't see nothing wrong with a little self-expression. The boy hair not hurting nobody.

The next time I wake up, the sun through the window is harsh on my face, and I hear the sound of the lawnmower. I glimpse a tall shadow through the curtains. From the thickness of the shadow, I realise Moses has taken up the task. I sigh, wondering how far "outside" Ashe has gone that he's not back yet.

He has become too irresponsible for words lately. Only interested in hanging out on the corner with those boys round the place. No matter how much I warn him from them. I mean, I'm not saying that they're bad boys, but I don't think they have the kind of discipline that we trying to give him. And, you know, they not as respectful as I think they should be. But what you goin' do? Everybody raise their children how they want. I don't have nothing to say about anybody. I just want him to come up different. I want him to learn some responsibility. Me and his father not too far removed when it comes to that. It's just, I guess, I have a softer touch. Although truth be told, I probably do more talking and nagging than Moses. But Moses firm. He mightn't talk much but when he talk, he talk.

I give up on the idea of sleep, get up to see about some coffee.

I'm blasting Short Shirt to drown out the sound of the mower and the washing machine as I clean. I'm singing, as I always do with Short Shirt: ". . .she want to go jump and play she mas just like an Antiguan. . ."

"Tourist Leggo." Now, that was kaiso.

The door opens, and in eases Ashe, and next thing I know he spinning me this way and that. I wouldn't mind if the boy could dance, you know, but he stepping all over my toes. But I'm high on calypso, and I'm happy, and I can't stop laughing. Ashe has that kind of effect on me. He is so much more outgoing and personable than his father. He always smiling and dancing, all when he walking. He was a happy baby, and is just so the boy come.

"Oh, you reach," Moses says, his voice booming over the radio. I hadn't even heard the lawnmower shut off. I reach for the knob, turn down the music.

Ashe just stands there, his smile becoming something else, something likely to push his father's buttons.

"Well, he here now," I interject. "Boy, go and do your work."

"It done do," his father says.

Ashe turns toward his room. His father grabs his shoulder, twists him around, "Boy, don't turn your back on me."

Ashe goes back to staring anywhere but at his father, his body language screaming insolence.

"What you good for, eh?" Moses wants to know. "Just eat, sleep, hang out on the corner, play video game, watch music video, play basketball, and run up my phone bill talking to that girl with the too tight clothes and the ridiculous high, high red braids."

Ashe's girlfriend, a too worldly though good-spirited girl named Dianne, is a sore spot with them. We worry about just what girl friend means in the world our son inhabits, which is a different Antigua than the one I'd grown up in. And I'd ended up pregnant at 18, way sooner than I ever wanted to.

"What you bringing up Di name for? What she do you?" Ashe demands, his tongue waking up.

"Oh, that get you going!" Moses says, "You piss bubbling now?! Well, you just watch who you raisin' voice to."

His hand twitches toward his belt, and I hold my breath. Moses doesn't like to talk. In fact, he's done more talking in these few moments than he normally does. But we'd spoken about this after the last time. Ashe is too big for that kind of discipline. I don't want my son to grow up beaten.

What I want is to lock them both in their rooms until Ashe's adolescence passes.

The phone rings.

"Moses," I say, interrupting the frozen tension. "Is Crab Louse."

Crab Louse is the captain of the steelband orchestra both my boys play with. My eyes flicker to the picture on the mantle, as Moses takes the phone. It is from panorama night. Father and son are decked in the band's yellow, red and green, looking like Flamenco dancers, both grinning ear to ear, surrounded by the other band members as they celebrate their victory. The band's first since before Ashe's birth.

Ashe disappears into his room, until later when Moses, dressed to go, calls out to him. "Boy, you not ready yet?" he demands. "I goin' leave you, you know."

There is no answer. Moses picks up his keys. Not being a morning person aside, he is a very disciplined man, can't stand being late. He butts heads often with Crab Louse and the others, since a pan yard by definition has a laid back attitude more suited to, say, Ashe.

"I'll bring him," I promise. It being my night off, I have plans to go watch them play anyway. Besides, Moses has to get there ahead of time with the van so that he can load up the pans and take them over to High Street for the Independence steel pan fiesta. He likes to do it all himself, since to his mind, the others never pack the van right.

He leaves.

I knock on Ashe's door. The imprint of the marker he'd used to write "Knock before Enter" was still there, despite his father standing over him two years ago demanding that he take it out. The boy is moving sluggishly. "What's your problem now?" I wonder. "I thought you loved playing pan." It is about the only thing they both still do, though technically, it isn't something they do together. Both play the bass, trading off between songs. Ashe had taken it up years ago when he was still young enough to want to be like his father.

I like to watch them play, though their styles are so different. Moses is all spare movements, and skilled, easy reserve. While Ashe is like a rubber band, bending this way and that, showing off for his girlfriend and his boys.

As he plays on High Street that night, once I've managed to drag him out after teasing him out of his sulk over his father's comments about his girlfriend, as it turns out, I can't help but smile. He is a joy to watch. His antics more than compensating for the self-consciousness of most of the rest of the band, a band of older players who, like his father, have been playing together since they were about Ashe's age.

Moses comes to stand next to me, hands me a cold malt. I lean into him. "He'll grow up soon," I say. "Don't worry."

He only grunts. But I smile. There is pride in his eyes too.

Soon, they trade places, on one of the classical tunes, "Air on a G string," I think. Not Ashe's speed. He stands a bit in the shadows with his arms encircling his girlfriend, decked as usual in a dress that embraces her fleshy breasts and wide hips, her hair just as high as Moses said. He wasn't exaggerating there. The girl is over done. Worry nips at me, but I shake it off, turning my attention back to Moses on the pan. Composed. Precise. Spare movements. I smile.

They are soon back in party mode. Latumba's *". . .hit man, number one, hit man, jammin' on. . ."*

Moses is still on the bass, turning this way and that in time with the faster rhythm. In his shadow, playing air pan, is Ashe, his movements an echo of his father's. If Moses notices, how could he not with the boy alongside him, he doesn't react, face as serene as ever. Ashe, the clown in a loose fitting rumpled top and baggy jeans, his big hair with some headband tied around it a contrast to his father's pressed black jeans and tucked in band shirt, perfectly trimmed hair. His elasticity, counterpoint to his father's measured movements. Their hands, keeping time, moving together.

I want to cry, and laugh at the same time. So, do both. Maybe if I could lock them in this moment, where the one seems at peace, the other immersed in joy, both in perfect harmony, until adolescence passes.

How to Revive a Faded Iris

Andrea Shaw

He tries to wash years and years of dust away in one morning, scrubbing a tea set that has not been used in over a decade. He dries the first teacup and puts it on the table, his hands trembling as he sets and resets her bone-white china, the one with slender purple irises. First he places the teacup on the left, then the right, turns the plate down, then turns it up. Pigeon feathers rustle in a cage on the front patio; a crisp, drying leaf on the banana tree outside sashays against the kitchen window in the breeze, at times getting caught in the iron burglar bars; sunshine peeps in; the living room clock chimes six weary gongs.

Rita, his wife, is in town. She flew into Kingston from Miami the previous day and is coming by this morning. He positions the second teacup on the table, alternately tilting his head and squinting at his haphazard place setting before shifting something else from one side to the next. He makes one final adjustment to a lopsided spoon—it is his sign of the cross, his benediction, his amen—praying that Rita will come inside the house one more time and join him for tea.

A few short steps and he enters the living room, bracing his weakened left side against the couch and catching his breath. He looks around the room, checking to see that everything is in order, and from the coffee table a ceramic figure of a boy in overalls playing a pipe stares back at him. The statue is oozing bubbles of Patex glue from an ancient wound across its shoulders—the glue calcified and frozen in time—and the boy sits amidst white folds of lace petals. After their children grew up, Rita crocheted everyday. He eases over to the coffee table and fingers the stiff arches that form interlacing patterns on the clean centerpiece. At least the washing girl used some of the starch he bought before sneaking it into her bag like so many other things in the house. He touches the boy's fragile pipe, which barely survived the day when Rita found out his receptionist was pregnant.

Lascelle, you are a blinking disgrace; sixty-odd year old man like you turning father after you just turn grandfather, and I must turn my back! Whattaway I must look to you like Granny Fool-Fool. Hmmph! Everyday bucket go to de well, one day de bottom going drop out!"

He barreled across the living room, knocking the piper to the ground. *Woman, what make you think you can talk to me like that in MY house?*

Your house?

In less than an hour she was packed, fitting everything into the suitcases she had brought with her when they married and purchased the house. All she took were her clothes and pictures—lots of pictures: their children graduating from college; their daughter Marlene's wedding; and the grandchildren, smiling against a JC Penney's painted backdrop of a log cabin and evenly spaced evergreens. A few days later, she flew over real pine trees while making her descent into Miami International Airport, hoping she might one day see a log cabin, but never wanting to live in one.

The crescendo of a sharp whistle from a kettle of boiling water calls Lascelle back to the kitchen. He pours some of the hot water over dried leaves in a teapot, and with the rest, he makes himself a drink. In a few minutes he is seated on his front porch where he crunches an Excelsior cracker and then slurps hot Milo, a thin stream of syrupy chocolate running down the left corner of his mouth. He dips another Excelsior cracker in his drink, and the pigeons chirp to the rising sun. After feeding the birds, he sweeps the leaves that have fallen from the huge Bombay mango tree in his front yard, and when he feels a damp spot in the seat of his trousers, he hurries in to change.

Before he gets back outside, he hears a sound like a small hurricane stirring in the leaves of the mango tree. "Those damn pickney from the primary school," he mumbles, going to his bedroom window to get a clearer view of the tree. At the same time a boy in khakis with Ninja Turtles backpack jumps from a lower branch of the tree and onto the freshly painted wall of the front fence. "Get away from there, bwoy," he yells, his voice not betraying his age or illness. "Get your damn self out of me tree!" The boy is busy balancing two luscious mangos in his arms; one falls when he hears the loud voice, and he takes off with the other.

Shortly after, just as Lascelle splashes on his second coat of Old Spice for the morning and picks from a vast array of comfortable house sandals and loafers, a car engine sounds outside. By the time he reaches the front door, Rita is entering the porch and the birds are in an uproar, flying into each other. She is wearing a turquoise pants suit that contrasts with her brown skin and her curly gray hair. Over her shoulders is a matching pocket-book, and in one hand she has a small Macy's shopping bag. By this time Rita's brother, Harvey, is under the Bombay tree using his cane to try and knock down a fuchsia tinged mango. Harvey notices Lascelle at the front door and walks over to greet him, offering a playful salute, a handshake, and a few words before resuming his mango hunt. Lascelle sees the shock in Rita's eyes as she gazes on his now misshapen body, and he eases lopsid-edly out onto the porch from the kitchen. "Rita—" he says, while her eyes pan the verandah avoiding his.

The wrought iron chairs sit kitty corner just as she left them, the floral pattern on the padded seats now faded from bright orange to a tame shade of peach, and in another section of the porch, under a baby's breath fern, she spots her old market basket.

"—sorry to hear 'bout your sister. Funeral is tomorrow, right?"

Rita nods, pursing her lips: "Thank you." She looks at her anthurium plant that she entered in the National Flower Show when her daughter Marlene was still in prep school. It is now bearing Goliath heart-shaped blooms and has been re-potted into a larger clay pot. "So how you doing, Lascelle? Sorry to hear about your stroke." A fretwork of multiplying pineapples hangs casually from the ceiling, exuding the smell of fresh paint.

"Well, I'm holding on, holding on—have to fight the good fight, you know." His lips begin to tremble, and he turns his head away from her, catching a glimpse of Harvey as he uses his cane to poke at a higher branch in the tree. She gingerly steps towards Lascelle and lightly touches the hand that is tightly gripped to the door jamb. His skin feels like damp leather. "It's all right. It's all right," she says tapping him lightly. "Never thought we would end up like this; never thought so at all, at all. But that's how it goes sometimes. We have to just make the best of things." Then Rita remembers how she cried every night for months after she left him, no one to gently tap away her sorrow, and she steps back.

She hands him the Macy's bag. "Marlene said you asked her to send these for you. Say you needed them right away."

Lascelle glances in the bag at a pair of house shoes—blue corduroy. "Oh yes, thank you, thank you, and tell Marlene thanks for me." He lingers with the bag in his hands for a moment then leans it against the bird cage.

"Yes, yes, yes, yes," he nods repeatedly as he speaks, trying to pump life into empty words. "So I was wondering if maybe you want sit down inside for a little and have something hot to drink."

He eases himself from the doorway, making sure that Rita can see the place settings, adorned with aging irises, on their dining table. "I know you like bush tea, and I have some black mint drawing for you inside."

"Well, I'm not really stopping," Rita says as she takes a step towards her kitchen, looking first at the dining table then the counter tops. She is amazed. Everything is precisely as she left it eleven years ago. Her blue canister set with the little Dutch girl smiling in her wooden clogs is stationed beside the window, only now rust is seeping through the girl's yellow hair. Beside that her Osterizer blender, then the toaster, then the narrow strip of wood with projecting nails for hanging citrus rind to keep flies away. Several stiff, darkened ribbons of orange skin, visibly coated with dust, seem suspended above the counter. Could these be the pieces of orange peel from the last breakfast she made on the day she left him to take complete ownership of his things?

Rita sticks her head further in the doorway, enticed by the faint aroma of her former life. She catches a glimpse of the sofa, light blue paisley swirling in a sea of beige and she feels her head begin to swim. She surprises herself and smiles, a dim reserved smile like what she used to have when she first met Lascelle, when she and the other girls at nursing school, huddled against London's cold and gloom, would giggle as the West Indian factory men called out to them while they all waited for the train at Victoria Station. The platform became her favorite place, as she looked for Lascelle's broad jaw and heavy eyebrows in the ocean of hopeful brown faces.

"You coming in, Rita?" The tension is evident in his eyebrows, now grey and thinning, his jaw permanently lowered.

"Long time I don't have mint tea. You still have that bush around the back?" she asks. His voice grows enthusiastic: "Would you believe that is the same mint bush stay and grow for all these year—" A loud rustle of leaves draws Rita's and Lascelle's attention to the Bombay tree, and they turn to see Harvey using the curve of his cane to grip a laden limb, violently pulling it up and down to displace a large bunch of mangoes. "Ayy, sah!" Lascelle's posture suddenly becomes more erect as he calls to Harvey. "Mind you break that branch on my tree; is long years now I have that tree growing. How many mangoes so you trying to get?" With barely a pause between sentences, Lascelle continues, "So you still take sugar, Rita, or you want your tea plain?" He turns and mounts the step to the kitchen, sure that Rita is trailing behind him, enraptured by the visage of the life she left behind, and transfixed by the imaginary scent of mummified orange peel.

Rita's shoulders rise up under her bright blue blouse, and she walks away from the front door to sit in a chair beside her anthuriums. When she opens her mouth to speak, the firmness in her voice startles Lascelle, and he almost loses his footing. "Remember when we first moved back to Jamaica from England? Must have been in about '57. We went to the country to visit Mama, and on the way back you bought soursop from some boys on the roadside—right by Flat Bridge—so I could make soursop drink for you. And I bought a plant from a man not too far away." Lascelle stands on the threshold of his house, wondering what Rita could possibly be talking about.

"The next evening after I came home from work, and as soon as I changed out of my uniform, I found a spot near the fence and put in that plant—watered it everyday until I was sure that it took root, and look at it now." She indicates the Bombay tree with a slight raise of her head. "But that tree is yours now—and the mint bush beside the gas tank, the banana trees outside the kitchen window, even my little June plum tree around the back, if it is still alive. And you know what, Lascelle, it may be a better thing to not confuse what belong to who after such a long time."

She looks wistfully at the anthurium beside her and gently caresses a blood-red bloom. "I have to go now." She rises and walks towards the gate where Harvey is fumbling with the latch as he bites into the orange meat of a juicy mango. At the same time Lascelle stands suspended between the doorjambs, his eyes fixed on the brilliant turquoise of Rita's outfit as Harvey waves goodbye then drives off.

Lascelle feels too weak to make it back inside, so he sits on the porch trying to savor the scent of Rita's hairspray and her perfume. When he has breathed in as much of her as he can, and all he senses is the acrid smell of paint, he goes inside to change his shoes, comes back out, and reaches for her market basket. He leaves the basket under the mango tree and goes to a back shed for a long, narrow bamboo pole—on the end is a curved piece of metal. Still feeling weak and walking with a slight drag of one foot, he hoists the stick into the air and begins to pick mangos—one after the other, after the other, often stopping to steady himself with the picking stick or leaning on the trunk of the tree to rest.

By that afternoon, when the nearby schools end for the day, Rita's basket is heaped with mangos and perched on top of the gate-column. Lascelle stays inside and peeps at the basket from behind his bedroom window, tears rolling down his face while the school children fill their bags with the ripe, juicy fruit.

Car Park Boy

Diana McCaulay

Been out here long, long, since around seven. Mumma send me
to beg lunch money for five of we. She don't know how it hard.
If I go home now, she a go beat me, say me worthless. She don't
understand the runnings out here. People don't like boys inna the
plaza; girls, now, they don't get chase like us. Not many girls out
here all the same. But we boys, me and Everton and Shelton and
Noel, we get chase all the time. Don't matter if you small like
Lasco, you still get chase. One time the security guard catch
Lasco and hold him down inna car park and beat him bad, bad.
One foreign white woman, she come over and she tell the security to leave the boy alone. The security say, "Mam, you don't
understand these boys. Them bad, them bad, them bad so 'til.
Them must beat like mule or donkey. Ghetto pickney must beat."
The white woman say she going call the police and the security.
He laugh. "Lady," he say—he stop call her Mam now—"the police
will beat him harder then me. These boys, them thief and cause
pure trouble. The management say we must run them *every* time
we see them." There is a white man with the white woman and
he say she must stay out of what don't concern her. The white
woman say it concern her, this is a child being beat up. The man
say them on holiday, don't know about things in Jamaica. Come
away, Lawra, or some name like that. Come away, he say. All
the time this going on, Lasco he just stand there, he don't cry. He
tough, Lasco. Where he come from make you tough like
coconut. His mother name him after powder milk, then she take
him to Maxfield Park home and leave him. He run away from
there before he twelve.

Me, now, I try make sure security and police never catch me.
If they catch me, I bawl living eye water and beg them not to beat
me. I say I hungry. I say I need money for school shoes for my
little sister. Most times they let me be.

I know one security name Sinclair. He tell me he like me
because I am mannerly, always say, Good Morning or Good
Evening and call him Sir. Sometimes he will give me a ten dollar or
a twenty dollar, if he have them in coin. Plenty place only want
paper money now, say not taking coin, especially not the red coin,
the ten cent and twenty-five cent. But enough coin will buy patty
and soda over at the gas station, so Sinclair, he give them to me if

he have them. He say he have a boy about my age, but I know he think I am twelve or thirteen, but I small. I am fifteen last birthday.

Sometimes I get coin from the boys who pack inna super-market. They hustling to take food to cars and they drop their coin. I find them half stuck in the asphalt. I have to careful how I pick them up. If the supermarket boys see me, they will beat me and report me to security. They hate us car park boys, even though some of them were car park boys before.

Lord, I hungry. Sinclair not on duty tonight. Best chance I have is staying round here in the shadow, behind expensive Chinese restaurant, and wait until movie house let out. Plenty rich people go to movie and when they come out, they don't like to see young boy inna car park. This don't work all the time, because late at night uptown rich people scared and go to their fancy car quick, quick. Car park dangerous place for them.

You have to pay mind to the movie showing too. Uptown people like movie 'bout love, they don't come out for shows with Kung Fu or plenty black people. They do come for certain kinds of black people, like that one Morgan Freeman with all the moles on his face, or Denzel, or that nice, nice gal Halle Berry. Wesley Snipes, Eddie Murphy, now, they don't come to see them so much. This movie tonight is about some kind of sun, a Tuscan sun. Never heard of that. I think plenty uptown people will be at this movie.

Uptown people can be black, brown or white, Chinese or Syrian. It bad they all have cell phones nowadays. They start talking on them as soon as they come out of the movie and then they don't see us car park boys. The uptown women they notice us, though, except the very young ones. The best kind of woman is not too young, white or Chinese, the kind that look like she have children already. Me, I think Syrian women have hard heart, always want tell you get a job. Black women now, they hard to read. Some of them sorry for us, but some just have to see us and they angry.

Aii. Foot bottom hurting. Barefoot on hot, hot asphalt all day is hard. Want two pair of shoe. Have only one pair and Mumma say it can only wear go school. When school over in the day, shoe come off. Then Mumma send me to plaza to beg. I like this plaza because the boys are small and you don't have to fight. One day, I did go down by Cross Roads and one big boy he beat me 'til I vomit. After that I stay here in uptown plaza even though the pickings slim sometime.

Movie is letting out now. People are laughing. That good; mean them not thinking about gunman on the way to them car. In Jamaica, you have to think about gunman all the time; them everywhere, like rat, lizard, cockroach, mosquito.

Trick is not to scare people, so they have to see you coming. Sometime that make them turn back and walk down a different row of car, but you have to take the chance, for if you surprise them, they angry for sure.

I get up and walk into the light. I pick a woman and a man to beg. It would be better if the woman was by herself, but uptown woman don't go to movie alone. The woman is right age, a browning, not too young. She wear jeans pants and a T-shirt with writing on it. She and the man a hold hands.

"Good evening, Miss, Sir," I say. "Beg you some money for school."

"No, thank you," the man say, quick, quick, and he steer the woman to one side. But she see me and she stop.

"What you doing out here so late?" she say.

"Miss, I have to get money for school."

"What's your name?"

"Miss, Delroy," I say. Is my pet name. My real name is Raymond.

"Where your parents?"

Too much talking now. How it work, if them don't give you money right away, probably not going to. People from the movie walk around the three of us. Some people look. Shoulda ask some other woman.

"Miss, I don't know my father; my Mumma, she at home with the other pickney."

The woman make up her face. "How old are you?"

"Twelve," I lie. Better they think you young.

"Where you go school?"

"Miss, Nightingale Primary." Another lie. I too old for primary school, I go most days to Papine All Age.

"How many brothers and sisters you have?"

"Miss, two brother, one sister." I want to get away now. This woman not going give anything and other uptown people leaving. I hear car door slam and engine start up. Look like tonight is a night for hungry bed and beating from Mumma. Aii.

"What you do for fun?" the woman say. For fun? This woman strange. I know must not tell her about jumping on back of pick-up truck stopped at traffic light and thiefing a ride from downtown, or cutting up seat on bus with Lasco knife. Must not tell about the time the police corner me and Everton and make us climb a chain link fence. While we up there, them lick us with a piece of two by four and how after—this is the fun part—we stick ice pick inna their car tyre. Must not tell how we find one old can a spray paint and write bad words on wall, or pull down posters for dance hall we car park boys can't go.

"I play draughts with my brother," I say. Draughts better to tell about than domino, even though domino need more brain and counting. Uptown people think domino for rum-head and worthless corner boy. "We make a board from old cardboard and use bottle tops for men. I teach him, my little brother. Me, I am the best draught player around."

The woman smile a little. The man say, "Come, Alice, it's time to go." He pull her hand. She just stand there, though. The man shake his head and he start take out his wallet from his back pocket. Yes, I think. Maybe he will give me a hundred dollar.

"Where you live?" the woman say.

Now I frighten. What she want know for? "Miss, Bell Town," I lie. Bell Town is next community to our own.

"If I want find you, how I find you?" the woman say.

"Miss, just ask for Miss Arlene. Everybody know her. She my Mumma. She keep a little shop on the corner, the deep corner at bottom of the steep hill."

The woman nod her head, yes. She step forward and she make up her face again. This time I know it because she smell me. She put her hand under my chin and she make me look straight, straight at her. "Do me a favour," she say, as if she talk to a big person. "When you get big, you don't have children and send them to the plaza to beg."

"Yes, Miss, for sure, Miss," I say, words all jumbled up. I don't like to look at her. At school they say is lack of respect if you look straight at a big person. I frighten of these two, want to get away. Maybe the man is police.

The man have his wallet in his hand now, but she shake her head at him and let go my chin. She take out her money from a little school bag she carry. She put five hundred dollar in my hand. I can't believe it; no way at all. Nobody ever *ever* give me five hundred dollar. "Miss, thank you; Sir, thank you," I say.

"Go home," the woman say.

I think about this woman sometime. I sorry she can't find me. Maybe she would help; you hear such things happen. Maybe I shouldna lie. That five hundred dollar last one long time. Mumma she smile when I bring it home. 'Course the bad part is, now she expect it again.

Maybe one month after, I at the plaza late again. This time I in front of pharmacy a talk to Sinclair. He tell me how the police lock up Lasco last week for theifing a cassette from the game arcade. He say his police friend tell him he see Lasco over at the station, handcuff to a railing. Then Sinclair look over my shoulder and say, "Evening, Mam?" I look around and the woman from the other night stand there, a look at me. This time she by herself.

"You don't live in Bell Town," she say. "I went there, I looked for you. I asked for Arlene but no one knew Arlene with three children and a shop. Why you lie?"

"Miss, I afraid you was police,"

"Come talk to me," she say. She walk over to the step and sit down *braps*. She pat a place beside her. "Sit," she say.

This woman definitely mad like dog on full moon night. She want me, a car park boy, to sit beside her, a uptown browning woman, on front step of plaza. If it wasn't Sinclair on duty, other security would run me already. I frighten, but I want to see what this crazy woman do next. I sit.

"I would like to meet your mother," she say. "I would like to help you go to school, pay school fees and buy books and shoes and all that. Would you like that?"

Shoe! Is all I hear. "Yes, Miss, yes, Miss, thank you, Miss."

"But," the woman say, "probably you have to leave your mother and go to boarding school. You know what that is?"

"Miss, when boys come from country to Bell Town they board with people in the area. You talking about school where pickney sleep."

"Yes. My husband, the man you saw me with the other night, he is on the Munro School Board. I have talked to them and they will take you in September. I want to talk to your mother about it."

I hear about Munro. Boys at Nightingale Primary used to talk about it, say it in the country, in St. Elizabeth, and how the wind blow 'til the trees all bend down in one direction, how the masters

beat the boys and how the water to bathe in ice cold. The boys
say you get food three time a day on long table. Seem like boys
get beat no matter where they is, but other things sound good. I
never see myself in such a place, though. Never like school
much—too much angry teacher, too easy to get into trouble.

"Come," the woman say. "Drive with me to your house."
House, I think. I wonder if she will call where I live a house.

She drive a little yellow VW, the old kind, not fancy like the
SUVs most uptown people have. Never see a uptown person
drive that kinda car. She don't talk. I wonder if she can smell me,
like the time she touch me. I wonder if she will leave her car window open when she park her car tonight, so the smell of me can
come out.

We go round the deep corner and I tell her to stop in front of
Mumma shop. Behind window and door people a look. Mumma
come out, she carrying Lissa. The woman get out of her car while
I still try open door on my side. I don't hear what the woman say
to Mumma right at first.

". . .I can get him into Munro and me and my husband will
look after his schooling. He will come home in the holidays, but
we think it is important for his education to get him out of this
environment," the woman say.

Mumma don't say anything. I know she figuring out "this
environment" business. Mumma, she don't go out the house
much. My second brother, Marlon, he do most of the shopping.
She don't ask the woman to come inside; she don't want the
woman to see that we thief light and shit in hole in ground out the
back; she don't want her to see cardboard under zinc roof for
leaks.

"Miss Arlene?" asks the woman. You have to give her that
she is a mannerly woman, lotta uptown woman would just say
Arlene.

Lissa start fuss and Mumma give her soother to suck on.
Mumma thin; you can tell she don't eat much. "Well, Missus,"
Mumma say, "for true I would like Delroy to go school. He bright.
But we woulda miss him round here." She don't say is me bring
home the money. She not going tell the uptown woman that.

"Well, think about it," the woman say. "Talk to Delroy about
it. I will come back in a week and you can tell me your decision."

"Yes, Missus. Thank you, Missus." I know Mumma hoping
the woman will give us another five hundred dollar, but she just

say good-bye to all of us and go back to her yellow car. She don't take me back to plaza, so I going have to walk. If I don't go, we don't eat tonight.

Mumma never talk to me about boarding school. Nobody have to say anything and I don't tell anybody, not even Everton or Sinclair. The week go by fast, fast and is Saturday morning and I know the woman will come today to hear Mumma decision. I wake up early and I climb up the hill behind our house and I hide in the macca bush. Sun go up and day is hotter and my stomach make hungry noises—not even sugar water I drink since morning. Macca bush scratch and I smell garbage fire. The yellow car drive up and I see the uptown woman get out. She carrying something in her hand. Mumma come out and the two of them talk. It don't take long. The woman turn to go back to car, she still holding the box in her hand. Then she go back to Mumma. The woman take something out of plastic bag and even from inside the macca bush I can see what she bring: Is a brand new draught set. She give it to Mumma and she go back to her car and I see her get in and I watch the little yellow car drive up the hill until I can't see it no more.

Calabash, broken

Kei Miller

1.

Is like he never understood boundaries or walls. Is like he never knew that to get from one room to another you had to find the door, open it, step through it. He always had the mind to just float through walls, like they wasn't even there—but people will stare if you do something crazy like that. They might even scream. They will think you odd. Think you is a duppy.

A duppy who have no conscience of concrete and walls and doors and boundaries and the things that separate us—a duppy who see the world as one open field. That's what he was like. You would be having dinner with lots of people and the talk is about politics, then all of a sudden he get up and looking to his mother across the table, and shout out, "Mummy! Mummy! I want to doo-doo! I need to doo-doo!" And everybody fork freeze in their hands and nobody even blinking and his mother closing her eyes tight, tight like she wishing this was another bad dream and him know that him do it again—his words come out like a man floating through walls. His words always crossing boundaries they wasn't supposed to.

Now somebody would hold Miss Gloria's hands. Her eyes still shut tight, but a tear squeeze it way out. She shake her head stiffly, "Why at sixteen him can't learn yet, eeh? Why!"

2.

The day Mary's boyfriend left she didn't cry, because it was raining. What the sense in tears when the world so full of water already? She only stand up there in the middle of the great, grey world where everything—the trees, the houses, the cars—was flickering between the lightning as if it was a black and white TV show and the picture not so good.

She stood up under all that water, her face fallen, her shoulders drooping and the rain beating down like young drummers. Wasn't no healing in that rain neither—no "lay down your burdens down by the riverside," no "dip them in the healing stream," no "sailing across Jordan." It was just water and water—her poor brain growing soft like water.

168

3.

. . .and because he forgot boundaries and walls, he would also forget the order of things. Like coming out of the bath one Tuesday, he put on a T-shirt without drying off. Then he forgot to put on underwear or shorts.

He climbed up on to his bed and picked up two calabash rattles, his favorite toys. You could make music with them and don't have to worry about keys and notes, octaves and sharps, rules— you never have to worry about eedyat rules. Just had to shake it—*shakashak! shakashakashak!*

Bouncing on the bed now: Jump—*shakashaka*, jump— *shakashaka*, jump—*shakashaka*. He grew hard.

His erect penis was something that frightened him. Him not telling nobody, but for two years him watching and getting worried about it—how it could all of a sudden get hard and ugly-looking—how with each year it was swelling bigger and bigger.

Jump, *shakashaka*. His member hitting him against his belly. Jump, *shakashaka*. Then is jump him jump straight off the bed (*shakashaka*) walking out the room and down the stairs (*shakashaka*) because he now decide to tell his mother—his mother who right then was talking to the new helper, the new helper who look up and almost drop down from shock. To get his mother's attention, him hitting her on the shoulder: Mummy! Look on my peepee! Miss Gloria look and feel shame. Shame because of the thing she see; shame because is pride she think she hearing in the boy's voice. "Jesus savior pilot me!" she whisper.

Pilot! Pilot! Now him start thinking of fly-cross-the-sky pilot! Airplanes. Being up there like a bird—imagine that! Him stretch him hands out like wings, running around the room, butt-naked and stiff, zoooooom zooooooom *shakashaka!*

"Philip! Philip! Stop that."

Him never take her on. The rattles in his hand sound like an airplane engine to him; the running about making him feel excited. Is all so much fun. Zoooooooom *shakashaka*.

"Philip!" Miss Gloria get up to grab him—but is out him run out of the room. She stumble behind him, cursing. Him run through rooms, run upstairs, run through the front door. She vex and panicking and screaming, "Philip, STOP!"

But he don't understand that she serious. Him think she playing with him again—finally loving him again. Him about to run into the road. She catch up and drag him by the shirt cuff. Him out of breath, look up smiling. "Mummy! You catch me!"

WAAAAP! Straight cross him face. His penis went limp.

"Why you must do this to me, eeeh, boy?"

She grab the two calabash rattles and slam them on the floor. One cracked open, red seeds pouring out.

4.

Is not drown Mary was trying to drown herself. Well-not really.

Remember the boyfriend left. Then the rain stopped. Now she always find herself walking past water and looking in—always the water would seem to open its doors and invite her singing, "Come just as you are." "This is the place where left-over-things rest." "When a man reach inside you, take out you heart and fling it weh careless; when you find youself as hollow as the tinman, this is where you belong."

Many days you would see her in Kingston Harbour, floating belly-up and if you didn't look close to see her stomach rising and falling, you would think she was a corpse some gunman had dumped into the sea. Is not drown she was trying to drown; is just that when every cell in your body turn itself into sorrow it will want to turn into water next. Out there in Kingston Harbour, she thought she would dissolve—become part of the ocean.

5.

Listen to a myth: living near to the equator, some days will feel like leather. That's if you believe the story that the world is a calabash broken in two and that a great snake has wrapped herself around the center to hold it together.

Some days if you step outside, lift your head in the wind, you will feel the belly of the snake resting against your cheeks.

6.

Sometimes, Philip just want to stay outside. He would climb up on the gate—don't care that him not a little child anymore. The middle of the gate had sunk in deeply from so many years of bearing his weight. He would sit there for hours just looking at the sky.

When you outside, everything is under one roof. The world is wide and without walls. Him feel more comfortable here. As the years go by it harder for him to listen to his mother when she calling him in. Sometimes him pretend him don't hear her—just so he can stay out there for an extra five minutes.

"PHILIP!" She look outside and see him humming intensely to himself, rocking on the gate. "PHILIP!" She could see his whole body tense and him just start to hum louder, rock himself more. God—she wonder—why life have to be like this? She step outside, all of the old anger in her voice and shout, "Philip, come inside right now!"

"No!"

"Philip. . ."

"No!"

Miss Gloria just can't find the strength to argue. "Well, fine. Have it your way. You is a big man anyway and Lord knows. . ." She slam the door shut, lock it.

That's how it started. He would sleep outdoors some nights—walk the streets, make friends with the stars and the moon-shining like a calabash lamp in the sky.

7.

At first it would scare people a little—make them heart skip a beat, when they first look out on the water and see this woman floating, her untidy locks spread out behind her like Medusa, her face as expressionless as formica. But they get used to it.

Nobody was going to call police on her, but Floating Mary started to break into Goodpeople's yards. Only reason rotweiler and doberman didn't bite her up is because they was too stunned when they see this woman, brazen as all hell, scaling fence and walking past them like nothing. And, also, they couldn't smell any fear in her.

So in the morning, Goodpeople would wake up and find this dirty woman floating in their swimming pools. They called police. Police came to haul her ass to jail. Between the water and the strong hands pulling her out, Mary shouting, "I have been poured out like water!"

Eh! Who would have thought that for her twenty-three years of sanity she had tried desperately to write poems but just couldn't do it. Now, when she speak, the red words tumble out like something straight from the Psalms.

8.

Is little white patches they attach to Mary's head. The patches were attached to thin wires, and the wires to an electric source—as if this kind of therapy could fix Mary's brain. Who tell them water and electricity could mix? It only fixing her from going into Goodpeople's swimming pool. It only stopping her from floating.

9.

He found the huge calabash tree growing in an open lot. It wasn't far from his house. This is where Philip now spent his days and even some of his nights. He loved the shade of the tree. He liked watching the green fruits for weeks—how they would swell up so big—how, eventually, their green skins would seem to turn into wood.

Sometimes he would yank one off the tree and shake it. It never sounded like his rattles. In fact, it never sounded at all. But he could feel the water moving inside it. Pure water. Water without boundaries or walls. Is like it was a perfect world inside that calabash.

And is because it was so perfect inside he liked to break them—liked smashing them against a rock and watching the river flow out.

10.

Listen to another myth: some people say if the world is really a calabash and God holds it in his hands, then every evening he gets clumsy and drops it. At that moment, we all bleed a little. The red on the horizon is the gathering of our blood.

11.

They finally let Mary out and she start to walk the streets. Electric and water currents bouncing in her head make her twitch with every move. Twitching Mary—that's what they called her now. Twitching Mary walking down Old Hope Road begging for 10 cents, or a dollar if you can afford it. Begging for a patty and a cocoa bread. Begging for someone to explain to her, please, why men must be so evil—why a man would promise you the heavens and then just leave you so—leave you for another big-bottom woman.

Twitching Mary walking up Lady Musgrave Road through New Kingston straight cross into Barbican. Twitching Mary walking around Kingston, begging. That's how she come across Philip under the gourd tree.

When she see what he was doing—picking the calabashes and smashing them on the floor—things start make sense. She see how out of pure idleness a man could break a world. Without any conscious intention, she found herself running towards him—and without announcing themselves, tears had finally risen up behind her eyes and were now falling out.

12.

Philip frighten to see this woman running to him.

"No! Stop it!" she was screaming, her mouth all full and angry with commands just like his mother, just like Miss Gloria. "Nonoonoooonoooonooostopit!"

So why people always telling him to stop? What damn rules him always breaking? He held the big, brown calabash in his hand, high up in the air, ready to smash it down like an idiot—god.

"No! Please!" She reached him, fell to her knees, face to the ground, her locks brushing his feet. "Please."

Philip don't know what to do. Him standing up looking both dignified and clumsy, the calabash swaying above his head. Him face fall into a frown, the gourd slip from him hands, bounce on the tree roots and then stop against a rock.

It didn't break bad. Just a little crack—just a little water dripping out. Mary scrambled over, picked it up, cradled it in her arms. Perhaps she was still a little bit mad and is that make her push the calabash up underneath her shirt, against her stomach—making her look more than nine months pregnant—water coming down her thighs—as if she was ready, right then and there, to give birth to another broken world.

And perhaps Philip still wanted his mother's love, and in Mary's newly pregnant state she was the closest thing. Perhaps that's what made him walk over timidly then rest his head against her belly.

13.

They say, in this world we are all splinters searching for our other parts—our unbroken selves.

Violin Dominicana

Calvin Mills

> *"Mi flamboyán es criolla*
> *adornada de mil flores*
> *que el recio varón caobo*
> *conquista con sus amores. . ."*
> — Pedro Mir

It was when I was two years old that my mother started me on the violin. It was not until I was eleven that I became a prostitute.

I was born here in Santo Domingo. My mother must have known already what she would do with me because she called me Música. I'm twenty-nine years old now. When I was fifteen I had a friend from America, an old woman called María. She asked me why I would not go abroad to study violin. She liked to tease me about my name, but I think she liked it very much. She didn't know what I did to make money or that I had been working from the time that I was very young.

Before María left to go back to the states, she asked me again if I would go to America to study violin. She did not hear me when I told her all the reasons I did not want to go. I don't like to travel. The only place I ever go is to Bayahibe, on the southern coast, to visit my cousin. But I would not like to leave the country because I couldn't stand to fly. What I couldn't tell her was that I also couldn't stand to see so many of the kind of men that are my customers.

I like to play the violin when I work. My mother was wise to have thought of it. She said, "You'll learn to play the violin so that you will remember the beauty of the music, and not the sweating faces of the men." Not only is it better for me this way, but now I have become famous on the island for what I do. I am the only Dominican whore who can play the violin. I always make love on top. And despite my mother's initial advice, and her having seen to it that I was given instruction on the violin, I do look at the faces of the men. The best part is that sometimes, if I am playing a sad song or a very beautiful piece, they cry. I like to have this power over them. And of course I do well and support my family.

Most of the customers are foreigners, Europeans who come here for the warm blue water. They come to see the Faro a Colón and the Zona Colonial, and of course, they visit prostitutes. Still,

I am happy, because in Santo Domingo the other prostitutes have to be dragged around town on dates, eating at restaurants, and drinking in bars before, or after. They are made to dance Merengue and Bachata in the clubs, or on the Malecón. For those women that are hungry and thirsty, too poor to eat and drink in those tourist restaurants, this sort of thing is welcome. But for me, I make enough to eat what I want. I would find it embarrassing to be with the white men in public like that.

Thankfully my mother, because she started me out so young, is accustomed to keeping things discreet. Now when I walk along the Malecón at night, I am on the arm of only one man. No one talks about me as I pass because only those who have been my customers know who I am by sight. Most of them are foreigners, long gone, and the rest, the locals, are rich enough to be embarrassed and keep quiet about it. To the other Dominicans on the street, I am not recognizable, but only a legend. They may have heard of me, but they don't know who I am.

A long time ago an American customer told me, "We call it sexual tourism." I thought at first that America must be a sad place if they have to leave to have sex.

But then he said, "In the states we can't get girls as young as you."

At the time I was fourteen. I don't question my mother about starting me out when I was so young. She had no idea how much I would make when I learned to play as well as I do now. In Santo Domingo you are not worth as much after you are sixteen, but I make more now, even more than I did then. The customers are usually foreigners, Germans, Italians, and Americans, most of them. But I have seen rich Dominican men. Most of them are of Spanish blood and have light skinned wives. Maybe I'm a cultural experience for them, like a night at the theatre. They don't often come to me more than once, these rich Dominicans. I think they only want to tell their friends they have had me and have heard my music. The music I play is not a popular style here. Classical music is nothing like our Dominican music.

I had recently taken a lover. He said that my music was the most beautiful thing on Hispaniola. Jean was Haitian and even darker than I am. He loved music and had traveled to nearly every city on the island, so he should have known if I was good or not, though I didn't need him to tell me this. He was jealous of the customers in the beginning. But because he was Haitian and he crossed the border illegally, he was unable to earn much here.

After a while he became accustomed to living with me. He knew he would always have a good life here. Also, I played a little trick with him, something I didn't do with any of my customers. Sometimes, I'd put down the violin and let him have me from on top without my even touching the violin.

For a long time now I have lived on Avenida Máximo Gómez, two kilometers from the ocean. When I leave the window open and the afternoon rains come, their fat clouds smothering Santo Domingo, everything inside is wet with the humidity. I usually play something slow and sad then, because my fingers slip against the strings. It is impossible for me to play the fast pieces. I like the slow songs too, because, so many times, it is during these that the customer cries, his tears sliding down his temples into his damp hair, like rain sliding along the waxy leaves of a banana tree. Sometimes a customer will talk about his wife. This made me happy after I had taken a lover myself. I liked to think that men knew something of love, something of what they were doing, of what they were losing with me.

Afterwards, I'd tell Jean about their crying and he'd laugh. Sometimes, for fun, Jean would speak French to me. There was a feeling I had then, while I watched his lips moving. A feeling that I could tell what it was that he was saying without understanding the words. I know today that I didn't understand anything he might have said but was charmed by the way the words slid out of his mouth so smoothly, like notes played on a cello.

My mother thought I would be worn out and worth much less by this time. I make more money than any prostitute she knows. I must remember this. She tells me this again and again, and smiles. I keep her in a small house we were able to buy near my apartment. She continues to arrange my appointments and in this way we support each other. She does all the cooking and brings me meals twice a day. She is a good cook, my mother, and because I bring in a good income for the two of us she is able to buy whatever she wants. She cooks a feast on the weekends and we eat at her house at a big round table with six matching chairs even though there are only the three of us. In the beginning she was cruel to Jean; she said it was because he was Haitian. But she had come to tolerate him when she saw that he would not keep me from working. The three of us would sit around the big table for hours eating my mother's Dominican and Spanish dishes. After the meals, we'd drink café con leche and listen to records.

On my free evenings I'd walk along the Malecón with Jean. He liked to drink Presidente and buy pastelitos there, and I liked to dance at the stands that played Bachata. I like Bacahta even better than Merengue because the songs are sad and much slower, and I liked to dance close with Jean. Last night Jean and I made love again without the violin. It was late, after a night on the Malecón. The apartment windows were open and the thick, wet air blew in across our bodies. Jean was asleep before long but I couldn't rest with the noise of the city coming in through the windows, taxis honking and motor scooters speeding along Avenida Máximo Gómez. Quietly, I left the bed and went to a chair by the window where I could see the park across the street. In the park there were chickens beneath the branches of a flamboyant tree that was in bloom. Their flowers are usually red or orange, but these were yellow. I could scarcely see the color of the flowers, which had all but closed for the night. They say that marriage is like a flamboyant; in the beginning it's all flowers but before long it goes to pod. I probably wouldn't have been missing much.

Sometimes I'd put the violin down and make love to Jean. But that night, the thing I wanted to do more than anything was only to play my violin, to be appreciated for this alone.

There is a beautiful theatre near the Plaza de La Cultura. I would like to play there. Of course I can never do this. I'm afraid that if I played my violin, the Dominican men from Gazcue and other rich neighborhoods would end up in the crowd. If they saw me playing they would recognize me. I would be there, playing beautifully, ignoring them, but they would still be there in the audience with their light skinned wives. They would use their influence to keep me from playing there again.

Jean never cried when I played the violin. But two days ago, when I put it down, I saw the light from the street reflected in his wet eyes. Then I felt the tears and beads of his sweat fall onto my breasts and my neck like a sparse rain. He was the only one who could be on top of me. He asked me once why wouldn't I run away with him to Haiti or to America where I could make a living as a musician and where we could be married.

"What about my mother?" I asked.

He looked disappointed. "But, she is the one who made you a whore," he said.

"She's also the one who gave me the violin," I answered.

"Fine," he said, after shaking his head for a long time. "You can send her money when we've settled."

"You don't understand," I told him.

I didn't allow him to talk about it again. Sometimes when we fought, or when I had a customer and Jean had nowhere else to go, he walked across the street to the park and sat beneath the flamboyant to wait for me. I'm sure he could hear my violin when I left the window open and I wonder now what he was thinking down there. There beneath the flamboyant where at the end of each summer, when the wind blows, a person is showered with the petals of a thousand dying flowers.

I try to picture him there now. I'm trying to understand why when I woke up this morning he was gone, along with my violin. My own violin, its beautiful red brown body, worn smooth, and shining with the oily touch of so many men.

Mother has scheduled appointments for me today. I wanted to go out to look for Jean, though I knew I would never find him. Instead, I'm at the window; the rain has come heavy and early today. The streets are flooded and a man pushes a stalled motor scooter through water to his knees. The rain has come. The streets swell its weight, and garbage floats along the gutters to the sea. The chickens are sheltering themselves beneath the flamboyant now. With both hands, I grasp the damp windowsill when there's a knock at the door, but I won't answer it now, not without my violin.

Special Section: Edwidge Danticat

Photo by Jayar Williams of *Caribe*

Edwidge Danticat was born in Port-au-Prince, Haiti in 1969 and, at age 12, she moved to Brooklyn, New York to reunite with her parents who had immigrated there nearly a decade earlier. Having won wide acclaim for her fiction even at a young age, she continues to receive accolades for her work. Danticat is the author of *Breath, Eyes, Memory* (1994), an Oprah Book selection; *Krik? Krak!* (1996), nominated for a National Book Award; *The Farming of Bones* (1998), an American Book Award winner; *After the Dance: A Journey to Jacmel* (2002); *Behind the Mountains* (2002); and *The Dew Breaker* (2004). Among other awards, Danticat was also a Pushcart Prize winner for her short story "Between the Pool and the Gardenias" which appeared in *The Caribbean Writer* Volume 7. In addition to producing her fiction, Danticat has edited two volumes of prose, *The Beacon Best of 2000: Great Writing by Women and Men of All Colors and Cultures* (2000) and *The Butterfly's Way: Voices from the Haitian Diaspora in the United States* (2001).

The Prize

Edwidge Danticat

Pierre was meticulously dressed, his starched, white Sunday shirt sticking to his back like the chestnut color to the rest of his skin. This was the day he would get his award from the mayor.

Pierre's mother, Aline, would be furious if she knew he was sitting in the playground, and was not at the bodega buying her stockings, as she'd ordered. "Always count on those darn things to run at the last minute," she had shouted before sending him out.

She was skipping and hopping around the apartment, changing from dress to dress, as if she were the one getting the award for dragging Georges' bloody body out of the way of cars in the middle of the street.

The playground was mostly empty now. Most of Pierre's friends were in school. He walked over to the swings, across from a trampled flower patch, where the early spring daffodils withered before they were fully out of the ground.

Pierre slipped his thin body between the swing's iron handles. The seat creaked loudly as he thrust himself higher, the wind tickling the inside of his nose while he soared and dived. Screwing his eyes shut, he saw stars swirling in a vertigo hurricane. This was Georges' favorite part of the ride. Raise the legs on the rise. Try not to scream on the fall. Pretend your head bumps into clouds.

The Marcus Garvey Neighborhood Center was pretty, once you were swaying back and forth in the swings behind it. On the side was a basketball court and a mural of children playing in a tropical forest filled with all kinds of palms: coconut, banana, cocoa, plantain, even breadfruit palms. The painter must have loved palms, reasoned Pierre's neighbors, mostly Haitians and Jamaicans, who often stopped to gaze at all the different types of palms painted on the outer courtyard walls, but the neighbors also paused to read the so-called Scroll of Respect inscribed in the indigo skies above these palms, mouthing the long list of names and pointing at the postage-stamp sized pictures of many of the children who'd died as a result of drug and gun violence in the neighborhood that year. The Scroll of Respect did not have the name of the dealers or guards, just the innocent kids who perished in the crossfire. Georges' grandmother was sitting on her usual bench, with some of the old ladies in front of Reverend Butts' church across the street from the center. She was wearing a flowered mumu, bedroom slippers, and rollers in her hair. Pierre waved, but she did not see him. She had her head down, reading a thick book. A female beat cop was strolling up and down the sidewalk, circling the area from which the chalk drawn around Georges' corpse had long faded since the night he died. The old women weren't far from the spot where Pierre had pulled the gun and drugs out of Georges' pocket and thrown them into the sewer. Georges was as good as any other kid on the block, everyone would probably have said. He just wanted to make some quick money for a cool pair of sneakers and a new video game. But if these things had been found on him, Georges' name would never have been placed on the Scroll of Respect.

A bunch of Georges' adult contacts were having a slam dunk contest in the center's basketball court even as Pierre was sitting there. Tartus was doing one-arm push-ups on the steps leading down to the court. Before Georges started dealing for Tartus, he used to joke that Tartus' head was so big, he had a five head, rather than a fo'head. Tartus was on what seemed like his millionth push up. Sweat was rippling off the large black muscle crevices on his back. Pierre hoped to have a body like that by the time he got to high school. He was going to join a gym, one like they advertise on TV.

Old man Hooper was sniffing a small paper bag as his free hand rummaged through the garbage can a few feet away from where George's grandmother and the other women were sitting. Old man Hooper was wearing a ripped sweater that was the same dried blood color as the bricks in the projects.

"Pierre Dominiques Charles!" Pierre's mother's raspy voice echoed louder than the basketballs pounding the rattling backboard.

Pierre couldn't instantly stop the swing. He had to allow his body to go up and down a few times, slap the ground with the bottom of his shoes, and dig his new pants into the metal seat.

His mother had finally settled on the silk pink blouse from her movie ushering uniform. Her pencil hips were lost under a pair of baggy black culottes.

Pierre quickly rushed over to her, stomping the doomed daffodils in his path.

"You know we have to be at City Hall in a half hour? I have a cab waiting."

She grabbed his wrist, and quickly shoved him into the back seat of a lime green gypsy cab, giving a furious glance to the cab's makeshift electric meter. She already owed two dollars and ninety cents.

"What the hell?" she said, pounding on the bulletproof partition that separated them from the driver. "I was out there for but a minute." She continued to chew out the driver, another Haitian, in Creole.

"Sorry," said the driver from behind a bushy mustache. "Even if you stop, I don't stop. I keep it running."

"Damn it, just go."

"City Hall, you said?" The man gave Pierre a quick look over, perhaps wondering what he and his mother would be doing there.

"Yes," shouted Aline. "And put a rush on it. We're about to be late."

Aline rolled down the cab window. Outside, East Flatbush was bustling with fruit and clothes vendors, calypso, meringue and rap blaring from cars and house windows and barbershops and beauty parlors. Young Fruit of Islam followers, selling newspapers, and shouting from megaphones: "You will wake up one day. You will open your eyes beyond this spring."

A prostitute jiggled her way across the street as the cab stopped for a light. Pierre moved closer to the window to have a better look. The girl looked barely sixteen. She was wearing a blue lycra skirt. Pierre's mother grabbed the back of his shirt collar and shoved him back into his seat.

"You want to end up like one of these bad kids out here?" Aline asked in the calm, pleading, guilt-laden voice that Pierre hated so much. "Why didn't you just go to the store like you were told? Why can't you appreciate the importance of a day like this? You got a letter from City Hall. The Mayor wants to meet you. Can't you show more appreciation?"

Pierre frowned and mumbled, "I don't see the big deal."

"It is a big deal," she said, "a very big deal."

As the car sped across the Manhattan Bridge, Pierre kept his eyes on the large red circles on either side of his mother's face. He raised his fingers to wipe off some of the Egyptian copper blush. It was either that, or the Nile bronze, which he also used when he ran out of paint for his watercolors.

His mother's glare was softening.

"Did I overdo the war paint again?"

Pierre nodded.

She fished into her purse and pulled out a small handkerchief with her initials AC, Aline Charles, embroidered on the corners.

"Take off as much as you can," she said.

Pierre rubbed the handkerchief over her soft high cheek-bones. Sometimes when he looked at her too long, she almost looked to him like a little girl.

The blood streaming out of Georges' mouth that night had been the same color as the cherry red on his mother's lips now. Georges had grabbed Pierre's wrist so hard before he died that Pierre thought Georges was going to stop both their blood from flowing.

The cabby took a sudden turn as they sped off the bridge. Even though he was wearing his seatbelt, Aline had to grab Pierre's shoulders to keep him from sliding off the seat. In the process, her cherry red lips brushed against his collar, landing a red blot near his neck.

"Take it easy!" Aline yelled at the driver in Creole. "Where do you want to take us? To the morgue?"

The cab was pulling into City Hall Plaza.

"You told me to get there quickly." The driver honked at a slow pedestrian.

"The money to clean this shirt comes out of what I'm paying you." Aline threatened the driver, but Pierre knew she'd never follow through with it.

"Does it look really bad?" Even though he couldn't see it too well, Pierre tried to blot the spot with his mother's handkerchief.

Aline quickly moved his hand away from the shirt. "A nice kiss just means you're loved," she said. "Besides, you're going to smear lipstick all over yourself."

The driver slowed into a spot near a hot dog vendor, as close as he could get to City Hall Plaza.

Aline spritzed a lemon-scented cologne between her protruding collar bones. Pierre closed his eyes as some fell on his face.

"The tab's going up while we're making ourselves pretty," complained the driver.

Aline slammed two twenty dollar bills into the swinging cash slot.

"Keep it all. Go play Lotto or something. It's a special day for my son."

Pierre clutched his mother's hand as they crossed the street and quickly marched up the endless steps leading to the City Hall building. City Hall looked exactly the way Pierre had seen on TV, like an all marble palace with lots of windows and old-fashioned

terraces. People were hurrying up the steps. Police men, business women, lawyers, and, Pierre noticed, a group of high school
and junior high school students, just like him. One of the girls
looked like she was having an asthma attack as she struggled up
the steps.

"We're here to see his Honor, the mayor," his mother explained
to a female guard near the metal detectors at the entrance.

"The award ceremony?" asked the guard, without looking at
them.

"That's right," answered his mother.

"Fourth floor, press room."

There were two spiraled staircases on either side of the lobby,
chandeliers floating from the ceiling and flags hanging on the bal-
conies.

Once they cleared security, they found the elevators nearly
packed, but rushed in anyway. The high school kids were talking
loudly. Someone threatened to vomit if the elevator made him
too dizzy.

When they got to the third floor, a teacher pushed his way to
the front to guide the students.

"The mayor's waiting," the older man said adjusting a slipping
toupee of curly blonde hair.

Aline pulled Pierre off to the side and waited for the others to
walk past them. The pregnant girl got off the elevator.

"Mister Casey, where's the bathroom?" She was holding her
back with both hands. Her body curved forward, which made her
look even more pregnant than when Pierre had first noticed.

"Follow the sign," shouted Mister Casey, who seemed to be
in his early twenties, though he might have been slightly older.

The girl wandered down the hall until she found a restroom
sign. Aline looked confused, but said nothing as they entered the
crowded conference room. The room was filled with kids between
nine and seventeen, black, white, Hispanic.

A tall, elegantly-dressed black woman walked over and handed Pierre and Aline a folded sheet of paper. She took them to two
seats in one of the middle rows. Aline scanned the program out-
lining the afternoon's proceedings: Mayor's Welcome, Presentation
of Awards, Reception.

Pierre could tell that his mother was fighting to maintain her
composure, trying to act as though everything was the way she
had both imagined and expected. He read a list of names in the

back of the program as his mother leaned over to talk to the woman sitting next to them. She too was black, but plump, and she wore bifocals, framing a moon-shaped face, capped with long, thick, salt and pepper dreadlocks.

"They're having the ceremony for all these children?" Aline asked the woman.

"I reckon they are," answered the woman.

Pierre found his name on the back of the program. Pierre D. Charles, East Flatbush, District 35. He tapped his mother's leg and showed it to her.

"Ah, you see. They've got you there." Aline smiled, even as the corners of her mouth were twitching.

There were a few reporters in the room now. A Chinese woman from the six o'clock news unwound the cord on her microphone. Some tried out a few poses for the cameras. Others were interviewing the kids in the front rows.

There was a stand set aside for the mayor, on a raised platform in front of a large unlit fireplace.

Georges would have loved this, Pierre thought.

It was almost a month now since Pierre had pulled him out of the street. Tartus and the others ran when they saw the Bronx dealers coming. Georges stayed. He hadn't been guarding long enough to know what to do. Georges had fallen in a flash of bullets. By the time Pierre had rushed over from the swings, Georges was barely breathing, except he still had that grip, that persistent, forceful grasp that refused to totally release his friend.

Pierre didn't regret getting rid of the coke and the gun that had been on Georges that night. The day after, *The Daily News* had published an old essay that Georges had written when they were both in the third grade.

"I want to be an astronaut" was the headline of the story. Somehow, the paper had found a picture of the two of them, Pierre and Georges at Georges' tenth birthday party.

The pregnant girl shuffled in and found a seat with some other girls near the front.

"What's she getting an award for?" Pierre heard his mother whispering to the dreadlocked woman next to her.

"Staying in school even though she's pregnant," the woman said. "That's why most of those girls are here."

"And your child?" Aline Charles asked the woman.

"I don't have a child," the woman said, raising her bifocals to better see Aline. She also glanced at Pierre, smiling at him approvingly, or so Pierre thought. "I work at Hale House with recovering teen addicts," she said. "I bring a couple of them once a month to get acknowledged by the mayor. I'm hoping it will keep them clean."

"I got a letter saying they were going to honor my son for trying to save a troubled boy in our neighborhood." Aline's hand crept around Pierre's shoulder.

"Most of these kids are here so they won't go from the bad they're in to something worse," the woman interrupted Aline. This time she looked directly at Pierre, fixing her eyes on him as if to hammer in a message. "Keep it up, young man," she said, nodding her head for emphasis. "Stay in school. Don't give up. Be somebody."

"But the letter had his name on it." Aline's voice was growing louder. "I thought it was addressed to him and him alone."

"They have a computer," the woman said. "All my kids get their own letters. We keep them in their recovery journals."

"We'll begin in a few minutes." The woman who had given them the program was now standing at the podium. "Please take your seats. The mayor is wrapping up a meeting. He'll be here shortly."

Aline grabbed Pierre's hand and quickly led him out the door. More kids were coming in, but Pierre and Aline walked by them so fast that they all seemed like the blurred image of one single person. Pierre kept his eyes on the flashing lights as they went down in the elevator. He knew something was wrong, that his mother was upset, but he wasn't sure yet how to console her. Instead he kept picturing Georges' name on the Scroll of Respect, his image among those on the mural of children playing in the thick green forest of a simpler, safer place. Georges Alexandre Toussaint, his calligraphic inscription read. Sunrise September 30, 1978—Sunset, February 7, 1992.

Outside, on the street in front of City Hall, people were rushing about, most of them to places they had some claim to.

"Maybe you ought to keep that lipstick on your shirt, it makes you look awfully debonair." Pierre's mother leaned down and planted a red kiss on his cheek. Noticing how embarrassed her son was, watching the curious passersby watch them, Aline straightened herself out, and patting Pierre's shoulders, she breathed in the crisp spring air as they moved on.

Je Voudrais Etre Riche:
A Trickster Tale
Edwidge Danticat

It was too good not to be true. Two women. One black. One white. One old. One young. The young black one, pregnant, with a slightly shrieking, wailing voice. The old white one hunched over under a red, ankle length coat, a fog of white hair creeping out under a crocheted black beret.

The old white one had a nice American lilt to her voice, a sing song, the kind of English you envy, the kind that overflows with ease and the rush of a stream, like the one behind my grand-mother's house in the old country. Yes, that stream, the stream of memory, measureless nostalgia that makes a person long for a palm tree-fringed ray of sunshine on a cold dark New York evening, the stream of yearning for the country that may never be its ideal, our ideal, the stream of yes—desires—that even makes us want to believe that sometimes people are nice here. This, and perhaps a bit of greed, is what led me to these two ladies on the upper West Side of Manhattan, ladies of apparent opposite worlds, one who—if not for the language—could be from back home, the other unmistakably from the new country.

Hey, girl, did you lose something?

Lose something? How much time did they have? How about my boyfriend of a few weeks now, my very popular, choir director boyfriend, the first of my whole nineteen years of life, who, just a few minutes before, had declared to me in the middle of a street on the upper Westside of Manhattan that he would not be going with me to a long-planned dinner at my college because "We'd have to be a couple there and it's obvious we're not a couple anymore." Obvious to whom? I wanted to ask. I guess I'd missed all the clues, the hints, the suggestions, thinking we were seeing each other less and less because we were becoming more and more busy with studying and work study jobs. "You're still one of the most important people in my life," he'd said. Still packages filled with trash had been dumped more carefully than this, so I must have been feeling vulnerable as well. Vulnerable and cold and sorry for myself. But more cold than anything else since I was dressed for the mild winter day that it had been that morn-ing, one at least twenty degrees warmer, a day which I had expected to end in a warm place with this man at my side. Did the voice asking what I had lost already know about all this? Could she tell? Before the voice had called me, I was about to decide whether to buy myself an egg salad sandwich for dinner— a recent favorite at the Deli across the street from the place where my boyfriend and I were supposed to have dinner. I must have been doing a kind of sidestep, which I'm told I do when trying to decide something. Go? Don't go! Buy that sandwich. Don't buy it! And finally I had decided against the sandwich because I only had fifty dollars in a Citibank account I had opened with high school graduation gift money and ten dollars total in my pocket, bringing the total sum of my assets to sixty dollars, not to mention the student loan debt I had already acquired as a sophomore at Barnard College, which meant that like most nineteen year olds, I had a super-negative net worth. I wondered if the old white woman knew all this when she moved from the end of a block and slowly walked a few steps closer to me in order to repeat her memorable question, "Hey, girl, did you lose something?"

Reaching into my small purse, in which I had a worn and extremely highlighted paperback of Zora Neale Hurston's *Their Eyes Were Watching God* book and a wallet filled with more pieces of identification than cash, I checked for both and made sure they were there. No, I hadn't lost anything tangible that I knew of.

The old white woman was holding a large blue plastic pouch with prints that made it look as though many had marched across it with wet shoes. As she pushed the blue pouch towards me, another woman, the black pregnant one, approached. The two ladies created a kind of half circle around me and the old white one said to the pregnant black one, "Did you drop this?" Like me, the pregnant woman shook her head no.

"Okay then, I'll open it," the old white lady said.

The white lady slowly removed a pair of black wool gloves from her hands, revealing heavily veined pink fingers. Carefully, she pulled open the zipper on the blue pouch and both the pregnant woman and myself leaned forward at the same time to have a look inside.

"Oh mercy no," the old white lady cried.

"Oh mercy yes," echoed the young black one. The peels of joy reminded me of church. I had spent the first twelve years of my life attending Sunday and thrice weekly Baptist services in Haiti and had later moved to Brooklyn, New York, where my parents belonged to a Pentecostal church, where a good part of the services was an hour-long song and dance fellowship that included shrieks of uncontrollable joy like this. So yes, mercy indeed, I thought peering inside the little pouch, which was filled to the brim with money, crisp green cash, dollar bills of a shade of green I had never lain eyes on before, all stacked together and wrapped around thick olive green rubber bands.

The white lady's eyes had grown wider than even the silvery buttons on her coat. We were now, all three of us, gaping at the pouch, taking turns clawing and leafing through what we quickly determined were thousand dollar bills. "Could there be that much money in the world?" The pregnant woman asked rhetorically.

"We'll split this three ways, okay?" the old one stopped groaning long enough to whisper. "People are starting to stare. My car's just around the corner. Let's go in there." No one was really staring. The man selling nuts from his cart was warming himself around a chestnut haze, the men selling watches for ten dollars each were making deals, the young woman selling reprinted movie scripts was mouthing a monologue to herself between customers. Still I followed them to the car, a beaten up gray station wagon, which was parked just across the street from the deli. The young black one introduced herself as Miss Sands before slipping in the front passenger seat. She signaled for me to get in the back seat behind her and asked me where I was from. I mumbled "Haiti" as the old woman slipped behind the wheel.

Miss Sands asked the old white lady her name.

"Call me Olive, dear," she replied.

From the driver's seat, Olive pulled a note from the pouch, a note that somehow had escaped my attention before.

Olive managed to place the note between the three of us and together we read what seemed like a quickly scribbled letter written by someone who was certain that its reader would have no trouble interpreting the nearly indecipherable handwriting. I am paraphrasing here, but the gist of the letter was this:

Dear Ben,
We won really big at the races. There is 75,000 dollars
here in 1,000 bills plus two bonds. Give Mom her share
and keep the rest for me until I get back.

"It's Christmas ladies!" Olive said. "Christmas in November."

"Let's split it," Miss Sands cried out, resting both her hands on her belly as if to contain not only her own excitement, but her fetus' as well.

If we were sharing, then of course I would get 25,000 dollars, a larger sum than I had ever seen or heard of anyone having at once.

For the first time since the encounter, I finally spoke.

"All right, let's do it. Let's split it."

My mind was spinning with the possibility of what I could do with 25,000 dollars. First my student loans. Then I would make a substantial payment on my parents' mortgage. I would give some to my three brothers then put the rest away for graduate school, whatever I would decide in the end, whether it was the MFA, EDD, or MBA.

"Oh, there's a small fly in our stew," Olive was saying, even as I'd already spent the majority of the twenty five thousand dollars in my mind. (I can't believe now how clichéd her language was.) "The fly in our stew is this," Olive said. "We can always dump the bonds. They'd trace them back to us anyway if they tried to cash them. The cash though is all in one thousand dollar bills." I had never seen thousand-dollar bills before. Did such things truly exist? I had a moment of doubt, but perhaps the ladies had foreseen this too. "There's no way we could cash something like that without getting arrested," Olive said. I thought of asking for my own money and deciding later what to do with it, but what if the letter writer and receiver were drug dealers or wanted criminals of a different sort? How would it look if I walked into the Citibank branch near Barnard College and asked to deposit all his money into my account with the fifty-dollar balance? Still I had no intention of walking away from twenty five thousand dollars, if I could have it without breaking any laws?

Before I could express my concerns, Miss Sands quickly came up with a solution. "I'm a certified cash messenger for a firm called Duff and Brown," she said. "Their office is right down the street. Mister Duff has an industrial machine that tests for fake money. If you two will trust me, I'll go and test the money in the office."

Now that we had decided to share the loot, I didn't want to split up. What if Miss Sands escaped with all our cash? Olive seemed less concerned about this than I was. I could see all the wheels spinning in her head. Miss Sands was pregnant after all. How far could she get on her feet? We could park in front of the Duff and Brown building and wait for her to come back out. But whatever Olive might have been thinking, had she brought it up for consideration, I would have been able to think of a counter argument. What if Miss Sands took the money and then called the police on us? What if she left the building through some side or back entrance that only an employee of that building would know about? But in the end, without much discussion—honor among thieves, I suppose—we drove to the Duff and Brown building, on the first floor of which were plenty of dentists and OBGYN offices, and watched as the pregnant Miss Sands wobbled in. As Miss Sands disappeared into that building, I looked through the side windows of Olive's beaten down station wagon and in that moment wanted to see something familiar, something that would prove that all of this was really happening, that I had lost the man I love and gained twenty five thousand dollars in one single hour.

Miss Sands was not long in coming back with the pouch cradled against her belly. She had to confess to her boss, she said as she slipped breathlessly into the car, that she'd found this money and her boss promised to help her. For his trouble, he would keep the bonds, which were ten thousand dollars each, but he would give us each twenty thousand dollars in smaller bills, 20, 50, 100 dollar bills that could easily be stuffed in pillows and mattresses, slipped into increased deposits at the bank, handed out as gifts, rewards, offerings at church. "Let's do it then," I said again, now eager for the whole thing to be resolved. Twenty thousand dollars was less, but still a whole lot of dough. I was ready for pay dirt. "Okay," Miss Sands said. And in the pause after that word, I would feel some further complication that she would soon be getting into. "What is it?" I asked. I was anxious not to let much more time go by. With time, the money was slipping through our fingers in very high percentages. Twenty percent of my fortune was already gone. I didn't want to sit there and watch the rest vanish. The trouble with being overly excited is that you either sound like a child or a brute when you try to speak. All the nuances are lost in your voice and you are only left with apish gestures to convey your deepest desires.

"There's one more thing," Miss Sands finally spoke, as I was sure she would. "In order for him to change the money, you need to make a deposit with your own cash so he can make it seem as though you're investing in his company."

"Company?" I ventured.

"Duff and Brown," Miss Sands reminded me. "That's the company I work for." She spoke very slowly as though I were really a deaf ape. And while Olive was saying "How much money do you have on you?" she and Miss Sands seemed suddenly of one mind, like even though they were seemingly of different races and generations, they were both from the same world. Suddenly, Miss Sands' face was moving closer to mine and Olive's attention temporarily shifted from me to Miss Sands.

"How much you got?" Miss Sands asked Olive.

"Twelve hundred," answered Olive. "I was going to the Citibank to deposit my rent."

"Give it to me," Miss Sands said. Miss Sands then took great pains to count Olive's wrinkled bills then handed Olive what seemed like a business card and pointed to the dentist and OBGYN building, telling the old woman, "Go and get your money, Mr. Duff will be waiting for you. I told him you were Miss Green and you, what's your name?" she asked me at last.

"Edie," I replied, which is a name I offer to people when I don't want to spend five minutes discussing my real name.

"You'll be Miss Brown," Miss Sands told me.

When I became Miss Brown, I realized that I was part of something that I could not easily leave, not without causing a scene or being called either stupid or lucky.

Miss Sands stayed in the car this time while Olive—now also known as Miss Green—walked into the building with her twelve hundred dollars of her rent money to surrender to Misters Duff or Brown.

"I can't believe our good fortune," Miss Sands said after Olive had disappeared into the building.

I began to feel a bit of remorse and even sympathy for Ben or whoever it was who'd lost all that money.

"You said you're from Haiti?" Miss Sands asked. I nodded, keeping my eyes on the round-bellied doorman at the building's entrance. "I was in Haiti once, on a cruise," Miss Sands said. "We got off on this beautiful island called Labadie. It was like paradise there. Great place."

"I speak a little French," Miss Sands added when I didn't respond. I was so deep in thought now that it was almost like meditation. Did Miss Sands have a gun in a pouch in her swollen belly? Could she lock the car somehow and refuse to let me out? Then as if to confirm my growing suspicion or my realization that I was the "mark" in a con game, Miss Sands uttered the most scripted of her clichéd dialogue thus far. "Je voudrais etre riche." And with that sentence, "I would like to be rich," she brought to mind a fragment of something I'd managed to retain from one of the endless sermons I'd heard at one of the many church services I'd attended since I was a child. It was a maxim from Ecclesiastes, not a fitting last prayer or verse, but one that was helping to hammer in the lesson I was perhaps meant to learn from all this: Lord, let me be neither too poor nor too rich. For if I am too rich, I might forget you. And if I'm too poor, I might steal and disgrace your name.

"Because of the job I do," Miss Sands added to fill the silence, "I'm insured with Lords of London for a million dollars."

For some reason, this struck me as impressive, and I was going to ask Miss Sands a few pointed questions about her work when Olive quickly slipped back into the car.

"Let me shake your hand," Olive extended a bony pink hand to Miss Sands. "I've never heard an employer speak so highly of his employee, especially a woman of color. Your Mister Duff while counting my money out for me told me how you're one of the most excellent carriers he has, insured by the Lords of London for a million dollars."

"See, what did I tell you?" Miss Sands said turning from me. I acknowledged this with a congratulatory nod, or what I hoped was a congratulatory nod. Olive now had her twenty thousand dollars in her purse. She was too afraid to display it, she said. Some evil eyes might be watching. Miss Sands had already decided that she was going to let her boss keep her money for her. He would use her salary as proof that she'd invested with him. So now it was my turn. Could I possibly have some cash on me that I could use for my transaction with Mr. Duff? I thought now that this was the moment I would get jumped, robbed or killed, the exact time that the car would speed away and I would be blackmailed into some horrible act at my destination. I mourned for the naïve me, the one who'd so willingly offered herself in sacrifice for a pouch full of cash.

"How much money do you have on you?" Miss Sands asked again very slowly. Her voice was gentle, not threatening at all. But there was an edge of urgency to it which signaled that she couldn't possibly be this concerned about someone else collecting money that if they failed to, she could harvest herself.

"We don't have much time," Miss Sands said. "It's nearly the end of the day. Mister Duff will be going home soon."

"Do you have a bank card?" she asked me. And this is when I expected the guns to come out, the other accomplices to flood in. This is when I was a hundred percent certain that I was the casualty, and not the perpetrator of a crime. And this is also when I slid closer to the car door, reached for the handle, pulled my purse closer to me, kicked the door open and jumped out. And even as I heard both Miss Sands and Olive cry out behind me, "What do you think you're doing?" "Where are you going?" I knew they would not chase me. They were older and weaker and didn't have the fright or flight instinct I now had, the kind of survival adrenaline pumping in my veins.

I must have ran five or six blocks before I stopped. Then I checked my purse again to see if my wallet was still there. It was. And it still had the same ten dollars that I had decided against breaking by not having my egg salad sandwich. For a second, I pondered finding a police station and filing a report. But I didn't think that it would do much good. To be almost the victim of a crime was not the same as being one. Besides, I was embarrassed. I imagine the policemen and women calling me gullible and laughing behind my back. Besides, even if the con had been carried out to its predictable conclusion, after an entire evening of spontaneous theater during which these women had to be on their toes at every step, they still would have only collected sixty dollars from me, a pittance for such an incredible display of creativity, skill, and artistry. The power of con artists is that they are dodgers. At least I had dodged them. But even if they had taken me for a whole ride, I still would have escaped the total horror of being a perfect mark.

Reading *Krik? Krak!* in Puerto Rico

Loretta Collins

Under the vaulted ceilings of la torre,
the grand Seville clock tower, where sun
paints the archways in brillant light
and warmth on marble floors, students
usually sleep or read, or sleep and read.
Sometimes the Conjunto de Clarinetes plays,
weak reeds gathering the heat and dust
of the tower into a somnolent splendor.
Or the strolling trovadores of the Tuna,
in crimson-lined black cloaks, black leggings,
and balloning bloomers, strum the islamic laúd,
bandurria, or guitarra. They crave the acoustics
of la torre as they sing about the lady love.
Perhaps, one disappointed trovador
let a sea breeze whirl up under his cape,
turning him into a vision of black butterflyhood.
Perhaps he flapped around the tower still,
as my students read "Children of the Sea"
in the last minutes before class, four women friends,
who breathlessly told me it wouldn't leave them alone,
an enormous black butterfly that battered one woman's face
and would not be deterred while they read Danticat's story
under the clock tower. They batted it away, and ran from it,
but it stayed on course, trying to light in Laurita's hair. . .
"and then, there it was, the black butterfly floating around us."
Jorge doodled in his art pad during class that day,
inking-in veined leaves and insets of a woman's nude back,
a pose between repose and labor, as if she were simultaneously
resting from a beating and rising up again. He replicated
her image in miniature, a morphed figurine whose spine
was composed of leaf veins, whose body assumed a crysalis shape,
and whose arm outlined a butterfly wing: "Mariposa negra."
Students talked about tennis shoes washed ashore, dehydrated groups
of Domincanos and Haitians routinely hunted down by La Guardia Costera,
drowned in the Mona Passage, hailed at sea, or corraled on shore

and deported from Puerto Rico. They admitted how little
they knew, though living just nextdoor, as islands go. From a botanica,
one student bought a framed Erzulie in her danto aspect,
the African madonna, with three bloody scars marking her face.
"Night women" walk the barrios of San Juan, too. She wrote
a poem about a prostitute in seven skirts, blue and white, who
with her hips, rocked the tides against the walls of the old city,
lulling the deambulantes and the residents of La Perla to sleep.
After reading "1937," one woman brought a cantaloupe to class.
She said that her mother, a devotee of espiritismo, had her own
annual ceremony at the sea. In Danticat's story, she said,
Haitian women needed to remember the baptisms of blood
their mothers received in the massacre at the river.
In Puerto Rico, we remember our massacres, too,
but we try, too often, to forget. A quintet played "La Borinqueña"
while women dressed in white walked with their children and men
down a street of Ponce. We remember that one, our "1937,"
when police blocked off the street, shot and clubbed Nacionalistas.
Once a year, my mother writes her bitterness
into a message, and inserts it into a melon, the student said.
She prays and throws the melon into the sea. It carries
her sorrows away. In a college classroom, where wobbling
ceiling fans stirred the heat, we each wrote our messages
for the cantaloupe, according to her instructions: a memory
from Danticat's writing, a phrase, an image, an allusion,
an action, a person impossible to forget. Students
chose the crow-women of the jail and hair that sprouted
from makeshift graves, but I chose the quilt stitched
in "The Missing Peace," a royal-purple, unravelling weft.
This semester, the students read *Kirk? Krak!* as closely
as they always do here, but this time they also responded
as artists and spiritualists with their own memories to craft.
Will they forget? This cantaloupe was for remembrance.
I don't know about its lasting effect as a pedagogical tool.
I don't really want to carry this thing around all day,
and we don't have a river or the beach around here,
the student told me after class. At home, I took
our messages out, cut the melon,
and thought about eating it. I didn't, though.
It was for remembrance.
The melon was so tart. It was so sweet.

The Immigrants' Storyteller

Kim Dismont Robinson

Reprinted with permission from *RG Magazine* (Bermuda) 8.8 (August 2000): 21-23.

Acclaimed Haitian-American author Edwidge Danticat talks to Kim Dismont Robinson about her novel *The Farming of Bones* and the challenges of writing from a "hyphenated heritage."

"In this theoretical world, people forget that creativity is magical," laughs Haitian-born writer Edwidge Danticat in her rich, musical voice. And Danticat knows better than anyone how to make magic—the 31-year-old writer has earned more critical acclaim already than most authors earn in a lifetime. Since the publication of her debut novel *Breath, Eyes, Memory* in 1994, she has used her lyrically powerful writing as a way of expressing what it's like to be a Haitian immigrant in the United States. Her 1996 collection of short stories entitled *Krik? Krak!* won a National Book Award nomination and *Breath, Eyes, Memory*, was one of Oprah's Book Club selections.

Like the protagonist in *Breath, Eyes, Memory*, Danticat left Haiti at the age of twelve for New York to reunite with her parents, who had tried to find more economic and political stability in the U.S. Since then, the fiction she's written has attempted to capture the unique linguistic and cultural challenges experienced by immigrants—challenges, she claims, will be even more important to understand as we move deeper into the 21st Century.

Danticat says there's a certain degree of suspicion directed toward artists such as herself with a "hyphenated heritage"—but she refuses to see a dual culture as being "tragic" in any way. "I'm always in the middle of this debate. Sometimes people are suspicious, and wonder if it means that people like me who write from the hyphen are 'less Haitian,'" she notes. "This debate is important because there's a whole generation of people who came with our parents and are creating in another country."

"But I think they *should* struggle with that, because we're going to have to deal with that issue more and more. People are being raised in between exile and assimilation. . .I don't think it's tragic, it's just that people who are more on one side (e.g. people born and raised exclusively in one country) have trouble understanding," she adds.

The stories that the sombre young writer has chosen to tell pack a serious punch. Her most recent novel, *The Farming of Bones*, is based on the 1937 massacre of Haitians at the border of the Dominican Republic. However, Danticat (who recently taught a creative writing workshop at the University of Miami) claims a key to writing is allowing a story to emerge on its own.

"A very difficult part for me was to find a way to enter the story underlying *The Farming of Bones*. The story already exists, and the drama was already there: you've got a river called Massacre River (because of all the Hatians that were killed), you've got one island which is split down the middle, a dictator. . .it's so full of drama by itself."

"Writing is such a solitary occupation. You have to get people out of your head to get back to the writing. You have to humble yourself, go back and get small; you almost have to forget you've been published," she says.

"Maya Angelou talks about that. She's written about twelve books, and each time she starts with a blank page. The less baggage you have starting over, the better it is for you."

In *The Farming of Bones*, Danticat raises some issues that aren't often discussed regarding the tensions between Haitians and Dominicans. The 1937 Massacre is still a sensitive topic, and so it's not surprising that Danticat has had mixed reactions from both Dominicans and Haitians about the book.

"There were so many Dominicans who knew this story in some way. They are so much more aware of us (Haitians) than we are of them. The only thing that made Haitians aware of Dominicans was that people went to work in the Dominican sugar cane factories. But Dominicans are taught about Haitians. . .for example, they celebrate the end of the Haitian occupation in 1844, not the Spanish occupation," says Danticat. "Some Dominicans thought *Farming of Bones* was one-sided, some thought it wasn't biased at all. . .and some Haitians felt I was afraid of the Dominicans and didn't 'go for it' enough."

Danticat's first novel *Breath, Eyes, Memory*, although critically acclaimed, was similarly not without its fair share of controversy. One of the core issues in the book surrounds the traumatic experience of a mother "testing" her daughter's virginity. Danticat says that she was heavily criticised for telling the story, since Haitians have been so poorly represented in the media.

It became obvious as Danticat discussed some of the negative responses to the book that it's still a sore spot for the soft-spoken young woman. But she made it crystal clear that her story, although important, is not intended to represent her entire culture.

"I'm not the bravest person in the world, but when I'm writing these things I'm not even worried—I feel like I have truth on my side, and something about writing makes me delirious. But for the Oprah edition, I wrote an afterword for *Breath, Eyes, Memory* because there was so much trouble," she said.

"I would tell the story again, but I'd also have a family that didn't 'test.' I don't think that would compromise. But it wasn't my intent. . ." she faltered, before trailing off. "I thought other people would see it like that, as one story—I didn't know that people would see it as the story. At some readings, people will come up to me afterwards and tell me stories even more horrifying—and it's not just Haitians.

"I'm glad that when I started off I was naïve. I went to the story and told it, even if I got a lot of hell for it. Because I was naïve, it's the purest manifestation of what I wanted to do," she notes. "Now I have more of a sense of 'what you tell'—and that will be with me for the rest of my life. But I'm glad I had the innocence back then to write that book," she adds.

Many of Danticat's characters experience a great deal of mental and physical trauma. She admitted that the troubling images in her fiction stem from a certain degree of melancholy and isolation in her own life.

"I feel like I'm writing about things that haunt me. Like (Antiguan writer) Jamaica Kincaid, I never was really writing to entertain and I don't know enough about the world to write that generally," Danticat says.

"I write about these things maybe because I haven't had much levity in my own life. Maybe it's not to do with being Haitian, maybe it's to do with my own disposition—separating from my parents at a young age, watching people disappear," she adds.

"I've always been drawn to the whole dilemma of how you deal with pain. It's not about being resilient, it's not about offering a model, it's about taking people and seeing how they cope.

"People deal with things differently. . .I think rituals help us cope. For example, Amabelle (the protagonist in *The Farming of Bones*) saying that she wanted to do the same thing every day is a way of bringing order and routine to life. But my way of dealing with tragedy is to work obsessively," Danticat says.

The class divisions which separate people in her native country figure as a painful reality for Danticat, who is often disturbed by how poor people are marginalised in Haiti. "There's a frustration that the people I'm writing about can't read my work. It's so vast, the difference. . .When I go back to Haiti, I go back to the mountains and think, 'My God, these people are marooned from the rest of the country.' There's an expression, *peyi ande yò*, which means 'the outside country'. . .can you imagine someone being considered living outside their own country?"

"One woman said to me, 'your peasants seem very bourgeois.' But I spent my childhood between the city and the country. . .these people have a complexity, and I wanted to write about them," Danticat adds.

As a Haitian-American writer often held accountable by her readers for the image of "home" she projects, Danticat's challenges are not necessarily unique to a Caribbean author. She recalled a conference where controversial Guadeloupian writer Maryse Condé was giving a lecture, and a member of the audience angrily confronted her about a book she wrote which gave a not-so-positive depiction of African culture.

"Maryse Condé had written about ten books since then, and all I could think was, 'You mean, I have to spend the next ten years defending this book I've written?'" she chuckled.

"I don't really do the conference crowd that much. By the time your book is published, you've gotten some distance from it and you want to move on. So I'm not going to put myself in the situation where I'm in front of a hundred people trying to defend my work.

"I had the 'pleasing disease' when I was younger, but I feel like I've aged a lot in five years. I've encountered a different kind of censorship than what I expected. . .for example, angry people claiming I was selling my culture for money.

"But it's good for me. I needed to take responsibility for what I'd written, to acknowledge that I'd made some people angry. But if my books make you angry, you have to think 'why' —especially since it's fiction.

"I'm glad that I've had negative reactions mixed in with the good things, because it keeps you focused on the work. If it had been 'all good,' it wouldn't have been good for me. It's important for a writer to have complexity."

The Ability of Water to Heal and Unify in Edwidge Danticat's *The Farming of Bones* and "Children of the Sea"

Magdalena Cohen

> *Aronse o zang nan dlo*
> *Bak odsu miwa*
>
> "Alert the angels down in the water,
> Back beneath the mirror"
>
> Common Opening to Vodou Ceremony

> The past is full of examples when our foremothers and forefathers showed such deep trust in the sea that they would jump off slave ships and let the waves embrace them. They too believed that the sea was the beginning and the end of all things, the road to freedom and their entrance to Guinin.
>
> Edwidge Danticat "We are Ugly, But We are Here"

In the works of Edwidge Danticat, water is a physical presence, nearly a human character. Through water, the beauty and the ugliness that have shaped and continue to shape Haiti are integrated as the lines between the past, present and spirit world blur. Through the integration of Catholicism and Vodou, water serves to integrate the political and historical atmosphere of Haiti. As it flows away from the main narrative to be a major character in the works of Danticat, water both cleanses and destroys. Danticat's Haiti is a country torn apart by political strife, with a history full of bloodshed. In *The Farming of Bones*, and the short story "Children of the Sea," water is an all-knowing godlike presence that has the power to hurt, to heal, to grant life and to take life away.

The Farming of Bones tells the story of the Haitian massacre of 1937 through the eyes of one woman and her personal loss of the man she loves. Through this one man, Danticat funnels the loss of the estimated twenty thousand people that died in the massacre. As the different rivers of the story separate, Amabelle's story emerges. Amabelle is an orphan, taken in by a wealthy Dominican family. She grows up with the family's only daughter, and as a young adult, continues to serve the Señora who marries and has children.

Amabelle lives as a servant in this wealthy house. She finds love with Sebastien, a cane cutter at a nearby mill, and they are learning "to change [their] unhappy tales into happy ones" (56). Then a presidential order instructing Dominicans to slaughter the Haitians and drive them back into their own country changes the course of Amabelle's life. Amabelle is forced to flee the Dominican Republic, and she tells her story of escape "from the other side of the river" (220). When the novel concludes, Amabelle is twenty-four years removed from the massacre, but still unhealed. She continues to hear the "weight of the river all the time," and in the novel's conclusion, she returns to the Dominican Republic to give her "testimony to the river, [and] the waterfall" (266). Amabelle visits briefly with the Señora, and says goodbye before returning forever to Haiti and her side of the river. Water appears throughout the narrative but what is perhaps most provocative is the way the river both begins and concludes the telling.

Water is present before the story begins. Danticat precedes the novel with an epigraph and a dedication. Water figures in both.

> Jephthah called together the men of Gilead and fought against Ephraim. The Gileadites captured the fords of the Jordan leading to Ephraim, and whenever a survivor of Ephraim said 'Let me cross over,' the men of Gilead asked him, 'Are you an Ephraimite?' If he replied, 'No' they said 'All right say Shibboleth.' If he said, 'Sibboleth,' because he could not pronounce the word correctly, they seized and killed him at the fords of the Jordan. Forty-thousand were killed. (Judges 12:4-6)

This Old Testament selection tells the story of the slaughter of forty thousand residents of Ephraim by the Gileadites, echoed in the massacre of Haitians by Dominicans in 1937. Both massacres took place at a river, and both used a single word to determine life and death. In biblical times the word used to determine life or death was "shibboleth" (Dedication and Epigraph). In 1937 the word is "perejil," the Spanish word for parsley. The role of the river in this Bible verse sets the tone for the importance that water plays in the survival of people worldwide. The choice of an Old Testament selection also establishes the presence of Christianity in Danticat's novel, in Haiti and therefore in Vodou.

The dedication that follows this epigraph will emphasize the role of water, while at the same time placing Christianity and Vodou in the same river. It reads: "In confidence to you, Metrès Dlo, Mother of the Rivers Amabelle Désir" (Dedication and Epigraph). Multiple objectives are established by this dedication. The Kreyòl language is introduced and then translated, assuming that readers will not be able to understand the words of Haiti's tongue, customs and religious traditions unaided. In the same sentence, the story to follow is given into the security of the Mother of the Rivers. "In confidence" is a unique phrasing that could be interpreted in several ways. There is an air of secretiveness about the word confidence, given the context, as if what is about to be revealed is for the personified ears of the water, and those ears alone. The tale is also being placed under the protection of the water, empowering the water, with the responsibility of revealing the story to those who need to hear it. In the dedication, water is a physical being, not simply a part of nature. This mythical mother of the rivers can also be read as reference to Lasirene, the feminine Vodou spirit of the water.

In Haitian culture, Vodou is an intangible part of everything. It is "infused into the very essence of living" (Yarbough 7). Amabelle may be unaware of the Vodou tradition she is embracing, but the dedication is an invocation of the spirit of the mother of the rivers. The invocation of spirits is a cornerstone of Vodou practice. A typical Vodou ceremony has two main parts: the "rite of entry" in which drums accompany the "orientation of the sacred objects, and finally the invocation of the Lwa" (Hubon 108). After the Lwa have been invoked, the Dañse-Lwa occurs. During the Dañse-Lwa, "the faithful who have been entered by the Lwa are seized by a 'fit of possession'" (Hurbon 108,110). These Vodou practices give additional meaning to this invocation, especially in light of the fact that this call to the spirits originates from Amabelle. Amabelle is looking to the spirit world for the strength to tell her story. At the same time, Amabelle is calling to Lasirene, who traditionally brings "good luck and wealth from the bottom of the sea" (Olmos112). As Amabelle's story unfolds, it becomes clear that she is seeking a type of wealth[1] from the bottom of the water. She seeks her parents and her lover, both swallowed by depths of the river. Amabelle needs their support, their company and their love. On some level, Amabelle is also requesting the return of all those who have vanished beneath the waters of the Massacre River.

Comparing the epigraph and the dedication provides an intriguing contrast. The two introductory selections share the presence of water, the literal river in the first account and the spirit presence of water in the second. The dedication calls upon the spirits of Vodou in the tongue of Haiti, while the epigraph tells an Old Testament story that foreshadows the massacre whose story is told in *The Farming of Bones*. The epigraph is full of bloodshed and hate, while the dedication holds out hope: the Mother of the Rivers will protect the fragility of this story that must be told. The tension between those who practice Vodou and those who do not appears in these two selections. It is this tension that has shaped Haiti's relations with the Dominican Republic and thus Haiti itself. In the story that follows these introductory pieces, water is responsible for bridging this gap and helping a single narrative to be born.

The Farming of Bones opens as Amabelle awakes from a nightmare. The nightmare Amabelle has "all the time, of [her] parents drowning" (1). Amabelle has been shaped by the loss of her parents, just as she will be molded by the loss of Sebastien. The loss of her parents is relived throughout the novel in vivid nightmares, until all the details intertwine to reveal what happened the day her parents drowned. That day, when the river first begins to define her life, she recalls that out "on the levee [are] a few river rats, young boys, both Haitian and Dominican, who for food or one or two coins. . .carry people and their merchandise across the river on their backs" (51). On this particular day they are not plying their trade. "The current is swelling, the pools enlarging. Even the river rats are afraid to cross" (51). The fear and hesitation of the river boys should act as a deterrent to those who wish to cross the river, but Amabelle's father remains stubbornly unafraid. He does not fear the water.

Instead her "father reaches into the current and sprinkles his face with water, as if to salute the spirit of the river and request her permission to enter" (51). This parallels the invocation of the water spirit that occurs in the dedication. In Vodou, it would be unthinkable to begin any venture without "a libation of water," to honor the spirits (Deren 197). Her father respects the power of the water spirits, but he does not fear that power. He has made his request and expects that the spirits of the water will now protect him from the wrath of the river, granting him a safe passage. Amabelle identifies her father's dabbing of the water as an appeal to the spirits, but his actions also mirror the Catholic tradition of dabbing holy oil on an infant's head prior to baptism (Desmangles 88). Vodou also has a rite of baptism. In fact, in his book *The Faces of God*, Leslie Desmangles claims that "to the untrained eye, the Vodou rituals might seem a replay of the Church's baptismal rites," so close are the two rituals in nature (88). This similarity of ritual demonstrates the impossibility of disentangling Catholicism from Haitian Vodou. In addition to evoking baptismal images, the sprinkling of water mirrors another Vodou tradition. "When a new-comer enters the family compound for an extended visit, courtesy requires that he or she make a small libation of water at the tombs, so that the ancestors will welcome the person" (But 1). This is a tradition throughout Haiti. When Amabelle's father sprinkles the water on his head, he is performing a similar ritual. He will soon be a newcomer in a river that has already taken thousands of lives. While he intends the sprinkling of water to be blessing, in light of the tradition, he is also consecrating his own tomb.

It is easier to identify the religious overtones when Amabelle's "mother crosses herself three times and looks up at the sky before she climbs on [the] father's back" (51). In contrast to her father, her mother observes a ritual that is uniquely Catholic. She cross-es herself in remembrance of the father, the son, and the holy spirit, hoping that God will protect her and her loved ones as they cross the river. This juxtaposition of Catholicism and Vodou echoes that seen in the positioning of the epigraph and dedica-tion, a pattern that is repeated throughout the novel.

In spite of all the prayers to different Gods, the crossing is doomed. As soon as her father steps into the river, "the water reaches up to [his] waist" and "once he is in the river, he flinch-es, realizing he has made a grave mistake" (51). Neither he nor his wife will survive this encounter with the water, because he has underestimated the power of the river. It is a mistake that will lead them to a watery grave.

Amabelle recalls her "mother turn[ing] back to look for [her], throwing [her] father off balance." (51) Her mother is both her father's savior and his death. In life she has been his partner, his support, but here in the river her mother also serves to throw off her father's balance. Water is present from the womb onwards, protecting and nurturing the unborn, but here it acts as a violent perpetrator of death. During the drowning, the sky opens and rain falls, adding strength to the river until it "springs upwards like an ocean riptide." (51)

The metaphor comparing the river to "an ocean riptide" seems out of place, given that the ocean does not appear at any other point in the narrative. It is possible that it appears here only because Amabelle is watching her parents die. She is devastated by shock and grief, and the grandeur of this comparison mirrors the enormity of her emotion. This could explain the absence of the ocean elsewhere in *The Farming of Bones*, which is significant, since the Dominican Republic and Haiti share a small island. In Vodou, Agwe, the Lord of the Seas, is generally associated with ruling the ocean. Unlike Lasirene, he lives above the water, and is male. His maleness and his life above the water exclude him from this story. This is one woman's story. She is speaking to give voice to all women who have similar stories, but have been unable to tell them. It is the story of women who have suffered great loss or died violent deaths, the story of many women from all over the globe. Given the enormity of that task, there is little space left for the male voice that the ocean represents. Amabelle, as a female, telling the story of women, needs female spirits to give her strength and guidance. As a result, she calls upon her mother, not her father, and Lasirene, not Agwe. Agwe is also absent from the narrative because he dwells above the water. Amabelle spends her life seeking the loved ones she has lost beneath the water. It is outside of Agwe's power to reunite her with her parents and Sebastien. The day her parents drown, Amabelle begins to seek riches beneath the water, and thus becomes a devotee of Lasirene.

Lasirene first begins to take precedence in Amabelle's life as she watches her parents die. While the loss of her parents makes her feel alone, as if the only company she has is the Lwa, in reality she is not alone on the river bank. The river boys stand beside her, and attempt to save her parents by throwing "a thick sisal rope to [them]. The current swallows the rope" (51). No one can save her parents from the river that has already claimed them as its own. As "the water rises above [her] father's head, [her] mother releases his neck, the current carrying her beyond his reach. Separated, they are less of an obstacle for the cresting river" (51-52). The struggle ends, and the river is victorious. It has violently taken lives, foreshadowing the violence that will take place in the coming years, and echoing the violence and bloodshed of the past. In this moment the river lives up to its name: the Massacre River[2].

Standing on the bank, Amabelle screams "until [she] can taste blood in [her] throat, until [she] can no longer hear [her] own voice. Yet [she] still hold[s] Moy's gleaming pots in [her] hands" (52). Standing in the rain, she finally makes a decision. She walks "down to the sands to throw the pots into the water and then [herself]" (52). The pots are a final offering before she joins her parents in the depths of the river. Amabelle does not want to be alone on the river bank. She wants to join her parents and become a child of the river. As she approaches, "the current reaches up and licks [her] feet. [She] toss[es] the pots in and watch[es] them bob along the swell of the water, disappearing into the braided line that is the river at a distance" (52). The pots take the same path her parents took moments before; the path she hopes to join soon, but "two river boys grab [her] and drag [her] by [the] armpits away from the river" (52). The delay caused by her fascination with the pots saves her life. If she had jumped into the river with the pots, the boys may not have arrived in time, but her fascination with the way the water plays with the pots gives them more time. Her fascination with the river, and other bodies of water, will follow her throughout her life; in the moment, she is stricken only by overwhelming grief.

In her memory of the boys who saved her, "their faces seem blurred and faraway through the falling rain" (52). This blurring is attributed to the rain, but the overwhelming presence of the river helps to blot out all other facets of Amabelle's memory. The rain justifies the blurring of the faces, and brings the river onto the shore. Even lying far from the river's edge, Amabelle continues to get wet. The water is healing, cleansing, while at the same time pounding into her forever the image of her parents sinking into the embrace of the river as the current carried them away.

The detail and emotion present in the recounting of this event, combined with its constant presence throughout the novel in Amabelle's dreams, indicates its importance. Later, in another telling, Amabelle talks about watching the river swallow her parents, describing the way the river current divided and conquered them. She is fascinated by the way the river first separated them and then sucked them under its surface, further personifying the river. The water has been misjudged. It is not in a mood to be friendly. Instead, it is violent, separating loved ones within the water, as well as from the loved one still on shore. The water takes two lives on this day, but figuratively it also takes a third.

Amabelle's first instinct is to join her parents and become part of the waters. Strangely, where moments before the water was threatening and violent as it separated and overcame her parents, as Amabelle approaches, the river "licks" at her feet (52). "Licks" may invoke pictures of a puppy playfully teasing its master, but it also drudges up painful images of whips licking at the backs of slaves or of the flames of execution licking at the feet of the condemned. The images this word calls up are either playful or violent and they serve to exaggerate and emphasize the significance of Amabelle's loss. In one instance, the river mocks her, teasing her playfully after violently sucking her family away. At the same time, the imagery ties her to generations of Haitians who have suffered pain and loss. In spite of these connotations, the licking of the water is not threatening because Amabelle is not fighting the river, but rather attempting to become a part of its current. While the river grabbed Amabelle's parents, the river boys grab Amabelle.

Both the river and the boys restrain their victims until they lie still. The river boys pose an interesting connection with the Mother of the Rivers, who was invoked in the novel's dedication. It is possible that the use of "river boys" is just a description of the boys that work on the river. However, the invocation of the Mother of the Rivers coupled with the appearance of these river boys who save the novel's main character appears intentional. The parallels between the violent way the river grabs Amabelle's parents and the way she is grabbed by the river boys lends strength to this premise. The boys' job is to serve the mother river, protecting those who wish to pass through her by carrying them on their backs. Amabelle's father did not listen to the river boys, who were staying out of the river the day Amabelle's parents died. The boys know their mother well enough to stay away on days she is angry.

Near the novel's conclusion, Amabelle reveals a minor detail of this day that she leaves out in earlier accounts. She recalls that on "the day [her] parents drowned, [she] watched their faces as they bobbed up and down, in and out of the crest of the river" (309). She believes that "together they were both trying to signal a message to me, but the force of the water would not let them. Her mother, before she sank, raised her arm high, far above the pinnacle of the flood. The gesture was so desperate that it was hard to tell whether she wanted [Amabelle] to jump in with them or move father away" (309). Amabelle claims that she "relived the moment often enough," but it does not appear in any previous account of her memory of this day. It does not appear when she shares her dreams, nor in the prolonged account of this day she gives earlier in the novel. This later telling places her parents in the position the pots occupy in the earlier telling, bobbing up and down in the water before sinking. In the earlier telling she does not recall watching her parents bob. In fact, Amabelle makes no reference to what occurs once they are separated by the current. The second omission is the more intriguing of the two. The tension created by water for Amabelle can be better understood through this omission. The final gesture of her mother calls to her still, over twenty years later, and Amabelle is still uncertain what it means. Amabelle's obsession with the water can be traced back to this gesture from her mother. Her trust of the rivers arises from her belief that her mother lives on underneath the water protecting her and watching over her from its depths. The presence of her mother as a protector is reinforced by the other two dreams that haunt Amabelle's existence.

One dream is about "the sugar woman," and the second about her mother. When Amabelle dreams of the sugar woman, she "is always dressed in a long, three-tiered ruffled gown inflated like a balloon," and "around her face, she wears a shiny silver muzzle" (132). The shiny silver muzzle loosely ties the sugar woman to Lasirene, whose "altar is decorated with. . .mirrors" (Olmos 112). At the same time, according to a Vodou song, all the gods live "in the water, down below the mirror" (Brown 110). In Vodou, the surface of the water is viewed as a mirror. The connection to the water is reinforced by the fact that when Amabelle speaks in this dream, "it is the voice of the orphaned child at the stream" (132). Amabelle is haunted by her inability to see the sugar woman's face, as she has been haunted by her inability to see her own, and the absence of her mother's. The sugar woman appears disconnected from Amabelle's other dreams about her parents, but at the end of the dream Amabelle asks the sugar woman why she visits. The answer is simple: she comes because she is "the sugar woman, [and Amabelle is her] eternity" (133).

"You are my eternity," says Amabelle's mother in the other dream. This time she is not drowning. She is smiling "a both-rows-of-teeth revealing smile" (208). In this dream, there is peace, not fear. Her mother comes to her "wearing a dress of glass, fashioned out of the hardened clarity of the river" (208). This account not only ties the sugar woman to Amabelle's mother but it visually unites the dress made of glass to the muzzle of shiny silver, and thus to the altar of Lasirene. The dress also further unites the images of glass with the river. The glass is formed by the "hardened clarity of the river." Amabelle has sought such clarity in the river many times since her parents drowned, and the river calls to her still.

Amabelle's fascination with the water is remarked upon by the Señora. She observes that when they were young together, whenever Amabelle disappeared, the Señora always found her "peeking into some current, looking for [her] face" (303). Without water Amabelle cannot see her face, but on a less literal level, without the drowning of her parents, and her own escape through the water, Amabelle lacks an identity. This obsession with being able to see her face is revealed in the dream about the sugar woman. Every time Amabelle has the dream, her voice asks the sugar woman if her "face is underneath" the silver muzzle. Amabelle is a fragile character, forever stuck in recollections of the past. Originally she is haunted by her parents, and later Sebastien and all the others killed in the Massacre join the spirits that haunt not only her dreams but her waking moments as well. When Amabelle finally returns to the Dominican Republic in hopes of laying the ghosts to rest, the Señora recalls: "when we were children you were always drawn to water" (303).

Amabelle returns to the Dominican Republic to give her "testimony to the river, the waterfall," to the spirit of Sebastien. Sebastien is dead, and Amabelle muses that "perhaps there was water there to greet his last fall, to fold around and embrace him" (282). Amabelle hopes he is granted the solace of the water, so she may join him beneath its surface. No one knows whether this was the case or not. What Amabelle knows is simple: "His name is Sebastien Onius and his spirit must be inside the waterfall cave at the source of the stream were the cane workers bathe" (282). When Amabelle returns to the Dominican Republic to find this waterfall, she is unable to locate it. Instead she visits briefly with the Señora before returning to Haiti.

When Amabelle leaves the Señora and the Dominican Republic, she knows she has seen her old home for the last time. She crosses back into Haiti and asks the driver to leave her on the banks of the Massacre River. When the driver hesitates, Amabelle claims: "my man is coming for me" (308). Amabelle has only one man, and he "stayed inside the waterfall" when she returned to try and find him, but on this night she hopes he will come to her from the river (306). Amabelle sees the water as the end of being, but in a comforting, healing way. In this final scene, Amabelle wants her body to be carried "into the river, into Sebastien's cave, [her] father's laughter, [her] mother's eternity" all a part of the river (310). The day her parents died, the river boys prevented her from entering the river, and surrendering her life, but on this night, with only the moon and the river for company, there are no river boys, no saviors present. On this day, if she is to survive, she must be her own savior.

"The water was warm for October, warm and shallow, so shallow that I could lie on my back in it with my shoulders only half submerged" (310). The gentleness of the water in this instance is so different from the picture painted on the day her parents died. The shallowness and seeming peaceful embrace of the water suggests no violence. Amabelle lies in the river with "the current floating [her] in a less than gentle caress," with "the pebbles in the riverbed scouring [her] back" (310). The water is not gentle, but neither is it threatening. The very use of the word "caress" suggests comfort and pleasure. As the pebbles scour her back, they are reminiscent of a pumice stone roughly removing all the dead skin as it cleanses the body. The pebbles here help to cleanse her mind and memory.

As Amabelle floats in the river, she "looks to [her] dreams for softness, for a gentler embrace, for relief from the fear of mudslides and blood bubbling out of the riverbed, where it is said the dead add their tears to the river flow" (310). This reflection is strange and a bit convoluted, because her dreams throughout the novel have been violent and frightening, and here she lies in a peaceful river, where blood is not going to bubble and tears have already been cried. It is only in her dreams and recollections that violence still exists. The embrace of the river blurs the lines between reality and dreams, between the past and present. Water has been present in every nightmare she has ever had, and as she lies in the river, she searches for pleasant dreams to drown out the voices of the past that are rapidly growing stronger.

Amabelle is "lying there cradled by the current, paddling like a newborn in a washbasin," dreaming of her parents and Sebastien while being watched by a man, who lost his mind to the

"the slaughter, the river" and now waits, like Amabelle "looking for the dawn" (309, 310). The professor, as the man is called, is a regular at the river. He wanders searching for his wife, who died in the slaughter. For years, he has observed without seeing all that goes on at the river. He can only see the past, where the river is filled with blood and screams. Amabelle is haunted by these same visions, haunted by flashbacks of her parents drowning, and her own brush with death as she escaped into Haiti through the river. The book's conclusion can be read as a baptism, a rebirth for Amabelle free from the memories that have weighed her down all her life. This reading is supported by her own description of herself "paddling like a newborn" (310). However, the ending can also be read as Amabelle's death. Not a violent drowning death like her parents', but simply a surrendering of life at a time when such a conclusion is appropriate, a calm sinking into the water that has defined her whole life. This interpretation is supported by her claim that "nature has no memory and soon, perhaps neither will I" (309). It is undermined by the shallowness of the water, and the way she seemingly floats in its comfort.

Danticat intends the ending to be both a death and a birth. In her essay "We Are Ugly But We Are Here," she explains that "in Haiti death was always around us" (1). Danticat states that she "has such a strong feeling that death is not the end. . .the people we bury are going off to live somewhere else" (1). In either reading, a part of Amabelle dies in the river. The question is whether her body dies, or the pain of her memory dies. Part of her returns to all the loved ones she has lost, journeying into the world after death to join them. Unlike the day her parents drowned, on this day she enters the river, finally joining all those the river has taken from her. In this way water completes the novel. In this narrative, Amabelle never emerges from the water. She is finally safe and untroubled, at peace in waters of the Massacre River. This is where the author leaves her, in the comforting embrace of the water, surrounded by all those she has lost.

In between the death of Amabelle's parents, and her own final immersion in the water, water affects the lives of many others. Ironically, the flow of the novel places the first reference to the death of Amabelle's parents next to the "raining sweat" of childbirth (5). While Amabelle's nightmare opens the novel in a vivid flashback, the current story begins with the Señora's waters breaking as she labors to bring forth new life (5). The drowning of

Amabelle's parents and the birth of the Señora's children are further linked when Danticat describes the Señora as "drowning in the depths of the mattress" (5). Danticat uses water to emphasize the cycle of life and death. As new life replaces old, it becomes clear that this happens both through birth and through the creation of new relationships. Amabelle loses her parents, but she finds love elsewhere, in Sebastien, and he finds the same in her.

Sebastien is no stranger to the pain and loss that water can cause. Sebastien lost his father to a hurricane. Lasirene, the spirit of the water, encompasses not only water but all "the volatile elements of the tropical storm: the gusting winds that precede the rain, the thunder and lightening that accompany it, and the rainbow that marks its conclusion" (Galembo 26). In this interpretation, the water includes all the elements of the storm. This connects his parental loss directly to Amabelle's, but there are differences too. Unlike Amabelle, who stood passively and watched her parents drown, Sebastien carries his father's dead body home: "you can see it before your eyes, a boy carrying his dead father from the road. . .The boy trying not to drop the father, not crying or screaming like you'd think but praying that more of the father's blood will stay in the father's throat and not go into the muddy flood" (34).

Biblical imagery, reinforced by the word "flood," streams into this scene, carrying with it comparisons to everyone from Noah to Moses. The reference to the father's blood joining the "flood" emphasizes the role water plays in this destruction, while also serving to put into perspective how much blood is being lost. In a more figurative sense, as Sebastien carries his father, so Jesus carried his cross (John 19:17). Unlike Jesus, who is surrounded by human chaos, the chaos surrounding Sebastien is caused by nature, but both men are quiet and strong, praying as they walk. Over the course of the narrative it becomes clear that on some level Sebastien is Amabelle's savior. He is the only human entity she truly believes in[3]. Sebastien comes alive as a Jesus-like figure in this scene, which appropriately is as painful for him, in retrospect, as the drowning of Amabelle's parents is for her. Sadly, the pain and loss of family does not end here. This scene is repeated in inverse, with the father carrying the son, when Sebastien's friend Joel is killed by the Señor.

Joel is killed on the night the Señora births twins. The Señor accidentally strikes Joel with his car, taking his life. Water took the life of Amabelle's parents, and Sebastien's father's as well (using the Vodou definition of water), but here water serves only to clean the body that is already dead. The cleansing of Joel's corpse is one of the few times in the novel that water's main purpose is to clean. After Joel's death, Sebastien and Yves, another cane worker, help Joel's father carry the body down to the river where they "washed him and cleaned all the blood off of him" (54). Joel was murdered by man, not by nature, and yet water readies his corpse for burial. Its job is to wipe away the signs of violence and cleanse his body. This river serves as a place of healing, where the blood of violence can be washed away forever, lost in the constant current that refuses to allow time to stand still. Joel's death foreshadows the slaughter that is soon to come, but it also shows water in a far less violent role.

Joel's death reveals the river as a meeting place, where the Haitians can talk amongst themselves. Joel's death worries the Haitians in the cane community, and it is in the river that these worries are revealed. The river unites the community of Haitians living in Algeria (a region in the Dominican Republic). The oldest women "start off every morning bathing in the stream," and on the morning after Joel's violent death, Kongo, Joel's father, bathes in the middle of the stream while everyone watches (61). The river is crowded by people who want to see how Kongo is going to react to the loss of his son, but he stands protected by Yves and Sebastien, scrubbing his own body with parsley and rinsing it clean with water. No one is allowed to approach, but there are other events occurring in the water as well.

Water dribbles down over the shoulders of Sebastien's sister, Mimi, as she bathes and converses with Amabelle. They talk with Felice, Joel's woman, about retribution and an "eye for an eye[4]" while they discuss the hate that comes with age (66). Formality dissolves in the water. Mimi can refer to her boss by her Christian name, and Felice openly discusses murder in the water. The water is a place of unity where secrets can be openly discussed, then lost in the din of the current and a community readying itself for another day. Perhaps the dedication to the Mother of the Rivers was intended in this spirit. The stories shared in the river are secret, protected from those who might use them for evil. Water in this instance is not violent. The water here provides cleansing, healing and a safe place to connect with other individuals. The community river is not the only time that water serves as a protector and witness to scheming and intimacy.

Sebastien and Amabelle first consummated their relationship hidden by the protective veil of a waterfall. The waterfall is the source of the stream where the cane workers bathe. It provides a safe place for the entire community, but in "a narrow cave behind the waterfall" Sebastien and Amabelle "first made love" (100). "When night comes, you don't know it inside the slippery cave because the waterfall. . .holds on to some memory of the sun that it will not surrender" (100). Hiding behind the protection of the waterfall there is eternal light and a rare safety from the reality of the outside world. For Amabelle, the cave behind the waterfall will become the place where she can be together with Sebastien forever. It becomes the home of a memory that provides comfort when she awakes in terror from another nightmare. It is not only the memory of the beauty and safety of the waterfall that comforts Amabelle, but the feel of flesh on flesh and the mixing of bodily fluids.

Fluids like sweat flush out pollutants, and cleanse the body's pores. Its presence as Amabelle awakes from a nightmare is a reminder of her fear, but when Sebastien is there to hold her, his body presses to hers. This creates additional sweat, turning sweat from a reminder of fear into a reminder of love. His touch draws forth, "a flood of perspiration from her body" and when he is not there, she lies naked and remembers him until the sweat rolls "down over [her] buttocks, down the front and back of her thighs" until there is "not a drop of liquid left in [her] with which to cry" (94). The joining of their bodies anneals Amabelle, preventing tears of grief from being spilled, as sweat replaces tears.

Tears are cried throughout *The Farming of Bones*. Some are tears of joy, but most are tears of grief. When the Señora's infant son dies, her tears show that grief has little respect for either race or class. The Señor holds the Señora as she tries "to find a comfortable place to sink into, within his arms" (98). In contrast to Sebastien, who uses his body to anneal Amabelle's grief, this scene between the Señora and her husband is reserved and sterilized. The Señor does not share her tears, and there is no sweat here to help her forget her pain. Instead there is an awkward silence.

"Perhaps he was suppressing his own tears, but the silence seemed. . .a sign of failure for this marriage" (98). He is unable to share his own tears, and without the combining of their fluids, there is seemingly no connection, no healing. There are sobs and tears, but no cleansing. The scene ends when the Señora abruptly stops crying, and her husband tells her he must soon leave for the border. This final verbal exchange amplifies the feeling of distance that begins with his inability to cry with her. In this scene, the water flowing freely from her eyes and the lack of water from his own, places a liquid barrier between them.

Sebastien's use of his body to anneal his lover is pagan in contrast to the interaction between the Señora and her husband. His use of the body is a type of ceremony, a ritual that has roots in Vodou. Vodou literally means "sacred energy" and is "first and foremost a system of movements that brings people together" (Olmos 102, 119). Sebastien's use of his body fits this definition well, but it is possible Sebastien is completely unaware that his actions have roots in Vodou. Sebastien and Amabelle are likely Catholic, but Vodou is the foundation of Haiti's culture. Sebastien may not have ever received any training in Vodou, but his culture tells him grief can be healed by the joining of bodies, whereas the Señora's Catholic-based culture is far less sensual, and more restrictive of its fluid exchanges.

The significance of shared fluids is further illustrated when the surviving twin, Rosalinda, is baptized. Baptism is a cornerstone of Catholicism. In the ceremony holy water is sprinkled on a baby's head to drive out the evil spirits and consecrate the infant as the property of the Catholic god. The baptism of Rosalinda is brief; "Farther Vargas poured water on Rosalinda's head welcoming her into the Holy Catholic Church" (118). This is the full description Amabelle provides about the actual event. No more details are shared. On this day of joy, Amabelle shares little compared to what she shared when the male twin died. As her account continues, Amabelle moves outside the church, where the Señora presents the newly baptized baby to Amabelle, who grazes" Rosalinda's cheeks with [her] lips" and discovers "her forehead [is] still wet where the priest had doused her with holy water" (119). Similar to the earlier scene with the grieving Señora, the recounting of the baptism is sterile. Amabelle shares the water with Rosalinda, as neither of her parents can. Echoing the earlier scene, Señor Pico emphasizes this sterility when he yanks "his wife's arm and pull[s] her away" as if Amabelle's kiss were some kind of poison. To a strictly Catholic Dominican, the mere possibility that Vodou could touch their offspring in any way would be horrifying. For Señor Pico, the sharing of the water between Amabelle's lips and Rosalinda's forehead is a type of Vodou contamination.

In the days following the baptism, Trujillo, the leader of the Dominican Republic, will express similar feelings of contamination. "Under the protection of the rivers, the enemies of peace, who are also the enemies of work and prosperity, found an ambush in which they might do their work, keeping the nation in fear and menacing stability" (97). His statement is illogical. His claims are similar to those made by Hitler about the Jews. Trujillo is attempting to establish the Haitian immigrants as scapegoats for any and all difficulties in the Dominican Republic. The claim that water has shielded the "enemies of peace," targets the Haitians by focusing on their religion. More than four-fifths of the citizens in the Dominican Republic "are adherents to the Roman Catholic church," while the majority of Haitians "are also practitioners of voodoo" (Britannica 1). In light of this religious difference, the accusation of water shielding the enemies of the Dominican Republic becomes less murky. The president's statement is condemning the Haitian immigrants as people who operate "under the protection of the rivers," practitioners of Vodou, but this is not the way they are segregated during the slaughter.

The pronunciation of parsley was the main way Haitians were identified during the slaughter of 1937. In this public address, the president is able to identify the Haitian immigrants and condemn them in a way that is seemingly innocent. Without knowing the history of religion in the Dominican Republic and Haiti, one would not be aware that those under the protection of the river are the Haitian immigrants. However, while people outside the area might find the President's words unclear, all of the people within the Dominican Republic would have recognized that the President was demanding the removal of Haitian immigrants.

This is exactly what occurs. Amabelle is among the Haitian immigrants fleeing the Dominican Republic. She flees across the Massacre River back into Haiti. Prior to her escape, she is badly beaten, her jaw "pried open and parsley stuffed" in her mouth forcing her "eyes to water" (194). Previously, water has seeped out of Amabelle's body from fear, and been used to heal that fear through passion. Here water seeps out of her eyes due to physical pain. However, this water serves a similar purpose to the sweat earlier in the narrative; it attempts to rid the body of pollutants and pain.

The night after being beaten, Amabelle crosses the river, back into Haiti. She remembers the events of that evening as she crossed with Odette, a friend:

The water was so deep that it was like trying to walk on air. When we were entirely submerged in the current, I yanked my hand from Odette's. I heard her sniffle, perhaps fearful and shocked. But I was only thinking of one thing. If I drowned, I wanted to drown alone, with nobody else's life to be responsible for (201).

This description of Amabelle letting go of her friend's hand is reminiscent of the scene where the water separated her parents, but here the separation is a choice. Amabelle decides that if she is going to die, she wants to die alone, with her remembrances of Sebastien and her parents, free of any connection to the present. The water allows her that sense of aloneness, and gives her a connection to her parents. Amabelle treasures that freedom for a moment before swimming after Odette and helping her to shore. Unfortunately, as Amabelle eases herself "out of the current," Odette's body lies lifeless. Her journey, like that of so many others that night, ends in the river (200).

As she dies, Odette utters a single word: "pesi," the Kreyòl word for parsley (201). Amabelle muses, "had the Generalissimo heard Odette's "pesi," it might have startled him, not the tears and supplication he would have expected, no shriek from unbound fear, but a provocation, a challenge, a dare. To the devil with your world, your grass, your wind, your water, your air, your words" (203). With this single utterance Odette gains the freedom that Amabelle struggles to find throughout the novel. Not the freedom of death, but the freedom of identity, of knowing who you are and exclaiming it with pride, not fear.

Included in Amabelle's interpretation of Odette's last words is a rejection of everything in the Dominican Republic including the elements: the land, the air, and the water. There are Vodou Lwa for every element she mentions, and this rejection of everything associated with the Dominican Republic is extended into the spirit world by her rejection of the elements. Amabelle is attempting to make a complete break with the place that has been her home for most of her life. This means rejecting the Lwa that inhabit the elements in the Dominican Republic who have failed to protect her along with her adopted country and its people. Her anger goes far beyond condemning the soldiers, the government and the people of the Dominican Republic. She rejects the spirits that live there as well. Her condemnation demonstrates water's ability to blur the separation between the spirit world and the human world.

In *The Farming of Bones*, water serves many purposes. It is present in every moment of the narrative, whether dramatically shielding lovers, drowning parents, helping new life come into the world or daily being used for washing, cooking, drinking and cleaning. Water serves as a constant reminder of the presence of the Vodou spirits, and it connects Amabelle to her parents and later Sebastien. Water's presence in *The Farming of Bones* is constant, but often flows through the background. That is not the case in the short story "Children of the Sea." From the title onward, water is impossible to ignore in this epistolary story.

"Children of the Sea" is one of ten short stories in the volume entitled *Krik? Krak!* It is told in a series of letters written by two young people, one male and one female. Both are aware that their letters will never be seen by the other, but they keep their hope alive by writing to each other. The young man, a political activist, has fled Haiti on a boat headed towards Florida. He writes to the young woman he has known since he "helped her pull out [her] first loose tooth" (3). She writes to him from Port-au-Prince, where violence rages as the Macoute soldiers murder and torture political activists and their families. As the story unfolds, the loving couple discuss their respective situations. The young man dreams of dying and living life "among the children of the deep blue sea, those who have escaped the chains of slavery," violence, and censorship of "the blood-drenched earth" (27). Meanwhile the young woman fights with her father, listens to her neighbors being beaten to death and finally escapes to Ville Rose where the nearby stream "is too shallow for [her] to drown" herself (22). Water sluices through the narrative, and introduces Guinin[5], a heaven beneath the sea, that hints at the importance of water not only to this couple but to their ancestors as well.

Out at sea, the young man dreams of heaven. "This heaven was nothing like I expected. It was at the bottom of the sea. There were starfishes and mermaids all around me. The mermaids were dancing and singing in Latin like the priests do at the cathedral during Mass" (12). This dream introduces the idea of a heaven beneath the seas, and unites Catholicism and Vodou. The speaker identifies the song and dance as a part of the Catholic mass, but he fails to inform the reader that the mermaid is a common embodiment of Lasirene, the Vodou Lwa that presides beneath the waters of the sea. This juxtaposition of Vodou and Catholicism demonstrates the fluidity of Vodou. In her essay, "Olina and Eruzulie," Kathy McCarthy Brown asserts: "Vodou is a part of the basic creation of meaning, the process by which a name is assigned to a moment in the flow of experience" (110). This means that if Catholicism is present in a given moment, it can become part of the flow of Vodou.

Vodou is less present in later discussions of Guinin. The young male narrator muses that he feels like he "is sailing for Africa. Maybe [he] will go to Guinin, to live with spirits, to be with everyone who has come and has died before" him (14). In this moment it is history that is emphasized, not religion, but Vodou does not differentiate between history and religion. Within Vodou everything is integrated. The narrator is connecting to the thousands of slaves during the middle passage that chose a watery death over slavery. This connection to his ancestors serves to emphasize his Vodou roots on two levels. Vodou came from Africa, and was shaped by the current of slavery. Also, the dead are heavily honored in Vodou tradition, because "whenever a death is acknowledged by society it brings acknowledgement to the living" (Hurbon 86). Death allows the living to "recover and assert their humanity," a need that began in times of slavery when the people of Africa were dehumanized (Hurbon 86).

The narrator is careful not to dehumanize his companions on the boat. There is a pregnant woman named Celianne who births a baby girl. The little girl never cries. Soon she is "purple like the sea after the sun has set" (25). The description of the baby looking like the sea foreshadows the events that follow her birth and death. The other people on the boat want Celianne to throw the dead child overboard, but on this issue the narrator remains silent. He refuses to add his voice to those calling for the child to be thrown overboard, perhaps because of his need to see the child as human. He cannot tolerate the idea of the infant's body being tossed overboard, no different from the other weight being tossed into the sea. Eventually Celianne gives in, reluctantly throwing her baby overboard "and quickly after that she jumped in too" (27).

The other passengers demand that the baby be thrown overboard because the boat is sinking. Everything that is not essential to life has to be thrown overboard in order to keep the boat afloat as long as possible. As a result, the narrator is forced to throw his book of letters into the sea. "It goes down to them, Celianne and her daughter and all those children of the sea who might soon be claiming me," he writes moments before throwing the book into the water (27). Prior to throwing the book away he muses on his future:

I go to them now as though it was always meant to be, as though the very day my mother birthed me, she had chosen me to live life eternal, among the children of the deep blue sea, those who have escaped the chains of slavery to form a world beneath the heavens and the blood-drenched earth where you live. Perhaps I was chosen from the beginning of time to live with Agwe at the bottom of the sea. Maybe this is why I dreamed of the starfish and mermaids having the Catholic Mass under the sea. Maybe this was my invitation to go. In any case, I know that my memory of you will live even there as I too become a child of the sea. (27)

This is the final letter from the male narrator. At the moment he writes, there is still the possibility that he will be rescued, but he is at peace with his fate. He believes he is destined to live forever as a child of the sea. When he first got on the boat to flee Haiti as a political refugee, he became a child of the sea, but here in the final moments of this tragic story the meaning of "child of the sea" changes. In the beginning, he was a child of the sea because he was trusting the sea to rescue him from the atrocities that were daily being committed in his country. In the end, he is child of the sea because his body will rest forever beneath the ocean waves.

In this final letter, he describes the depths of the oceans as preferable to the "blood drenched earth" where the girl he loves still lives. As young as he is, he has seen enough to understand what made his ancestors choose death over life as a slave. This raises the comparison of political unrest and oppression to slavery. Through this character, the aforementioned hopelessness of slavery comes alive in the present. For this young man, death is a certainty if he stays in Haiti. His only chance of survival is to throw himself upon the mercy of the sea. However, the sea cannot save him. He romanticizes the idea of death in this letter, claiming that really his death at sea is a homecoming, where he will live on for eternity. This is the essence of Guinin. At a time when the world treated its black citizens as slaves, Guinin was a place of acceptance, where African people were welcome and celebrated.

Unlike the first time Guinin is introduced, here there is a direct reference to Vodou. The speaker claims that he will go and live with Agwe beneath the sea. Strangely, Agwe traditionally lives above the seas. He is the Lwa who protects navigation, shipping and fishing (Hubon 142). He is "the lord of the sea," often represented or even referred to as an Admiral (Deren122). It is his consort Lasirene who is often associated with mermaids, whales, and the creatures beneath the sea. This inconsistency serves to reinforce the difficulty in studying Vodou. Vodou is ever changing. Spellings and even the names of Lwa vary from source to source. What remains constant is the presence of spirits, the importance of ancestors, and the way water connects the spirit world to the human world, and the human world to the life after death. Guinin "or Africa is the home of the gods and lies either below or far across the water" on the African coast (Brown 110).

The female narrator remains on land, but water is no less present in her life. She grieves for the loss of the lover she hopes took "a boat to heaven knows where" (13). Her mother consoles her with these words: "all anyone can hope for is just a tiny bit of love. . .like a drop in a cup if you can get it, or a waterfall, a flood if you can get that too" (13-14). In equating love and water, three connections float to the surface. First, the presence of the water connects her to her lover who is out at sea. Second, this comparison of love to a flood suggests the danger that is always present in love. Finally, the presence of the waterfall here in this sentiment of love ties this female character to Amabelle, from *The Farming of Bones*, and her experience of love protected by the waterfall.

The two characters are also connected by the presence of water nearby. Out in the country the girl lives near a stream. It is "a stream that is too shallow for [her] to drown [herself] in" (22). This consideration of death joins her with Amabelle, who looks at the river as an escape into death, shortly after the drowning of her parents and again in that novel's conclusion. It also connects her to the boy at sea. More importantly, this reference to the shallowness of the stream, shows a mindset similar to the one held by the male narrator. Death would allow her to escape the same reality that forced her lover to escape. It is a reality where "you can let them kill somebody because you are afraid, they are the law" (17). The reality is the law daily commits atrocities, often forcing sons to lie down with their mothers, and daughters with their fathers (12-13). Like her boyfriend, this girl reaches a level of hopelessness where death is preferable to life. This mental state echoes the mindset of many in the generations of Haitians that preceded this tale's two narrators, people who have kept the legend of Guinin alive.

The concept of Guinin rains new meaning upon *The Farming of Bones*. Throughout the novel, Amabelle views the river as a place where life continues after death. While "Children of the Sea" amalgamates the heaven under the seas to Haiti's slave past, Amabelle's belief that life continues beneath the water is far more personal. Amabelle has lost too much in the river to believe that it is anything but a comforting place that holds her loved ones until the time when she will be ready to join them. Through Amabelle, Danticat has created her own version of Guinin beneath the waters of the Massacre River. In her Guinin, the horrors and atrocities of Haiti's bloody history can be annealed. The Massacre River connects the two countries that share the island of Hispañola, and holds out hope that one day the unity and peace that exist beneath the river might follow the waves up onto both sides of the shore.

Endnotes

[1] *The Oxford English Dictionary* defines wealth as "the condition of being happy and prosperous; well being."

[2] According to Michele Rucker's article, "The River Massacre: The Real and Imagined Border of Hispañiola," the Massacre River was originally named for the colonial-era Spanish slaughter of French pirate buccaneers. In 1937 it became the site of El Corte, the common name given to the Dominican slaughter of 30,000 Haitians.

[3] While bathing in the stream with Mimi, Amabelle recounts a discussion she had with another woman: "She asked me if I believed in anything and all I could think to say was Sebastien" (65).

[4] Exodus 21: 23-25: "And if any mischief follow, then thou shalt give life for life, eye for eye, tooth for tooth, hand for hand, foot for foot, burning for burning, wound for wound, stripe for stripe."

[5] In her essay "We are Ugly, But We are Here," Danticat discusses her forefathers believing water was "the road to freedom and their entrance to Guinin" (2). However, I have also come across reference to this mythical heaven beneath the sea as Guinèa. In deference to Danticat, this mythical slave heaven beneath the seas is referred to as Guinin. It may also be important to note that Guinea is a country in West Africa.

Works Cited

Brown, Karen McCarthy. "Olina and Erzulie: a woman and a goddess in Haitian Vodou." *Anima* 5 (1979):110-116.

But, Mambo Racine Sans. "The Ancestors in Haitian Vodou." www.sheps.com/ancestors/mamboracine.html.   16 March 2004.

Danticat, Edwidge. *The Farming of Bones.* New York: Penguin, 1998.

_____. *Krik? Krak!* New York: Random House, 1995.

_____. "We are Ugly, But We are Here." *The Caribbean Writer,* Volume 10.

Deren, Maya. *Divine Horsemen The Living Gods of Haiti.* Kingston: McPherson, 1991.

Desmangles, Leslie G. *The Faces of the Gods: Vodou and Roman Catholicism in Haiti.* Chapel Hill: University of North Carolina, 1992. 174-181.

Galembo, Phyllis. *Vodou Visions and Voices of Haiti.* Berkley: TenSpeed Press, 1998.

Hurbon, Laennec. *Vodou Search For The Spirit.* New York: Abrams, 1995.

Olmos, Margarite Fernandez and L. Paravisini-Gebert. *Creole Religions of the Caribbean.* New York: New York University Press, 2003. 101-130.

Rucker, Michelle. "The River Massacre: The Real and Imagined Borders of Hispañiola." www.haitiforever.com/windowson-haiti/w99021.shtml. 11 April, 2004.

Crushed Like the Cane:
Traumatic Borderlands in Edwidge Danticat's *The Farming of Bones*
Kim Dismont Robinson

If a traumatic history is also one that can be said to repeat itself, Haitian history contains a number of violent and uncanny repetitions strangely reminiscent of the nature of rememory, the memory of a past event which contains within itself the possibilities of "happening again."[1] There are several pivotal events in Haitian history that contain the seeds of uncanny echoes from the past. One of these events, linked to the landscape and Hispaniola's uncertain borderlands, is the slaughter at the site of a river. The Massacre River, which was said to run red with the blood of tens of thousands of murdered Haitians during the 1937 genocide, was originally renamed as such because of a previous bloodletting which occurred during colonial times.[2] During the 1937 Massacre, there was a testing which conflated language with racial and national identity. The linguistic testing carried out by Dominican persecutors was a defining point of the 1937 Massacre. Haitians unable to pronounce the word "perejil" (the Spanish word for parsley) without the telltale Haitian accent which made the word sound more like "peweji" or the Kreyol "pèsi" were murdered with machetes on the spot.[3]

These historical echoes have reverberated in Haiti's literary imagination, resulting in Haitian-American writer Edwidge Danticat's work of fiction based on these tragic events. *The Farming of Bones* fictionally re-imagines the Haitian Massacre of 1937 which occurred during the thirty-one-year-reign of the Dominican dictator Generalissimo Rafael Leonidas Trujillo Molina (1930-1961). The real and fictitious casualties of the 1937 Massacre were victims of Trujillo's deeply oppressive nationalist project. Danticat draws upon history, legend, oral narratives and imagination to create human, albeit fictional, faces representing the casualties of a tyrannical nationalism.[4] *The Farming of Bones*, the cultural production of an imagination shaped by the particularities of a sometimes traumatic history, reflects a concern about the effect of nationalistic violence on individual and cultural identity as well as the gendered significance of such violence.

In 1955, political activist Jacques Stephen Alexis published his first novel, *Compère Général Soleil* (recently translated into English by Carrol F. Coates as *General Sun, My Brother*). Alexis, the son of a Dominican woman and a Haitian ambassador who claimed Jean-Jacques Dessalines as an ancestor, created a novel which explored the harsh realities of Haitian peasants, some of whom chose to work in the Dominican canefields in an attempt to create a better life.[5] The text culminates with the protagonist Hilarion and his wife Claire-Heureuse attempting to escape the nightmarish 1937 Massacre. In the novel's grim conclusion, the couple has managed to cross the Massacre River into Haiti, but not before their infant son Désiré has been killed by dogs and Hilarion has been shot in the stomach by Dominican soldiers. As Hilarion lies dying on the riverbank, he delivers an eloquent soliloquy to Claire-Heureuse about the hardships of his life and the necessity for Haitians to reclaim their own country and "find a season to live without misery" (289). He urges Claire-Heureuse toward survival as message-bearer who will help bring to birth a new nation:

> In a little while, you will have to go away alone and find your way without turning back. You must give birth to another Hilarion, other Désirés, and only you can create them. You have to go forward to other mornings of love, other Saint John Days, begin a new life. Now you know what's in the belly of misery, and you know that all the marvels that our land can yield are not for black people like you and me. You know why white Americans are the masters and why there are new tears in people's eyes each day, why people don't know how to read, why men leave their native land, why sickness ravages our people, and how little girls become whores. . .General Sun! See him! He's right on the border, at the doors of our native land! Don't ever forget, Claire, never, never! (289-290)

Joan Dayan has rightly pointed out how many male-authored texts such as *General Sun, My Brother* have portrayed one-dimensional female characters who are usually primarily foils for their male counterparts.[6] In the preceding passage, Alexis provides an example of how the woman's role in nation-building has traditionally been perceived by men as witnessing, surviving, and producing "new life" both by moving forward into the future, as well as by giving birth to the next generation of heroes—"another

Hilarion, other Désirés."[7]   As the vision of the Haitian countryside unfolds before his eyes, Hilarion dies with a smile on his face; however, the stark final line of the novel shifts the focus back onto Claire-Heureuse: "She was alone" (290).

In addition to being a significant achievement in its own right, Edwidge Danticat's 1998 novel *The Farming of Bones* has also been considered as a companion text to *General Sun, My Brother*. Danticat, clearly inspired by Alexis's work, offers the following acknowledgement in her own novel: "To Jacques Stephen Alexis, for Compère Général Soleil. Oné. Always" (*The Farming of Bones* 312).   Despite the obvious respect Danticat has for her literary forebear, an intertextual reading reveals the ways Danticat's novel offers a challenging "woman version" of the massacre.[8]   Danticat's text could be said to begin where Alexis's ends; Claire-Heureuse, "alone" following the murder of her partner, provides an eerie counterpart to Danticat's Amabelle Désir, a "survivor" of the massacre haunted by the memory of her murdered lover Sebastian Onius.   Danticat responds to Alexis's call ("Don't ever forget. . .never, never!") through the historical fiction she has created.

In Danticat's woman-version text, Alexis's charge assumes gendered significance. Claire-Heureuse, given the task of bearing "other Désirés," manages instead to produce a Désir through the intertextual conduit of Danticat's literary imagination.   However, this "other Désir(é)" is female instead of male; and her relationship with Haiti has nothing to do with a desire to bear male children who will liberate the nation.   In fact, the consequences of Amabelle's life lived primarily as witness are precisely what stand in the way of her imagining the kind of contradictory future that Hilarion wished for his widow Claire-Heureuse to "begin a new life. . . . Don't ever forget, Claire, never, never!" Amabelle reflects:

> It is perhaps the great discomfort of those trying to silence the world to discover that we have voices sealed inside our heads, voices that with each passing day, grow even louder than the clamor of the world outside. The slaughter is the only thing that is mine enough to pass on. (*The Farming of Bones* 266)

In this sense, Danticat's text represents not only a testimonial for those slaughtered in the massacre of 1937, but also for those who physically survived, only to experience an existence crippled by the insistent weight of memory. Amabelle Désir thus remains true to another submerged meaning of her name, since Désir echoes the Spanish word "Decir"—a word in the language of Amabelle's adopted Dominican homeland which means "to say" or "to tell."

Amabelle, narrating in the present tense, speaks only of her memories of Sebastian, her drowned parents, and her life before the massacre. In the first chapter, Amabelle recalls that as a child, she often played with her own shadow, "something my father warned could give me nightmares" (4). She adds, "There were many shadows, too, in the life I had beyond childhood" (4). Amabelle's shadowplay suggests an introductory trope foreshadowing the illusory nature of her connections with other human beings, a life overshadowed by remnants, specters and memories more real and enduring than the living. However, this moment also suggests a strange kind of twinship, a doubling with a phantom self which, in Amabelle's adult life, reemerges as shadows that sometimes threaten to engulf her.

The significance of such shadowplay is heightened in the following chapter when Señora Valencia, the woman the orphaned Amabelle serves, gives birth to twins—the firstborn, a cream-coloured boy and the second, a dark-skinned girl. The girl, Rosalinda, seems initially to be the one in peril; less than half the size of her brother, she is born with a caul covering her face and the umbilical cord curled "in a bloody wreath around her neck, encircling every inch between her chin and shoulders" (10). Utilizing the twins as metaphor, Danticat constructs a powerful trope for the representation of Haitian-Dominican relations concerning the issue of race politics. Señora Valencia believes her daughter is cursed because of what is suggested by the choking umbilical cord, and because of her deeply bronzed skin. Señora Valencia exclaims, "My poor love, what if she's mistaken for one of your people?" (12). Her maternal concern highlights the dangerous nature of Dominican national identity, constructed on the precarious foundation of skin color in a racially mixed country, the results of which become evident during the massacre when dark-skinned Dominicans are slaughtered along with the Haitians. The mentality which effectively produces such a divided sense of nationhood is evident in Señora Valencia's reaction to Rosalinda's skin color. She says to Amabelle, "My daughter is a chameleon. She's taken your color from the mere sight of your face" (11). When the doctor suggests Rosalinda has "a little charcoal behind the ears"—a strain of African blood—the señora's father scolds him for his "very impolite assertion" before offering an extensive family genealogy and blaming her coloration on her father's lineage

(17-18). There is a sense that Señora Valencia has accepted her dark daughter, but in the way usually associated with Dominican racial politics. She describes her children as "my Spanish prince and my Indian princess," adding proudly, "look at that profile. The profile of Anacaona, a true Indian queen" (29).[9]

The dialogue surrounding Rosalinda's skin color and racial ambiguity allows Danticat to reveal the ways in which blackness/Haitianness within a Dominican context is traditionally associated with contamination and contagion either through tainted bloodlines, as with Señora Valencia's husband Pico, or through close contact as the señora implies is the case with Amabelle. Although the señora voices her comments half-jokingly, the potential for violence surrounding these issues becomes startlingly evident on the day she invites a group of cane cutters in for coffee. She refuses to allow a cane cutter to touch her infant daughter, and when Señor Pico later learns that she used their imported tea set to serve the Haitian workers, he shatters the china against the walls of the outhouse, "one by one" (116).

In his essay entitled "Hairlips and Twins: The Splitting of a Myth" in *Myth and Meaning*, Claude Lévi-Strauss observes similarities between different Native American myths regarding twinship, which suggest a general belief "that twins result from an internal splitting of the body fluids which will later solidify and become the child" (30). According to Lévi-Strauss, "When there are twins, or even more children, in the womb of the mother, there is usually in the myth a very serious consequence because, even if there are only two, the children will start to fight and compete in order to find out who will have the honour of being born first. And, one of them, the bad one, does not hesitate to find a short cut, if I may say so, in order to be born earlier" (32). This myth finds expression in *The Farming of Bones* when Doctor Javier questions whether the umbilical cord wrapped around Rosalinda's neck resulted from her brother's attempt to strangle her in the womb, adding, "Many of us start out as twins in the belly and do away with the other. . .sometimes you have two children born at the same time; one is stillborn but the other one alive and healthy because the dead one gave the other a life transfusion in the womb and in essence sacrificed itself" (19).

Lévi-Strauss notes that a basic characteristic in Amerindian twinship myths is the eventual splitting of twins, who often have different fathers and different individual fates as adults. He relates a Tupinamba version of the myth in which a woman gives birth to twins, one of whom is fathered by her husband and the other by a Trickster god. Lévi-Strauss states, "since these false twins had different fathers, they have antithetical features: one is brave, the other a coward; one is the protector of the Indians, the other of the white people; one gives goods to the Indians, while the other one, on the contrary, is responsible for a lot of unfortunate happenings" (27). He adds that regardless of the version of the myth, "nowhere are the two heroes really twins; they are born from distinct fathers. . .and they have opposed characters, features which will be shown in their conduct and in the behaviour of their descendents. So we may say that in all cases children who are said to be twins or believed to be twins. . .will have different adventures later on which will, if I may say so, *untwin them*" (28, my italics).¹⁰ Although Señora Valencia's twins do not in actuality have different fathers, they clearly resemble a pair of "false twins" on the basis of skin color and gender; with Rosalinda representing a frail, dark-skinned, feminized Haiti choking at the hands of her twin—the stronger, cream-colored Dominican son Raphael, named for the dictator Trujillo who ordered the massacre.

Pairing Lévi-Strauss's observations on Amerindian twinship myths with the fates and physical descriptions of Señora Valencia's twins in *The Farming of Bones* reveals Danticat's underlying thinking on the twinned nations of the Dominican Republic and Haiti. Ironically, although Rosalinda seems the weaker of the two children and less valued by her father because of her skin color and gender, it is Raphael who dies inexplicably a few short days after birth. Within the context of Señor Pico's accidental murder of Joel, a cane cutter's son, as well as the impeding massacre, Raphael's death becomes one of many to occur that season; and the anguish that Señor Pico and Señora Valencia experience functions symbolically as a reminder that, in the words of the grieving cane cutter, "[Haitian] lives are precious too" (66). Although Danticat constructs a narrative which reveals the fragility of all life and the indiscriminate nature of loss, the fate of the "untwinned twins" seems to suggest that not all losses are equal. When Joel dies as a result of Señor Pico's carelessness, the Haitian community suggests one death should be repaid with another as "an eye for an eye" (110) and there is a sense that Raphael's death is linked, at least metaphorically, to Joel's. However, while Rafi is given a beautiful funeral, Joel is all but forgotten by the very people responsible for his death.

The death of Rafi is also significant when considered in the context of Rosalinda's fate. Although initially considered a potential victim of her "Dominican brother," Rosalinda manages to survive and indeed thrive. As a symbolic marker of the Africanized, feminized Haitian side of the twinned nations of Hispaniola, Rosalinda's ability to flourish in contrast with Rafi's demise suggests that Danticat envisions Haiti as a nation that will endure against all odds. However, the way in which Rafi is mourned by his family also suggests a critique of the way Dominican lives have been seen as more valuable than Haitian lives: Raphael is honored more in death by natural causes than either Joel, who was carelessly killed by Señor Pico rushing home to his new children or Rosalinda, who even as a baby seems to want to make amends "for having lived in her brother's place" (112). When Amabelle returns years after the massacre to visit Señora Valencia, she realizes the portrait of Rafi, "a bone-white baby boy, watchful and smiling, in an ivory pearl and satin baptism dress with a matching bonnet framing his water lily-colored cheeks," (294) overshadows all other portraits in the room. His looming painting has replaced that of his namesake, the Generalissimo, whose "enormous presence" in the form of a portrait once dominated the room (43).

The disparity between the two communities of Haitian and Dominican people, represented symbolically by Señora Valencia's twins, is both heightened and blurred by the massacre itself since dark-skinned Dominicans as well as mixed families pay the price of Trujillo's nationalistic project. For example, during Amabelle's escape to Haiti, she travels for a time with two Dominican sisters, one of whom lost her Haitian lover when he was taken from their bed in the middle of the night (176). Similarly, when Amabelle awakes in the survivor tent on the Haitian side of the river, there are many black Dominicans in the room, including one who'd "been mistaken for one of us and had received a machete blow across the back of his neck for it" (217). Although initially aimed at Haitians, the entire border community suffers as a result of the massacre to greater and lesser degrees; but it is the "wayfarers," cane workers and other people defined by the uncertainty and liminality of borderland culture, who suffer the brunt of the brutality.[11] Even prior to the Dominican Republic's ethnic cleansing, Sebastien, Amabelle, and their friend Yves are all haunted by dreams of past traumas and nightmares that prefigure the losses they will eventually suffer as a result of the Massacre.

Although Danticat's historical fiction illustrates the ways in which the Trujillo regime's anti-Haitian, anti-black policies were the driving force behind the Massacre, her characters also reveal the failure of the Haitian government to protect its people. Tibon, attempting along with Amabelle to escape the violence of the Massacre, declares that Haiti's poor were "forsaken" by Haiti, stating: "Poor people are sold to work in the cane fields so our own country can be free of them. . .When you stay too long at a neighbor's house, it's only natural that he become weary of you and hate you" (178). When the survivors are prevented from relaying their testimonials to Haitian government officials on the pretext that victims' compensation money has run out, the crowd burns Haitian President Sténio Vincent in effigy. Appropriately, the first part of the image to burn is "the shiny medal of the Grand Cross of the Juan Pablo Duarte Order of Merit, given to him by the Generalissimo as a symbol of eternal friendship between our two peoples" (236). By constructing a narrative which is critical of President Vincent's own feeble concern for his countrymen, Danticat points out the link between the two leaders of the Hispaniolan nations, both of whom instituted policies which stress the divisions, rather than the bonds, between individuals and the state. The medal Trujillo gave to Vincent, which the people of Haiti symbolically burn, emphasizes the ways in which these leaders' collusion undermines people whom they supposedly represent.

The Massacre itself occupies the center of the text, and Amabelle's escape to the border is punctuated by murder, butchery and impossible choices made for the sake of survival. When considering the effect of national violence on the individual, perhaps the most significant insights offered in *The Farming of Bones* emerge not only from the senseless and horrific murders that occurred in the name of nationalism, but also from a consideration of those who survived with this experience embedded in their consciousness.

The survivors' camp on the Haitian side of Massacre River reveals a nightmarish landscape of human beings mutilated in body and spirit. When she first arrives at the camp, Amabelle is taken past a row of people "with burns that had destroyed most of their skin, men and women charred into awkward poses, arms and legs frozen in mid-air, like tree trunks long separated from their branches" (206).[12] Amabelle describes her own body as "simply a map of scars and bruises, a marred testament" (227), a vehicle for recording a fragment of the Massacre's damage. However, Amabelle's physical wounds serve to reflect her emotional state. Following her rather dubious "survival" she, like the burn victims, seems awkwardly frozen and mentally trapped in a place where the Massacre never ends. There is a moment following the death of her companion Odette when Amabelle takes a last look at her face, stating: "I must have been standing over her body for several hours. *Wherever I go, I will always be standing over her body.* No farewell could be enough" (205, my italics). Amabelle's post-Massacre experiences suggest an internal splitting has occurred, so that as in her childhood shadowplay, she is always mentally two places at once: both in her present context and in the moments relating to the Massacre.

In an interview with Cathy Caruth, Robert Jay Lifton suggests that "extreme trauma creates a second self" since the experience itself changes the individual so irrevocably. He states:

in extreme trauma, one's sense of self is radically altered. And there is a traumatized self that is created. Of course, it's not a totally new self, it's what one brought into the trauma as affected significantly and painfully, confusedly, but in a very primal way, by that trauma. And recovery from post-traumatic effects, or from survivor conflicts, cannot really occur until that traumatized self is reintegrated. It's a form of doubling in the traumatized person. And in doubling, as I came to identify it, there have to be elements that are at odds in the two selves, including ethical contradictions. . .But in doubling in the service of survival, for life-enhancing purposes, as I think is true of people who undergo extreme trauma, as with Auschwitz survivors, as they say, 'I was a different person in Auschwitz.' ("An Interview with Robert Jay Lifton" 137)

Although Yves fills his post-Massacre time by attending to practical tasks such as tending his father's land, there is a hollowness in the exercise—not an embracing of life, but rather a time spent "plant[ing] and sow[ing] to avoid the dead season" (263). Similarly, Amabelle's traumatized "second-self" cannot escape her memories long enough for another attempt at living. Remembering the other survivors in the camp near the river, Amabelle realizes she has been emotionally deadened by the genocide, but seems unable to find a way past her paralysis. She states, "I wanted to bring them out of my visions into my life, to tell them how glad I was that they had been able to walk into the future, but most important to ask them how it was that they could be so strong, what their secret was, how they could wash their lives clean, if only for brief moments, from the past" (247). So while Yves plants to avoid the dead season, for Amabelle the dead season is "one never-ending night" where she dreams of offering testimony "to the river, the waterfall, the justice of the peace, even to the Generalissimo himself" (264). Like Yves, Amabelle spends her time working as a means of consolation but nevertheless grows old waiting for news indicating for certain whether Sebastian died in the slaughter although this news never arrives. Memories of her lover haunt her, and Amabelle's narrative reveals the ways in which she has self-admittedly chosen a "living death" rather than fight for a future. Remembering Sebastien, she declares, "His absence is my shadow; his breath my dreams. New dreams seem a waste, needless annoyances, too much to crowd into the tiny space that remains" (281).

At the novel's conclusion, Amabelle returns to the Dominican Republic for the first time since the Massacre to find a waterfall where she hopes, at least symbolically, she will discover Sebastien waiting for her. She instead finds an equally aged Señora Valencia whom she encounters like an awkward memory. Amabelle's return does not bring her any closer to understanding, and she soon returns to Massacre River which itself has become both monument and witness to the slaughter. Standing by the water, Amabelle reflects on the day her parents drowned in the river:

> The day my parents drowned, I watched their faces as they bobbed up and down, in and out of the crest of the river. . .My mother, before she sank, raised her arm high, far above the pinnacle of the flood. The gesture was so desperate that it was hard to tell whether she wanted me to jump in with them or move farther away. I thought that if I relived the moment often enough, the answer would become clear, that they had wanted either for us all to die together or for me to go on living, even if by myself. I also thought that if I came to the river on the right day, at the right hour, the surface of the water might provide the answer: a clearer sense of the moment, a stronger memory. But nature has no memory. And soon, perhaps, neither will I. (309)

The Massacre River, as a symbolic location for Amabelle's losses, does not provide her with any further answers than the ones her own damaged psyche is able to produce. The novel concludes with Amabelle once again crossing the border, this time choosing to lie down in the river that is the border. Although this can be read as a kind of rebirth, particularly since Amabelle describes herself as a newborn "cradled by the current," her positioning suggests otherwise. The river is shallow enough for Amabelle to lie on her back with her shoulders "only half-submerged" (310); the water is neither deep enough for full submersion as one might expect for baptism, nor for her to be swept away like her parents and be drowned. Instead, she embodies the crossroads of Ghede, vodoun god of life and death who "is wise beyond all others" (Deren 37).[13] Bathing in the river, Amabelle balances between her four worlds: the borderland between Haiti and the Dominican Republic, as well as the border between the living above the river and the "spongy bones" beneath. Although the novel's conclusion is somewhat open-ended, perhaps the only nationality Amabelle can truly claim is the one at this quartered crossroads.

Endnotes

[1] Toni Morrison's concept of rememory, which emerges in her neo-slave narrative, *Beloved*, suggests that since the past never dies, what once occurred can "happen again" to someone who did not experience the original event.

[2] Fernando Valerio-Holguín cites Vega's *Trujillo y Haiti* in endnote 41 of "Primitive Borders: Ethnic Cleansing in the Dominican Republic," where he states that the river formerly called the Gutopana was renamed Massacre River following the murder of 30 buccaneers by the Spaniards in 1728. According to Valerio-Holguín, the massacre ordered by the Dominican leader Rafael Trujillo is also prefigured by the primordial moment at the beginning of the sixteenth century during the slaughter of Jaragua, where Spanish governor Nicolás de Ovando ordered the murder of thousands of Taino Amerindians (82). When Jean-Jacques Dessalines ordered the slaughter of 3,000 French during the Haitian revolution, no gunshot was allowed—only hatchets, knives and bayonets so that others in nearby towns would not be warned of the impending attack (Dayan, *Haiti, History, and the Gods* 4). During the 1937 Massacre, the same order was given to

Dominican soldiers when murdering the Haitians so that the slaughter might be brushed off as a proletarian conflict rather than a government-sponsored attack. When considering the compounding echoes between these various historical events, it is also a great irony that many Dominicans refer to the 1937 Massacre as "El Corte" meaning "the cut" or "the harvest." Although casualty estimates for the Massacre vary, Michelle Wucker notes that no less than 15,000 and possibly as many as 35,000 people may have been murdered (Wucker 50-51).

3 This event, too, carries historical echoes. There is a biblical parallel in the Old Testament where 42,000 Ephraimites were killed by the Gileadites after mispronouncing the word "Shibboleth" in a similar test. In Hispaniola's history, according to Wucker, "Jean-Jacques Dessalines, the general who declared Haiti's victory over the French and then became the new nation's first emperor (Jacques I), ordered that all the French who remained in Haiti be killed. Some of the colonists tried to pass as Creoles who had grown up on the island and had African blood. Dessalines devised a test to weed out the ones who had not spoken Kreyol all their lives; they had to sing *'Nanett alé nan fontain, cheche dlo, crich-a li cassé'* (Nanette went to the fountain, looking for water, but her jug broke). The French gave themselves away when they could not properly pronounce the Kreyol or duplicate the African cadences of the melody. Their lie uncovered, they met the bayonets of Dessalines's men. (More than a century later, black Haitians would die for failing a similar test in the Dominican Republic)" (Wucker 37).

4 Julia Alvarez was personally affected by the harshness of the Trujillo regime since she was forced into exile in the United States along with her family shortly before the murder of the Mirabal sisters as a result of her father's participation in a plot against the dictator. See the Postscript of *In The Time Of The Butterflies.*

5 This biographical information about Alexis is included in Carrol F. Coates's introduction to the English translation of *General Sun, My Brother* (ix).

6 Joan Dayan cites an earlier part of the novel when Hilarion personifies misery as a woman. She notes, "He will later meet Claire Heureuse (his beautiful helpmate named after Dessalines's wife), who promises regeneration from a barbarism represented as female. Hilarion's négritude, as in so many other dramas of

men finding themselves, defines itself against the familiar conceit of the double Venus, women cloven in two as beneficent or savage, virginal or polluted" (*Haiti, History, and the Gods* 48).

7 This point is made rather explicitly by Anne McClintock in *Imperial Leather* when she states: "All too often in male nationalisms, gender difference between women and men serves to symbolically define the limits of national difference and power between men. . .Excluded from direct action as national citizens, women are subsumed symbolically into the national body politic as its boundary and metaphoric limit . .Women are typically constructed as the symbolic bearers of the nation. . .but are denied any direct relation to national agency" (354).

8 The term "woman version" is borrowed from Evelyn O'Callaghan's text by the same title. She defines a woman version as follows: "what I suggest is that we approach [West Indian women's writing]. . .as a kind of remix or dub version, which utilizes elements from the 'master tape' of Caribbean literary discourse (combining, stretching, modifying them in new ways); announces a gendered perspective; adds individual styles of 'talk over'; enhances or omits tracks depending on desired effect; and generally alters by recontextualization to create a *unique* literary entity" (11).

9 Torres-Saillant explains this kind of cultural identification and its heightening during the Trujillo regime when many Dominicans tended to identify with Hispaniola's indigenous Taino inhabitants, rather than with the African side of their ancestry. He states: "The regime gave currency to the term *indio* (Indian) to describe the complexion of people of mixed ancestry. The term assumed official status in that the national identification card gave it as a skin-color designation for the three decades of the dictatorship and beyond. While, in the minds of most Dominicans who use it, the term merely describes a color gradation somewhere between the polar extremes of whiteness and blackness much in the same way that the term *mulatto* does, the cultural commissars of the Trujillo regime preferred it primarily because it was devoid of any semantic allusion to the African heritage and would therefore accord with their negrophobic definition of Dominicanness" ("The Tribulations of Blackness" 139).

10 Although somewhat different from Lévi-Strauss's formulation here, the metaphor of twins-who-are-not-twins emerges elsewhere in Danticat's writing such as in her previous novel, *Breath,*

Eyes, Memory, and is linked to a concept found in vodoun. Describing the *Marassa* concept of twinship, Danticat states: "the idea is that two people are one, but not quite; they might look alike and talk alike but are, in essence, different people" (Shea 385).

11 The plight of Haitian sugarcane workers in the Dominican Republic is a recurring source of tension between the two nations since the workers are both needed and despised, and there have been several studies (including the documentary *Black Sugar*) which highlight the inhumane conditions to which the workers are subjected. The plight of the workers are obviously a concern of Danticat's also; the final line of her acknowledgements in *The Farming of Bones* is "to the constant struggle of those who still toil in the cane fields" and, in one interview, Danticat expresses some of her own concerns about the possibilities of the Massacre recurring: "There were people in my family who had gone over to work in the sugar cane in the 1970s and 1980s and when they were gone off and people didn't hear from them. . .people would talk about this thing that happened in 1937 and wondered could it happen again" (Interview with Jacqueline Trescott 2J). For a different perspective on the lives of the sugarcane workers, see also Catherine C. Legrand's "Informal Resistance on a Dominican Sugar Plantation during the Trujillo Dictatorship."

12 The kind of trauma experienced by survivors of the Haitian Massacre, both in Danticat's fiction and in actual accounts, eerily mirrors some of the emotions experienced by Holocaust survivors from which the current research on trauma theory and post-traumatic stress disorder has emerged. Historical parallels emerge when considering the fact that Trujillo had strengthened ties with Adolph Hitler and Nazi Germany during the time leading up to the Massacre, and had even accepted a gift of *Mein Kampf* publicly. According to Wucker, Trujillo offered 100,000 visas to Jewish refugees following the Haitian Massacre for two reasons: to rescue his international image following the Haitian Massacre, and also in hopes that the Jewish refugees would intermarry with Dominicans, thus assisting with the nation's "whitening" process (*Why the Cocks Fight* 56).

13 In the section of the text entitled "The Cosmic Mirror and the Corpse on the Cross-Roads," Maya Deren explains that "the sign of the cross appears everywhere, whenever communication or traffic between the worlds is to be indicated. The vertical

dimension comprehends both the abyss below and the heavens above the earth, the dimension of infinity; the horizontal comprehends all men, all space and matter" (37). In becoming an elder who has lived a life divided by both physical and metaphysical worlds, Amabelle embodies some of Ghede's aspects; he is considered "the greatest of the divine healers" and, significantly, Amabelle recalls that "births and deaths were my parents' work" before she midwifes Señora Valencia's twins (*The Farming of Bones* 5). This also suggests another reading of the earlier twinship trope, since Ghede represents: "the corpse of the first man, who, in his original twinned nature, can be thought of as a cosmic totality segmented by the horizontal axis of the mirror divide into identical twins. The worship of the Marassa, the Divine Twins, is a celebration of man's twinned nature: half matter, half metaphysical; half mortal, half immortal; half human, half divine" (Deren 38).

Works Cited

Alexis, Jacques Stephen. *General Sun, My Brother.* Translations and introduction by Carrol F. Coates. Charlottesville: University Press of Virginia, 1999.

Caruth, Cathy. "Interview with Robert Jay Lifton." *Trauma: Explorations in Memory.* Baltimore: The Johns Hopkins University Press, 1995: 128-147.

Danticat, Edwidge. *The Farming of Bones.* New York: Penguin Books, 1998.

Dayan, Joan. *Haiti, History, and the Gods.* Berkeley: University of California Press, 1995.

Deren, Maya. *Divine Horsemen: The Voodoo Gods of Haiti.* New York: Dell Publishing, 1970.

Legrand, Catherine C. "Informal Resistance on a Dominican Sugar Plantation during the Trujillo Dictatorship." *Hispanic American Historical Review* 75.4 (1995): 555-596.

Lévi-Strauss, Claude. *Myth and Meaning: Cracking the Code of Culture.* New York: Schocken Books, 1995.

McClintock, Anne. *Imperial Leather: Race, Gender and Sexuality in the Colonial Conquest.* New York: Routledge, 1995.

Morrison, Toni. *Beloved.* New York: Plume, 1988.

O'Callaghan, Evelyn. *Woman Version: Theoretical Approaches to West Indian Fiction by Women.* London: The Macmillan Press, 1993.

Shea, Renee H. "The Dangerous Job of Edwidge Danticat: An Interview." *Callaloo.* 19.2 (1996): 382-389.

Torres-Saillant, Silvio. "The Tribulations of Blackness: Stages in Dominican Racial Identity." *Latin American Perspectives* 25.3 (May 1998): 126-146.

Trescott, Jacqueline. "Her Tales of Haiti Eloquent, Melancholy." *The Palm Beach Post*, Sunday, October 17, 1999, 2J.

Valerio-Holguín, Fernando. "Primitive Borders: Cultural Identity and Ethnic Cleansing in the Dominican Republic." Translated by Scott Cooper. *Primitivism and Identity in Latin America: Essays on Art, Literature, and Culture.* Eds. Erik Camayd-Freixas and José Eduardo González. Tucson: University of Arizona Press, 2000: 75-88.

Wucker, Michele. *Why the Cocks Fight: Dominicans, Haitians, and the Struggle for Hispaniola.* New York: Hill and Wang, 1999.

The Terrible Days Behind Us and the Uncertain Ones Ahead: Edwidge Danticat Talks about *The Dew Breaker*

Renee H. Shea

In *The Dew Breaker*, her latest work, Edwidge Danticat draws on her early childhood in Haiti during the Duvalier dictatorship. The central character is a quiet man, a husband and father living in Brooklyn, whose past in Haiti made him, as he tells his daughter, "the hunter. . .not the prey"—a torturer. Danticat explains that she translated the title, the English version of a Creole expression, *Choukèt laroze* "in the most serene sounding way I could." In a series of interconnected stories, we meet his victims and survivors as Danticat moves between past and present, Haiti and New York, redemption and guilt, despair and hope.

    The Dew Breaker has already gathered strong reviews. In *Time Magazine* (8 March 2004) Pico Iyer praised "Danticat's gift" that "combine[s] both sympathy and clarity in a moral tangle that becomes as tight as a Haitian community." Writing in *The New York Times* (10 March 2004), Michiko Kakutani called *The Dew Breaker* "as seamless as it is compelling," and described Danticat's "fierce, elliptical artistry. . .her piercing, indelible words."

    Currently living in Miami with her husband Faidherbe Boyer, Danticat toured seventeen cities when *The Dew Breaker* came out in March. She and I talked early in April in Washington, D.C., before a reading at Vertigo Books in College Park, Maryland.

RS: Are you surprised by how well the book is doing?
ED: You can never predict how any book is going to do, but, yes, I am a little bit surprised. I couldn't have gauged it at all. First of all, it's stories, and not a traditional novel and you never know what people are going to be interested in. I'm pleasantly surprised by the wonderful reaction people have been having to these stories, these characters who are so close in many ways, so important to me.

RS: In the Acknowledgement, you said that your cousin Hans Adonis "is the book's parenn, because of all the Duvalier-era research he so lovingly bombarded me with." Did the idea originate with him?

ED: I've always had the idea of writing about the Duvalier era, and actually I had started writing a novel about a woman named Madame Max, who has a small cameo in *The Dew Breaker*. She was the head of the female section of the Tontons Macoute, so I wanted to write about her, but the more I learned about her, the harder it was to humanize her because pretty much all that is known about her is pure evil. The fact that she was still living also made it tricky. But I wanted to write about that period in the aftermath of the 29-year Duvalier dictatorship because it's really the last period I spent in Haiti—the last time I lived there. I wanted to write about what people make of that time period and the idea of migration, that you have this mixture of people who were victims of the dictatorship and those who were perpetrators of it living now in a different country, in the United States, especially in New York.

The whole book actually started with one story, the first story, "The Book of the Dead," which was published in *The New Yorker Magazine* in 1999. It's a story about a father, the dew breaker, and his daughter Ka on a trip from New York to Florida. The daughter is a sculptor, a wood carver, with only one subject so far, her father. He is so moved when he sees her sculpture of him that he feels unworthy and confesses. When I was done with that story, I became very curious about the father's past and wrote a story to flesh it out. Then everything I wrote after that for a couple of years became part of the father's world. After the father became very clear in my mind, then his wife, the mother Anne, surfaces, and she intrigued me, and I wrote "The Book of Miracles" about her.

So these three stories were linked formlessly, but all centered around this one person really, the dew breaker. The book itself became about solving a puzzle, looking at this person from all these different angles.

RS: I'm fascinated by the intricate ways the characters and events intertwine, but you're telling me that you didn't plan all that ahead of time?

ED: No, the stories came as I myself was trying to understand these people's connections to one another. Really, the book started with two people—Ka and the father. I remember when I was writing it, there was this barber, this dew breaker, and then I realized there had to be an equally strong person to fight him, so the preacher, his nemesis, came out of that puzzle, too. Then there was Anne, his wife, and his relationship to her. So it was a whole series of surprises to me. The only people I knew who would be shadowy presences in the book were the dew breaker and Gabrielle Fonteneau, the famous Haitian-American actress who everyone in the book watches on television. They all love and admire her just as much as they fear the dew breaker.

RS: Is she based on a real person?

ED: Yes, sort of. There's one really stunning Haitian woman on television that everyone's very proud of. She's on *NYPD Blue*; her name is Garcelle Beauvais, and she's the pride of the community, so I had this idea that almost everybody in the story would be watching her on television. In the editing she came out of some of the stories because I didn't want to give the impression that everyone was either being scared of a torturer or watching the television all the time. But the famous actress and the dew breaker were the only two people I planned to have in all the stories, whether they were actually in the foreground or the background. However, I wanted the reader to have this feeling that when "entering" one of the stories of wondering if the dew breaker will surface. So that feeling is there for the reader, wondering is he going to surface, almost a fear, kind of a fearful dread or searching for him in every place. Just as one of the characters thinks he's in every house on every block she's ever lived in. I wanted the reader to share that fear, that dread that he might show up anywhere.

RS: Why did you reveal who the dew breaker was right away in the first story instead of letting it unfold?

ED: I didn't want to dangle this false mystery. So much of the structure of a mystery is that discovery of who did it that you lose sight of everything else. I read mysteries, and sometimes I feel I miss so much because I'm in such a hurry to find out who the killer is. I didn't want to set up this atmosphere where you're wondering who is he, but rather what did he do and why? That for me was a more important question than who he was. There were so many people like this dew breaker in the 29-year history of the dictatorship. So many vanished and blended into ordinary life and you don't really care who they are so much after a couple of decades—but people care and want to remember what they did and why and what the aftermath of their deeds are.

RS: Apparently, you've baffled your reviewers about whether *The Dew Breaker* is a novel or a series of short stories. Which is it?

ED: The publisher didn't want to label it. For me, it was always short stories, and we decided to compromise and not say anything on the cover, leaving it up to the reader to decide.

RS: The same people recur in several of the stories, and there's a strong narrative thread running throughout all the stories. So it seems more of a novel.

ED: But I think if I had started it with the idea of writing a novel, I would have written it differently. It turned out in the end that whatever it is, the structure fit it really well. I tend to write more linearly with novels, so for me it's a matter of intention. I never started thinking I was writing a novel.

RS: But at some point you had to say "This is done" because it seems you could always add another story.

ED: Actually, someone asked me if I could have taken one out, and I said, no. Then they asked if I could add one more story, and I said no. So, they said, "It's a novel!" I feel that it's its own kind of universe. Whatever it is, the structure fits it, and maybe it's one of those accidents of design. It just works, like a puzzle; the different pieces fit where they are meant to, and I am very glad it's comprehensible at all. Even when I was writing *Krik? Krak!*, I tried to experiment with the interconnectedness of the stories, but there was never a confusion about that because they were so clearly separate. There's just a lot more overlap in this book. Some pieces echo here and there more than others.

RS: I read that the minister's story is taken from your own experience, that he's an actual person you remember from when you were growing up in Haiti?

ED: There is a minister in the last story, who is simply called "the preacher"; he has no name. His character is based on a real minister I knew growing up, a man, who was the pastor of the church, L'Eglise Baptiste des Anges, as it's written in the book, in the Delmas area of Port-au-Prince. He had written something against the dictatorship and was taken outside of his church and beaten severely one night. He was a revered minister with a radio show, and he had baptized me when I was a child, he had married my parents. I remember hearing that he was grabbed and beaten but survived. He was the first case I knew of a religious figure being attacked. I am not saying that there were not others, but he was the only church leader I knew personally who was attacked this way by Duvalier's Macoutes. I remember because my uncle was also a minister, and I felt if even people of the church weren't safe anymore, then it was not a sanctuary—even though the minister we knew was taken outside of his church and was beaten as he was leaving. I remember feeling very struck that my uncle was in danger. It was really unsettling.

RS: That sanctioned national prayer that is in the story "The Dew Breaker," that begins "Our father who art in the national palace, hallowed be thy name. Thy will be done, in the capital, as it is in the provinces. . ." Is that true?

ED: Yes, Duvalier the father, the elder, wrote that prayer. Actually, when I was doing research for *After the Dance*, I came across a *Life Magazine* article that my cousin gave me where a reporter asked Duvalier "What do the Haitians have?" and he said, "I'm their father, and the Virgin Mary is their mother." It was very extreme, a kind of intense madness. Even the Macoutes—he took a childhood legend, a myth, and made that scary bogeyman figure real. Then it becomes everybody's nightmare come to life.

RS: You said in an interview that this work is something new for you because you have male protagonists, but aren't Anne and Ka very central as well?

ED: Yes, but this book has the most male characters I've ever written. Actually, the story that was the most fun to write was "Monkey Tails," the one with the little boy who's in love with every-one. That's the one I enjoyed most. Doing the voice of that little boy was almost a way for me to channel my brothers. I have three brothers, so I grew up in a house outnumbered by male siblings.

RS: I'm very interested in the intertextuality in the novel. You made reference to Abner Louima, Jacques Alexis, Patrick Dorismond, Emmanuel Constant, among others. I know most of them, but who is Emmanuel Constant?

ED: He's a man who started an organization called FRAPH, and they were notorious in the early 1990s. He was Duvalier's godson by some accounts. The CIA recruited him, by his own account. When they were about to deport him, he went on *60 Minutes* and said he was recruited by the CIA to create an organization that recycled some of the old Macoutes, and they killed something like 5000 people during the coup of the 1990s. Then he fled to the U.S. where he has family, and he's been living in Queens. Actually, just a couple of days ago there was a demonstration in front of his house. This has happened several times because people want him repatriated or detained. But there was a point right after he came here when people would say, "I saw him here, I saw him there," so he was a sort of a notorious celebrity in the Haitian community. There were "Constant citings."

I tried to add these real people in some ways more for me than the reader because I need a kind of anchoring truth in the fiction. Even when I'm writing it, just the interaction of my characters with real people and events makes it seem a little more real to me, so it makes it seem like the characters really exist. It's fun because you might not know Emmanuel Constant, but if you do recognize him, it has another layer.

RS: Like the passages written in Creole?

ED: Exactly!

RS: Another kind of intertextuality is the title, which echoes Jacques Roumain's famous novel, *Masters of the Dew*. Were you intentionally connecting your work to this earlier classic?

ED: Yes, the title is a tribute in some ways to *Masters of the Dew*, the great Haitian novel that was translated by Langston Hughes and Mercer Cook. Roumain's book was such a powerful one for me. It was the first time I had ever seen Haitian peasants, people like many in my family who live a rural life, in a book. I've read it many times and taught it. He presented another approach to this expression, *laroze*, the dew. He was trying through the characters in this book to show a different approach to building a country, one village at a time, one dew drop at a time. My book is in some ways a nod to him, a tribute to show my appreciation for how much the book touched me, but it also acknowledges that in some way the struggle for our country has always been a battle between dew breakers, *choukèt laroze*, and dew masters, the masters of the dew of his title.

RS: Now what about the "Book of the Dead" and the dew breaker's interest in Ancient Egyptian art and culture? What led you to include those elements in your work?

ED: People are always asking what's autobiographical, and I borrowed from my own interest in Ancient Egyptian culture for this. I've been fascinated by Ancient Egyptian culture since I was in junior high school here in the United States. . I went to school right across from the Brooklyn Museum, and we were always taken there on field trips. I thought that all the mortuary rites were so amazing, almost as though you could negotiate your eternity.

RS: You wrote this about the dew breaker: "But what he admires most about the Ancient Egyptians is the way they mourn their dead." The juxtaposition of the great disregard for life and then the great regard for life that never ends is so powerful.

ED: I think maybe it's part of his configuration of his current life. It is a very striking legacy of the Duvalier dictatorship that they managed to "disappear" many people, people whose families had no idea what happened to them. In the Acknowledgments, I mentioned the case of Patrick Lemoine, who wrote a book called *Fort Dimanche, Dungeon of Death.* There he writes about being in prison for three years, and by the time he comes out, his wife has a new family. She thought he had died. So many people just vanished without ever even having a funeral. Even when their bodies survived, something else died in them. So the dew breaker's whole reconfiguration of his life is perhaps about whether he could have done things differently, saved rather than destroyed. I'm sure that if he could erase his past, he would. The Ancient Egyptian rites, on some level, allow for that, for you to still have a good eternity even if you had a bad life, the same way that Christianity does for his wife. His fascination with this culture shows a shift in his thinking.

It's interesting, too, that what this organization FRAPH, Emanual Constant's organization, in the 1990s—and there are accounts that human rights organizations have documented—used to do is to mutilate people's faces so they would not be identifiable. That's something people are saying now is happening again, that when people are killed their faces are basically removed. So what a contrast to the Egyptians' right of preserving people for eternity—which is much closer to our ancestral beliefs, much closer to preservation of ancestors in the indigenous culture. The mortuary rights of the Tainos are very close to the Ancient Egyptians in that people are buried with what they prized most. Now, in Haiti, you see a dead baby or a corpse on the street, and people just walk by. The elders would say this is the degradation of a society because there is no respect for the dead. People just walk by. Part of that is that there've been so many deaths. Some are afraid to take their loved ones out of the street for fear of what will happen to them when they go and claim these bodies.

Respect for the dead is something that rural Haitian culture shares with the Ancient Egyptians. When you go to the countryside in Haiti, you see graves very close to the houses looking sometimes better than the houses. For the story, "The Night Talkers," which I had written first as an essay for *Calabash*, I went in 1999 to see my aunt who had never left the country. I saw the grave of my great grandmother for the first time since I was a child during that trip. My aunt had her own grave all set next to her daughter's (she had died of AIDS very young), both right next to the house. The connection is very deep there between the living and the dead.

RS: In the first story, "The Book of the Dead," we're told that Ka's name means "a double of the body. . .the body's companion through life and after life." Is that the same doubling from *Breath, Eyes, Memory*?

ED: I hadn't thought of that. The doubling in *BEM* is based on an historical event. The myth of Dessalines and the idea that he was only defeated because he had this double. That he was resting—this is something my grandmother said a lot. He was not fully in force, his other part was somewhere else. I recently had this experience driving with a friend, and someone jumped in front of her car, and she shouted, "What's your problem? Is your good angel at home? Your *ti-bon anj* sleeping?" This idea is that you're completely bare, there's a part of you missing if you're not completely aware at all times.

With Ka, I was exploring both the idea that your *ti bon anj*, your good angel, your *id*, your good sense, that part that helps you to make good decisions is in someone else, someone, as in the dew breaker's case, who represents your future, your child, your progeny. But also the literal meaning is "your good angel," which is how the father also took it. He sees the wife and daughter as the good angels on his shoulder, the ones who have saved him from doing more wrong. And what a burden that is, even to someone who knows fully what you've done in the past, but think of it for someone who didn't even know and didn't choose that role.

RS: The epigraph of the work is from the Russian Osip Mandelstam: "Maybe this is the beginning of madness. . .Forgive me for what I am saying, / Read it. . .quietly, quietly." Is he especially important to you?

ED: I've always been moved by him, particularly I just love that poem. I had the whole poem sitting on my wall as I was writing. "Forgive me for what I am saying" is a great point, imagining things unsaid, and a way to connect things to the way things were done during the dictatorship—you were told to speak quietly, do things quietly. Not complete silence but forced quiet.

RS: Actually, voice and voicelessness seem a theme in *The Dew Breaker*. Ms. Hinds literally cannot speak because of cancer, Nadine cannot force herself to call her parents, the dew breaker can't tell about his past.

ED: Silence is at the core of a story like this, just as it is during the dictatorship. There's so much you're not allowed to say. The Duvaliers silenced—by killing a whole generation and stunning many of the survivors into silence. My parents still have trouble speaking of that period, for example. So there are many ways to be silenced. Migration also silences you. You're in a country where you don't speak the language, don't know the names of things, so there's a silencing there as well. In the story, "Water Child," the nurse who works with Ms. Hinds, the woman who loses her larynx to cancer, tells her that she'll never speak for the rest of her life at the same time that she's helping immigrant children who suffer from selective muteness, a psychological disorder of sorts, to speak again, and she is silenced herself by the distance from her loved ones in Haiti. So, yes, there is a lot of silence in this book, but the fact that we have the stories, that these characters tell their stories in different ways, to the reader, to other people, breaks that silence too. So the book shows where silence meets the breaking of silence.

RS: Anne's life is described as "a pendulum between forgiveness and regret." She seems happiest in church—the Christmas mass. I'm not sure what you're doing with religion. It seems her only solace. You weren't raised Catholic, were you?

ED: No, I wasn't raised Catholic, but I went to mass every week when I was at school in Haiti and have later gone to mass in New York, so I have seen a lot of the rituals.

RS: Anne says that part of a good life is time for mass; she calls it "enchantment." Religion seems a solace, yet I don't feel you're criticizing her for choosing a kind of "easy" way out.

ED: I think faith is very important in a situation like that. In Haiti you find a lot of people with faith, be they Catholic, Protestant, or Vodou practitioners. Sometimes the situation is so difficult that you need something larger to surrender yourself to. Anne acknowledges that she knows that she is comforted by her faith. There is nothing wrong with that. Even Francois Duvalier, Papa Doc, linked faith to his power. That's where you get into the kind of misuse of faith or religion that requires criticism. Papa Doc didn't rewrite "The Lord's Prayer" to place himself in it for

Renee H. Shea

nothing. This whole notion of him as the father of the Haitians and the Virgin Mary as the mother was a misuse of religion, but he did use it. He used Catholicism, he used Vodou, all to maintain power. The preacher in the story is fighting as much against religion as opiate as he is against the dictatorship itself. So I guess he was an early liberation theologist; he is not renouncing his faith or his church, but he is using it as a tool to ignite a fire under his people.

RS: Church for Anne is a place of peace and rest, for the minister a place of agitation and unrest.

ED: That's right for Anne. Her faith allows her to forgive the unforgivable. That's part of her going to mass daily—to help herself forgive her husband, to deal with the choice that she has made. The church, just like the Ancient Egyptian mortuary rites, gives you ways to negotiate your own personal anguish.

RS: There is so much tension in *The Dew Breaker*, the half truths, the accommodations of living with what we can bear to know and leaving the rest. It feels like a negotiation with the truth, which doesn't seem one of those things we should negotiate.

ED: When the book was done and Robin [Desser, Danticat's agent] read it for the first time, she said, "Are you sure you want to say this?" I thought these are the characters' choices. This is how they are dealing with this torturer. Some forgive, and some don't. Anne did. She even grew to love him. It's easier to write the condemnation than the forgiveness, but Anne forgives every day. She's lost everything, just as the dew breaker had, and all of a sudden, this man gives her a mission in life. She could be saintly. If he hadn't come, what would she have done? She feels as though she literally stands between good and evil; she's the gatekeeper.

RS: Anne gains clarity when she has to tell her daughter. She says, "He's a seed thrown in rock. You, me, we make him take root." Once she confronts that truth with her daughter, everything changes. What was it like to write in the mind of the dew breaker?

ED: I know it sounds strange, but it was like writing anything else. With everything, you have to sort of put yourself in that person's place. Did I feel sympathy? I had to or I couldn't have written it. So, I had to bend over backwards to find something to feel sympathetic about in this person, just as I did in every other. I didn't start to feel really bad until the preacher struck him, and he had that gash on his face. When he was most vulnerable—in that scene when he was telling his daughter about his past—I felt more

250

sympathetic for him than I did even for her. Maybe without those small things, those vulnerable moments, I could not have written him. There are times when he does things every once in a while that soften the character; when he tries to sing in church with his wife, for example, he's most human in those moments. I had to find things like that from some deep places to make him come alive. I couldn't have written about him from a place of pure evil. It's those gray spaces that are interesting.

RS: Well, actually, he doesn't seem driven by the desire for recognition or pure malevolence but by some sense of duty.

ED: He was a reluctant abductee [into the Tonton Macoutes]. Like many now who are enrolled in these groups, there were few choices available to him. Everybody who was powerful was a Macoute, so if he wanted to be powerful, he had to copy these things. This is not to excuse him because not everyone followed the same path he did, but he's seduced by that kind of power as many young men of his time were, especially those who were poor and had no other options. That's also why he doesn't have a name in the book. He could have been anybody; anybody could have fallen into that situation. I feel like I had to put myself in his shoes to create him.

RS: How will Ka think of herself now that she knows who her father is?

ED: She's probably found a cause. She'll probably be among those people marching in front of Constant's house now! But she'll still have the fear, wondering if people will recognize her as so-and-so's daughter. She'll probably go more deeply into the community. I see her as an artist activist.

RS: Is she ever going to understand?

ED: I think she already does. I think on some very instinctive level, she always knew. Maybe the daughter didn't know, but the artist in her knew. She said, "Oh, that's why we don't have friends, we don't do this and that. . ." so I think on some level she knew something was off. I think the artist in her knew, and that's going to go deeper. She may not forgive. She's very judgmental, and I think there will be clashes, painful conversations—and silences with the parents. But she'll find out more and eventually she'll deal with it. That's the kind of person she is. The first stop with something like this is denial, then separation, so when she finds this out, the question she's trying not to ask herself is, "Am I also evil?"

RS: She's a great character. . .I hope she comes back.

ED: People keep asking me about that! Will she come back? I'm not sure.

RS: In the Acknowledgements of this book, your first line is, "For my father who, thank goodness, is not in this book."

ED: People thought that was my mother in *Breath, Eyes, Memory*, and that was a bit inconvenient to both of us, but having them think that my father is in this book could be outright dangerous, so I felt I had to make that distinction very clear.

RS: At the end of "The Funeral Singer," the women toast to "the terrible days behind us and the uncertain ones ahead." Is this Haiti today? How discouraging is it for you?

ED: It could be Haiti at so many moments. There are definitely uncertainties ahead. There are some terrible days behind us, but we've always had terrible days. I'm really sad that on the bicentennial of independence, we have foreign troops, especially French troops, on Haitian soil—my ancestral pride is burned on that one. It just seems like such a whipping for the last 200 years. It makes me ashamed that after all of these years, we aren't able to handle our own problems.

RS: I wanted to ask you if the move from New York to Miami affected your work? New York is where you grew up, home in a sense, yet Miami has such strong associations for the Haitian community.

ED: When I went to live in Miami about a year and a half ago, I was revising this book—after I realized it was a book—and then I was really nervous. Even when I moved from Brooklyn to New Rochelle, I wondered, "Can I write in a new place?" I purposely started a young adult book right away in Miami and I was able to finish it, so now I think, "Okay, I can write in Miami." It's a different environment for me, I'm still adjusting, and I think I can write there. Do I have the great Miami novel in me? I don't know. We live in Little Haiti, but I don't think I'm there collecting stories. If something surfaces there, I will be very open to it.

RS: But I understand you are working on something new— more than just an idea?

ED: The best advice I ever got from Laura Rushka of Soho Press, my first editor, was that before anything comes out, just start something new; before you even get any reaction to the one you've just done, write something new so you can prove to yourself you can do it again.

RS: And you've done that consistently, including now?

ED: Yes, I've written a young adult novel called *Anacaona, Golden Flower*, about a Taino queen named Anacaona. I was fascinated by Anacaona, who came from the same region where my mother was born, Léogane,—and I have always wanted to write about her.

RS: So there's not another novel on the horizon?

ED: Not right now. I have something percolating, but I don't want to start too soon. I have to calm down from the book tour. I want to rest a bit, travel for fun, go on vacation, become reacquainted with my husband and then become reacquainted with my ghosts. Hopefully then I'll start the whole joyous and painful writing process all over again.

Special Section:

Virgin Islands - Two Cultural Icons

Charles Abramson   06/11/45 - 05/23/88

Charles Abramson:
A Dream of Life and Victory
Edgar Othniel Lake

> "We are ourselves sculptures awaiting a dream of life that may draw upon us when we engage differently with a pace that is secreted everywhere."
> — Wilson Harris

I met the artist Charles Abramson in 1971, a veteran teacher in the New York Public School system; he taught Science all day and painted at night. That evening, I cheated him of his art, as we talked until dawn. I was recently released from the US Army; he had been a US Air Force serviceman; both of us were Vietnam War-era veterans, with birth celebrations days apart in June. What I didn't know initially was that I had met one of the most remarkable artists of my generation, and that this encounter would unlock a rich and complex African Atlantic tradition from which we had sprung.

I write that Abramson was an 'artist,' because Abramson embodied many disciplines—in fact, his life was a performance of artistic generosity, and his legacy remains a life-force still echoing across friendships and frontiers only now to be fully explored. Yet, though many of his canvasses remain lost, his many dynamic artifacts in installations were, like his sculptured pieces and murals, real and fleeting; perhaps elusive in their custodianships, yet haunting in their recurring meanings.

At the old Studio Museum in Harlem around the corner on Fifth Avenue and 126th Street, the Trinidadian Bronx painter Leroy Clarke was doing battle with Wilfredo Lam's drawings, and his own lines, depicting Trinidadian 'Duende' mythology. Abramson was taking classes with the sculptor Valerie Maynard; she, armed with her patented head ties and smiles, was slaying her own dragon—a French Citroen in which she commuted to Washington, D.C. Her car was notoriously sluggish on wintry evenings, and one sees, now, how The Reichhold Center for the Performing Arts, at the University of the Virgin Islands, St. Thomas, would easily beckon her to curate its African Collection in the 1970s. Across the street from the museum, WBLS's Radio Personality Hal

Jackson—who promoted "Ms. Black Teenage America" in the Virgin Islands—lived on "the block:" Fifth Avenue and One-two-five (125th Street). This was a popular Caspar Holstein numbers combination, and it sat just up the avenue from the "Uptown Jazz Club," where the upstate commuter busses slowed to a crawl, at Mount Morris Park.

Charles Abramson was born in Harlem, and grew up across the street—126th Street between Madison and Park, the block of the Studio Museum in Harlem. His father, Lionel Abramson, was a merchant seaman, and although frequently absent, Abramson was very close to him. Abramson had researched Holstein's life, an unobserved influence in the Harlem Renaissance's "Powerful Ten." He had ritually included pieces of Holstein's *Washington Post's* full-page photogravure, a multi-image depiction on the Virgin Islands, in his earliest installations. Abramson believed Holstien's photogravure to be the forerunner of a "Black Harlem" collage tradition, for which he believed Holstein deserved some credit. But, beyond this, Abramson's feathery trope in his early installations hinted at the 1928 Gale, a hurricane that wasted his parents' home on the island of St. Croix, when all the fowl population perished and had to be plucked, transforming the estate farmlands and village yards into plumed fields. Holstein's relief efforts to those families most needful is inherent in Abramson's aerial feathers: a forest of plumed votives to the fraternities that shaped Holstein's generation; an aesthetic still carried on in present-day Virgin Islands Carnival tradition.

Abramson was taking printmaking classes with Maynard in 1971. Concurrently, he studied at the Arts Students League on West 57th Street, taking Life Drawing, Painting, and Composition classes. There, Abramson met great teachers in Norman Lewis, Knox Martin, Richard Mayhew, and Morris Kanto; he also studied Elements of Drawing with Marshall Glasier.

After participating in his first exhibit, "Contemporary Caribbean Painting," he painted in his mural with that now-recurring theme of his life, "Dream Stages in 4 Parts," for the Center for Multi-Handicapped Children in New York City. Immediately after, he visited his parents' hometown in St. Croix, a place where he had spent his youth, and was encouraged to paint his next mural with a 'dream' motif: "Queen Mary: A Dream of Life and Victory."

Abramson worked at the Association for Alternative Development in Washington, D.C.; and, later, he was employed at the New York Urban Coalition's office. He worked as an art director for Nok Publishers, providing graphic illustrations for Rhonda Mills's book of poems, *Dark Heat When the Sun Goes Down.*

In 1974, Abramson returned to fill a third floor space at the Studio Museum in Harlem. He exhibited "Kwanza 74," with black volcanic sand from St. Vincent and an oversized bleached-white brain coral from St. Croix. Suspended overhead with nylon string were Gullah rocking chair parts from St. Helena Island and Southern plantation wooden bullock collars; torn photographs, mirrors, razors and iridescent feathers gave the room a numinous quality and effected a deep hush on the mandatory bare-feet audience.

Between 1973-75, he worked with Diane McIntyre and her Sounds in Motion at the Clark Center in a New Choreographers Concert. That same year, his exhibit of "Old/News" opened while he was an Artist in Residence at the Henry Street Settlement/Arts for Living Center, on the Lower East Side. This was a vibrant space—bordering Chinese, Eastern European Jews, and newly-arrived Hispanics—where productions of Eric Bradley Burton and Gus Edwards, two playwrights who had once resided in the Virgin Islands, were staged. Additionally, Larry Neal's blues/jazz masterpiece, "The Beautiful Monster in the Bell of the Horn," was musically choreographed by Max Roach.

The next stage of Abramson's expressionism came in the 1975 one-man mural exhibition, "Rivers of Honey and Color," a dialectical salute to Fanon's "Years of Blood; Rivers of Darkness." It was the same year that Abramson received his initiatory Yoruba rank, Weusi Nyuma Ya Sanaa.

Many of us came to love the "stacked shop" environment of Master Printmaker Bob Blackburn on 16th Street, between Sixth and Seventh avenues, where accommodations were tempered through punctuality, compliance and time management. After a long day, Blackburn, walking alongside his famed black bicycle, could be seen on his way sampling tea in Second Avenue tea houses and East Village noodle shops.

Once I talked to Blackburn at a Second Avenue Tropical Bar, a bar and restaurant where waiters wore colorful Miami Keys print shirts, but otherwise mauled Blackburn's soft encouragements by the ice-cubed rattling of daiquiri blenders. Many of our earnest conversations were about the post-World War II whereabouts of Blackburn's friend Ronald Joseph, the first African American Abstractionist, who had settled in Belgium from Harlem after originally migrating from his native home, St. Kitts.

Talk would inevitably turn to the post-60's influx of dancers from various Brazilian Capoeira dance schools, coming to New York City. In turn, there was a lively African American exchange of artists among the collaborators filmmaker/Art historian Daniel Dawson, who had accompanied Abramson to Brazil in 1983. (Dawson would return to Brazil more than two dozen times, once even to give Charles's son, Daveed, a collection of his late father's exhibition catalogs.) On one of these subsequent earlier trips, Dawson and fellow-filmmaker Ronald Gray returned to Brazil to shoot their film "Capoeira." Some of the Chuck Davis African Dance Company members—principally among them, Monifa Olajorin and Sandra Burton—who went to Brazil, had also attended the 1977 Second African and Black World Festival of Arts and Culture in Lagos, Nigeria. Abramson had earlier worked with the Davis dance company as a Set Designer and Props Manager, from 1973-1975.

During the early 1970s, Dawson, David Hammons and Abramson had done rigorous commuting to New Haven, attending classic lectures by Yale Master/Art Historian Robert Farris Thompson: "Twin Images among the Oyo and other Yoruba Groups;" "Yoruba Artistic Criticism: The Traditional Artist in African Societies; Aesthetics in traditional Africa;" "An Introduction to Transatlantic Black Art History: In Anticipation of a Coming Golden Age of Afro-Americana."

In Brazil, Abramson was interested in hearing the *cordells*, the epic Brazilian poems and the *hepatistas*, extemporaneous songs of the favelas (akin to the early calypso form of female praise-songs for the stick-fighters). Abramson, who spoke Brazilian Portuguese, was looking for songs about Crucian heroine Queen Mary's banished son. (Highfield, *Society of Virgin Islands Historian Proceedings*, 1988-92).

On returning from Brazil, Abramson had proudly told his longtime friend, John Richards, of his painting a mural in Bahia during his visit to Brazil. Fellow-traveler, Dawson, later surmised that it may have been done on one of Abramson's surreptitious excursions into the streets.

Blackburn knew Abramson well, at least as well as he knew another Virgin Islander, the painter Ademola Olugebefola. Abramson had earned a scholarship to study Lithography with Blackburn in 1975, although he had studied printmaking under Micahel de Leon and Roberto de Lamonica.

Ademola, like Abramson, was an accomplished muralist and painter. He too was an agent of the west-coast Black cultural religious movement, Kwanza. He was the founder of the Grinnell Gallery; and its publishing house, Gumbs & Thomas Publishers, promoted many of the earliest Kwanza publications. Ademola, like Abramson, had successfully included many symbols into his design canvasses. It is a significant African American Art tradition that these two artists share in Virgin Islands art history, complimenting each other's personal sagas to continental Africa, and synthesizing her Caribbean religious Shango retentions.

Ademola's 1967 masterful woodcut print, "Faces of Shango," is still a hallmark; and later, his 1969 pen and ink drawing, "Shango," inspired other African American performance celebrations. Both were ancestral tithes, echoing Abramson's installation classic, his 1985 "Altar to Chango" (Thompson's "Faces of the God" 243).

Blackburn admired these two artists; their strong fraternal commitments triggered his memory of his association with the "306" Group on 141st Street in Harlem, in the 1930s. It was "the American equivalent to a Parisian salon" (Patton: *Memory and Metaphor: The Art of Romare Bearden.*)

In the Sixties, the Weusi Academy in Harlem was the spiritual house for these two abiding priestly artists of African and African American culture. The subtleties of kinships and enduring legacies are myriad and hint at labyrinth presences—too sober for the uninitiated. Weusi Academy is, still, simply one of the most venerable African American artist cooperatives in America.

An account by Otto Neals describes its fraternal legacy succinctly. Once, there had been a Weusi Academy reunion at the Jamaica Arts Center, which Abramson had attended, although he was not a Weusi Academy founding member. Clearly, the West African tenets of the Harlem-based cooperative group's visions appealed to Abramson's evolving Yoruba insights. The roots were collegial, but more enduring.

When Weusi Academy evolved from its 1967 vanguard cadre of 20th century creators, at some point, Abdul Rahman and

James "Jimmy" Phillips were tenants in Abramson's loft. When Weusi founding member Nii Ahene Mettle Nunoo extended his family's hospitality in Ghana to fellow-Weusi Academy artist, Otto Neals, it spearheaded a fountainhead of lifelong missions between these corresponding African American artists. Between 1969 and 1979, James Scipio and Nii Ahene were invited by Abramson to visit and work in the Virgin Islands.

It is a measure of the African artists' cooperative traditions, so intensely believed by this longest-standing African American artistic group, that accounts for Nii Ahene Mettle Nunoo's twenty-year sojourn as artist-teacher and Resident Curator at the Fort Frederick Museum tithing his talents in Abramson's homeland, St. Croix, U.S. Virgin Islands.

In Frederiksted Town, Fort Frederick was the portal of the 1848 Emancipation and the venerable site of the Africans' mass formation demanding Freedom. It was also the locale for their initial collective act of freedom of expression. A veritable historical shrine for the African people of the Danish West Indies is the coalescing of the Living Arts.

While his father, Lionel Abramson, was a native of Christiansted, Abramson's mother, Mary Springer, was from "Freedom City" Frederiksted. He returned to St. Croix, and Frederiksted Town, with his parents when he was fourteen years old.

II

"My Stepfather, Horace Truell, was a very good drafts-man. He would draw my mother over and over, again. He drew Black People from memory. . .He was the only person I'd seen who drew Blacks from memory."
— Abramson Interview, by Dawson: 1979

Conceivably, Abramson belonged to the Third Wave of Virgin Islands artists, artists with an eye to forge a vernacular beyond the Folk aspects of their culture.

In New York City, Abramson and I talked about young artists on St. Croix in the Seventies. (His first murals are now forgotten on the island, concealed behind faded scaffolding in the Lost Dog Bar & Restaurant; another lay forgotten in the John D. Merwin warehouse, where he once worked as a clerk.)

After his mid-Sixties stint in the US Air Force, and a tour in the Vietnam War theater, he returned several summers in the 1970's visiting siblings, and completing his 1973 mural, while talking with young artists of a budding muralist tradition on St. Croix. Those visits placed Abramson as a catalyst in the indigenous Art in Public Spaces movement, already popular among many artists and activists. Darwin King, a deputy under Governor Cyril King's Youth Administration, remembered Abramson's presence and encouragement. Abramson was active in both towns, but King remembered him in Christiansted, his father's native town, where as a boy he roamed Gallows Bay, site of the rebellious slaves' public hangings, and the town's waterfront where Alexander Hamilton swam with his Ghanaian slave friend, Ajax.

Retired New York City artist Leo Carty had taught and brought along several student groups—novice mural painters, if not virtual initiates—who had completed several public murals, including "Sunday Concert at Christiansted Port," and "Sunday Concert at the Frederiksted Port." Both murals were installed at the Estate Whim Gardens Senior Citizens residence. Leo Carty, the late Tom Feelings, and Otto Neals were African American co-spirit guardians of the African Atlantic epic. In the 1970s, each was attracted to the Caribbean although it was Carty who adopted St. Croix as his home. Neals and Feelings headed for Guyana. Yet, they remain in the vanguard of a vision to which many other sojourning African American artists were dedicated.

Abramson's youth was spent at Estate Whim. The family house—a stone residence, now unoccupied—belongs to the historic architectural line, the Homestead model buildings. Not surprisingly, it is the neighboring St. Croix Landmarks Society, located at Estate Whim with its Museum and Archives, that hosts the historic 1990's UNESCO Slave Project conference, bringing delegates from as far away as France, Ghana, and Brazil to join Caribbean UNESCO delegates in an ongoing worldwide historic project.

El'Roy Simmonds, a pioneer native Crucian painter and teacher, had studied at Denmark's Royal Danish Kunst Academy (Copenhagen) Intensive Language School K.I.S.S. and, later, New York's Pratt Institute. He set out to create a bold style and a fiercely self-liberating manifesto of images—first, in pen and ink a signatory orange tinge highlighting some part of the otherwise stark canvass. The technical excellence of El'Roy's folk portraits and his graphically abstract *Fort Frederik Series* are without par.

In 1982, Simmonds, assisted by Paul Youngblood, posted a huge (20x40') futuristic mural, "Crucian Eclipse," in Christiansted. Although now partially obscured, it stands as a neighboring portal to Christiansted Town, long before Youngblood flexed his mural skills on the Red Brick public housing building, posting his multi-faceted 1984 mural of Crucian folk hero, D. Hamilton Jackson. Once popularly visible, it has since been erased. It would have stood to amplify the aesthetic presence of D. Hamilton Jackson—as does a lone bust in Christiansted, a rare and enigmatic posting on the National Park Service grounds at Fort Christiansvaern.

Others had helped to articulate this St. Croix muralist tradition which Abramson embraced. Nathaniel Mack had painted his now-notorious 1994 Emancipation mural in the Frederiksted Post Office, had even cast a life-size figure in bronze of Queen Mary.

These muralists teachers closed ranks with Wrenford Grouby's mural "Bob Marley" in Grove Place; and the late Lloyd "Dove" Braffith's self-taught renderings of our architecture and his earlier folklife series.

In the broader arena of post-Sixties New York City Art, as African American artists strove to infuse Contemporary American Art with ancestral icons, pyramidal landscapes were best seen in Olugebefola's 1972 crossroads-bound drawing, "Atomic Thought Vision Sound." Against this, a geometric essay on several planes surfaced again in his 1976 collage "Pyramidical Equation with Eye of Ra." Along with another 1972 thunderbolt drawing, "Unison," it establishes Olugebefola as the best graphical surveyor of this field. Olugebefola's pyramidal vision proves more exquisite with his 1989 masterpiece, a collage titled "Assemblage." Its pharaoh-like figure in the foreground, echoing Reiss's commanding Aztec-like visage of African Fantasy, also hints at Hansen's 1928 photograph of Lindbergh's landing in the Virgin Islands. It was as though Olugebefola answered, definitively, to the Cartesian draftsmanship of Margarita Vargas's pyramidal arrangement in her "Door: Honor to the Ancients."

III

"He told me to come back home (St. Croix). 'The city is too hard for you,' he said. 'Go back, Griles, boy.' That's what he said to me. Now, I take care of the only thing he left us—his mural."
         — Isidore Griles (Mural Preservationist/St.
         Croix Folk Musician)

Nestled in the valley between the mythically named Wheel of Fortune and Mars Hill, St. Croix, is the 60x20' mural, "Queen Mary: A Dream of Life and Victory." Abramson, encouraged by school principal and community band musician, James Sealey, painted the mural in his childhood neighborhood school, the Alexander Henderson Elementary School. On a 1973 visit to the school, and a short distance from his father's house, he gives the Virgin Islands its only visual glimpse of his intricate art: its posting. Each morning, with the sunlight pouring in, as alternately theatrical glow and dim, the Abramson mural is animated serving as a backdrop to urgent whisperings and glances down the school's crossroads hallways.

I have twice assisted in preserving Abramson's only existing Virgin Islands mural. In 1997, Raymond Ross, my former 1966 photography colleague at then College of the Virgin Islands, first sent me pictorial evidence that Abramson's mural existed at his school. An astute student of Caribbean children's literature, Ross intrinsically understood this important posting; Abramson's mutual bond had reunited us. Ross wrote:

It was restored by the Virgin Islands Council on the Arts. 'May be worthwhile to speak to Mr. Ulric Carrington on St. Croix. He seems to be a 'force' behind the creation of the mural. Let me know if you need more shots. 'Wall prevented me from getting the whole mural with my camera. Sorry for the delay.
         — R. Ross

Raymond Ross, like Abramson, was born in New York City of Crucian parentage, and had returned to spend his youth in Frederiksted, St. Croix. Ross made annual pilgrimages to New York City attending Children's Literature conferences; but he also attended cultural events and institutions in Harlem.

On that first Friday afternoon visit, as I arrived from neighboring St. Thomas with my lighting cables and Lowell lights, Ross greeted me like it was in our old college times. He introduced me to Isidore Grilles, the school's maintenance engineer and friend of the late Abramson. Griles, a community folk musician, had stayed with Abramson after his US Army stint, but he was encouraged to return to St. Croix. Now, in the spirit of their childhood friendship, and of his own lifelong commitment to the collection and preservation of native art forms, he became a veritable guardian of the mural and its legacy.

Though many symbols of Abramson's mural whisper his twin heritages, a white horse, so reminiscent of Romare Bearden's1974 "Fall of Troy," registers Abramson's stewardship with his Arts Students League alumna. The hedgehog silhouette of gingerbread houses allude to the phoenix spirit of his mother's Frederiksted Town.

In 1998, I would bear a check from this modest St. Croix elementary school to a copper engraving company on New York's Sixth Avenue and 32nd Street—a crucial scissors-crossing of Sixth Avenue and Broadway—a second floor shop, facing my grandfather's Twenties furrier store. In exchange for this ironical reminiscence, I bore away a copy of Coreen Simpson's full-sized profile of Abramson, wearing friend David Hammons' top hat. It is now embedded in the wall, beside the school's mural. Its legend, which I crafted, reads:

Charles Oliver Abramson: painter, son, priest, father, husband, teacher, Babalu-aiye. 6/11/45 — 5/23/88

Abramson's two other Crucian murals have disappeared under a benign neglect policy towards public space art; in fact, territorial agency employees routinely paint over murals by outstanding Virgin Island artists. Regrettably, there have been public debates about images painted by our students of art; some art teachers have been deemed pariahs by the official art barons for posting black images in public spaces and instructing students in this lofty mural tradition.

IV

"Black is, 'cause Black ain't ain't."
— Charles Oliver Abramson

In the mid Eighties a decade before leaving New York City, I frequently met Abramson dressed impeccably in white clothing. He was fulfilling the requirements for his receivership of the rank Babalu-aiye. He had already received his priestly rank of Obe Ogun in the Awo Osu Society, initiated as a Yoruba priest, Ibu Oknala, in 1978.

As we walked through the crowds of Times Square, climbing backdoor stairs to pay his Set Designer Guild dues, Abramson intermittently checked sets with professional stagehands at several Broadway theaters.

Abramson had long-contributed to the post-1960s renaissance of the National Black Theater, as well as to the American Broadway Musical Theater traditions.

O'Neal Able, a photographer and Master Dancehall Instructor, with a catechism of the Palladium dance Mambo steps, was an artist with strong Virgin Islands family ties to the island of St. John. O'Neal knew Abramson. O'Neal was a much-sought dance instructor at the time of the famed 1981 Lena Horne production, *The Lady and her Music*, a Broadway review production of her musical career. Abramson's set designing skills were associated with the award-winning production.

Similarly, when the revamped 1975 Broadway production of *The Wiz* invited aboard Director Geoffrey Holder, the theater émigré extraordinaire from Trinidad, production managers sought new set technicians like Abramson for the radically spatial Tony Award-winning production at the Virginia Theatre.

I remember accompanying Abramson backdoor to the set of *Dream Girls*, a 1980s breakthrough of an American musical, allegedly adapted from the Motown Records "Supremes" pop legend. Only Ossie Davis's 1971 musical production *Pearlie* and Melvin van Peebles's 1973 one-man musical production *Ain't Suppose To Die A Natural Death* preceded its long consecutive-week run.

Abramson's priestly stewardship, posting vibrant murals of light and spectral vision across New York City, included neighborhoods in Harlem, Brooklyn, the Bronx and the Lower East

Side. I remember seeing murals painted by Abramson at Second Avenue and Houston Street (an Eastern European community); Lexington Avenue and 125th Street (an Hispanic community); Amsterdam Avenue and 130th Street (an African American community).

Once, on the eve of Nelson Mandela's release, when the clash between street merchants and the police had grown especially severe, Abramson brought his step-ladder and started painting a beautiful mural of pastel colors on the underground garage of the New York State Office Building. Perhaps the outrage of the merchants had been fuelled by recent triumphs: the regeneration of the Apollo Theater; the Harlem visit of Mandela; the eve of the election of Harlem-based NYC Mayor Dinkins; and State Senate election of Adam Clayton Powell, Jr., Abramson sketched and painted his last mural on 125th Street. A powerful ritual of faces and figurative poses recreated across the wooden facades; partial friezes moving horizontally and, sometimes, scrolling vertically, when the motorized garage doors were activated.

Consider one typical space where Charles posted his now triple text of prophetic scriptural messages and subtle interlocking sacred and secular traditions. It is posted at the Church of Believers of the Commandments of God, at Broadway Avenue and 127th Street, nestled next to a neighborhood funeral home, and showered in the laced shadow of the elevated Broadway subway tracks. In an open-book motif, floating in the white fleecy clouds, are the painted scriptures—excerpts of the Book of King James Bible: St. John and Isaiah on the twin frontal windows. On the rear window, Abramson posted Hebrews.

There are firstly, the obviously interdicting texts of Charles' illuminating mission: "Marvel not that I said unto thee, Ye must be born again." (John 3: 7); "Come now, and let us reason together, saith the Lord: though your sins be as scarlet, they shall be as white as snow; though they be red like crimson, they shall be as wool." (Isaiah 1:18); "Are they not all ministering spirits, sent forth to minister for them who shall be heirs of salvation?" (Hebrews 1:14).

V

"I see myself as an African American. I say 'African American,' because I'm living in America; and my heritage is African. And, 'African America' because the two cultures are meeting within me."

Interview: Daniel Dawson, 1979

It is without great surprise that I discover Abramson's work, post-mortem, in the annals of post-Twentieth Century Afro-Americana, embodying Thompson's Yale lectures.

In The Smithsonian Institution, in the voluminous category where his file exists, his stewardship is self-explanatory: "Artists Collaborating in the 20th Century." In a file (Artist Files, 1978-1984) he is catalogued, rightfully, with his peers David Hammons and Jorge Luis Rodriguez. [Smithsonian Institution Archives Record Unit 481, Box 26, Folder 2.] This category only hints at Abramson's erstwhile impact and formidable integrity.

Robert Farris Thompson, a leading and prolific scholar of African American Art at Yale University, wrote of Abramson's work. His 1985 article, "Santos Del Monte: An Impression of the Work of Jorge Luis Rodriguez and Charles Abramson," is an exhibition review of Abramson and Rodriguez at the Museum of Contemporary Hispanic Art in New York City. Thompson wrote:

New York Afro-Catholic consciousness, moving always in terms of the creative exchange of idiom and ideas, is accelerating. At the vanguard of this seething world stand Jorge Luis Rodriguez and Charles Abramson. (1)

Thompson writes a lengthy essay complimenting the exhibition's catalog on which appears a striking black figure, *El Nino de Atocha*, "transformed by the Yoruba of Cuba into a patron of the childish and irrepressible elements that dwell in all of us and over which the Yoruba trickster, Elegua, traditionally presides. Rodriguez's Africanizing interpretation of the child-saint is strikingly complex: the saint holds a basket, and a staff to which a calabash is affixed, behind him." Thompson reminds us in Iberia the calabash symbolizes pilgrimages while pointing out that Rodriguez has the saint perched on one foot, "about to start dancing." Thompson is meticulous, cataloging the Nigerian Yoruba tradition's meaning of *elese kan* (one-footed dancing), echoing "an ancient Yorubaland dance on a single foot, held among the

Egbado to symbolize the breaking out of argument and dissension not to be ended until Elegba has placed both feet securely on the ground."

Then, Thompson adds this counter-profile of Abramson's remarkable contribution:

Charles Abramson, himself one of the most important avatars of the renaissance of New York sacred Yoruba and Kongo art, in effect furthers the allusions to the child-like propensities of Elegua by garnishing shrubs before the icon of the dancing saint with 'candies and dolls and all the things Elegba would take.' It is not an altar in a conventional sense, then, with frontal icon and tiers. The wall becomes the altar and the mixture of living greens and flashing baubles for a child are particles of visual speech, praising and qualifying the impact of this most important transatlantic deity. (1)

Thompson in his 1987 "Rediscovered Masterpieces of African Art" published by the Dapper Foundation in Belgium, further wrote of Abramson in a long essay, "People of the Word: Remarks on Yoruba and Yoruba-Atlantic Art." In a section, entitled "Coda: Honey is the Knife—The Answering Yoruba Vision of Charles Abramson," he affixes him to one of the most prominent Cuban folk artists of the twentieth century:

[Manual] Mendive has a kindred spirit, a leading Afro-American artist in New York City: Charles Abramson. I consider the work of Abramson at this point because it follows so logically, and so closely, the charm and intensity of Mendive. (52)

Thompson points us to one seminal clue about Abramson's spiritual initiation. "In 1975, he was introduced to New York's Yoruba religious life by Stephanie Weaver, priestess of Obatala, and also an artist. She played Orisha-oriented music by Justi Barreto, a black Cuban composer, while she painted." Abramson had taken me to meet African Cuban Tania Leon, a leading New York composer working with the Brooklyn Symphonic Orchestra, as well as several concurrent Broadway productions.

By 1978, Abramson's peers, with Black Critic Larry Neal among them, were struggling with folklore and reincarnation. Neal, who was considered the architect of the Black Aesthetic, had issued forth a strategic connection between the Blues and the emergence of Yoruba deities:

The blues god's an attempt to isolate the blues element
as an ancestral force, as the major ancestral force of the
Afro-American. What I always say about the blues god
is that was the god that survived the middle passage. It's
like an Orisha figure.

— *Drum Magazine*, 1978: 11

Then, just after Abramson's enlightenment, Thompson chronicles his encounter with Abramson in that pivotal year, 1978, when
the artist becomes initiated ("Ibu Okanla") Priest of the Sun, by his
Godmother, Sunta Ascencion Serrano ("Osu Unko"). Abramson
solo exhibits a water-shedding piece, "Esu Ebo," at the Cinoe
Gallery. (The exhibition would later go on tour at the Brooklyn
Academy of Music, in Brooklyn, New York.) Thompson, author of
the 1983 groundbreaking tome *Flash of the Spirit: African and
Afro-American Art and Philosophy*, writes most perceptively of the
urban maelstrom in which Charles' flashing wit and brilliance
thrived: "Three years later, Abramson was exhibiting an image of
Elegua Laroye, at Fifth Avenue and 14th Street in all that com-
merce, in all that people, a perfect setting for him."

By 1981, when Abramson was an Artist in Residence at the
Studio Museum in Harlem, he had traveled—in just the previous
year—to Watts Tower Arts Center in Los Angeles, California for his
exhibition, "Shadow Dac." He also painted a mural there.

As Artist in Residence at the Studio Museum in Harlem,
Abramson had a show, "Spaces V," of installation pieces with
David Hammons and Jorge Rodriguez. Hammons told me in a
hallowed tone, so reminiscent of Abramson's voice:

There were many abandoned buildings in the surrounding area at the time of our residence at the Studio
Museum in Harlem. We gathered about 50 large boxes
of abandoned material. We found some mosaic tiles,
which we glued to sofas, walls, any surface. It was the
last installation before the museum moved from the old
neighborhood. (Phone conversation, April 2004)

William Zimmer, a reporter enamored with a romantic image
of Harlem, "The Cotton Club and the young Ella Fitzgerald" era,
wrote this about the exhibit in *The Soho News* (1981):

Having no real title, the installation is the collaborative
effort of Charles Abramson, David Hammons and Jorge
Rodriguez—all artists-in-residence at the museum this
year. The three obviously got along swimmingly, which
is appropriate to an installation that would fit nicely into

an Olympic-size swimming pool. They merged their specialties and styles while suspending their egos, and very early on in the experience of the installation, the viewer ceases to be concerned with who made what and goes with the flow.

Zimmer gets eloquent, carried along in this environment. He waxes mytho-poetic about what he feels, some of it hauntingly contemporary.

The feathers and tiles immediately conjure ancient splendor, imparting the feeling of an African Islamic kingdom. But the fragmented character of the tiled areas indicates that paradise has been lost, or at least displaced to make way for something more contemporary. The tiled areas on the floor are a multitude of islands, an archipelago. At the entrance of the installation is a crate of detritus obviously taken from one of the neighborhood's many hollow-eyed tenement buildings. Such buildings had classy art deco detailing like the tiles and bathroom remnants— and the three artists have used this salvaged material to summon a magical Africa. . .For the record, the special contribution of Abramson was most likely anything that resonates clearly of Africa, for he is currently engaged in painting a Yoruba myth over a hundred panels.

Then, Zimmer makes the remarkable adaptation of Ishmael Reed's series of essays, *Shrovetide in Old New Orleans*, to the interiority of this Abramson/Rodriguez installation experience:

Reed's outlook could be that of the Studio Museum artists, when he writes: 'I see life as mysterious, holy, profound, exciting, serious and fun. The so-called humor which appears in my work is affirmative, positive. It teaches me to be humble.'

VI

By the Eighties, the Modern Black Arts Renaissance in the United States, and the nascent South African national theater, had begun to fuse, mightily or vice versa. Abramson elucidated this in his 1987 exhibit, "Defeat of My Enemies through Witchcraft, Presented by Dr. Buzzard," at the TWO RAW Gallery in New York City.

Robert Thompson elucidates this exhibit, prophetically, and with great critical refraction of Abramson's interior psyche:

Thus in one exhibit of the early Eighties, meant to combat the multiple witchcrafts of racism, he refracted his own image photographically over and over again. This recalls modern-traditional photography among the Yoruba in Nigeria. (Rediscovered African Masterpieces 527)

(But Abramson had been struck by photography in the late Sixties, and its transformational power early, during his Vietnam stint, when Armed Forces overseas personnel relied heavily on the *Stars and Stripes* newspaper. He had seen the era's under-representation: how cameras as accomplices helped race divide America against itself. And it was through contemporary American art and cultural thinking, started in the 1960s and 1970s, that reclaimed images used in collages and employed large-scale in murals began to inform the national landscape.)

Thompson reminds us that "Abramson in the Spring was working on an altar for Oshun. 'My road to Oshun,' he told me, 'is Kole. She moves where the vulture moves.'" This, apparently, is Thompson's recollection of Mendive's image of her. Abramson continues, "In this camino she destroys what needs destroying. She sweetens and illumines the world with honey. Honey is the knife; she cuts with sweetness, she cuts with love." Thompson is relentless in his outpouring of the twin-heritage aesthetic, shared by Mendive, the Cuban painter, and Abramson, the New Yorker, born of Virgin Islands parents. "Abramson works in spiritual affinity with Manuel Mendive. As Abramson brings a pot of honey and places it on an altar for Oshun in Brooklyn, he knows he is adding, to her image, the necessary wildness, the necessary alive which activates and safeguards her mercy." (527)

Thompson's witnessing is a rekindling between two peoples, since the 1968 Welterweight class boxing classic was remembered as a tragic metaphor of Pan-Caribbean collisions. Cuban champion, Benny "Kid" Paret, and Virgin Islander world champion, Emile Griffith, fought to a tragic end. Despite Griffith's generous overture to Paret's family—a psychic shattering was long felt.

Once again, in his 1993 classic book, *Face of the Gods: Art and Altars of Africa and the African Americas*, Thompson displays Abramson's Altar to Shango in a chapter titled "Shango: Storm on the Edge of the Knife." Thompson chronicles the diversionary paths for Yoruba manifestations in two of the world's largest African-populated cities—two strongholds for the deity's presences.

In both Brazil and New York an extension of the thunder god's power and mystery has been discovered in electricity itself. The stratagems are simple: in one Umbanda center in Maceio, when a priest begins to sing the praises of Xango he turns on a redlight, flooding the altar, filled with oricha/saints, with the color of the god's righteous fire. And, in Brooklyn, in the winter of 1985, the late Charles Abramson captured in red paint on white sheeting a giant silhouette of Chango with looming axes on his head. This he caused to be back-lit, giving the impression that Chango himself stood behind the cloth, guarding an altar elaborated within a closet. (240, 242)

Under the right edge of Abramson's double axe, hangs a white shirt on the outside of the closet, emphasizing the double occupancy of two worlds.

Yet, instructively, we cannot overlook Abramson's remarkable curatorship in the "One-Plus-One" exhibition, a collaborative event between Black female and male artists at the Dr. Martin Luther King, Jr. Cultural Center in New York City.

VII

African Arts published a 1999 article featuring auspicious remarks by Dr. Lowery Stokes Sims, now Chief Curator of the Studio Museum in Harlem. Dr. Sims had correctly cited Abramson in a 1998 Metropolitan Museum of Art symposium, "Perspectives on African Art: A Dialogue with 'Tradition.'" Dr. Sims and Alisa LaGamma had organized the symposium's conclusion around a panel, "Contemporary Artists: Issues of Individuality and Tradition."

It was ten years since Charles Abramson's death. Dr. Sims, an expert in Twentieth Century Art, placed his name correctly in the company of his peers:

We invited three important presences on the contemporary art scene—Arturo Lindsay, Jose Bedia, and Manuel Vega—to discuss their involvement with concepts, beliefs and aesthetics that are grounded in traditional African art and culture, specifically that of the Yoruba.

Dr. Sims, who was then the only African American 20th Century Modern Art curator at the Metropolitan Museum of Art, continued her opening statement on the panel:

> In my opening statement, I noted the context for this discussion could be found in the 1996 publication 'Santeriia Aesthetics in Contemporary Latin American Art' edited by professor Lindsay. Lindsay also contributed an essay in which he outlines some of the main points that predicate the consideration of the work of these artists and their contemporaries who have been interested in marrying their cultural realities with the imperatives of western critical paradigms, be they modern or postmodern. The pioneer in this effort was the Cuban artist, Wlifredo Lam, who in the 1940s conceived a sysnthesis of Cubism, Surrealism, and motifs from the Afro-Cuban philosophy and religion known as Lucumi or Santeria.

Whenever I read this passage, I am forced to remember Andre Breton's post-Algerian War sojourn along with his provocative advocacy of Surrealism, including in Surrealism's intellectual constellation the Haitian "art schools of the Bush," when he discovered the Haitian folk master painters, Bigaud, Jacmel and others.

Dr. Sims amplified her insights and threw-down challenge to some of the finest contemporary artists present, and sitting on the panel:

> This process of introducing cultural specificity into the language of contemporary art was continued by a number of artists in the 1960s and '70s, the best known being the Cuban-born Ana Mendieta, Carlos Alfonso, Juan Boza; the Puerto Rican-born Jorge Rodriguez; and the African American artist Charles Abramson.
>
> ("Art as a Verb" catalog)

Dr. Sims and Dr. Leslie King-Hammond, perennial scholars, were co-curators of a two part exhibition, "Art as a Verb." The exhibition ran from November 1988 to January 8, 1989, a year after Abramson's death. According to a joint statement, it was a concept and theme they had earlier developed, and expressed thusly:

> These artists firmly focus on the dilemmas of their existence within the technological society of the United States at the end of the 20th Century.
>
> ("Art as a Verb" catalog)

Together they co-wrote further, these pioneering artists' legacy has already begun to take root in the word of the younger Afro-American artists who are beginning to come to the attention of the art world.

Barbara Price of the Maryland Institute, College of Art, wrote then of the 13 showcased African American artists:

They were artists who operate outside the main-stream of the contemporary currents of the art world, yet are very contemporary and represent most of the dynamic work being done by artists in the black community.

Abramson's belated profile—tributes by colleagues, with two striking photographs—is the first entry of the "Art is A Verb" exhibition catalog.

Even here, existentially, Abramson literally kept his eye on the present, while appraising the narratives of the past. The 1983 photograph these co-curators respectfully included in their 1988 catalog shows Abramson lighting an installation, "Palo Mayombe," at the opening reception of Fred L. Emerson Gallery's exhibit, *The Regentrified Jungle*. Dr. Sims and Dr. King-Hammond thereby facilitate Abramson's image and presence—still enlightening the gathering ever-present eye on the present work at hand.

One of Abramson's last created works is a 1988 installation, "Homage to Jack Johnson" (mixed media on Installation board) at the Urd Decker Gallery, Maryland Institute of Art, Baltimore. It shows a large white room, its wall festooned with black shapes and red-pistils. In the room's center, and situated on a black eight-pointed star, sits a wire-mesh cage with a rooster poised between two feeding bowls. One can surmise they are filled with corn feed and water. Yet, the row of flickering lit candles creates a life-force border between the self-stalking rooster and its silhouetted death-flight shadowings on the walls. This shows how Abramson not only created the rarefied space of mediation between the physical world and the temporal realm, but the cautionary tale between the caged fighting rooster and its inflamed destiny.

Kelly Jones, Visual Art Director, Jamaica Arts Center, New York City, paid this tribute to Abramson's life: "Abramson worked from an Afro-centric perspective although he also appreciated Western abstract art, particularly surrealism. Art was extremely personal to him, paintings and installations were private explanations of life and dreams."

Homage to Jack Johnson

Photo courtesy of Urd Decker Gallery,
Maryland Institute of Art, Baltimore

Charles Abramson

Wey' Pa Butty Dem?:
Repositioning the Poles — A New Consciousness and Cultural Identity Politics

Clement White

So meson' ah was wondering "Wey Butty"?
Because 'tis a long time ah ain hear from he.
Wha he name say he see him some place one day,
Walkin' wid he han' behin' he back, he wen down by dey
    bay.

He don been to housin' and talk to dey lil' ones dem dey,
Done do he rhyme dem; ah need to find him right away.
Bu' ah carn find Butty at' all no matter how hard ah look;
And remember, nobardy ain' evar put he name ever in no
    book.

I came to this poetic moment in the 1970's when I was obsessed with the notion of personal legitimation of the Virgin Islands cultural codes. In reality, I was fighting a silent, maniacal battle which can be best characterized as an impulse to reappropriate our cultural signs and relocate them in a space that would allow me, I thought, a kind of mental reconfiguration of Virgin Islands culture. I was re-visiting *Butty*! During the 1950's I, along with many other Virgin Islands children, had sat down in Savan, the Pearson Gardens Housing Project, and other areas and listened to *Butty*—a rather surreal St. Thomian, who was very real at the core. This mystical man of mythical proportions frequently walked the streets of the island, shoeless, adorned with a rope as his belt, and girded with many shirts and various pairs of trousers. His was a simple mission, one of love, of educating, driven only by a strong sense of African, Caribbean, Virgin Islands, and "West Indianness." Butty spoke non-stop from his deep reservoir of knowledge and his infinite well of culture, and oral traditions. His oral performances were so sophisticated that in retrospect I can now see that the form of elaboration approached the level of the message; content and art merged with gratifying results for his appreciative audience. For Butty, then, and subliminally for us his young listeners, the art of telling was not at all merely tangential or peripheral to the multiple folk themes that he narrated.

In point of fact, the primacy of the form, of repetition, of suspense, of alliteration, of biting irony only added to the constant creation of a kind of cultural-mythical matrix. It was folk telling at its best. He told of Shango, Oshun, and Obatalá, Bru Nancy, Tuckama, Yemaya, Queen Mary, the Jumbie, and the Obeah Man. He interwove moments of Virgin Islands history, juxtaposing them with Virgin Islands myth and often transfixing, transferring and relocating them in an African context. Butty was the Master of the masters! What happened to Butty, Shango, and the Obeah Man?

I would like to situate Virgin Islands folk tradition within a wider overarching cultural problematic, and show that the dislocation of these figures is not at all arbitrary. Our cultural lines have been blurred and problematized by our duplicitous relationship with the United States. Seen in the framework of post-colonial discourse, Virgin Islands culture has been subverted by the hegemonic imposition of a super culture that continues to cause us to interrogate the very grounding of our own local culture. The consequences of this are grave for they have aided and abetted in our gradual distancing from our other Caribbean neighbors, and have created the most ghastly, painful fear—the fear of ourselves. In the Virgin Islands after the Fountain Valley tragedy in the early 1970's, the deluge of philosophical, social, and political debates have asphyxiated themselves in abstraction because they have been decontextualized from the cultural upheaval seething in the underbelly of an ever shifting culture. Indeed, paramount to our understanding of ourselves is a compulsory relocation of culture as central—a kind of re-contouring of our cultural and identity politics. This re-centering, and re-situating would not impinge on, nor invalidate other existing realities. For example, it would not (nor even could not) deny that the United States Virgin Islands exhibit traits that are characteristically American. However, it would emphasize and accentuate our "West Indian selves," for too many years subjugated by prevailing concocted socio-political and cultural ideologies and incessant ideologues. So, "wey Butty?" What happened to the Green Face Man that Butty narrated?:

The Green Face Man was all about;
The Devil knew him well, there was no doubt.
You couldn't find him in the day; he was always out of sight;
My father told me once he had seen him in Savan one night.

Daddy was on patrol wid dey police lookin' fo' him.
According to Daddy the Green Face Man climbed trees
And jumped from Limb to limb.

Then he would return anew to scare de life out-a all ah we;
Butty say he belong' to Satan—'cause he was God's adver-
sary!

In the 1950's people spoke incessantly about this figure,
rumored to be seen by many, but, of course, having no specific
point of origin. Yet, we claimed him as our own—part of our West
Indian being. But, as Virgin Islanders, we have fallen prey to the
not so subtle subversive ideology that has convinced us of the
idiocy of our own folktales. We began to suppress our cultural
sentiments, relegating them to the deepest enclaves of our subconscious, afraid that if they reveal themselves, they will ultimately expose us—tell us who we are. In actuality, then, the
Green Face Man did not really disappear. We misappropriated
him in our schizophrenic zeal to subscribe to the tenets of what
Louis Althusser refers to as the ISA—or Ideological State
Apparatus.[1] We practice the rituals of the apparatus—the rituals
of self-delusion and self-deception. The Green Face Man's dis-
placement is closely tied to our own penchant at disavowing our
Caribbeaness. Contemporary essentialist debates on the essence
of Virgin Islands identity locate at center stage political and geographical interplay but largely ignore, by conscious design or by
subconscious fear, the crossing and crisscrossing of cultural
boundaries between the U.S. Virgin Islands and our neighbors.
Such debates ignore culture as a common denominator and con-
nector. Essentialist notions of a "Virgin Islander" place our history on the backburner and fallaciously attempt to define us
through legal and constitutional constructions. Thus, the new,
anti-historical definition of the Virgin Islands emerges uniquely
and almost exclusively affixed to our "territorial," colonial, relationship to the United States. Such modern interpretations of who
we are, forged from within the context of a shadowy hegemonic
reality, have created the nomenclature that ultimately defines us.
But definitions rising out of this limited and proscribed United
States-Virgin Islands interplay, by their very nature, de-empha-
size, devalue, and discourage Virgin Islands and West Indian inter-
sections. It is essentially this construction, resulting from dominant ideologies, that is responsible for the cultural and traditional
distancing often seen on our islands.

This is not meant to ignite an irresolvable quarrel concerning the current political debates stirring on our islands on the definition of a Virgin Islander. Instead, the intent is to argue that our creation of a binary paradigm of exclusivity is problematic. In essence, by claiming the Obeah Man do we, then, disclaim the "hechicera"[2] or Vodoo man? I recall that my grandmother, who was Nevisian, would mix Crucian folktales with anecdotes and beliefs centered in the annals of Nevis folk tradition of the early part of the last century. Simultaneously she claimed her *nevisianess* through the Nevisian folk songs and socio-cultural history while affirming her *Crucianess* and her *Virgin Islandness*. Each time she proclaimed her *Nevisianess* she also de-essentialized me, and I became Caribbean-Nevisian-Virgin Islander, cultural lines which intersect at various points, and run parallel at others. Our cultural inner linings are in constant hemorrhaging, symptomatic of the ruptures suffered from the pulling away from our West Indian "selves," a kind of identity crisis nurtured from the blood lines of a history of contradictions and distractions. It is a strange, polarizing dynamic which results from being marginalized and "othered," yet somehow feeling privileged, a clear inversion linked to the collision of our culture and that of the United States. The false consciousness and the resulting fragmentation of our self-image conspire against our impulse to seek refuge in the enclaves of our surrounding neighbors' cultures—which in their reflective capacity ultimately would show us our true selves. For we know that once we can relocate the lines of intersection then we gradually become whole. It is within this space of renewed consciousness that the Virgin Islands can truly begin to comprehend the totality of who we really are.

Does this mean, then, that in this journey toward a new consciousness the Virgin Islander will be transformed into an Antiguan? Puerto Rican? Nevisian? A Cuban? If this is our concern, then we implicate ourselves in the debate, admitting by default that our embracing of American culture while distancing ourselves from the rest of the Caribbean, speaks to a greater fear: the fear that recognizing ourselves in other Caribbean folk traditions somehow makes us cultural appendages of the United States, subtextualized as secondary characters. What happened to Butty and his folk narratives? Where is the Obeah Man? They have themselves become "othered" and marginalized in a cultural backlash where we gradually shifted in constant flux to fit the paradigm of our notions of true Americanism. Part of this paradigm includes by praxis the rule that the association with the Big Primary culture implicitly demands the dissociation from the Small Secondary culture. The Obeah Man has lost his way, and so did Shango! To some extent they lost their way due to a cadre of cultural operatives. I remember them all too well—these operatives who spewed a kind of distasteful venom of oppositional cultural politics, the focal point of which was axiomatic: *The Virgin Islands have no story to tell. You have no narrative.* In our islands, folk narratives gradually became, as Shakespeares's Macbeth tells it, like: "tale[s] told by idiots, full of sound and fury, signifying nothing."[3] The 19th century Argentine writer, Domingo Faustino Sarmiento in his explication of Argentina's so called "*atraso cultural*," or cultural backwardness, points to what he terms barbaric cultures and civilizations, among them indigenous peoples, gauchos, and Blacks. He argued that the only salvation for a bright Argentine future was the suppression of these cultures, for the europeanization of Latin American culture.[4] Sarmiento's attempt at socio-culture analysis of Argentine and Latin American reality was unmistakably intertwined with ideological distortions, which rendered the non-European as inherently barbaric.

In a similar way, and through the Ideological State Apparatuses, to use the althussearean model, such as schools and churches[5] we in the Virgin Islands too were being taught that our narratives were barbaric. This was done through a relentless process of cannibalization of culture. Not surprisingly, then, gradually as Virgin Islands children we began to accept the often unstated dictum that to narrate our folk tradition was to be self-accusatory, for it spoke of one's lack of education, one's ignorance, one's "West Indianness." No doubt, the underlying ideological agenda collided and conflicted with our own struggles to authenticate ourselves.

Interestingly enough, though, a closer look at the cultural dynamics of the 1950's reveals a secret, well kept and persevered in an ironic mold. For while school children were being explicitly or implicitly distanced from our folk traditions and those of the rest of the Caribbean, older folks were going to Guadalupe, Haiti, the Dominican Republic where they sought intervention by the Obeah Man and where they were also able to see themselves reflected in the narratives of those islands. This was a confidence builder for a people who deep in their spirits did not wish to be complicit in the dislocation and rupturing of our cultural blood vessels. Their pilgrimages to these neighboring islands tacitly confirmed that there has always been resistance to the ongoing process of cultural fragmentation. Anthropologist Fernando Ortiz, poet Nicolás Guillén, and short story writer Lydia Cabrera, each in his or her own literary medium emphasizes the African presence in Cuba. Ortiz, in a thorough, if at times patronizing study, traces the island's beliefs and folk traditions to Lucumi[6] roots. While Guillén in such works as *West Indies, Ltd*, and the *Entire Son* challenges the prevailing negative notions of Cuban folk traditions by bringing these traditions to poetic center stage.[7] Cabrera validates folk traditions, incorporating them in her text as central motif and protagonizing them in a kind of thematic schema. I posit that the works of these literary giants reflect *Butty*, and I see in them the same ethos represented in our folk traditions.

Like Butty's narratives, Cabrera's and Guillén's works delve into the psyche of a people who cling to deep-seated beliefs, which circumscribe and define them. As preservers of culture, whether writers or oral elaborators, they become cultivators of mythic consciousness, or to quote K.K. Ruthven[8], they become "a sort of evolutionary throwback, a living fossil." The obeah man or woman who boils bush, fixated on a singular purpose of claiming another as property is not unique to Virgin Islands lore. He roams the Cuban text, the Brazilian narratives, and shows his face in the Panamanian Carlos Guillermo Wilson's works.[9] He is not exclusively ours—only that we in the Virgin Islands often take special steps to maintain sharp cultural lines of demarcation, to keep him apart. For in so doing, we essentialize ourselves as Virgin Islanders—tacitly constructing a paradigm which in short reads: 1) they are not Americans, 2) they are not a part of who we are, thus 3) they do not reflect us. In point of fact, however, Butty's obeah woman shares center stage with the Cuban hechicera.

Also etched in the annals of Virgin Islands lore is the legend of a rather mysterious phenomenon—"the box." For those not familiar with this tale, I offer this brief chronology. According to this folktale, a box appeared one day on the St. Thomas waterfront. Its unique nature lay in the belief that it had no well-identified place of origination, or mode of transportation from point to point. It was axiomatic that its transference from one location to another was accomplished through a mysterious process, understood only though an allegiance to and comprehension of our islands' cultural signs. Through a kind of cultural consensus, there were at least five intrinsic truths: 1) the box by its very appearance was inherently evil, 2) it was incapable of being probed or scrutinized adequately, 3) its presence was clearly linked to an act by an obeah man or woman, 4) the intended target was by no means a collective one, but an individual who probably suspected his or her own susceptibility, 5) the box had a designated duration period, known only by the conspirators and co-conspirators:

The box was square, or round, or oval some had said;
No one lifted it, but it was light as a feather or heavy like lead.
It was seeking vengeance for a deed unknown,
Most likely for some evil deed that had been sown.

No one saw it, but every one saw it up close;
It could transfigure you, especially if it saw you as foe.
Everyone kept a distance from this object, seen and unseen,
For it could cause misery—this box, so obscene.

But then, suddenly, the box sort of went away;
No one could tell where, no one could say.
Supposedly to another isle for more vengeance sake;
It was heresy to consider this thing a fake.

What happened to the box? Did it truly disappear? No, its absence in the narratives of our islands can be traced to the penchant for disconnection and disassociation. Today, as Virgin Islanders, most of us are probably not willing to discuss such a phenomenon with any degree of seriousness because it points the trigger back at us. It creates for us a position of awkwardness and reawakens in our subconscious that tragic state of cultural denial. The box, with its undetermined contour, origin, and questionable aim best metaphorizes our own uncertainties, and through a symbolic gesture this real, or imagined object, reminds us of our cultural conflicts. In the 1960's, talk of the box was commonplace conversation among islanders. In general, there was no inhibiting sense of relating one's knowledge of this object. On the contrary, people were persistent in relating their own awareness of the supposed origins and possible ultimate destinations of the box. In contemporary Virgin Islands society to now express such an interest, or worse, such a belief, would be self-incriminatory, an acknowledgement of an adherence to a cultural system which the dominant culture convinced us was linked to the "uncivilized."

Translation: "Such backward beliefs are connected to Africa, to Lucumi, to the Congo." So in this psycho-philosophical milieu what eventually happened to the Box? Essentially, it went the way of Butty, the Jumbie, and the Obeah man. It went the way of the Cow Foot Woman who roamed St. Thomas freely, seeing everyone, meeting no one, and harming none. Now, she too has been de-oralized, the pages of her oral narration unceremoniously ripped apart, and used to hide our confusing images of ourselves.

In the cultural backfirings we have wounded ourselves. But can we still revisit Butty, and reconfigure our cultural signs? Can we find the Obeah Man and Woman and relocate them where they can regain their value and be appreciated? Or, are we as Virgin Islanders doomed to the notion of an essential Virgin Islander, caught somewhere between a frenzied courtship with "Americanness" and the rejection of our Caribbean essence? This is by no means an indictment of the United States, but it dramatizes the fact that the onus is on us to reexamine what it means to be "*American*" in a Caribbean context, an interrogation that should never be considered heretical, blasphemous, or sacrosanct. If in this re-examination we find it necessary to distance ourselves from the Obeah Man and Butty, then our understanding of the relationship between our neighbors and ourselves becomes stuck in the quagmire of cultural distortions. At the base of our self-identify crisis lies a powerful ideology deeply rooted in faulty premises and syllogisms, an ideology which privileges that which is American over any other. As children growing up in the Virgin Islands in the 1950's we were consciously and subconsciously Carribbean—West Indian—Virgin Islander. This in no way represented split personalities but a well constituted identity, each complimenting the other. As the pace of immigration and emigration became more intense, the paradigms began to shift and we began to view ourselves in the context of Washington and New York.

This new way of self-reflection dramatizes the fact that this is ideology at work—at its very best—as Althusser so emphatically posits: "Ideology is a representation of the imaginary relationship of individuals to their real conditions of existence,"[10] the notion of "real" here used in the Marxist sense of an objective reality. In essence, who we are and who we interpret ourselves to be are conflicting realities, emanating from well-established and deeply entrenched ideological roots. It is what results in geographical discrimination and prejudice against other Caribbean peoples; the same mechanization at work yields rejection of that which is considered West Indian, opting for that which is American. Thus, for example, for many years we have been discouraged from speaking in our own local vernacular because, for many, to do so attested to our ignorance, our miseducation, our Caribbeaness. Moreover, admitting that we do in fact speak differently shakes the very foundation of our image of ourselves within the framework of our notion of Americanism, since in point of fact linguistic allegiance is one of the main features of cultural adherence. This socio-cultural linguistic sabotage created in its subjects feelings of inferiority, conflicting issues of allegiance, and numerous doubts about self-worth. In reality, then, our language (I reject the idea of *dialect* in this debate) was consistently used to pit us against ourselves, to interrogate the very essence of our cultural identity. No one is arguing here the rejection of alternative forms of speech, whether it be American or British. In point of fact, no one would seriously challenge the stance that it is to everyone's advantage to be open to a variety of linguistic mediums. The problem is, however, that we have approached our own language with much trepidation, and its social censorship is inextricably linked to our interrogation of our own self—actualization. In the early 1950's, for example, some missionaries coming to the Virgin Islands were informing the people that singing calypso was sinful, and children were often led to believe that even speaking in our vernacular was somehow linked to some kind of moral corruption.

Consider the fact that there are those who would speak our language only during special occasions, i.e. parties, Carnival, other cultural events. Place this within the context of harboring a secret—"keep it within the home," the family would often think. Many were admonished to speak "calypso" in the house, but not to be heard speaking that "gutter" language outside of the protective confines of family; here was a systematic demonization of speech. The fact that this language is confined to the domestic sphere is a result of a systemic cultural repression, a kind of linguistic imperialism. Its usage in the public domain, for example, in the schools, the churches, the senate, would undoubtedly be considered by the cultural operatives as an act of subversion. The time has come to broaden the spaces to include works of art written in the vernacular, to affirm and validate it, and to move away from the apologetic nature of its elaboration. I argue that it is impossible to reject language without rejecting "self," without disavowing identity, without distancing oneself from who one truly is. Thus, our many years of language annihilation over-lapped with a sustained process of self-victimization. This heavy-laden conscious and automated act ignored for the most part the idea of language as culture, as ideology, and viewed it only as lin-guistic articulation.

What happened to Butty? In many ways many of us are accomplices, participants in his disappearance. We are implicated by our acts of resignation, our posture of silence, by our apathy. There have been too many missed opportunities to provide count-er hegemonic discourses. Too many lost chances to challenge and interrogate our deeply held notions of who we have been defined to be. It is true that our interpretation of ourselves is not at all stat-ic, since in fact culture is always shifting, feinting, slipping. In the case of the Virgin Islands, however, the shifting and the constant motion seems only to move unilaterally. It is a moving away from our Caribbean region, ripping apart from our ontological selves. Educating ourselves and those in our midst, especially our young requires a special commitment, for our journey in comprehending the world must begin with our resolve to know ourselves. As Paulo Freire would argue[11], subjecting our young people, the future standard bearers of our culture, to the mere banking method of teaching, may not be adequate enough to change attitudes. Freire's revolutionary pedagogical approach departs from the lin-guistic and cultural universe of the community. What is required is a purging of sorts, a cultural catharsis. Insisting on our West Indianness inverts the ideology of "American Virgin Islands," reconfigured to read Caribbean Virgin Islands, a cultural/psycho-logical realignment, which does not impose on nationalistic identi-ty. Virgin Islanders in this restructuring of the psyche are not trans-formed into different islanders. Identities are not necessarily exclu-sively constructed; in this cultural mix the inference is not that one must choose one culture over the other. Indeed, there is enough space for the interlocking of various cultures.

The truth is, however, that for many years now many of us have made a conscious effort to erase the West Indianness in us; even though this may very well be an impossibility, the fact is that the mere effort to do so creates a kind of automatization that transforms the conscious into the subconscious. In the final analysis we react, as Foucault would argue, in a mechanized way.

Certainly, Foucault's notion of the Ponopticon is relevant here, as we have succumbed to the constant surveillance[12] of the guardians of culture, the self-made ideological-cultural police who have installed socio-cultural condemnation as their principal method of castigation. This notwithstanding, once we begin our new assertive, affirmative journey, with counter hegemonic and counter ideological postures and strategies, then we will be well on our way to reposition the poles of our culture; to find where the obeah man really roams—there with Shango, Oshun, Obatala, Yemaya, and narrated with dripping, biting suspense and irony by our beloved Butty!

Endnotes

[1] See Louis Althusser's interesting discussion on ideology in "Ideology and Ideological State Apparatuses" in *Critical Theory Since 1965*. Ed. Hazard Adams & Leroy Searle. Tallahassee, Florida: University Press of Florida. 1992. pp. 239-250.

[2] sorcerer; enchanter.

[3] Macbeth's response to Seyton in Act V, Scene V.

[4] For a better understanding of Sarmiento's socio-political ideology read his *Civilization and Barbarism.*

[5] In Althusser's argument there are two broad categories of discussion; one is the Ideological State Apparatus (ISA), and the other is the Repressive State Apparatus (RSA). Whereas the police and the armed forces fall under the second, the church, school, and family fall under the first as they exude an ideology which at times may not always be so obvious. According to Foucault, the ISA functions primarily by ideology, whereas the RSA functions principally by repression. He emphasizes, however, that both (the ISA and RSA) use both repression and ideology; there is just a question of degree.

[6] Yoruba.

[7] Undoubtedly, Guillén's work was groundbreaking, introducing as it were the Black and Mulattoes as poetic protagonists. And in so doing the poet highlights the African aspect of the Afro-Cuban reality.

[8] Ruthven's study *Myth* offers a clear, well formulated discussion of this concept.

[9] In Wilson's fascinating novel *Los nietos de felicidad Dolores* set in Panamá, there are numerous references to obeah. Wilson,

who traces his heritage to the English speaking Caribbean, reveals in his novel century old beliefs with roots in several African countries.

[10] Althusser, p.141.

[11] Paulo Freire's work *The Pedagogy of the Oppressed* is an excellent work which probes pedagogical strategies for overcoming oppression.

[12] In his "Discipline and Punish" (1977) from excerpts in Antony Easthope, & Kate McGowan's *A Critical and Cultural Theory Reader*, Foucault argues that over a period of time, as subjects we react automatically to the norms and dictates of the dominant culture. There comes a point where surveillance is no longer necessary because the automatization of the socio-cultural machinery is already set in its ideological place. This is the mechanization of the subject's activities based on the fear of punishment: ". . .the major effect of Panopticon {is to} induce in the inmate a state of conscious and permanent visibility that assures the automatic functioning of power." (p. 85). . .It [the Ponopticon] is an important mechanism because it automatizes power (p. 86) And echoing Marx and Althusser, "A real subjection is born mechanically from a fictitious relationship." (p. 86)

Bibliography

Althusser, Louis. "Ideology and Ideological State Apparatuses." *Critical Theory Since 1965*. Eds. Hazard Adams & Leroy Searle. Tallahassee, Florida: University Presses of Florida, 1992. pp. 239-250.

Augier, Angel. Nicolás Guillén. *Obra poética: 1922-1958*. Editorial Letras Cubanas, 1980.

Chang Rodriguez. *Latinoamérica: su civilización y cultura*. New York: Harper Collins. 1991.

Focault, Michel, excerpts from "Discipline and Punish" in *A Critical and Cultural Theory Reader*. Easthope, Antony & Kate McGowan, eds. 82-89 Toronto: University of Toronto Press. 1992.

Ruthen, K.K. *Myth*. London: Methuen, 1976.

Wilson, Carlos Guillermo "Cubena." *Los nietos de Felicidad Dolores*. Ediciones Universal. 1991.

BOOK REVIEWS

Nancy Pistilli

Songs of Light and Darkness

Shara McCallum, *Songs of Thieves*. Pittsburg, Pennsylvania: University of Pittsburg Press. 2003. 72 pages. p.b. $12.95.

> "And I grew up fostered alike by beauty and by fear"
> — Wordsworth

Contradictions are often the stuff of life and McCallum's new volume including its telling title, *Song of Thieves*, celebrates contradictions-turned-ironies. The music of nature—the rattle of Caribbean winds, fogs peeling off the ocean's face, rustling cane fields, the clacking of breadfruit leaves, and moonlit silver branches may have fled with maturing years and the move to *foreign* and to snow; but she has preserved them, not by a dynamic painting, but by a potent poetic art. Hers is a controlled contradiction suffused with the seductive lyric quality of her verse. Even in her riddles of folklore, contradiction is evident.

> Lemon tree very pretty
> And the lemon flower so sweet.
> But the fruit of the poor lemon
> is impossible to eat. (33)

Here, appearance is certainly not consonant with reality.

McCallum's poems strike a strong autobiographical note; and issues of racial identity arise because two bloods and cultures appear to meet in the chief persona of the poems who is seemingly a mulatta and probably an octoroon, for: "Blood's the bar I cannot pass" (50). She gropes after wholeness to arrest "coming apart like petals falling from their stem;" and questions of identity are faced head-on: "That face that knows my name: / Is it you? / Is it me?" (48-49) she questions.

The crisis of identity is aggravated by migration, for the poet must navigate the straits between two countries and cultures, indeed between two worlds mirrored in "Autobiography of My Grandmother," by Trinidad and Canada, each with its distinct disadvantages. In both cases, vigorous teachers proffer advice especially regarding the discovery of "the sea between my legs," and she is torn this way and that:

> don't trust a world covered in ice;
> don't trust a world of constant green

is the admonition.

Religious resonances and allusions are plentiful in the volume and religion weighs in with well-meaning but problematic moral precepts: "Keep your skirts down, / your legs shut tight," counsels the nun, but this comes with a price, for "All night, the cold enters / my bones" (41) filling her with unfulfillment. The conflict is palpable.

The poet explores issues of family with courageous, almost brutal frankness, and the result is an emotional richness and a hurt that haunts. The father embodies both good and evil like the devil and the washed-up god of "A Story;" "So he took a broom / to my mother's head / until blood bloomed / on her face, until / her elbow splintered and he saw / what he had done / and it was not good" (p 4). What a misguided god he was! In her artistic control of the experience McCallum almost distances herself not just with the alliteration of 'blood' and 'bloomed,' but with the graphic and surprising juxtaposition of those two imageries. Thus she preserves her smile and her sanity in the poem and in life. The nexus of the painful and the felicitous is a characteristic of McCallum's style in this volume. And, yes, there is strength in family; and mother, sister, a grandfather's unsettling wisdom and a child who is a "little once cassava" (20) (what a novel way to express tenderness) all get a bar in the song. But family also conjures up pernicious feuds and tribal divides, epitomised in the archetypal family of biblical Abraham. Modern Isaacs and Ishmaels with a religious overlay spring up across the world in Africa, Asia, "Cambodian killing fields" and elsewhere "clamouring for God's ear" (68). The poet recognizes a universal malaise in contemplating a personal dilemma.

Light and darkness is a dominant imagery in the book. Consciously or not this reflects the checkered experiences of the poet, her clouds and sunshine and thorns and roses. The "dark and light twinned" of "Fate" (6) may well be the unresolved complications of a mulatta life and the shaded light of her "divided worlds" generally (50). A painful tension and harrowing *inbetweenity* is evident in "Mulatta."

Sometimes, there is a magic about blackness and light as in "Wolves" (17) where these states stimulate the imagination, and *duppy* stories become real before the loss of innocence robs them of their truth. Fortunately, light sometimes illumines darkness as in "Teresa of Avila (1515-1582)" (51), although: ". . .When she moves / her hips, she is no saint / but a woman beneath / her cassock." McCallum is ever sensitive to subtle ironies, recognizing as she does here, the fragile curtain between flesh and spirit, between the sensuous and the religious, and that even light which is truth can be terrible. It is this kind of magical balance which she explores to such moving effect, and she has the artistic tools to do so. There is a wit in the Teresa poem and others not unworthy of the English metaphysical poets of the seventeenth century.

I find the book emotionally aching to read, but enthralling. It may be the poet's terse and simple diction and yet profundity of thought; it may be that her heart is heaved into the songs; it may be painful realities made flesh without being oppressive; it may be that the poems are born of bitter-sweet experiences personal to her and in many cases to us. It may be that all of this is skilfully textured into the unique tapestry of her verse and more.

"More" certainly includes the creative use of "home-grown imagery" from the Caribbean landscape which not only speaks to her but has become part of the grammar of many of her songs. Like her speaking "Spider" she carves messages in stone; the sound of the sea and the wind speak a language of comfort in contrast to the father's rasping voice (6). She is a flower blooming out of season, a symbol of rare beauty in spite of untoward environments; and songs are caged birds searching for expression, beating wings against the scaffold of her ribs (12).

McCallum employs techniques that one is accustomed to, to explore themes that are not new, but the compelling product is her own, and a distinctive image is stamped on her pieces. There are many poems which one would wish to return to again and again if only to savour their sweet sadness and their magical quality withal. McCallum is poised to be a leading Caribbean poet in "exile." Exile is relevant, in a manner of speaking, and she does not paint the islands as any paradise either, if we are to take the Sodom analogy seriously. "Think of Lot's wife," she writes, in "Six Ways of Envisioning Loss," "leaving home / without warning or choice / I am she / I am the one looking back" (64).

There is tension in looking back, but happily, it is creative tension. I welcome this new voice to the Caribbean creative writing fraternity.

Howard A. Fergus
Montserrat

Slender Lines, Terse Snapshots

Velma Pollard, *The Best Philosophers I Know Can't Read or Write.*
London, England: Mango Publishing. 2001. 87 pages. p.b.

Velma Pollard's poetry collection, *The Best Philosophers I Know
Can't Read or Write*, uses slender lines with well-chosen line breaks
to give us a staccato vision of things, a world of terse snapshots.
The strength of her line breaks provides the only end punctuation
throughout the book, save an occasional question mark. Indeed,
a line of six or seven words is long in most of these poems where
we enjoy the direct strength of cut-to-the-chase images:

> Is lunch I used to bring
> help down the basket
> salt fish and casi
> boil food
> and cool mauby (9);

or the tight complete,

> new room
> new life
> God
> thanks (27);

or consider this evocative juxtaposition:

> But no
> gun hills
> like yam hills
> grow gun
> shoots
> so (57).

Pollard, who was born in Jamaica and continues to teach at
the University of the West Indies, writes essays and fiction as well
as poetry. Her novella, *Karl*, received the Casa de las Americas
literature prize in 1992. Her other titles include: *Crown Point and
Other Poems* (1988), *Considering Woman* (1989), *Shame Trees
Don't Grow Here* (1992), and *Homestretch* (1994), as well as *Karl
and Other Stories* (1994).

The 40-some poems in this collection are a global lot from
memory pieces and Jamaican observations with dialect to poems
that travel to New York, Toronto, Iowa, Grenada and Tortola,
among other places. Many have parenthetical dedications that
intrude on the writer-reader dialogue; it's difficult to become
immediately engaged with that niggling, well,-this-poem-isn't-for-
me beginning. The one dedicated poem that didn't use paren-

thesis except for the date was less bothersome. The variety of locales and subjects is reflected in the titles of the poems which range from the enticing to the more pedestrian. Consider: "A scientist speaks of relationships: the snake is his metaphor;" "Armageddon needn't be a war;" or "Beware the naked man who offer you a shirt," as opposed to "Mule," "Bird,", "Name," "Chance," and "Old Age." This noticeable dichotomy is also present in the poems which wind between pieces with sharp clear-voiced language and those more ponderous where the poet overtells or forces the issue. For example, giving us a complete picture of thankfulness and then saying she gives thanks.

My favorites here are simply the photographic vignettes where the language invites the reader to see and sort as in the evocative "We are our grandmothers" with its lovely opening stanza:

Perhaps I do not
ride side-saddle
Sunday morning miles
brushing the horse's rump
with stiff starched drill (31).

Another such gem is the aptly titled "Bridges" where an

old man with serious eyes
is urging bridges
for emergencies (76).

And, really, what is a better bridge over the ravines of human isolation, than the hand-knotted words of poem?

Carol B. Fleming
Chulla Vista, California

Another Face of Nicolás Guillén

Nicolás Guillén, *El gran zoo/The Great Zoo*. Translated by Roberto Márquez. London: Mango Publishing. 2002. 95 pages. p.b.

The late Cuban poet Nicolás Guillén (1902-1989) delighted his readers with this collection of poetry—*El gran zoo* or *The Great Zoo*—when it was published in 1967. At the time, Guillén was well established nationally and internationally as a poet, writer, and social activist. He was a major force in making Afro-Cuban literature a part of the Spanish literary canon.

The Great Zoo was Guillén's 13th book. Apparently, he wrote the first poems for the collection while he was in exile in Buenos

Aires, Argentina in 1958. Then, after Fidel Castro overthrew Fulgencio Batista's government in 1959, the poet returned to Cuba. Nine years after he started it, the book was completed.

Roberto Márquez, who translated this edited version of the work from Spanish to English, is a leading authority on Guillén. Currently, he is a professor of Latin American and Caribbean Studies at a college in the United States. His translations of 39 poems that make up this centenary edition are excellent.

Apparently, the popularity of *The Great Zoo* was due, in large measure, to its versatility. It can stand as a collection of juvenile poems, crafted to delight and entertain. For instance, an eight-line poem "Lady" is playful enough: "This enormous lady/ was harpooned in the street" (33). The poem "Guitar" is another fun piece. Its opening lines declare, "They went out hunting guitars / under the full moon" (19). These wonderful lines invite readers into a fabulous world. However, the appeal is not without a problem, as the final lines of the poem contain a warning.

Indeed, many of the poems in this collection have elements of danger or disaster. Perhaps this is the reason for the book being read as something more, a work of serious social commentary. Guillén has gathered animals, objects and humans and their "types" or "conditions" and placed them behind bars where they are easily observed.

Once behind bars, the poet's keen eye explores and describes "Hunger" and "Gangster" and "KKK" to name just a few of the subjects and the titles of three of the poems. These are not designed to be entertaining, unless of course the horrendous appeals to you.

Even a short poem like "The Tiger" transports the reader from one scary reality to bigger and more frightening ones. From a simple tiger, the reader is taken, through metaphors, to even more terrible human threats. The poem's second stanza is composed of a list of metaphors depicting human tigers: "A boxer / A jealously-enraged lover" (49). The final stanza gives readers some relief. Indeed, we are more vulnerable to human evil than we are to the paws of any real tiger. It's a nice twist at the end of that poem.

Readers will find that Guillén writes with great insight, wit, irony, and literary skill—he's clearly a master with a sense of humor. Those who are concerned about reading works in translation should know that Márquez is quite skilled at bringing Guillén's world into the English language.

Marisella Veiga
Alexandria, Virginia

Family Values

Louie Laveist, *The House That Jack Built and Other Plays.* St. Martin: House of Nehesi Publishers. 2003. 97 pages. p.b. $15.00.

Readers should welcome these three plays by Louie Laveist, who has long been St. Martin's foremost playwright. Since his teens LL has dedicated himself to drama as actor, writer, director, and producer. As outlined in a balanced introduction by UWI lecturer Funso Aiyejina, the theatre of Louie Laveist self-consciously sets out to dramatize the most pressing issues facing St. Martin society; family values, to put it coyly, is uppermost on the list but the three plays tackle the way drugs can break up the family, how marital infidelity undermines the daily and necessary grist between couples of sharing confidences and difficulties and the tensions between parents and children, particularly those tensions pertaining to parental ambitions foisted upon the freedom of choice of their offspring. In this sense he is a social dramatist. He dedicates the art to the betterment of society, art as instruction in the Brecktian sense, and art as the forum for exploring national issues as, say, in the best work of the Irish playwright Michael Frayn.

In "Forbidden Love," first performed in 1993 in St. Martin and revived for Carifesta VI at the Little Carib Theatre in Port of Spain, the lead character, Samantha (Sam in the play) tries to convince her parents, principally her dictatorial father, about her love for a Rastafarian. But her father (played by Laveist) who is very aware of his middle class standing and what he wants for his only child, wants Sam to court and marry a respectable young man, Andrew, who is a deputy manager in the father's supermarket. Sam wants nothing to do with it but comes up with the ruse of a family dinner first with Andrew and then with her true love, the Rasta Butch (later changed to Berhane). The first dinner happens off stage for the most part and goes smoothly. The second dinner is a rowdy affair with a shocked and semi-comical reaction from the father and a starched collar if slightly wooden show by the boyfriend whose predictable utterances, it must be said, would try the patience of the most liberal of parents. LL's point in the portrait of the Rasta is to present a challenge to the middle class family model. In this sense the Rasta looks like a threat and acts like one (though dignified). Just when everything threatens to collapse for the family by Sam's fear that she may be pregnant which draws violent responses from both of her parents, it turns to be a false alarm and the noble Rasta backs away from his love and opts for a more softly, softly approach. The Rasta's decision to try and fulfill the father's expectations of a success man for his daughter regains the play's harmony centered on the precious family unit. In his direction it is clear that LL means us to view this as a morality play, particularly instructive to the young as seen in the portrait of Sam and Butch's courtship which presents the main challenge to the sacrosanct family unit.

In "Who's Fooling Who" the main character and head of the household, Bobba, succumbs to a drug habit which destroys his status and breaks up his family. His cocaine habit is presented as worse than marital infidelity in terms of its effects, and the house is literally torn apart to support his expensive habit. There is a motif in the play of the self-reflecting mirror. Bobba looks into it and with each view his sense of himself progressively disintegrates. The drug dealer, Big Daddy, is a veritable Mephisto, malevolent and merciless and somehow made from the dregs of the very society founded on the continued success of a family man like Bobba. Interestingly, Bobba is not a youth but an adult who should know better. The fact that he is vulnerable to drugs and the penalty of losing everything in order to feed his habit foregrounds the drug problem in a unique manner. As before, the society is predicated on the health of the family, and the lesson for us all is that drugs eat away at the heart of societal values. I missed a more existential approach to the issue, but I bow to Laveist's sociological project whose importance cannot be underestimated.

The title-play and third in the trilogy is perhaps the most accomplished. It appears to be about marital infidelity but changes to how grief—in this instance the death of a child—can drive a wedge between husband and wife. I found the quarrels between the couple wonderfully nuanced (the exchanges always on the verge of physical violence, the verbal excesses always stopping just short of sudden sex breaking out as if the words were a kind of rough foreplay) and the resolution convincing.

As before, the direction and writing by Laviest (and the part he plays as the husband) are all geared to restoring the primacy of the family under the most debilitating circumstances as when lawyers become involved! Just when things are about to mash up between the couple, love is restored and it is a great payoff for the reader and audience. The surprise character here is the classic mother-in-law, Jack's mother. She adds comedy to the mix, and in her superstitious talk she reminds us all how much of a force those old-time sayings and practices still exert on our reasoning. She helps to bring the couple together at the end when she has a stroke, and her mean utterances towards the wife are disarmed by her invalid status; in fact the husband and wife form a united front against the bullying and hectoring of the mother-in-law. Love acts as a palliative for grief and the family endures because it is founded on love.

Fred D'Aguiar
Blacksbury, Virginia

Negotiating the United States

Edwidge Danticat, *Behind the Mountains*. New York: Orchard Books. 2002. 167 pages. h.c. $16.95.

Edwidge Danticat's third novel, *Behind the Mountains*, is distinguished as a first on two counts—as the author's first novel for young readers, ages 11-15, and as the frontrunner in the First Person Fiction series, works for children depicting the experience of coming to America.

The story begins in October 2000 with 13-year-old Celiane's first entry in her diary, which she affectionately calls "*ti liv mwen*," my sweet little book. In it she innocently records the details of her simple life in Beau Jour, a Haitian village in the mountains. She is preoccupied with her school work, daily chores, longing for her father, and love for the tranquil setting.

> I love the rainbows during sun showers. I love the short-cuts through the cornfields, the smell of pinewood burning, the golden-brown sap dripping into the fire. I love sleeping on a sisal mat on the clay floor in Granmè Melinda and Granpè Nozial's one-room house and eating in their yard while listening to Granpè Nozial's stories.

Her peace and security are shattered when she and her mother visit her aunt in Port-au-Prince, the exciting but dangerous capitol. There the political turmoil sparked by the upcoming presidential election flares up in her life when she and her mother are seriously injured in a pipe bomb explosion. This incident hastens their plans to leave Haiti along with her 19-year-old brother and join her father, after a long five-year separation.

In Brooklyn, Celiane faithfully and candidly continues to record her impressions. The city is cold, and the skyscrapers remind her of the mountains of home. While she struggles at school with learning a new language and making new friends, her parents and brother struggle with making a living. All of them struggle to re-establish a happy family, one based on reality rather than on the "stream of their dreams." Gradually, Celiane does make friends at school, her father and brother resolve their differences, and the family moves into a larger apartment. Optimistically, Celiane looks forward to the day when her words and her brother's paintings will tell the story of how the Esperance family left a place where "Behind the mountains are more mountains" to overcome a "mountain of obstacles."

Although the exposition of background material occasionally seems mechanical and at one point, in a letter to her father, the child's voice seems uncharacteristically mature, this is a clear and moving story that will help young readers understand and empathize with the trials of Haitian immigrants.

In a six-page afterword, Danticat highlights some of the parallels between Celiane's story and her own. Like her protagonist, Danticat grew up in Haiti without her parents, who had moved to New York for economic reasons. And she has precious memories of growing up in Port-au-Prince and spending summers in the mountains of Beausèjour, at the family's ancestral village. This terrain—growing up without parents who have migrated and then moving from Haiti to New York—undergrids much of Danticat's work, especially her first novel *Breath, Eyes, Memory* (1994).

In her mid thirties, Danticat has already produced a body of work that is impressive both in its depth—political turmoil, women's issues, and Haitian history and culture are other recurring subjects—and its range, with one short story collection, four novels (including *The Dew Breaker,* 2004), an account of carnival figures in a Mardi Gras celebration (*After the Dance*), and an anthology of essays and poems which she edited (*The Butterfly's Way*), and numerous miscellaneous pieces such as her foreword—described by one reviewer as "lyrical but trenchant"—for a collection of oral histories, *Walking on Fire: Haitian Women's Stories*, and her many contributions to *The Caribbean Writer*. It's no wonder that she is being hailed as a "major American writer!"

Roberta Q. Knowles
St. Croix, U.S. Virgin Islands

Insidious Colonialism

Kester Branford, *Rufus Who?* Leicestershire, England: Upfront
Publishing. 2003. 208 pages. p.b. £8.99.

In the long tradition of Caribbean coming of age novels, Kester
Branford has brought this genre up to date by his setting the story
in the early 1970s, in which long-standing questions of race and
class continue to be examined. The main character, Rufus Linton,
who was born six years after Trinidad's independence from
England, has no direct knowledge of life under colonialism, but
suffers its effects through his family relationships, his schooling,
and the actions of the government. As the title indicates, Rufus
is in search of his self identity.

Rufus has been raised by Auntie Mavis, his unmarried aunt,
who with a major in Economics from a noted British university,
had risen from a civil servant to a prominent bank official. In
Trinidad, the Linton family of mixed ancestry was considered, as
the novel indicates, "French Creole" or "red" (23), meaning they
were descendants of the Whites born on the island who had in the
past "segregated themselves from the Black majority" (Brereton
3). Everyone refers to the family as "upright. . .maybe more
upright than others" (63).

Rufus knows that his Auntie Mavis had "volunteered to take
total charge of the children her brothers had fathered out of wedlock" (29). In the household there are two other such children.
Unlike Rufus, they know at least the identity of their fathers, and
they are unconcerned about their parentage. Throughout his
formative years, however, Rufus is continually being criticized as
the one who always asks the embarrassing questions as his determination to know the identity of this mother is continually met
with the answer that she was "temporarily in Venezuela" (11).
Rufus also knows that everyone considers his Uncle Clive, the
family drunkard, to be his father. "Clive never had denied that
Rufus was his son" (42).

While Auntie Mavis is proud when he receives high grades
and that he is accomplished in playing the piano, she "withheld
encouragement" when he shows an interest in playing a steel
orchestra instrument (24). He again demonstrates his interest in
music when his interview with a family friend about his parentage
quickly reverts into a discussion about the intricacies of being a
calypsonian.

Upon receiving a basic degree which allows him to teach English, Rufus is desirous of studying abroad. To obtain a passport, he seeks a copy of his birth certificate at the Trinidad government administrative office center located in the massive colonial structure, Red House, in downtown Port-of-Spain. This symbol of the government is conveyed menacingly throughout this novel and is pictured on the cover of the paperback edition. The building looms in his life like a friend who has let him down.

After several attempts to procure the birth document, he learns that his name has been registered as "Prince Linton." Directly underneath his name, Rufus sees the word "Illegitimate." "That word offended Rufus, without, however causing him any sense of shame" (41). The narrator explains that in secondary school he had written an essay on the unfair stigma which is attached to such children. At the end of his paper, Rufus concluded his thoughts with a play on words which was praised by his teacher: "In the final analysis, no so-called illegitimate child conceives himself as illegitimate. The illegitimate conception is that of his parents" (41). Besides learning his real name, the document shows that no father's name is listed, and that of his mother is "Miss Linton." Once again he questions Auntie Mavis, who refers him to his grandmother, who then tells him to ask a neighbor, who then sends him back to his grandmother with the words, "Let the high and mighty Lintons wash their own dirty clothes." (69)

In learning that Mavis's sister, Carmen, is his mother, Rufus is much ashamed by the way she and her prestigious husband and child treat him. Unlike the simple chores Auntie Mavis expects of him, Carmen treats him shabbily and has him do heavy household tasks. Through Carmen he eventually realizes the convoluted series of lies and deceptions which his entire family has engaged in order to give Carmen an opportunity to marry properly and to keep the secret of his birth and parentage away from not only him but from the world. Rufus explains to Carmen:

'If you had any kind of human feeling, you would feel guilt. Not because you had a child without being married. To me that is not a crime. But you carried on a pretense for years, and made me feel as if I dropped from a tree and didn't belong to anybody. *That* is the crime'. (115)

Branford has written the novel much like a mystery story in which Rufus unravels the various details. The frustration Rufus experiences in finding the truth leads to rage. His normally calm demeanor cracks as he bursts out and throws bottles against the wall during a family party.

The novel is quite predictable to this point. Rufus's rage at being talked about behind his back turns to violence and sub-consciously he kills Carmen, calls the authorities, and lies in her bed waiting for the police to arrive. His subsequent imprisonment is curious. Rufus admits his crime but is not remorseful. He has a change of character in that he becomes philosophical about the larger questions concerning life and death, guilt and sin. Thus, he continues to ask embarrassing questions of the chaplain and the warden, once again, making those around him feel uncomfortable.

While the educated and independent Mavis represents the modern woman in the Trinidadian workplace, her responses to the actions of her siblings and their children are steeped in tradition. Kinship relationships and family standing as perceived by society certainly take precedence in preserving their family name. The novel demonstrates that while independence has thrust the country into the modern world, institutional dictates on morality and everyday prescriptions still linger. Rufus, the sensitive child, is hampered by the restrictions imposed upon family by both society and government. These institutions have made him dependent, "emotionally deprived," as the defending attorney attempts to explain while he pleads Rufus's case (129). His crime of matricide and his resultant reaction of lying in Carmen's bed are seen as the highest felonies by the community, and Rufus will ironically hang for his actions in Woodford Square, next to the Red House, where all his problems had begun (195). Rufus's experiences have been steeped in class and race conflicts that are beyond the scope of his ability to rise above. The novel is recommended for high school level reading, and guided follow-up discussion would bring out these themes.

*Bridget Brereton, *Social Life in the Caribbean 1838-1938*. Oxford: Heinemann CXC History, 1985.

Elizabeth Rezende
St. Croix, U.S. Virgin Islands

Orgasm and Politics in the Caribbean

Jacques Stephen Alexis, *In the Flicker of an Eyelid*. Translated by Carrol F. Coates and Edwidge Danticat. Charlottesville, Virginia: University of Virginia Press. 2002. 278 pages. h.c. $59.50. p.b. $19.95.

This is the love story of El Caucho, a strong, honorable Cuban mechanic, thirty years old, now working in Haiti, and La Nina Estrella, twenty six, a Cuban whore in a Haitian bordello servicing American marines. They are immediately aware of each other and attraction between them grows gradually, in a series of chapters, based on the senses. Initially they see each other. Then they are aware of each other's odor; from his scent she can tell that he smokes Cuban cigarettes, and works with machines. In the third chapter, he hears her cry out "Down with the Jwif" (Jew) during a carnival celebration, and she hears his "Let me through" when he saves the life of a child. In the following chapter they taste each other in a kiss, and the fifth sense, touch, occurs when they finally are in bed together. They then realize that they knew each other as children in Cuba. The slow progression of their knowledge of each other is very erotically portrayed. When, finally, for the first time in her life La Nina reaches orgasm, their union is complete, or almost. She has tried to lose all memory of her innocent life as a child, and now feels she must find herself, establish an identity beyond the bordello, before uniting with El Caucho. Having a man is not a goal in itself. *In the Flicker of an Eyelid* is in many ways a feminist novel. Its portrayal of the other prostitutes is sympathetic. La Nina is a fully developed character, not so idealized as El Caucho.

Alexis's style is very rich, full of long enumerations, many images, much use of color. Antoine has an "ivory black" complexion; Celia Cruz's voice is "red and black." La Nina's body is the color of honey. (Her clitoris, however, is described in the translation as "cerulean.") Here is their first taste, in a kiss:

> On the nape of his neck, she discovered a pepper shaker; the cinnamon of hard flesh, balsamic; the resin of that coarse pineapple, his neck, the spicy salad of hair. His shoulder is a ripe tamarind that sets the teeth on edge. . .the scents she had already inhaled from the body of this man suddenly became real like a salami or salt pork. (164-5)

Written shortly before the Cuban revolution, the novel has a political message. La Nina's orgasm could be seen as a precursor of a revolution. The pair are types of the exploited—the prostitutes brutally taken by the marines, or the workers with few rights under Caribbean dictators. Prostitutes, El Caucho thinks, are proletarian and "like good work, work that's well done" (34). Mechanics, on the other hand, can be compared to sex workers: "The exhaust pipes fart in their faces, the storage batteries piss acid on their arms, the valves ejaculate their thick, black, greasy sperm on them" (80). Proletarians both, they are part of the "uncounted army struggling humbly, stubbornly, and without useless posturing or shortsighted rebellion. True, valid heroism lies within the obscure existence of the humble" (197).

This is, Alexis often tells us, a "Caribbean" love story. "We, the peoples of the Caribbean, are children of truth and light, children of water and corn, children of the surging sea" (193). Many of the characters have parents who come from several islands, and travel often among them. They are sons and daughters of the Caribbean.

Alexis intended another novel about La Nina and El Caucho, in which they would meet again in Cuba, perhaps after the Caribbean Federation for which he dreamed. A founder and leader of the "Parti d'entente populaire," Alexis tried to return to Haiti to organize against the government in 1961, at the age of 39. He was tortured and killed by Duvalier's agents, before he could complete another novel.

Alexis's novel, originally published in French in 1959 (*L'espace d'un cillement*), is the second of his works to be translated in the CARAF series of Caribbean literature in French. The translation is sometimes awkward, using latinate vocabulary which is acceptable in French but sounds pretentious in English. La Nina's hair is a "heavy, capillary cascade" (40). The scholarly notes and documents published at the conclusion leave a great deal to be desired. The translators do not inspire confidence when they mention their ignorance of the role of the Virgin of Pillar in the Caribbean. They publish letters from Alexis to his daughter, and her comments on the novel written many years after his death, and only later introduce this material to the reader. The popular 1940s song "Sentimental Journey" becomes "Sentimental Journal." Worse, the discussion makes many citations from the novel, which are all identified as occurring on page 000. Such sloppy editing is unforgivable, particularly in a university press publication.

Adele King
Paris

The Burning of Dreams

Lyonel Trouillot, *Street of Lost Footsteps.* Translated by Linda Coverdale. Lincoln, Nebraska: University of Nebraska Press. 2003. 115 pages. p.b. $16.95.

Street of Lost Footsteps is a prophetic and disturbing novel set in Port-au-Prince, Haiti. The story is centered around a day and night of violent chaos as the revolutionary forces of the mysterious Prophet clash with the military regime of the great dictator Deceased Forever-Immortal. The novel takes its name from the imaginary *Rue des Pas-Perdus*, or Street of Lost Footsteps described as the "zone of utter oblivion, where they burn dreams, memories. . ." (21).

The metaphorical street lies somewhere in the city, at the intersection of the four cardinal points. The reference is to the Vodou Papa Legba, the loa or spirit of the crossroads. The text is interwoven with other references to Haiti's Afrocentric religion, appearing like *veves* or symbolic designs in the personal history of the three main characters in the book.

Trouillot's highly poetic and intense language lavishly explores Haiti's complex composition. Interwoven scenes blend descriptions of tropical splendor with disturbing stories of human and environmental destruction. The tragic/comic progression of events could be described as surreal if not for the factual evidence that all of it is too, too real.

The novel is structured around three alternating first person narrators: a former teacher turned postal clerk; the aged Madame of a brothel; and a wounded taxi-cab driver fleeing for his life through the city. The three personal tales share a combination of disturbing recollections, bitter regret and immediate terror at the horrors occurring around them.

The postal clerk is caught in a lackluster love affair with a pretentious, emotionless woman. His best friend Gerard is a disillusioned intellectual impotent with fear and befuddled by rumors and conspiracies. Their friend Andre is described as a pretend-radical locked in his own delusions of social evolution. Gerard provides a sanctuary for the postal clerk and his lover during the night of flames. But this apparent seclusion offers them no escape from the disruption occurring around them.

The retired Madame is filled with loss and dim intimations of a better time when Haitian society functioned in a normal way. Her wistful memories describe her struggle with poverty and her attempts to maintain dignity in the midst of perpetual violence. Eventually, her brothel is closed and the girls who worked for her are drawn into the rebellion, seeking revenge for a life of poverty. "Because what feeds you and makes you the way you are, is poverty." (94)

Written as a cross-section of Haitian society, the book narrates a bloody tale of rampage and murder and changing class order that knows no limits. The constant manipulation of warring political parties eventually creates a society caught in divisive self-destruction. "Here terror goes on and on, changing sides, target, speeds." (77)

The cabdriver is caught in the cross hairs of revolt, shot in the leg and dumped into the ironically named *Ravine les Innocents* along with a madman with a map who is trying to find *Rue des Pas-Perdus*. The madman drowns in the Ravine which is filled with the slime and detritus of a poverty stricken nation. The cabdriver escapes through the city giving an eyewitness account of the atrocities committed on every street corner.

Haiti's precarious position as a society on the brink of destruction infuses the book with despair. The country is ripped apart by conflicting powers, remnant colonialism, racism, foreign occupation and a history of political disasters. The populace is so defeated that "What's missing is the imagination to imagine happiness." (47)

The disruption of natural order is not something new to Haiti. The novel could well take place on any number of possible days in Haiti's infamous political history. As far back as 1492 there were perhaps as many as six million Arawak and Carib Indians in the Caribbean Islands. A few generations later Spanish cruelty and disease had destroyed the native culture and more than 20 million African slaves were imported.

Haiti was created from the first successful slave uprising in history when Toussaint L'Ouverture, a former slave, led a rebellion in 1791. In 1804 Haiti was the first black-ruled state outside of Africa. From that date to the present the country has been disrupted by an endless succession of corrupt dictators.

This cycle culminated in the infamous Papa Doc Duvalier (1957-71) and his son Baby Doc (1971-86). The Duvalier family and the clandestine Tontons Macoutes expertly eviscerated every institution of Haitian society. Rampant crime and unemployment plagued the citizens. Strikes, attempted coups, demonstrations, assassinations, and mob executions reduced the country to "An epic failure factory." (1)

Trouillot expertly weaves his stream-of-consciousness narratives together, mixing past and present, real and imagined, psychological and physical damage in a nasty brew. Behind it all the enticing image of a smiling woman on the day in 1938 when the first American invasion of Haiti was ended offers promise and hope.

Is hope possible? Trouillot's book is a testament to the yearning voices of Haiti's population who haven't been given a chance to escape its bloody history. Regrettably, contemporary events have further confirmed the absurdity of Haitian politics and the brutality of regime change. The book proves as relevant today as it was when it was written. "As tension mounts, the occupation forces stand guard over the ruins of a broken fountain." (81)

At the end of the book the cabdriver, in a hallucinatory passage, locates the Street of Lost Footsteps at the bottom of the *Ravine des Innocents* where it is populated with images of dictators, prophets, commandants, murderers, "and a few million sick children." (108)

Stephen F. Soitos
Northompton, Massachusetts

Haitians on Foreign Shores

Marie-Hélene Laforest, *Foreign Shores*. Montreal, Canada: Les Editions du CIDIHCA. 2002. 187 pages. p.b.

Oral tradition prevails in Haiti where the illiterate masses (90% of the population) have traditionally relied on the memorization of rituals, folk tales, songs and dances to keep their culture alive. It has become evident, for instance, that all the written and published material on Vodun is authored by Haitian scholars or foreign writers rather than Vodun priests or believers, and that the transmission process in that religious tradition depends entirely on the contemporary idiom of living practitioners. However, the opposite can be witnessed in the so-called diaspora where Haitian immigrants, a minority, seem to take full advantage of the written medium and publishing means available, particularly in North America. It was interesting to learn recently from a public librarian in Miami that the recorded book production per capita by Haitians in Florida, USA, surpassed by far that of other larger immigrant communities of that state. This new interest in written culture reflects an eagerness to preserve and celebrate things Haitian, and is perhaps fueled by nostalgia about the homeland and an elan of protectiveness towards a cultural history perceived to be in peril at a time of accelerated change.

The new book by Marie-Helene Laforest entitled *Foreign Shores* provides a good example of this trend: Unmistakably a work of Haitian literature both by its subject matter and its author's origins, it is written and published abroad (Italy and Canada), it is also a true work of English prose—not a translation from French or Kreyol. *Foreign Shores* is a compilation of eighteen short stories articulating the kernel of survival in the community of Haitian immigrants. Set over the course of the Duvaliers' era, the stories are grouped sequentially in four self-explanatory sections: "Island Life," "Some Drifted," "Many Stayed," "A Few Returned." They touch on a variety of topics and depict various social environments both in Haiti and the United States: from quiet scenes of Haitian country life to the job market in the bustling American cities and later the nursing homes for the aging, we encounter Haitians from all social classes, and experience with them the deterioration of the traditional structures in the island, the reality of exile, and even the attempt by some to bring change back home after years abroad.

Writing from foreign shores herself, Laforest amazingly manages the kind of storytelling that highlights the deep truth about the quintessential Haitian character by cleverly exploring the ingredients that define culture—religious, racial, and historical identity. In the Acknowledgments, the author thanks her parents who have not ceased to tell her stories, suggesting that she draws somewhat on personal history and experience. Only two of the stories are narrated in the first person and it is not clear whether most of the material is autobiographical since she so consistently stays out of the way as a narrator, even when speaking in the first person, and lets the story be. However, there is clear evidence of memory practice, and whether retold or imagined, her stories are written with the revived wonder of one recounting something felt deeply and experienced intimately.

Laforest exhibits the power and skill of a true storyteller with a striking ability to recount and make real, introducing the right mixture of homeland folklore to flavor her tales without allowing them to become social or psychological fables. Personal and collective memories are preserved, updated with current experiences, transformed and passed on. Remembering and new beginnings come together beautifully in brief accounts (some stories are only one page long) as she renders the lives of Haitian immigrants through the use of a steady accretion of telling details, encapsulating simultaneously the reality of nation and an individual family.

In "Language of the Gods," following the train of thought and reminiscences of a widow hours after her husband's funeral, we review the complete trajectory of their lives together, typical of so many immigrants, from their native village in Mon Kabrit to the United States, their steady relationship with Adventist missionaries in Haiti and the U.S. Flashbacks, in the casual flow and easy conversational manner of her prose, bring to life significant moments of the couple's years in New York's Haitian community, their courtship, raising a family, their language issues; then burying practices here and in the island are compared, leading seamlessly to a clash in her memory with the "wrong Gods" that her time and involvement with the Adventist church have not managed to erase from her soul. "[M]ourning, then half-mourning, that's what they said back home. . .Death in a family, black dress ready overnight. . .for a ceremony to the wrong gods, those that come from Guinea. . .Goatskin drums, the deep sound of hollow bamboos resounding in the countryside, beating in her head now. In the dark night flashes of red kerchiefs in the shadows of vast trees. . .White forms trash to the ground. The other gods, which her family renounced. . .That disorder in her head, those strands of memory, they had come so unexpectedly, so wrongly. . ." (114) Mysteries are suggested without being spelled out through lines of a Vodun song, *Soley o atidan iboloko. . . Mwen se neg ginen o. . .* "A song," she said to her inquisitive daughter, "when I was a girl. . .The church not yet built, dressed in white, at night. . .wrong words," she shook her head, "wrong gods, wrong food, wrong clothes, wrong tears." *Atidan iboloko. . .*May [her daughter] did not understand Kreyol, how could she understand *langaj*, the language of the gods. (114)

Laforest finds her impulse and drama in the dreams and experiences of those affected by migration and she skillfully crafts new language capable of relating those experiences to a wider audience. She reports on aspects of Haitian life which have disappeared with time or due to change in population. The idea of home has shifted from Haiti to elsewhere. The reader is placed in cultural history that sketches back simultaneously a few years of a single family's life as well as two centuries of national history. We see the far reaching hand of US consumerism affecting customs and the Kreyol language in Haiti and New York. Words like kenedi (Kennedy) have entered the Kreyol vocabulary to designate second hand clothing donated by US charities. She described the city landscape through the eyes of a newly arrived Haitian.

> [W]hen she saw a garden of fireflies below, she knew it was New York. People who had been abroad had told her about the many voices making announcements. . .Once in a room where people were being checked, she would show the green cards. Then she would really be in New York. . .She didn't know the doors would open by themselves into rooms that were like avenues and she would not know what to do. . .Annette saw tall constructions that looked like police stations or churches. 'It's a city of churches,' she said. When the car stopped, the street was lined with two-story houses. . .'People here don't live in a whole house. It's bits of houses people live in'. . .Her bit of house was a basement with a table and four chairs as soon as the door opened, and a real cooker in front. A square plastic sack with a long zipper partitioned the rest of the room. . .Her heart pounded like when she boarded the airplane, like the day the money arrived, or when she went for the papers. Two years ago she took the bus to Port-au-Prince always wearing her good dress, the green kenedi from Madame Luce, a Grande Rue woman, the only wealthy woman whose clothes did not constrain her shoulders and did not need letting down. . . (120)

A new chapter of Haitian literature is being written within exile communities throughout the world by a generation who possesses yesterday's reality in their minds, retelling their stories in new tongues, making them part of the fabric of their current lives and environments, making them available to a younger generation of Haitians abroad. *Foreign Shores* represents something reassuring about the state of Haitian letters abroad, and hopefully contributes to keeping the gap in comprehension between Haiti and the World from opening up wider.

Maud Pierre-Charles
St. Croix, U.S. Virgin Islands

Even if You Can Go Home Again, Maybe You Shouldn't

Maeve Clarke, *What Goes Round*. Birmingham, England: Tindal Street Press, Ltd. 2003. 299 pages. p.b. £7.99.

Frank Galimore leaves his home in England to return to Jamaica, the land of his birth, to bury his father who has just died there. This is the first time Frank has returned to Jamaica since he immigrated to England. Traveling with him is his fifteen year old daughter, Jewelle, who has never been to Jamaica, and Frank's deceased wife's sister, Aunt B, who is also a native Jamaican.

Upon arrival in Jamaica Jewelle meets her grandmother, Miss Jess, a "Big Momma" type person recognizable by black people the world over. She also meets Jake, a young boy her age, who performs odd jobs for Miss Jess and becomes her first serious love interest. A good portion of the book concerns the development of Jewelle's romance and her coming to terms with her Jamaican heritage and culture. The other main character of the book is Rose, who had a torrid (and somewhat injurious) relationship with Frank before he married his wife Beth. Now that Frank is single and back in Jamaica, what will happen between Frank and Rose? Will Frank fatalistically accept his destiny?

What Goes Round is a first novel by Maeve Clarke who was born in Birmingham, England to Jamaican parents. She is a graduate of Manchester University's MA in novel writing and the author of a short story "Letters A Yard" that appeared in the "prize winning anthology" *Whispers in the Walls*, also published by Tindal Street Press.

To my mind, Ms. Clarke turned into a novel something that probably would have worked much better as a short story. The ending turns on an ironic twist that is not a big enough payoff after reading almost 300 pages. It is contrived, implausible yet anticipated. Along the way we meet a multitude of characters who are in the main very ordinary West Indians who impart nothing special in the way of insight or knowledge with respect to Jamaican life, history, or mores. People who have familiarity with the Caribbean already are familiar with what Ms. Clarke's characters do and say. In addition, most of these characters play no significant role in advancing the plot.

Most of Ms. Clarke's characters speak Jamaican patois, and although Frank has been away from Jamaica for many years and speaks acceptable London English, he quickly reverts to his old speech patterns. While this change is in character for Frank, the fact that most of the characters speak patois becomes distracting instead of increasing the characters' authenticity. I found myself questioning whether the author should have used "dey" instead of "dem," or vice-versa instead of concentrating on the content of the characters' speech. Also, when all of the characters speak patois, it detracts from the comedic effect of any character whose humor is largely based on the peculiarities of Jamaicans' speech patterns.

Roland B. Scott
Sandia Park, New Mexico

The Song and the Scent of Trust

Alba Ambert, *The Passion of María Magdalena Stein*. London, England: Mango Publishing. 2002. 263 pages. p.b.

Currently Writer in Residence at Richmond, The American International University in London, Alba Ambert has an impressive list of credits to her name. Besides dedicating herself to academic concerns, mostly in articles and books on bilingualism, this Puerto Rican writer has also published five books of poetry, three children's books, two plays, a work of non-fiction about Greek topics (she lived in Greece for a while), a collection of short stories, and a novel which won the 1996 Carey McWilliams Award, *A Perfect Silence*. *The Passion of María Magdalena Stein*, her second novel, clearly demonstrates the author's skill at telling a story that is at once poetic, dramatic, and very well crafted in surprising ways.

Between the first two sentences, "A song can make the world forget. And remember," and the last, "The scent of jasmine erases the memory of blood from her mind," Ambert slowly reveals the "passion" of her protagonist, María Magdalena Stein, from the age of five, when she is living in New York and her mother marries a Greek man who introduces her to the nostalgia of *rembetiko*, music from his country, until she is twenty-eight, a singer living alone in Boston and emotionally healed years after running away from the abusive environment created by her second stepfather, Mr. Creed, in Arecibo, Puerto Rico. This part of her story is told in the seven odd-numbered chapters of the novel through a distant limited omniscient narrator and a series of flashbacks with very effective transitions. The six even-numbered chapters, however, are a first-person narrative of Mary of Magdala, the woman María Magdalena becomes in her dreams, the only way she feels she is alive. In them, she lives in the Palestine of Roman times as a healer, visionary, prophet, someone who can bring the dead back to life, and a cross-dresser who assumes Christ-like characteristics that emphasize the need for love and compassion in a world marred by human and animal sacrifice and a patriarchy in which females are afforded very little value. Throughout each of these narratives that are ultimately about the same character, Ambert establishes parallels that make the plot cohere, thus avoiding the danger of digressing. In both parts she includes images (scents and sounds being the most prominent), objects, songs, names, symbols, and allusions that express something of the same nature in the chapters that follow one another. Through the dreams that she faithfully describes in her notebook, María Magdalena starts to emerge from her nightmares and sees possibilities for herself. She learns to trust again.

Alba Ambert revealingly dedicates this book to uncommon women, convulsionaries, sorceresses, victims of war and "all the other crucified women," and in the novel describes this world as one in which Peter the Apostle "usurped what could have been a renewal of faith in women healers and instead built a church that reflected his own image" (262). She also establishes an evident intertextual relationship with the Spanish Golden Age play by Calderón de la Barca, *La vida es sueño* or *Life is (a) Dream*, which she quotes in one of the three epigraphs she puts in the book: "In the world, all those who live, dream." The play provides some of the means through which she'll describe the dream or desire for a world in which healing is possible. Obsessed by the idea of life as theater, shadow and dream, Calderón, too, created a female character, Rosaura, who cross-dressed and was abandoned by her father. "The hurt of the fatherless daughter" (76) is the strongest bond uniting María Magdalena and her best friend, Vanesa, who writes her own play based on Calderón's, and whose advice during one of María Magdalena's most stressful moments is to pretend that it's a dream from which she will wake up one day.

In *The Passion of María Magdalena Stein*, Alba Ambert also relates opposite versions of mother-daughter relationships. Like Jamaica Kincaid, she includes parts in which the mother is the spokesperson and agent of a limiting and even abusive patriarchy, and like Esmeralda Santiago, she describes instances of supportive mothering in spite of obverse circumstances that could easily put the relationship at risk. In the end, though, it's the daughter's well-being that is at stake, and she assumes responsibility for her personal healing. Through her, Ambert succeeds in blending a story of personal grief with a history of women healers, and by doing so she proves herself to be an excellent storyteller. Along with this unique layering of life experiences, her skillful use of artistic language, which at times is almost poetically complex, inserts this novel in the ongoing discussion about the telling of women's lives. Here, for one, is a story that picks up where others were forced into silence.

María Soledad Rodríguez
San Juan, Puerto Rico

Silence and Sunshine

Curdella Forbes, *Songs of Silence*. Oxford, England: Heinemann (Caribbean Writers Series). 2002. 154 pages. p.b.

Paulette Ramsay, *Aunt Jen*. Oxford, England: Heinemann (Caribbean Writers Series). 2002. 105 pages. p.b.

Curdella Forbes and Paulette Ramsay are two gifted Caribbean writers from Jamaica who both published short books of fiction in the same year (2002) and with the same press (Heinemann). Their books are set in Jamaica's recent past and feature young rural girls as the first person narrators. Since the authors hope to reach a wide range of readers, each book includes a helpful Glossary in Standard English that explains local sayings and phrases important to fully understanding and enjoying their fiction. The events in *Songs of Silence*, by Curdella Forbes, take place in the 1960's. The eight linked stories, or "songs," and the epilogue are all narrated by the observant, precocious Marlene, who reflects on the places and people of her home district after she has left her family for Kingston and the teacher's college there. Most of Paulette Ramsay's brief epistolary novel, titled *Aunt Jen*, spans a four year period, from 1970 to 1974. A teenaged girl named Sunshine writes all but the last letter. All of her letters are addressed to one person, Aunt Jen, really her long-absent mother, telling her in vivid detail about the family and Jamaican village she has left far behind.

As her title indicates, one word—silence—is explored in great depth throughout Forbes' collection of evocative tales in *Songs of Silence*. Each of Marlene's stories is chosen by her with care, judged to be "worth the telling, surrounded with the kind of drama and rarity that make it sweet to tell" (5). The major character of her first narrative is Effita or Effie, "a woman who sang of death like a tribal griot" (15) making "plenty noise" as she wailed and spun in a tranced frenzy. Marlene and the other villagers can depend on the old woman to announce whenever anybody in their district dies—until her beloved fourteen year old nephew, Son Son, has a fatal seizure at school. After this tragedy Effie is quiet for a long time, refusing to look at anyone directly; eventually she fades into the shadows, almost forgotten. Marlene is fascinated by how tragedies, great and small, can silence even vocal, vibrant people like Effie. She explains:

> I understood silence. I understood the stone prison and the snail's secret house of being unable to speak. For me, from the day I went to school. . .language was a shame I could not bear to use, except when I was allowed to write it down. Speaking made people laugh at you, especially if you spoke too softly and hung your head so you could not be heard. Children mocked you, adults teased. Speaking opened your body to betrayal, speaking allowed you to be seen. . .For years I could not speak, silence was my snail's house on my back that kept me safe. (18-19)

Eventually Marlene changes schools and finds a welcome release from her self-imposed, protective prison-shell of silence—with the help of Miss Herfa, a teacher who is able to provide "an oasis beyond my mother's and my sister's skirts" (18). However, she does not lose her habit of quiet, acute observation or her fascination with strange secrets and dark shadows. She is her Uncle Curthbert's most avid audience when he tells "magnificent" folk tales "that no one rivaled" about rolling calves quarrelling with three-footed horses, for example, or duppies with no feet and teeth like monsters who haunt graveyards, cotton trees and "hushed, moonless roads" (98-99). No wonder the wide-eyed young girl with her vivid dreams and boundless imagination finds an uneasy hero in Long Man, a lonely wanderer she describes as "a dark red ghost" (99) who sometimes visits her family while he does some itinerant work in the district for a few days, or a few weeks; then melts "away into the dark. . .slid easily into the night.

. .smooth and silent and glidingly belonging. . .one of that elusive species, a traveler. . .he came and went like the wind" (102-103).

Marlene's discussion of Long Man, and his mesmerizing effect on her family gives readers important insights into the close, nurturing relationship she has with her mother and father. "I loved Long Man's coming," she confesses. "Even though his presence faintly disturbed me, I loved Long Man's coming, because when he was there, all day my mother sang" (100). Later she explains, "Instinctively I felt him stand between my mother and me, and for this reason I dreaded him" (100). When she was very small she would hug her mother's legs tightly whenever Long Man first arrived, trying, without success, to stop her mother from looking at this tall rival for her young daughter's affection and attention. And when Long Man swung Marlene easily onto his shoulder she would feel "both exhilarated and offended. . .because this was my father's place, his shoulder was where my father hoisted me every evening when I ran out screaming to meet him coming home from work, and where he carried me the long way to the clinic when I was sick" (101). She would watch her father closely when Long Man stayed with the family, watching for signs of anger or jealousy but "in fact they got on quite well, and that helped to assuage my disquiet and my unknown rage" (101).

In the end, in spite of Marlene's attraction to "old wives' tales and black people gossip" (129), it is the solid, warm, living reality of her mother's family stories about growing up in Jamaica that infuse Marlene's own life with hope. Even more so, it is her father's dependable, enduring love that inspires her: ". . .how lucky I was my father stayed and that he left his dent on things that he sat on and touched. . .I was happy because I was holding my father's hand and we were laughing as I went with him out into the open yard" (130). Although she eventually comes to realize, "I knew them all" in her home district in spite of their different secrets "because they were all the people I had been and there was no me before there was them" (152), her father is her guiding muse. He is the person she is most determined to keep alive "by the skeins of stories" she weaves in her head, "sacred as a book of prayers, bright scarves of stories in green and blue and red and gold and the soft grey light of afternoons" when it rains and "the whole sky over the sea" is "bright and tender like the soft inside of shells" (128).

In Paulette Ramsay's novel, *Aunt Jen*, the narrator, Sunshine, is also a young girl with a head full of strange dreams and secrets. Like Marlene, she feels driven to weave stories on paper about the people and community she observes, although, unlike Marlene, she never seems to have a problem speaking aloud. In her case her compulsion is fueled by her longing to somehow communicate with "Aunt" Jen, her long-silent and mysterious mother, who lives in England. Some of Sunshine's letters to her absent mother, written in anguish and never actually posted, are found twenty years later, in 1993, by Angel's daughter, April. It is April who concludes the book with a letter of her own, addressed to her recently discovered—but never seen—"Dear Grandma Jen."

In a sense, then, "Aunt" Jen, the narrator's mysterious, long-silent mother, is Sunshine's muse even though the girl has no memory of her and possesses not even one photograph of her. She is more like a fantasy than a reality to Sunshine, whose everyday world is dominated by the large and colorful family in Jamaica who raise her—Uncle Johnny, Aunt Sue and Gramps, for example, and especially Ma, her maternal grandmother. It is Ma who makes history "real real" (73) through her stories of their maroon ancestors. It is Ma who is Sunshine's hero, "so strong and fiery" even in old age that her granddaughter declares, "I come from a line of fighters! I will never let anything in this life beat me. I'm going to be a lion like Ma" (73).

It is only after Ma's death that Sunshine's mother finally decides she wants a chance to not only meet her daughter, but have the girl come live with her. She begins to suddenly besiege Sunshine with letters and plans for their future together. But Sunshine's replies reveal that she too is experiencing a drastic change of heart. "Sometimes I think that a mother is not just the woman who gives birth to you, but is someone you have important memories of like the ones I have of Ma plaiting my hair, tying my dress-band, ironing my clothes and cooling my favorite corn-meal porridge" (92), she explains. "The fact is, life has a totally different meaning for me now. . .I'm not the Sunshine who used to make daily trips to the post office hoping to get a letter from you" (97). Sunshine has already rejected the idea of living with her father, a bullying braggart whom his daughter dubs "Mr. Big Mouth Smith" (32). Although she promises to consider her mother's offer, she makes it clear she has other, and perhaps more compelling, choices—she may decide to stay in Jamaica with Aunt Sue or move to America and live there with Uncle Roy.

Aunt Jen is a strong novel, well worth reading for its pathos, clever plot, and quick pace. Indeed, Curdella Forbes and Paulette Ramsay are both accomplished writers who create intriguing characters and situations. Certainly both authors explore themes that are capable of holding a reader's attention. But Curdella Forbes has a gift for painting memorable word pictures which shimmer and glow with life—even when she is describing darkness and death. It is for that reason her *Songs of Silence* is destined to become a Caribbean classic.

Patricia Harkins-Pierre
St. Thomas, U.S. Virgin Islands

Love in Sligoville

Garfield Ellis, *Such As I Have*. Oxford, England: Macmillan. 2003. 132 pages. p.b. £4.95.

Garfield Ellis, author of *Flaming Hearts* and a past winner of the Canute Brodhurst prize for fiction (*The Caribbean Writer*), has created in *Such As I Have* a story about the redemptive value of love. In this novella, we watch the main character, Headley, a stubborn, self-absorbed young man, as he is transformed by Pam, the object of his love, into a caring, responsible man. Yet it is also a cautionary tale about love that can shatter a fragile ego unprepared for the change that must happen with love—a shift from the concerns about oneself to another. Finally, it is a story about loyalty—a characteristic that Headley's best friend, Dezzy, displays throughout the novella and which, in the end, proves to be key to Headley's salvation.

There is so much to be said about Ellis's novella: the confident storytelling he displays from the opening words of the story: "Sligoville people love to tell stories about Headley—especially the old men when they sit at the bars and engage in the detailed and technical discussions on cricket that only they can" (4); an exploration of outcast status in Jamaican with its roots in race and class prejudice; the use of cricket as a metaphor for understanding the protagonist's motivation; the precision of word choice and images drawn from Jamaican life to reveal character: "Headley was the brash and flamboyant one, with a temper like a scotch bonnet pepper" (77); and the vivid descriptions of the Jamaican countryside. All of these, however, would be distractions from this beautiful West Indian love story.

When we first meet Headley, he is walking out to the cricket pitch: "He had the same old walk—ass cocked in the air, chest high like a game-fowl and the same old sarcastic smile played across his face as he teased the fielders on his way across the Puddin' Pan" (4). Then he meets Pam: "His eyes caught the unmistakable flash of the red blouse and the red floral band on the big straw hat that shaded the jet black face" (4). After their fateful meeting, Ellis skillfully leads us through the wooing, the chase and the early missteps that occur in all love relationships. He also highlights the conflict that these two lovers must overcome. Headley is a local hero who has been sheltered by his mother, his friends, girlfriend, and the entire village from the rigors of everyday life. Headley has concentrated his entire life on playing cricket and has never had to make any of the necessary choices that transform a boy into a man:

> Headley did not work. For him cricket was work. He put more of his time, dreams and energy into cricket than most men put into two jobs. His mother took care of him. What she did not have, his father sent from England, and for whatever else he wanted, the people of Sligoville were there. (9)

Headley also takes his friends, even his girlfriend, Maizy, for granted and tramples over their feelings to get what he wants. They all forgive Headley while he remains oblivious to their sacrifices. Pam, on the other hand, as the daughter of the town's outcast—the obeah woman—has steadily overcome all of the village's biases, but still carries the wounds of the race and class prejudices embedded in her nicknames: *African Perch* and *Junjo Head*. She has made all the choices that Headley has never had to make—a point she drives home after one of their initial meetings when Headley tries to boast about his prowess in cricket:

> "Is we Sligoville men who give Sligoville playing field and put Sligoville on the map," he sneered at her.
>
> "Cricket can eat?" she said sarcastically, half to herself. (13)

Gradually Pam draws Headley out of the cricket-bound world of Sligoville and he gains a broader perspective. Ellis also paints a beautiful picture of Kingston—a reversal of the usual point of view that many Jamaican writers employ. He describes Kingston from a rural viewpoint: "He looked away from her across the hills, following the arc of her waving hand. He made a quick scan of the slopes of the darkening hills, the trees with leaves bristling and entwining against the backdrop of the skies, the twilight mauve of the Caymanas flats and the neatly partioned pastures" (54). In this pivotal scene, Pam admonishes him, "You don't see out in front of you? You don't see the lights? You don't see Kingston?

You don't see the sea? And then, you don't see the planes lift off for other places? Sligoville is just the edge, the dark part" (57).

And when tragedy strikes, Headley, who because of his self-absorption has been totally unprepared for life, goes to pieces. He is rescued however by his friend, Dezzy, who counsels him at every turn, and along with Pam's love finally transforms Headley into the man he is to become. Dezzy, by his example, teaches Headley the true meaning of friendship by sticking with Headley through all of the hard times and the fights and never leaves Headley's side. Even when they disagree, Dezzy remains loyal, "The truth," Dezzy said, "the truth. When last me can't tell you the truth? Is that bother you, don't it. Is not the talk bother you, is not the talk that is the problem—is the truth. You don't want hear the truth. You don't want to face it" (121). Without Dezzy's help Headley would have succumbed to his self-pity that verges on self-destruction, but Dezzy's friendship rehabilitates this broken man. We leave Headley at the end of the novella using the same words as at the start: "How much runs you want?" (130). But it is a confidence tempered by loss and devoid of the empty bravura that had previously consumed his life.

Such As I Have, the first offering of the revived Macmillan Writers Series edited by Judy Stone, is a touching love story that engages the reader's attention with all the traits of true storytelling: careful plotting with unforgettable characters drawn with an eye for detailed descriptions, a unique point of view with memorable turns of phrase, and masterful use of dialogue and tone to guide the reader through the narrative. This may be Ellis's first novella, but from the abilities he has displayed in *Such As I Have*, he has built a strong base for a receptive audience for years to come.

Geoffrey Philp
Miami, Florida

Descent into Hades

Geoffrey Philp, *Benjamin, My Son*. Leeds, England: Peepal Tree Press. 2003. 185 pages. p.b. £8.99.

Geoffrey Philp is the author of four books of poems and a collection of short stories. For his debut novel he has chosen a genre, the mystery thriller, which is more often associated with airport best-sellers than with serious literature. Philp has succeeded in infusing some literary complexity into the genre, but at the expense of some of the urgency that ordinarily characterizes the genuine plot-driven whodunit. While the novel is fast-paced and tightly plotted, what is most compelling about it is not the plot, which revolves around the narrator's somewhat diffident search for the killer of his step-father, whom he hated, but the portrait of a society in the process of devouring itself. In the final analysis, the novel is too poetic to make it what blurb-writers call "a real page-turner," nor, one senses, was that the author's real aim. He sometimes seems to get distracted by the scenery, and seeing he is giving us a conducted tour of Hell, the scenery is the fascinating part. Like his protagonist, Philps was born in Jamaica and attended Jamaica College, which figures prominently in the novel; like his protagonist, he now lives in Miami. One gets the feeling that an actual return to the scenes of the author's youth lies behind his detailed description of his homeland and of his *alma mater*, and one can distinctly feel his dismay at their deterioration.

The novel has two epigraphs: the passage from Dante's *Inferno* where Virgil offers to give the poet a guided tour of Hades, and a quotation from Mark 3:25: "A house divided against itself cannot stand." This was the reply Jesus made when the scribes and Pharisees accused him of casting out demons by the power of Beelzebub, the prince of demons: "How can Satan cast out Satan? If a kingdom is divided against itself, that kingdom cannot stand. And if a house is divided against itself, that house cannot stand." The house divided against itself in the novel is contemporary Jamaica, where rival political parties and their allied gangs, combined with poverty and guns, drug trafficking, and AIDS, have converted a potential tropical paradise into a fair substitute for Dante's *Inferno*. The narrator's description of the ghetto area of Standpipe echoes Dante's description of the circles of hell:

> The men left us on a washout overlooking Standpipe.
> The thatched huts and tin shanties wrapped themselves
> around the hillside, circles and circles of mud, plywood
> and zinc that exposed the limestone underbelly yellowed
> by the sun. (71)

His descent into Standpipe, again, is reminiscent of Dante's descent down a washout into the lower regions of Hell, reserved for the violent:

> We descended through a washout strewn with plastic
> bags. A flock of John Crows, mobile black dots, hovered
> over the carcasses of dead dogs while others swooped

down, then climbed into the upper blue, gliding on the air currents that lifted them higher and higher into the sky.

Standpipe was a gangrenous artery of Kingston. Lives oozed in and out, clogged between the splintering light that fell through the tamarind trees to the rubbish-strewn ground and the aerial spiral of the John Crows who, like gregarious mutes, remained detached from the heat. (71)

Other echoes of Dante include the narrator's ambivalent relationship with his old mentor Papa Legba, who plays a Rastafarian Virgil, his ultimately redeeming love for his girlfriend Nicole, starring as Beatrice, and his visits to various former friends and acquaintances, who all seem to be writhing in some form or other of torment. The literary allusions add a layer of complexity to the novel which provokes thought, and as a result sometimes prevents the reader from actually turning the page. One lingers, not so much drawn forward by curiosity about what is going to happen next, as fascinated by the varieties of torment being played out before one's eyes.

Jason Stewart, the narrator and central figure of the novel, is an unlikely hero; indeed, Philp seems to have gone out of his way to create an unsympathetic character as protagonist. First of all, the man is a telemarketer; it is humanly impossible for anyone in his right mind to feel sympathy for a telemarketer, "one of those guys that rip off senior citizens and scam old people out of their pensions and social security checks" (129). As an economic fugitive from Jamaica, Jason has completely bought into the American dream of divorce, credit-card debt, and bar-crawling, while retaining enough self-righteousness to look down upon those who have stayed behind. Here is his opinion of his native land: "It's just full of people who lie and are dunce, lazy, slack, and arrogant" (12). Although he seems to make a habit of leaving his friends in the lurch when they get into tight places, he is stupid enough to try to intervene in a knife fight over a domino game, risking his life for a perfect stranger, who, as his more street-wise companion points out, is only getting what he deserves. His naiveté at times borders on criminal negligence, as when he deserts his friend Trevor in a situation likely to get him killed by the police, or when he reveals his informant Reuben's real name after having sworn not to tell anyone. This latter indiscretion results in Reuben's arrest and death under torture by the police; Jason never seems to make the connection between the two events, but the reader does. Jason's cowardice and insecurity lead him into a senseless fight with his girlfriend; when he is too immature to admit he was wrong, she storms out, and as a direct result is kidnapped by his father's killer. Jason does manage to redeem himself in the end—but I have to stop here, lest I reveal the surprise ending.

Unlike your ordinary thriller, this book is complex enough to require rereading; unlike your ordinary thriller, it is also rich enough to repay rereading. I recommend it highly.

David Gould
St. Croix, U.S. Virgin Islands

Life's Irony: Bitterness Results in Sweetness

Alan Cambeira, *Azúcar! The Story of Sugar.* Kearney, Nebraska: Morris Publishing. 2001. 290 pages. p.b.

Alan Cambeira's first novel resonates with the irony that provokes the saying: "the more things change, the more they remain the same." Slavery has been abolished, but the sugarcane workers at Esperanza Dulce, "Sweet Hope," experience another form of slavery. The conditions under which they live are an extension of "plantation slavery" (2). Old Don Anselmo reminds everyone that the systems implemented are ways "of very efficient control and exploitation" (77). *Azúcar* is, indeed, the story of sugarcane ("maldita cana") and the story of the protagonist, ironically named Azucar. Azucar's early life is anything but sweet, having lost her mother at her birth, her father to a brutal murder, her virginity to rape and abuse, and her twin daughters to the spirits. But in the end, life becomes sweet for Azucar as she finds true friendship in Marcelo and Dr. Harold Capps, the Canadian scientist. These two gay men "maricones sucios! Dirty faggots," (131) "perveros," are the catalysts that lead to her finding true love and much happiness. Azucar is a veritable embodiment of the sugar industry and its role in the Caribbean.

Cambeira captures the essence and flavor of the Caribbean and the plight of the workers who seem trapped in an industry that exploits them for the profits of some local people like Diego Moncalvo, "capataz" or overseer, and his inhumane sons. The author's realistic portrayal of the characters through their diction adds truth to his work. The novel is rife with the creole, French, patois and Spanish of the workers and the overseers' family. As the readers follow the characters in the "batey" they learn the history of sugarcane as Cambeira uses Don Anselmo, Mama Lola, Dona Fela and even Azucar herself to educate the readers about the painful life they live. They seem trapped in a hopeless situation where the basic necessities of life are denied them. Instead, "the open sewage trough that meandered through the entire length of the decrepit housing compound" contributes to the stench of the "batey" (2).

The spirits are an integral part of the sugar workers' lives. They are very real to the believers, and their mandates must be obeyed. The Haitian tradition mixed with that of the Dominicanos presents a vibrant interaction and invocation to the spirits. Not only do the worshippers seek protection, but they plead for revenge and they sacrifice Azucar's twins to "clear the way for her," something she doesn't understand until later.

M' hijita dulce. I did what I had to do to save you. . .It was all accordin' to the loas that we traditionally obey. To disobey would be a frightful mistake. Raisin' those twins would have meant your doom. . .and theirs, too. Someday you will understand all this. . .My duty was to have the powerful spirits of our ancestors protect you. (173)

The wisdom of the older ones—Anselmo, Fela and Mama Lola—is dispersed throughout the book in their sayings. Azucar understands when she returns "kaka pa pikan, men kan ou pile-l fo' kou bwete! Shit never stinks but you nevertheless tiptoe when you do walk through it" (184).

Azúcar! describes one girl's journey from the batey to a fulfilled life, with all the people who helped along the way. Azucar's story is the ultimate irony that her happiness is bound up in those connected with her island.

Valerie Knowles Combie
St. Croix, U.S. Virgin Islands

Mikey's Self-Appointed Crusade

Brian Meeks, *paint the town red*. Leeds, England: Peepal Tree Press, Ltd. 2003. 115 pages. p.b. £7.99.

Brian Meeks's *paint the town red* is a compact tale of love, disappointment, idealism, disillusionment, class structure, rebellion, and death. The author described writing this book as a "cathartic experience," as he attempted to explore the rebellion of the 1970s in Jamaica: "There are so many painful unanswered questions about Jamaica in the 70s, some of which may never be resolved by the historian or social scientist," he said. Through his protagonist, Mikey, Meeks expresses "his concerns with the theme of rebellion and the existential condition" not only of Mikey, Rosie, Carl, Caroline and Jamaica, but of the peoples of the Caribbean region. In that sense, the book becomes an account of the experiences of the peoples of the Caribbean.

paint the town red introduces Mikey being beaten in prison, then through flashbacks, the author uses Rohan to tell the story. Significantly, the story is not very different from the present, when the killings continue and blood still flows on the Jamaican soil. *paint the town red* tells the story of political uprisings and the involvement of young intellectuals. This book describes the human condition and the vicissitudes of life that impact most people; however, the most important message it teaches is the resilience of the human spirit, as is seen in Mikey.

Class plays a very important role in Meeks' book. Those with connections will be saved: "Tek de brown man alive!" (104) is the mandate from Caroline's father that saves Mikey's life, but it does not save him from imprisonment. His being alive haunts Mikey who wonders why the others were killed while he was allowed to live. That sends him searching for Caroline, a former lover, who reveals the arrangement. But Mikey is not content. He prefers to be dead than to carry the suffering of his friends' death. Like him, Jamaica and the Caribbean will survive, but their future will remain blighted by the stigma of incarceration as is expressed in Charlie's words as he tells Mikey that his mother would "neva recover. . .from de fact dat ar one son tun prisoner" (105).

The reggae music and the Rastafarian presence are themes that run through the book, juxtaposing the real with the ideal to show that the fabric of Jamaica society is intertwined in its people and its music. Mikey's last words to Rohan are prophetic:

"Remember Rohan, Marley say, 'Rise up fallen Fighters. . .He who fights and runs away lives to fight another day.' One day, the heathen back shall be against the wall and I an I shall return" (114).

Meeks' ingenious literary style introduces the reader to Jamaican landmarks, reviving memories in those who know Jamaica and can identify the various locations such as Spanish Town and Half Way Tree. The language of the book, interspersed with the Jamaican dialect, and the Rastafarian flavor, authenticates the story and keeps the reader reading, wanting to know more.

The introduction of different characters' perspectives is an added dimension that helps to balance the story. In Chapter 8, Carl convinces Mikey to visit his neighborhood, where Mikey is introduced to the elders. At the end of that chapter, as is done in other chapters, Carl gives his perspective on Mikey where he alludes to a self-imposed test that he administers and which Mikey passes. Carl calls Mikey a "cool yout," because "im always willing to share" (36). That character portrayal is important, because it prepares the reader for Mikey's role in the unfolding history of Jamaica, and his ultimate incarceration and release.

Meeks combines romance with politics and warfare, but he shows that for those youth, commitment to their political persuasion supersedes their personal comforts such as romance. When Rosie and Carl disappear, she has no qualms; the party comes first. In 115 pages, Meeks captures the fervor of the time, encapsulates it in a few well developed characters, and leaves the reader reflecting on Jamaica then and Jamaica now. Times have changed, people have changed, but the warring factions seem to remain the same. The book ends with Mikey loping "hungry lion-style down the sidewalk,". . .slowly fading "in the blue haze of the frantic traffic" (115).

Valerie Knowles Combie
St. Croix, U.S. Virgin Islands

Cycle of Fear

Gisèle Pineau, *Macadam Dreams*. Translated by C. Dickson. Lincoln, Nebraska: University of Nebraska Press. 2003. 215 pages. p.b. $20.00.

Gisèle Pineau's *Macadam Dreams* is an engaging, yet painful account of life in the shantytown of Savane Mulet, Guadeloupe. The lives of the main characters, Estelle, Rosette, and Angela, epitomize the state of women in their surroundings, living between cyclones—between despair and more despair. Here, the women's dreams are all intertwined, and Pineau makes us aware that, individually and collectively, these dreams are as fragile as the shacks that the dwellers erect and are forever reconfiguring.

First published in 1995 and only recently translated, *Macadam Dreams* is Pineau's second novel; since then she has written three, the most recent being *Chair Piment* (2002). *Macadam Dreams* is the story of wasted existence of a people who seem to be abandoned on the edge of survival in a place that was founded by a dreamer and (ironically) dubbed "the Good Lord's paradise" (17). Others, however, saw the harshness and the mule-stubborn nature of the environment, hence the name Savane Mulet. True to their prediction, paradise is perverted, and now its inhabitants forever live in a state of primitive barbarism or in ethereal suspension. Either way, life is bleak. It is Savane's female characters that forever try to escape into a dream world, yet it is they who see and experience reality at its harshest. Estelle, the main protagonist, lives in a state of perpetual memory-lapse brought on not by age but by a trauma experienced during her early childhood. This has left her emotionally paralyzed, unable to embrace the present with any passion and compassion—"her heart safely barricaded" (34). Her life is a state of arrested hesitation and lamentable "should haves." Time has snatched her one dream of bearing a child; hence she dulls the pain through her frequent escapes into her dream world and in her (futile) attempts to alienate herself from the sufferings of the neighborhood. She does not succeed in remaining aloof, however, and distancing only intensifies her pain. Behind the veil she suffers at every neglected opportunity to help—reduced to cowardice, petrified by her own inertia.

Rosette, in contrast, bears the weight of the entire ghetto (and more) on her soul—"the accursement of the black people, the calamity of misery, and the dead dreams on the earth" (34).

But Rosette is also the consummate dreamer, spending time "exalting in her paradise, busily hanging stars in the sky" (176). For her "happiness is [forever] at the tips of [her] lips" (177); she never tastes it, however, and always searches for the ultimate escape from life as she knows it. Her escape finds rest in her dreams that are every bit prophetic; only, the finger of doom constantly points in her direction. Her dreams are nothing but numbing euphoria, and, ironically, she feels the pain of all except the one closest to her—"[seeing] nothing, [hearing] nothing" (176).

Angela, the youngest of the main characters, is the most tragic, representing both the progeny of a morally debased family and the victim of a generational curse. Her one source of hope lies in her smashing the façade of the happy family her mother tries so hard to create and rebuilding her life with Estelle as her new mother. One wonders how deep are her psychological scars, though, and to what extent she will propagate what is clearly a damaged gene. If the youngest generation is blighted by a family curse, then one questions the ability of that generation to engage in productive existence. Angela therefore represents the now, the future of Savane Mulet, an attempt to rebuild from a disaster only to live with the constant menace that at any time there may be another—the end is the beginning.

One cannot read this book without noting Pineau's use of nature to alter the course of life of the people of Guadeloupe, specifically the dwellers of Savane Mulet. Here nature is eternally harsh—the hot sun, the dust, the cyclone. Long ago when Savane Mulet was being settled, many came thinking that they could drive away the ghosts, clear the land, and establish an existence. The land, however, has proved as stubborn as a bad memory, and the only measure of growth is in the ever mushrooming bellies of the women, each gestation hoping for reprieve.

In reading *Macadam Dreams*, much attention should be paid to the structure of the story. The plot is simple with many layers, stories within (frame) story, repetitive, cyclic, wheel within wheel—the end is the beginning, much like the lives of the main characters. Without the constraints of chronology, the story itself is like a series of bad dreams that recur, each time acquiring more horrifying dimensions. The narration is also typical of Creole story-telling—varied voices, different points of view so that the reader sees more intimately into the lives of the characters, and questions remain unanswered.

Having the book translated into English, Pineau has widened her readership to include the English-speaking Caribbean, and indeed, the wider English-speaking audience. Most of us can relate to the ambivalence of the tropical climate, and the constant need to break free, yet conform to the dictates of nature.

This book should definitely be added to our list of Caribbean must-reads.

Consuella Bennett
Atlanta, Georgia

Revival of a Forgotten Genre

José B. Alvarez IV, *Contestatory Cuban Shot Story of the Revolution.* Lanham, Maryland: University Press of America. 2002. 140 pages. p.b.

At last an audacious scholarly scrutiny that challenges the well-entrenched privileging of the Cuban theatrical, novelistic, poetic genres. Prefaced by an insightful introduction by Professor William Foster, José Alvarez IV's study, *Contestatory Cuban Short Story of the Revolution* is a bold affront to literary traditionalists unwilling to locate the rich Cuban literary tradition outside of pre-scribed genres. Alvarez does not purport any heroic investigatory mission. In fact, the author's words epitomize the forthrightness of his research: "The primary objective of this study is to explore and analyze the evolution of the constestatory element in the Cuban short narrative that emerges as a consequence of the censorship-resistance dialectic" (Alvarez 15). Clarity, however, does not portend arbitrariness, for Alvarez's study reflects years of scholarly exploration—trips to Cuba, reviewing countless documents, and interviews with prominent literary and political Cubans. Alvarez's fresh approach succeeds because of a style that allows profound philosophical and ideological concepts to flow unobstructed by opaque language or idle morphological constructions. His language is appropriately simple (not simplistic) yet sophisticated.

In order to present his reader with a clear notion of "the censorship/resistance dialectic" (10), Alvarez divides his work into four chapters, and an appendix with a spirited roundtable discussion with four Cuban intellectuals. The introductory first chapter offers clear historical and theoretical guidelines along which the study is to proceed. This strategic contextualization of the text permits one to navigate it with a clear sense of its limitation of scope and its primary goals. Among other issues, the writer outlines the successes of the Revolution in the context of socio-political and literary productions. Alvarez's referencing of various Cuban writers and his citing of the formation of important cultural and literary organizations are two primary examples of his thorough approach. Chapter Two concentrates on the works of the better known writers of three separate post-revolutionary periods: 1959-1965, 1966-1970, 1971-1976, and 1977 to literary productions during Senel Paz's generation. Alvarez's convenient denominations—Golden Quinquennium and Gray Quinquennium—position the short story in the context of a swinging pendulum that sways according to the ideological and political winds. In this chapter he analyzes, among others, short stories by Nicolás Pérez Delgado, César Leante, and José Soler Puig. The latter's work, "Mercado libre" ("Free Market"), centers around the Machado dictatorship of the 1930's and shows the hypocrisy of that government. Alvarez points to Pérez Delgado's "Gracias Torcuatico" and Leante's "El esposo" to dramatize the role that violence played during the Batista era. This chapter ends with an insightful discussion of the "new literary process," the period beginning 1975. Gradually, according to Alvarez, this generation initiated a revival of the aesthetic accomplishments of the golden era. The critic devotes much attention to Senel Paz's writing, because of the "authenticity and freshness with which" (34) Paz treats serious topics. The chapter ends on an optimistic note, affirming that the "narradores de la búsqueda" (Writers in Search) are carving out new paths. In essence, while they revisit traditional themes, these writers also explore unexamined areas, among them, homoeroticism and internationalism.

Borrowing Salvador Redonet's terminology *novismo*, in the third chapter Alvarez discusses the contribution of writers born between 1959 and 1972. Rejecting the traditional notions of the short story, they have opted for irreverent approaches that force a new formula: reader/accomplice. No longer can the reader passively enjoy the ride, but must, for the ultimate construction of the new text, be an active participant. The interplay of reader/writer and the intersection of competing literary techniques, including dialogues with the reader, position the *novismos'* Cuban short story within the framework of textual experimentation. In Chapter four, Alvarez resists the temptation to locate homoeroticism within oversimplified parameters. Instead, he posits his discourse within a larger overarching socio-cultural-political problematic. It must be noted that Alvarez privileges the term "homoerotic" over "homosexuality" for fear that the latter conjures and unleashes a string of stereotypes. Neither anti nor pro Castro in his discussion, he offers a balanced analysis of the ideology of the Cuban Revolution and how its far-reaching tentacles impinge on the notions of individual freedom. Moreover, Alvarez argues that "in post-revolutionary Cuba there is and has been prostitution, homosexuality, indiscriminate repression of citizens. . .hidden by Castro's government" (10). The chapter is replete with references to works that highlight the homoerotic theme. In the section "Gays in the Revolution" Alvarez cogently analyzes the image and the treatment of this minority class in Cuba. Marginalized by the government and viewed as aberrations of a Marxist system, gays were unabashedly repressed; no surprise to the critic since their sexuality is in ideological conflict with the ideals of the Revolution. This chapter skillfully discusses the intersection of patriarchy, machismo, homophobia, culture, gay identity, and hegemony in order to explain and properly position the Cuban homoerotic text. Despite negative responses by the government to the "dissident" gays, Alvarez contends that "the long evolutionary process of homoerotic texts in Cuba is finally reclaiming its legitimate space on the island's literature" (103). This upswing, argues the critic, is not a transitory moment in literary history. In fact, he posits, the ideological and other challenges by the government have only served to highlight the tenet that the fundamental thirst for freedom and civil rights can never truly be quenched.

The spirited interview in the Appendix offers the reader opposing and converging interpretative viewpoints of Cuba's socio-political realities. In a free-flowing discussion, Alvarez allows his interviewees to expound on such topics as Marxism, liberty, and existentialism. Wisely, the author avoids imposing himself on the debate, mainly formulating questions that evoke various exchanges among the intellectuals. Their introspection and analyses of Cuba compliment Alvarez's efforts in the previous chapters and help to crystallize his representation of the evolution of the short story. Alvarez's decision to focus on the Cuban short story is in and of itself a significant contribution, but the fact that he has done so with ample historical, sociological, and literary insight places his work in an even more unique category. The penchant by scholars to emphasize the novel, or poetry, at the expense of the short story must now be re-examined, because Alvarez has made it impossible to continue to ignore this most important genre. If we heed his words, ably defended in this well-researched text, we will walk away with a truth, hidden for years under the onslaught of novelistic and poetic critical evaluations: the Cuban short story deserves its legitimate position in the literary trajectory of Cuba. Alvarez's timely study goes a long way to reclaim this right.

Clement White
Providence, Rhode Island

Islands of Legends, Dreams and Lies (190)

Jacob Ross, *A Way to Catch the Dust and Other Stories*. London, England: Mango Publishing. 1999. 208 pages. p.b. $14.95.

The Caribbean of Grenadian Jacob Ross's collection of short stories, *A Way to Catch the Dust*, is a place of small villages, unending cane fields, deep forests and bountiful yet forbidding seas. It is a place that exists in a time before digital; a place where the supernatural is taken for granted; a place where Anancy may still hold sway. It is a place populated by people of the soil and the sea who speak to each other and to the reader in the vernacular of the common man and woman of the Caribbean.

Ross fashions his human relationships in broad swathes of Caribbean iconography. There is the long-suffering mother who sacrifices endlessly for her boy child. There is the wily and wise elder who is not as completely at the mercy of the powerful as circumstances and appearances first suggest. There is the light complexioned, socially prominent father who rejects his darker complexioned daughter—the product of a short liaison with his nurse. There is the acquisitive white foreigner for whom the local population is invisible except when it serves a purpose.

The natural environment plays a major role—often adversarial—in many of these stories. Nature sustains, but it also challenges the human community whose relationship with it is intimate and immediate.

She headed for The Mouth. There, with an almost experimental distraction she allows its pull to take hold of her, forcing herself to drift with it until she felt the silent, sucking cold. Then, with a violent flash of limbs, a sudden twist of rage that both surprised and pleased her, she pulled herself loose from its grip and headed for the beach. (45)

Whatever its manifestation, nature is always a powerful and mysterious entity, indifferent to the affairs of the human characters who regard it with respect, fear and awe. Sometimes it is accessible.

Times like these, he thought he understood the vast unnamable forces that kept the world on a pendulum; the mysterious precision of things; the forces that synchronized the rise and fall of moon and tide; the time that birds and fishes spawned and died and spawned again. (79)

But more often, it is a menacing, impersonal entity upon which humans have given ominous titles in homage to its terrible, unfathomable power.

. . .the Point of Shadows, is the rock they used to call The Sound—a jagged chunk of granite that rears its mighty head out of the water and straddles the air like some horned beast. Its great, twisted mouth is turned up at an angle to the sky in a timeless scream that remains silent even in the murderous hurricanes, which from time to time, sweep in from the north and west. (121)

Departing somewhat from the general sensibility of this collection, Ross devotes a series of three stories to Ku-Kus Stanislaus. Ku-Kus is a woman to be reckoned with—rooted in her culture and imbued with a robust self-possession and a keen native intelligence, curiosity and common sense. She also has a good man to back her up. As such, she is akin to Alexander McCall Smith's Mma Precious Ramotswe, owner of Botswana's *No. 1 Ladies Detective Agency*. Indeed, it is hoped that Ku-Kus will continue the sleuthing she began in "Ku-Kus: Woman of Letters" for it would be a shame—as Ku-Kus styles it—for the "fun an dramatics" (164) to not continue.

These are eerie, unsettling tales where there is a fine boundary separating the mundane and the extraordinary and where Ross has created a world that is at once literate and steeped in the oral tradition.

Mary Alexander
St. Thomas, U.S. Virgin Islands

Surviving the Crossing

E.A. Markham, *Taking the Drawing Room through Customs.*
Leeds, England: Peepal Tree Press. 2002. pb. 354 pages. £9.99.

This is a short story collection for the connoisseur. Markham's imagination is fertile and his craftsmanship superb. The response to the text is cerebral as the author moves the reader through digressive monologue to imaginative literary excursions, through philosophical ruminations about being and becoming to the mundane concerns of island life told with masterful control of Montserratian Creole.

Markham's characters move on a grand stage of infinite variety. In the background is a cadre of scholars, creative writers, diplomats, and literati presenting papers at seminars or speeches at conventions. Occasionally, these players move down center to become the hub of the action. In the foreground, commanding center stage, are the main characters who enter and exit as scenes play out, held together by a variety of themes.

Sometimes women command attention as Markham sketches tender vignettes of "La Contessa," the mother stories, or romantic liaisons with "Whatsername;" or the troubling current of female abuse in "Skeletons," or the ambiguous passion of "Miss Joyce" for Bobcat's machine, or the memories of grandmother Animal Pound in "The Pig Was Mine." At other times, there is the rough and tumble of West Indian life in Britain, colonials from the West Indies paying their dues and graduating to take their places in their new world, or bemoaning the demise of West Indies cricket, or reminiscing about the world they left behind, or like Pascoe looking for their roots, or planning illicit liaisons unknown to their wives or mistresses.

But what holds the stories together, the main strand of the plot, is always a discussion about roots, about transplantation, the West Indian immigrants settling in a new country and the threat to the West Indian family. In the post-war era, West Indians were moving to England in great numbers and Britons were being asked to move over, to make room and accommodate the colonials. Some West Indians, even those comfortable with the new life in the metropolis, were fighting to resist assimilation into the Mother country as the trickle of immigration grew into a steady stream in the 50's and 60's. Regardless, Markham's thesis is that to emigrate is to go backwards before moving forward to square one, and advancing from there takes time.

In "Preacherman," Markham presents a picture of hope for the hoards of people making the crossing from the Caribbean to Britain on the boat, anxious to "distinguish themselves" in a place where they "should demand to be treated with respect," (134) a big enough place, where in the words of the cynical professeur, a person could "fart in public" without the world knowing (135).

The West Indians are to suffer a culture shock. Mrs. Stapleton was somebody in Montserrat, a woman "who never worked for people" (13). The first day at the factory she is undeceived. Factory hands do not know "her place in society" (10). She moves from task to task at the miniature assembly line and rejects this topsy-turvy world. "A Short History of Employment in Britain" is told with sympathy and an underlying painful humor. However, confusion comes like a mighty wind uprooting La Contessa's world. Is she a seamstress or machinist? Is she using thread or cotton? Is it her hearing or her accent that is problematic? And to top it all, the people are uncivilized and should be taught manners.

"Madeline" details how Pewter's mother's great trunk is lost on the voyage to England in 1956: the silver spoon, the wedding dress and shoes, family photos, pictures of the houses, the crockery, the family Bible—all lost. The image of the lost trunk with its invaluable possessions is symbolic of disconnected roots and the fractured family. British immigration officials and customs try everything to cut the families loose from their anchor. Pewter knows that "once you start dismantling the house you might as well demolish the whole thing " (199).

"Our Man in KL" focuses on the drawing room story and what survives the crossing. The symbol of customs helps to frame Markham's discussion. In the final analysis, Pewter argues, it is taking the drawing room though customs that brings an anchor to the lives of the Stapleton family. And the author understands this well. Born in Montserrat and living in Britain since 1956, Markham brings an inside perspective to the theme. For Pewter, the drawing room "convey[s] a sense of what the family thought they had brought to England from the West Indies in 1956, and how little of it seemed to survive" (193). Even if Madeline managed to get her dog through customs, it only tells Pewter that England preferred animals to people.

What survived the crossing was the drawing room wit, a certain drawing room manner, Sunday afternoon sessions in the old house, going upstairs to talk. The family house in Montserrat was an anchor; life in England offered no interiors, no anchors for the soul—"other people had images to confirm their interiors, we did not" (240).

So in the new life in Britain where men like Pascoe look for roots in a society that "patronized black people" (27), somehow the West Indian immigrant survives. Some go back home for funerals to return again; others to show off new clothes, new accents, and new women; and still others like Miss Joyce with great expectations of a cultured life.

Often the return has tragic dimensions. In the delightful story of "Miss Joyce and Bobcat," the heroine wants to become a lady, only to fall in love with Bobcat's machine. To use her words, she had endured "cleaning racists in hospital beds, hoping to live again like a human being when she returned to the island" (263). In the end she is disillusioned and must settle for sex.

When Pewter returns to Montserrat, the family house no longer stands. Pewter notes: "When the house, my grandmother's house collapsed, the village came and took it away in pieces" (248). It became part of other houses. In Britain only customs preserved the family.

This is a serious work; beneath the humor is serious commentary about life and family. Markham's humor is delightful. Pewter's mother is sitting on the horse, getting her portrait taken. They labor to lift her on Ruby, the groom and the painter being "careful where they put their hands." The horse takes a few steps forward; the mother screams. Sometimes it is subtle and situational as in "Mammie's Form at the Post Office." She wants to send money HOME, not abroad. But beneath it all, Markham is inventing islands; he is also reshaping minds.

Trevor Parris
St. Thomas, U.S. Virgin Islands

A Real African Lion on London

Faith Smith, *Creole Recitations: John Jacob Thomas and Colonial Formation in the late Nineteenth Century Caribbean*. Virginia: University of Virginia Press. 2002. 224 pages. h.c. $59.50.

Smith's *Creole Recitations* evaluates the intellectual life of John Jacob Thomas while at the same time documenting the social conflict between the colonial elite and the working class in late 19th century Trinidad, where the British had recently replaced the French as colonial rulers.

Thomas, an educator, is best known for his polemic study of Trinidadian Creole Grammar, and *Froudacity*, a polemical work that takes issue with the ethnocentric remarks made by Oxford Professor Froude about Trinidadian society, and by extension the entire Caribbean.

Smith asserts that although Thomas was in many ways a product of his patriarchal, colonial Victorian education, he actively supported the professional advancement of intellectually talented women of all races and classes.

Like CLR James, the pre-eminent intellectual of the early 20th century Caribbean, Thomas was born in humble circumstances in Cedros, Trinidad. Like his Virgin Islands contemporary, Wilmot Blyden, Thomas used his pen to champion the cause of working class people in Trinidad and elsewhere. An advocate for West Indian literature, folk music, the quadrille dance, the use of organic reading in French creole in the school curriculum, this self-taught linguist and classical scholar saw education as the vehicle for upward social mobility among the poorer classes. Boldly insisting on his African identity, Thomas criticized British and French colonial policies in West Africa and North America.

In addition to demonstrating that creole has an orthography, an etymology, a syntax, and semantic rules, Thomas documented idiomatic expressions, proverbs, as well as translated excerpts of fables by Aesop, Perrin and La Fontaine. One of the proverbs, **Ravette pas jamain tni raison douvant poule** "Cockroach is never in the right where fowl is concerned" (p. 99), corresponds to similar sayings throughout the Caribbean and West Africa. Smith is careful to remind the reader that although Thomas' research in African etymology for creole expressions sometimes betrayed his lack of formal training in philology, Thomas' pioneering scholarship places him squarely in the company of world class radical innovators in humanitarian and educational scholarship.

Thomas' scholarship attracted mixed reviews from the international press, especially after 1893 when he presented a lecture on his Creole Grammar to the London Philological Society, perhaps the highest recognition accorded the Trinidadian legend during his lifetime.

Although the typical tendency of periodicals like the *Spectator* was either patronizing or blatantly racist, a few reviewers were more liberal in their response. In 1869 the *London Spectator* described Thomas' Creole Grammar as ". . .the first grammatical work composed by a person of negro descent, and has a certain historical value from this point of view. Otherwise, except so far as its subject matter is concerned, it has nothing particularly remarkable about it." (67) In 1873 the *Trinidad Chronicle* commented on Thomas' lecture at the London Philological Society as follows: ". . .It is not every day that they catch a real African lion on London, and of course they make mush of him when they do." (67)

As the above examples suggest, readers will note that Smith's analysis of Thomas' life and scholarly work does more than highlight social conflict in Victorian society in Trinidad. It also reveals ironic situations that survive in post-colonial Trinidad and the rest of the Caribbean.

Educators and culturally inquisitive readers should find this study an informative, fascinating, thought-provoking experience.

Vincent O. Cooper
St. Thomas, U.S. Virgin Islands

Selvon, Tiger and Moses

Martin Zehnder (ed.), *Something Rich and Strange: Selected Essays on Sam Selvon.* Leeds, England: Peepal Tree Press. 2003. 159 pages. p.b. £14.99.

Something Rich and Strange, compiled while Martin Zehnder was writing an M.A. dissertation for the University of Warwick, brings together seven essays, two interviews and a bibliography. The bibliography acknowledges indebtedness to Susheila Nasta's in *Foreday Morning: Selected Prose 1946-1986*.

In one of the finest pieces, John Thieme argues that "*The Lonely Londoners* may reasonably be viewed as the seminal West Indian carnival text, since it combines an oral narrative voice with the parodic, egalitarian and subversive comedy of Baktinian carnival."(55) The discussion includes an illuminating comparison between two versions of a common story, the aborted crucifixion in *The Lonely Londoners* and V.S. Naipaul's "Man-man."

In another outstanding essay, Maureen Warner-Lewis examines with detailed authority "Selvon's Linguistic Extravaganza" in *Moses Ascending*. "The overall dissonance of language register functions. . .as a thematic device as well as a formal means of character delineation." (71) While language, she writes, "accounts for a large part of the humour in the novel, it is itself a metaphor of Moses's ambivalent, ambiguous and ironic situation." (74)

Harold Barratt's contribution—"Sam Selvon's Tiger: In Search of Self-Awareness"—centres on *A Brighter Sun* and *Turn Again Tiger*, placing them in relation to other books by Selvon and work by other West Indian writers. Some commentators, he notes, "have given Tiger's bond with the land short shrift; recognition of this bond, however, is essential for an understanding of Tiger." (33)

Victor J. Ramraj considers the treatment of political militancy in *Moses Ascending* and *Moses Migrating*. "Selvon conveys his pejorative assessment of political zealots primarily through his skilful characterisation of the two Moseses, who, though they share the same name and several characteristics, are quite different individuals in their respective novels." (78) *Moses Migrating* "is less a continuation of *Moses Ascending* than a separate work." (82) Selvon, in *Moses Migrating*, "discourages taking Moses's frantic militancy seriously, playing it simply for laughter as an end in itself." (83)

Kenneth Ramchand, contending that Selvon in his later novels uses comedy "to evade troubling issues," speculates on the relation between the author and his work.

I would hazard the intuition that the increased reliance upon broad comedy in the two later Moses novels, and the uncertainty of purpose in Selvon's expression of the loss of belief and intensity in the Moses character are a function of the author's own problems of belief (to put it moderately), not unrelated to his departure from England for Canada in 1978. (88)

Ramchand anticipates some possible objections.

Part of the evidence—the language Moses uses to describe his feelings—may be inadmissible: the language Moses uses is Moses's language, and cannot technically be deemed the author's voice. In the second place, an argument that an author evades the challenge and logic of the situation he has created runs the risk of turning out to be a declaration that he did not write the book one wanted him to write. (101)

The Lonely Londoners is nevertheless wielded as a stick with which to beat the author for two very different enterprises.

If the comic response in *The Lonely Londoners* is profound, it is so because almost every episode contains an acknowledgement and defiance of tragic dimensions ('they only laughing because to think so much about everything would be a big calamity'), and every comment of the narrating voice is heard as the wisdom of one who has seen and suffered all. (86)

In "The Odyssey of Sam Selvon's Moses" John Stephen Martin, seeing in all three Moses novels an "ironic pattern of complicated responses" (110), considers Moses "an unstable verbaliser of his own life" (108) "Who is the real Moses? The reader cannot be sure." (111) "*Moses Migrating*. . .tells of Moses's Odysseus-like attempt to return to his Trinidad home after almost three decades of subtle anglicisation." (112) But "Moses has nowhere to go but back to England, the home of the transformed immigrant he is." (114)

Paola Loreto's "The Male Mind and the Female Heart: Selvon's Ways to Knowledge in the 'Tiger Books'" says love "is the form of knowledge that comes from an attitude of patient expectation and surrender to a powerful, superior force" and that the male and female characters in Selvon's novels "reach this form of knowledge by different routes." (40) But "As far as he gives each of them equal credit, the male and female psychologies of knowledge, or ways of coping with existence and its harshness, are truly complementary in Selvon's fiction and, evidently, in his view." (48)

The two interviews reflect contrasting approaches. John Thieme concentrates on eliciting information. His questions are succinct, modest, open-ended. Alessandra Dotti, on the other hand, is often asking the author to confirm or challenge critical assertions.

In his Introduction, Martin Zehnder makes a case for every item. He commends and recommends attention to Selvon's Indian heritage, a stronger presence in *A Brighter Sun*, he believes, "than. . .Selvon himself was sometimes willing to admit." (15) With reference to Loreto's contribution, Zehnder notes that there is further scope for study of the female characters in Selvon's books, "in particular a reading of the women against the background of an Indian aesthetic." (17) He mentions recurrent commentary on literary allusion in Selvon's work, and he himself contributes, suggesting the usefulness of reading *The Lonely Londoners* against *The Quest of the Holy Grail* as well as the *Bible*, Dante, Virgil and Homer.

Mervyn Morris
Jamaica

A New View of V.S. Naipaul?

V.S. Naipaul, *Literary Occasions*. New York: Knopf. 2003. 202 pages. h.c. $24.00.

While widely admired for the quality of his observations and his lucid prose, V.S. Naipaul himself has been described variously as "dyspeptic" and "snappish"; labeling him a "curmudgeon" seems almost kindly. This is the man who recently accused Tony Blair of promoting an "aggressively plebian culture that celebrates itself for being plebian" and who denigrated both *The New Yorker*, the magazine which has published so much of his work, and Oxford University, his alma mater. This is the man who, when judging a poetry contest, insisted that he could award only a third prize and then begged one poet to abandon poetry altogether. And this is the man who once wrote of his native Trinidad and the entire Caribbean with such scandalous contempt that he is still not wholly forgiven.

And yet. And yet. Critics have rightly called *Literary Occasions* a "literary autobiography" and the essays collected here, such as "Reading and Writing," "Prologue to an Autobiography," "Forward to the Adventures of Gurudeva," and the Nobel Prize lecture, "Two Worlds," reveal the origin of many of Naipaul's themes, including the impact of colonialism and what he terms his lack of a literary mythology, but, surprisingly, they also reveal a different Naipaul, a nostalgic side to a man celebrated for anything but. Literary occasions, as evidenced in these pieces, are essentially occasions for Naipaul to reminisce about his childhood in Trinidad and especially about his father.

Consider how often Naipaul has been retelling his life's story: how in Trinidad at age 11 he determined to become a writer and how he set himself to the task so fervently. He repeats this account in varying lengths in more stories, essays, and interviews than I can count: five times in this collection alone. At first it seemed he was simply repeating his standard how-I-came-to-be-a-writer speech, but then I wondered—might it be comforting for him to hark back to his past like this, to reiterate his early history? He doesn't, after all, reminisce about the early years of his first marriage or his student days at Oxford. Is he, then, really—when it comes to childhood and Trinidad, at least—an old softie?

There's more evidence here. When Naipaul won the Nobel Prize in 2000, he infamously quipped that the award honored his home of England and his ancestral home of India—omitting entirely his true home of Trinidad. In "Two Worlds," he discusses the origins of his art and he speaks primarily about Trinidad and its connection to India. While Naipaul once again talks about his early determination to leave Trinidad, he also details life in Chaguanas, and he asserts that those "areas of darkness" around him as a child later became his subjects.

Most revealing of this nostalgic side of Naipaul, however, is the repeated homage expressed towards his father. Seepersad Naipaul is discussed in the Introduction to the collection by Pankaj Mishra, and then Naipaul himself writes of him in "Reading and Writing;" the lengthy "Prologue to an Autobiography;" "Jasmine;" in his forward to "A House for Mr. Biswas," a novel inspired by his father; in "Two Worlds;" and even works him into the essay on Joseph Conrad.

But Naipaul reveals the depth of his affection for the man he called "The best man I knew" (Letters 265) in the introduction he wrote for the publication of his father's book of short stories, *The Adventures of Gurudeva*, published in 1975 and reprinted here. Getting his father's stories published was clearly an act of devotion, a debt paid, it would seem, to a man who wanted nothing so much out of life than to be a successful writer. The elder Naipaul made "the writing life seem noble" to his son and was unquestionably the major influence on his son's life. If V.S. Naipaul vowed to be a writer and struggled to turn himself into one despite many obstacles, it was his father, Seepersad Naipaul's dream first. Naipaul's published letters reveal the depth of his father's determination towards this end: When their father had a heart attack in 1953, his sister wrote to him in England, that only the publication of his stories would make their father well again. It took over 20 years to fulfill his father's wishes—his father was by then long dead—but as Naipaul writes the introduction to his father's only published collection, he writes it with his father's very own fountain pen.

Besides revealing this softer side of Naipaul, the essays published here confirm the world's assessment of him for both the insightful quality of his prose, his range of intellect, and his "incorruptible scrutiny" (to quote the Swedish Academy). Naipaul reviews a biography of Rudyard Kipling and talks of the Indian writer Nirad Chaudhuri's "extra-literary personality" (149). His provocative essay on Joseph Conrad reveals that he felt Conrad had come before him as a man offering "a vision of the world's half-made societies as places which continuously made and unmade themselves. . ." (170).

At first I was skeptical of *Literary Occasions* (a companion to *The Writer and His World*, which reprints Naipaul's travel pieces); both books were obviously packaged to take advantage of Naipaul's new-found audience since winning the Nobel Prize. But the value of *Literary Occasions* is clear to me now: it offers the advantage of accessibility in one volume and is also a bargain compared to purchasing the numerous publications on their own. Plus, this collection offers noteworthy insight into the vast reach of Naipaul's intellect, his "genius for noticing" (according to the *New York Review of Books*)—and a worthwhile perspective on his famously testy disposition.

Erika J. Waters
South Freeport, Maine

A Culture of Meaning

Edwidge Danticat, *After the Dance - A Walk through Carnival in Jacmel, Haiti*. New York: Crown Publishers. 2002. $16.00.

Edwidge Danticat's *After the Dance*, subtitled *A Walk through Carnival in Jacmel, Haiti*, details the author's journey to Jacmel, Haiti during the carnival season. However, the text is much more than a travel narrative. The book serves as a psychological portrait of both a literal and allegorical return and journey. On the literal level, the narrative functions as a type of travel journal, exploring the preparations and the history of the Carnival parade and associated celebrations in a small town on Haiti's southern coast. On a symbolic level, the text explores the narrator's allegorical journey into the depths of her subconscious. The carnival and telling the story of the carnival become a catalyst for psychological growth. The narrator systematically explores her own fears and reservations about making herself vulnerable and about establishing emotional connections not just with others but with her ideas of a homeland. The text also links the author's interior journey with the development of Haiti's emerging identity and other artistic representations of Haiti's development. Specifically, Danticat refers to paintings depicting the lush and forested landscapes when, in reality, Haiti's forests are rapidly disappearing. The paintings, her text suggests, attempt not only to compensate for the loss but also to build an imaginative forest that can then serve as a place for cultural and creative growth.

Danticat begins her story by writing that she "had as intense a desire to join the carnival as some peculiar American children have of joining the circus" (13). Her longings persisted, despite her uncle's warnings that the carnival represents danger and makes one vulnerable to licentious behavior. The carnival also, Danticat reveals, comes to symbolize her fears of political violence. "At Carnival, there were always militiamen and soldiers clubbing people over the head with sticks or rifle butts" (14). She also confesses that the carnival also evoked her fear of crowds. However, she ends her first chapter with a determination to "confront" those "carnival demons which" she "had been so carefully taught to fear" (15). Subsequent chapters systematically chart Jacmel's geography, simultaneously connecting the author's literal and spiritual geography.

Danticat seeks out a graveyard and, while touring the tombs and markers, recalls an English travel writer's despair at the desolate grounds and decaying tombs. Danticat, in contrast, notes the signs of life among the markers of the dead. She stumbles on condoms and the signs of sexual encounters, recalling James Joyce's hero Leoplold Bloom's discovery of similar signs of life in the funeral car in *Ulysses*. At the close of the chapter, Danticat links the graveyard's various signs of life, that also include legends and flowering vines, to her own creative efforts, writing that she "wants to spin her own tale" (35) and that she "think[s] perhaps it is the trembling shadows from the cemeteries, sending us sparkling signals from across the waters." (35)

Her book goes on to lay side by side perceptions of life and death. She explores colonial forts, plantations, the life of slaves, bringing these images together within the symbolism of carnival. Her work acknowledges the violence of Haiti's history, including various United States' invasions and the abuses of Haitian governments. Danticat's story transforms the brutal, faceless violence of militarism by seeking out the human presence of individual soldiers.

She tells the story of an American soldier who has become a legend and even a figure in carnival because "he was a powerful man who wanted to use his power to defend" (76) the Haitian people. She names the soldier "Makanani" (77), and she notes that he "became included not only in the history, but also the legend of Jacmel" (78). Significantly, Danticat does not attempt to gloss over or ignore the faceless brutality of military involvement. Rather, she acknowledges it. In another story of an American soldier, Danticat tells how "Captain Lawrence Rockwood, a counter-intelligence officer from the Tenth Mountain Division who had left his assigned barracks in the middle of the night to inspect a Haitian prison for human rights abuses, would later be court-martialed" (77). Not only does Danticat name the soldier, she names his unit. She gives him a complete identity, in the same way he sought dignity for political prisoners. Significantly, she also notes how a faceless bureaucracy destroyed him. American soldiers and Haitian civilians find themselves united not only as victims of oppression but as people who strive to see the humanity in themselves and others.

Danticat's narrative culminates not only in the literal celebration of carnival but also in her re-integration into Haitian culture. She establishes a metaphor linking emigrants and the disappearing forest of Haiti. Even as she despairs over the loss of Haiti's natural heritage, she wanders into a forest and notes that "even the echo of my voice, bounced against the trees, sounds like a series of other voices all together" (108). Her suffering and sense of exile find a resonance with the spirits of the dead and the living. She returns and discovers the power of her voice and its ability to echo and project her suffering and the suffering of others and even the suffering of the natural world.

Ultimately, she acknowledges a culture of meaning that moves beyond the carnival of Bakhtin and others. For Bakhtin, the freedom of carnival ends with carnival, as the revelers take off their masks. For Danticat, she ends her story by acknowledging the reality of carnival. She writes that "it did happen" (158), that she "had really been there" (158). She goes on to say that "Even as others had been putting on their masks, just for one afternoon, I had allowed myself to remove my own" (158). Danticat's story culminates not simply in an escape from the individual pain of emigration and exile and not just in a temporary sense of freedom from the traumas of Haitian history. Her story ends with an integration into Haiti's rich and meaningful culture that has endured and grown despite the sometimes dehumanizing events of Haiti's sometimes turbulent past. Danticat's story, then, is Haiti's story, the human and beautiful picture of a nation far too often seen as a place only of violence.

Bernard McKenna
Madison, New Jersey

The Person Ignores the Material

Kellie Magnus, *Little Lion Goes to School*. New York: Media Magic. 2003. Illustrated by Michael Robinson. 16 pages. Ages 3-8. $9.99.

Kellie Magnus has written *Little Lion Goes to School*, the first in a series to be written about the adventures of a young Rastafarian named Little Lion. Having a book series available to children written and illustrated by Caribbean authors and illustrators is a welcome addition to Caribbean children's literature. Caribbean children should be exposed to representations of themselves. They need books that help them identify with their unique culture and surroundings.

In *Little Lion Goes to School*, Papa wants Little Lion to have the best education and enrolls him in a new school. The main character, Little Lion, is very apprehensive about leaving his friends at his old school and going to the new one. To tell this story, the author juxtaposes Papa's thinking and the running story with the italicized thoughts of Little Lion as he goes through the first few days of school. In this way, the reader has a better understanding of Little Lion's inner thoughts and feelings.

Papa encourages Little Lion saying, "Your new school will open the door / Tomorrow will be a new beginning / With a good education / You can be anything." While Little Lion is thinking, "Oh, no. Oh no. This isn't cool / Don't make me go to that new school / Why can't Papa change his mind?" Once inside the new school, Little Lion feels even more out of place, especially as children begin a Show and Tell time and talk about gifts, toy cars, and phones. He has none of these fancy things to tell about. Little Lion is even more afraid of being in this school as he thinks about how different the children are from him. As he worries about his turn for Show and Tell the next day, Papa tries to encourage him to "stand tall" and remember that it is what's inside a person that counts. But, Little Lion is still thinking that "there's nothing special about me." He warily waits and is the last person to take a turn. As he is called forward, he becomes embarrassed when the teacher has trouble pronouncing his given name. The children laugh. Just in time, Little Lion remembers his father's words, closes his eyes, and sings a song that tells about him, his life, his father, and other Rastas. The class is soon clapping and swaying to the music and cheering him on. Little Lion learns an important lesson that day. He thinks, "Wow. Papa was right. . . / My special gift is inside me."

Magnus teaches children the life lesson that what is important is what is inside each person and not material possessions. Teaching through story is a characteristic of Caribbean tales that is also found in this book. In addition, the poetic, deconstructed style brings to mind the lilt and cadence of Caribbean languages. Michael Robinson's colorful, caricature-type illustrations authentically represent the Caribbean, from shuttered windows, to fishing boats, to the diverse children in the classroom. This book is a welcome addition to the growing body of Caribbean children's literature.

Sarah F. Mahurt
West Lafayette, Indiana

CONTRIBUTORS

Madeline Meehan

Contributors

Mary Alexander earned a B.A. in English at the University of the Virgin Islands where she has been a member of the Humanities Division since 1981. She is also a poet and a farmer. She is a founding member of the Rock Collective which produces open mic experiences every month on St. Thomas, Virgin Islands.

Lauren K. Alleyne, born in Trinidad, is currently pursuing her MFA in Poetry at Cornell University. Her poetry has appeared in *Sketch and Sexing the Political: A Journal of Third Wave Feminists on Sexuality*, *The Caribbean Writer* and *The Sydney Hampden Review*. Her essay entitled "How to Leave Home" is forthcoming in the anthology *Leaving the Nest: Mothers and Daughters on the Art of Saying Goodbye*.

Nigel Assam was born in Trinidad and moved to the U.S. at fourteen. While living in New York, he studied art and graduated later with a B.A. in Literature. He currently lives in Baltimore, MD.

Mary Kate Azcuy's poetry has been published in literary and academic journals, two collections, *nantucket* and *key west*, as well as local and regional newspapers and magazines. She currently serves as an English Instructor at Monmouth University in New Jersey.

Consuella Bennett has published in *The Caribbean Writer* and *CLA (College Language Association) Journal*. She also has an essay in *Changing Currents: Anglophone, Francophone, and Hispaniophone Literary and Cultural Criticism* (University of Florida Press), edited by Emily Williams. She is currently a UNCF/Mellon fellow, completing her dissertation; her discipline is Rhetoric and Composition.

Susan Broili, a journalist, has published non-fiction, journal writing and poetry, most recently in the anthologies *The Caribbean Writer*, *Poets for Peace* and *Earth and Soul*.

Richard James Byrne is a writer living in New York. He is working on his first novel and is the Director of Communications for the PBS public affairs series *NOW* with Bill Moyers.

Kathy Carlson received a BA in Education from Kean College and a Masters in Math from East Strausburg University. She has been a teacher for over 25 years and an artist for over four decades.

Magdalena Cohen recently graduated from Lewis & Clark College with a BA in English and a BA in Psychology. She currently resides in Torrance, California where she will begin Law School this summer in Los Angeles.

Loretta Collins is an Associate Professor of Anglophone Caribbean literature and creative writing in the English Department, University of Puerto Rico, Rio Piedras. Her poems have appeared in several journals, including *The Caribbean Writer*, *Poui*, *Black Warrior Review*, *TriQuarterly*, *The Missouri Review*, and *Antioch Review*.

Valerie Knowles Combie is an associate professor of English at the University of the Virgin Islands. She has written book reviews for past editions of *The Caribbean Writer*.

Vincent O. Cooper lectures in English and linguistics at the University of the Virgin Islands. A widely published linguist, poet and literary scholar, his most recent poetry publication is *Tigers in Paradise*, which is co-authored with David Gershator and Patricia Harkins-Pierre.

Alba Cruz-Hacker was born in the Dominican Republic and also lived in Puerto Rico for several years. Her work continues to appear in various literary magazines and she's also a 2003 Pushcart Prize Nominee. She resides in Southern California with her husband and three children.

Fred D'Aguiar's most recent books are a novel, *Bethany Bettany* (2003), a verse novel, *Bloodlines* (2000), and his new and selected poems, *An English Sampler* (2001) all from Chatto, London. He is on extended leave from University of Miami and is Professor of English at Virginia Tech.

Garfield Ellis's first published collection of stories, *Flaming Hearts*, and a later unpublished manuscript, *Till I'm Laid to Rest*, both won the Una Marson Award. He has also won the Canute A. Brodhurst prize for fiction (*The Caribbean Writer*) and the 1990

Heinemann/Lifestyle short story competition. His second collection, *Wake Rasta and Other Stories*, was published in 2002, and his first published novel, *Such As I Have*, has recently been published by Macmillan. A second novel, *For Nothing At All*, is forthcoming.

Howard A. Fergus, Professor of Eastern Caribbean Studies at the University of the West Indies (Montserrat), is a widely published author and poet. His most recent book is *A History of Education in the British Leeward Islands* (UWI Press, 2003) and his *Volcano Verses* will be published by Peepal Tree Press this year.

Carrol B. Fleming is the author of *Adventuring in the Caribbean: The Sierra Club Guide to the Caribbean*. She has published two chapbooks of poetry and numerous articles in national magazines. She currently teaches poetry in California.

David Gould teaches English at the University of the Virgin Islands, St. Croix campus.

Cecil Gray retired from the University of the West Indies and has since published four collections of poetry. He was awarded *The Caribbean Writer's* Daily News Prize for poetry in 1996.

Patricia Harkins-Pierre's poems may be found in two recent collections, *Akpasa: Poems That Dance* and *Tigers in Paradise*. She received her doctorate in Creative Writing (fiction and poetry) from the University of Southern Mississippi and has studied with distinguished Caribbean writers Mervyn Morris of Jamaica and Nobel Prize winner Derek Walcott of St. Lucia.

Tonya Haynes is a 21 year old Management Studies student at the University of the West Indies (Cave Hill Campus) and the inaugural winner of the John Wickham Memorial Prize of the Frank Collymore Literary Endowment.

Donna Hemans, Jamaican born, is the author of *River Woman*, which was a finalist for the Hurston/Wright Legacy Award in 2003. Donna served as the Spring 2004 Lannan Visiting Creative Writer in Residence at Georgetown University in Washington, D.C. where she taught fiction writing. She lives in Maryland and is at work on her second novel.

Joanne C. Hillhouse, an Antiguan, is a freelance producer, journalist, and writer. In 2003, Macmillan Caribbean released Hillhouse's first work of fiction, *The Boy from Willow Bend*, with another, *Dancing Nude in the Moonlight,* scheduled for release in 2004. Hillhouse self-published her first poetry collection, *On Becoming.* She was associate producer and production manager, respectively, on Antigua's first and second feature films, *The Sweetest Mango* (2000) and *No Seed* (2002).

William Hudson was born near Black Rock, in Lawrence County, Arkansas. He writes from Spokane and Usk, Washington.

Hilda Lewis Joyce was born in St. Thomas, US Virgin Islands. She recently retired from the University of the Virgin Islands where she served as associate professor in Business Administration and director of Academic Administration. She is the author and self-publisher of seven short story books in which her charcoal illustrations are included. Her work was previously published in the *Virgin Islands Daily News* and *The Caribbean Writer.*

Adele King, Professor Emeritus in French, Ball State University, now lives in Paris. Her most recent book is *Rereading Camara Laye.* While most of her work has been on French and African literature, she has written on Maryse Condé, Myriam Warner-Vieyra, and Gisèle Pineau. She contributed the chapter on "Postcolonial African and Caribbean Literature" to the *Cambridge History of African Literature.*

Roberta Q. Knowles is a former English professor at University of the Virgin Islands, St. Croix campus. She co-edited *Critical Issues in Caribbean Literature* (1984) and wrote *Arona Petersen: Famous Virgin Islander* (1991).

Edgar Othaneil Lake is a writer lilving in St. Croix, whose forthcoming novel, *The Devil's Bridge*, is to be released from Athena Press & Book Publishers this spring. He is currently working on a larger manuscript on Charles Abramson and his most recent paper, "Virgin Islands Cultural Gifts of the Jazz Age: Charles Lindbergh's Landing, 1928" was presented at the 13th ACASA Triennial at Harvard University in April 2004.

Laurence Lieberman has published 13 books of poems. *Hour of the Mango Black Moon*, poems with paintings by Stanley Greaves and others, has just appeared from Peepal Tree Press. Other recent books include *Flight from the Mother Stone* (2000) and *The Regatta in the Skies* (1999). He is the editor of the Illinois Poetry Series and Professor of English at University of Illinois.

Sarah F. Mahurt, a former professor of education at the University of the Virgin Islands, St. Croix, is now the director of the Literacy Collaborative at Purdue University. She has published articles on Caribbean children's literature in the *Journal of Children's Literature*, *The Five Owls*, and *TELLing Stories*.

Patti Marxsen manages publications for an international peace and justice institute based in Cambridge, Massachusetts. She is a former French teacher and has spent time in Haiti through her association with Hopital Albert Schweitzer.

Diana McCaulay is a Jamaican writer and environmental activist. She was the author of a weekly opinion column for the *Gleaner* between 1994 and 2000. Her short story "The Mango, The Ackee and the Breadfruit" won the *Lifestyle* magazine short story competition in 1992. She is the CEO of the Jamaica Environment Trust and is currently working on a novel entitled *Jamaican Born*.

Bernard McKenna teaches English at Drew University. He served on the editorial board of *The Caribbean Writer* for Volume 17 (2003).

Rachel Davis McVearry has published in newspaper articles and her poetry has appeared in high school and college journals and *Poetry.com*.

Madeline Meehan was born in Cuba and now lives in St. Thomas, U.S. Virgin Islands. Her book, *Golden Beaches, Crystal Waters: An American Paradise in Drawings*, was published by the Honey Press.

Anesa Miller, a foreign language teacher for 15 years, has also worked as a freelance writer and editor since the late 90s. Her work has been published by the University Presses of Michigan and Massachusetts and appears in recent issues of *Cimarron Review*, *The Cream City Review*, *Kenyon Review*, and *South Carolina Review*.

Kei Miller has been a visiting writer at the York University in Canada, and the Department of Library Services in the British Virgin Islands. His work has appeared in *Red River Review, Paumanok Review, The Caribbean Writer* and *Caribbean Beat.* He is currently pursuing his Masters in Creative Writing at Cardiff University, Wales.

Calvin Mills, born and raised in California, later attended the College of the Redwoods before moving to Little Rock, Arkansas. Mills finished a fine arts degree in 1998 at the University of Arkansas at Little Rock where he is currently studying writing.

Mervyn Morris, now a Professor Emeritus, taught at the Mona campus of the University of the West Indies. His books of poetry include *The Pond, Shadowboxing, Examination Centre* (New Beacon, London) and *On Holy Week* (Dangaroo Press). He is also the author of *Is English We Speaking and Other Essays* (Ian Randle Publishers).

Trevor Parris is a full tenured professor of English at the University of the Virgin Islands and Director of the Virgin Islands Writing Project. He has studied English at the Universities of the West Indies, Toronto, and Hull (England). His literary publications include a children's novel and contributions to a number of poetry anthologies.

Jeff Percifield is a freelance writer and ex-US military serviceman who grew up in New Mexico but now lives in the San Francisco Bay Area. He studied writing at University of California at Berkeley and his stories have appeared in *Santa Monica Review, Beloit Fiction Journal, Minnesota Review,* and upcoming in *The Caribbean Writer* and *Sulphur River Review.* He is currently working on a novel about post-9/11 America.

Geoffrey Philp is the author of the novel, *Benjamin, My Son,* and four poetry collections, *Exodus and Other Poems, hurricane center, Florida Bound* and *xango music.* He has also written a book of short stories, *Uncle Obadiah and the Alien.* Philp's reviews, articles, poems and short stories have also appeared in numerous publications including *The Caribbean Writer, Florida in Poetry, The Oxford Book of Caribbean Short Stories,* and most recently, *Whispers from the Cotton Tree Root.* He teaches writing at Miami Dade College.

Maud Pierre-Charles is a native of Haiti and a visual artist living in the Virgin Islands. Her series on the Caribbean market place was featured in *The Caribbean Writer*, Volume 4.

Nancy Pistilli holds a BFA in Art from the University of Connecticut. Her work is represented at the Christiansted Gallery in St. Croix and The Pink Papaya Gallery in St. John. She has been painting in the Virgin Islands since 1972.

James Plath is a Hemingway scholar who presented a series of lectures at the Nobel laureate's home in Cuba and at the Instituto Internacional de Periodismo José Martí in Havana. He was a Fulbright lecturer at the University of the West Indies in Barbados, and is currently Professor of English at Illinois Wesleyan University.

Rohan Preston, Jamaican-born, New York-reared and Yale-educated, has authored the poetry collection *Dreams in Soy Sauce* and co-edited the multi-genre anthology, *Soulfires: Young Black Men on Love and Violence*. His work is widely anthologized in many publications including *American Poetry: The Next Generation*; *Beyond the Frontier: African-American Poetry for the 21st Century*; *Bum Rush the Page: a def poetry jam*; and *Catch the Fire: A Cross-Generational Anthology of Black Poetry Pyromaniacs*. He currently serves as the lead theater critic at the *Star Tribune*.

Toodesh Ramesar, from Trinidad, has been an English teacher for 22 years; he is currently vice-principal of a junior secondary school in south Trinidad.

Thomas Reiter, a recipient of 2003 fellowships from the National Endowment for the Arts and the New Jersey State Council on the Arts, holds the Wayne D. McMurray Endowed Chair in the Humanities at Monmouth University. In 2004 Louisiana State University Press will publish his next book of poetry, *Powers and Boundaries*.

Elizabeth Rezende serves as an adjunct professor of social sciences and is currently teaching history at University of the Virgin Islands. She holds a doctorate in history and has published articles in several journals including *Kruispunt* and *La Torre*. Additionally, she has written reviews for *The Caribbean Writer*.

Kim Dismont Robinson is an assistant professor of English at the University of the Virgin Islands. Her critical writing focuses on the links between Caribbean literature, psychoanalysis, and spirituality. A Bermudian poet and journalist, she also works as a freelance writer and oral historian.

María Soledad Rodríguez teaches women's, Caribbean, and postcolonial approaches to children's literature at the Rio Piedras campus of the University of Puerto Rico.

Clemens Schoenebeck is a retired dentist who discovered poetry rather late in his life. He has been published in a number of small press poetry journals, including *The Dan River Anthology*, and *The Midwest Poetry Review*. His 9-11 poem, "For the Angels Unwinged," was published in the *Aurorean*, and nominated for the 2001 Pushcart Prize.

Roland B. Scott, a former Army officer and a retired attorney-at-law, lived in St. Croix for 24 years. He presently resides in New Mexico where he devotes time to reading historical and biographical works.

Marci Sellers is a retired professor of English from Erie Community College, Buffalo, NY. Her poems deal with connections in a multi-cultured world. Past works have appeared in *ELF*, *The Buffalo News*, *Lyric*, *Poetica*, and other publications.

Berkley Wendell Semple was born in Guyana and immigrated to the US where he is currently a school administrator in New York. He has previously published fiction in *The Chabot Review* and poems in *Callaloo*, *Votsee* and *The Caribbean Writer*.

Andrea Shaw was born and raised in Jamaica and now resides in South Florida where she is an M.F.A. student in Florida International University's Creative Writing Program. She is working on her first novel and has just completed a Ph.D. in English literature at the University of Miami.

Renee H. Shea, professor of English and Modern Languages at Bowie State University in Maryland, has published widely on Edwidge Danticat in *Poets and Writers Magazine*, *Macomere*, *The Journal of Haitian Studies*, and *Callaloo*. Guest editor for

MaComere in 2002, Renee has published articles on other Caribbean authors, including Zee Edgell, Marilene Phipps, and Michelle Cliff.

Sue William Silverman's memoir, *Because I Remember Terror, Father, I Remember You* (University of Georgia Press), won the AWP Award Series in creative nonfiction. Her second memoir, *Love Sick: One Woman's Journey Through Sexual Addiction* (Norton), is under development for a *Lifetime* television original movie.

Stephen F. Soitos is the author of *The Blues Detective: A Study of African-American Detective Fiction.* The book has won many awards as the first critical and historical survey of African Americans who worked in the mystery field. He has also authored three novels and has written many essays on African-American and Caribbean authors, art and culture.

Virgil Suárez, born in Havana, Cuba, arrived in the US at the age of twelve. He received an MFA from Louisiana State University and is the author of three new poetry collections, *Palm Crows* (University of Arizona Press), *Banyan* (Louisiana State University Press), and *Guide to the Blue Tongue* (University of Illinois Press). This year, *Infinite Refuge*, a memoir sequel to *Spared Angola*, was published by Arte Público Press, University of Houston.

Anne McCrary Sullivan teaches in Florida at the Tampa campus of National-Louis University. Her poems have appeared in many literary publications including *The Gettysburg Review*, *Southern Poetry Review*, and *Tar River Poetry*.

Marisella Veiga's poetry, fiction, and articles have appeared in various publications. She is a past recipient of The Daily News Prize from *The Caribbean Writer* and won an honorable mention from The Pushcart Prize. She is now working full-time as a freelance writer and living in Virginia.

Cassandra Ward-Shah teaches English at the University of Delaware and has published poems in *The Schuylkill Valley Journal* and *The Caribbean Writer.* She has new poems forthcoming in *The Hampden-Sydney Poetry Review.*

Erika J. Waters was formerly a professor of English at the University of the Virgin Islands, St. Croix, and has published articles and reviews on Caribbean literature for over 25 years. She co-edited *Critical Issues in West Indian Literature* (1984), edited *New Writing from the Caribbean* (1994), co-edited *Contemporary Drama of the Caribbean* (2001), and was the founding editor of *The Caribbean Writer*. She now lives in Maine and teaches part-time at the University of Southern Maine.

Clement White is a professor of Spanish/Latin American literature at the University of Rhode Island and Director of the Graduate Program in Spanish. He has published several articles, and poetic entries in *Sun Island Jewels, Pacific Stars* and *Stripes*, and *Yellow Cedars Blooming*. He is also the author of *Decoding the Word: Nicolás Guillén as Maker and Debunker of Myth, Wey Butty, and Networks of Spheres*.

Marvin E. Williams, from St. Croix, teaches at the University of the Virgin Islands. He edited *Yellow Cedars Blooming* (1998) and published a collection of his poems, *Dialogue at the Hearth* (1993). He is the current editor of *The Caribbean Writer*.

Research in African Literatures

Edited by John Conteh-Morgan

Research in African Literatures, the premier journal of African literary studies worldwide, serves as a stimulating vehicle in English for research on the oral and written literatures of Africa. *RAL* also provides information on African publishing as well as announcements of importance to Africanists, and it frequently prints notes and queries of literary interest. Special issues and clusters of articles reveal the broad interests of the readership.

VOLUME 35, NUMBER 2
HAITI, 1804–2004 LITERATURE, CULTURE, AND ART

Martin Munro
Can't Stand Up for Falling Down: Haiti, Its Revolution, and Twentieth-Century Negritudes

Nick Nesbitt
Troping Toussaint, Reading Revolution

Jean-François Brière
Abbé Grégoire and Haitian Independence

J. Michael Dash
Nineteenth-Century Haiti and the Archipelago of the Americas: Anténor Firmin's Letters from St. Thomas

Rafael Lucas
The Aesthetics of Degradation in Haitian Literature

Donette A. Francis
"Silences Too Horrific to Disturb": Writing Sexual Histories in Edwidge Danticat's *Breath, Eyes, Memory*

Cilas Kemedjio
Postcolonial Mythologies: Jean Metellus and the Writing of Charismatic Memory

Lizabeth Paravisini-Gebert
The Haitian Revolution in Interstices and Shadows: A Re-reading of Alejo Carpentier's *The Kingdom of This World*

George Lang
A Primer of Haitian Literature in Kreyòl

Jean Jonassaint
Beyond Painting or Writing Frankétienne's Poetic Quest

Subscription Information
Published quarterly; ISSN: 0034-5210
Subscriptions
Individuals, **$42.50**
Institutions, **$107.00**
African Instiutions, **$70.00**
Foreign surface postage to Africa, **$10.00**
Foreign surface postage elsewhere, **$14.00**
Foreign air mail postage, **$30.00**
Single issue price, **$13.95**
Single issue shipping, **$5.00**

Send Orders to:
Indiana University Press
Journals Division
601 North Morton Street
Bloomington, IN 47404 USA

Order by phone: **1-800-842-6796**
Fax orders to **1-812-855-8507**
Email: **journals@indiana.edu**

Order online at: **http://iupjournals.org**

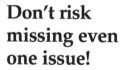

small axe
a caribbean journal of criticism

small axe
a caribbean journal of criticism

Small Axe focuses on the renewal of the
practices of intellectual criticism in the
Caribbean and includes fiction, nonfiction,
poetry, interviews, visual art and reviews.
Small Axe recognizes the tradition of social,
political, and cultural criticism in and about the
regional and diasporic Caribbean, and honors
that tradition. *Small Axe* provides a forum for
rethinking many of the conceptions that guided
the formation of Caribbean modernities and
an informed and sustained debate about the
present, its political and cultural contours, its
historical conditions and global context, and
the critical languages in which change can be
thought and alternatives re-imagined.

March 2004   15

Number 15, March 2004
Special Issue
Guyana: The Present against the Past

Subscription Information:
Two issues per year; ISSN: 0079-0537
Subscriptions: Individuals, $34.50
Institutions, $60.00
Foreign surface postage, $11.50
Foreign air mail postage, $23.00
Single issue price, $17.50
Single issue shipping, $5.00

Send Orders to:
Indiana University Press Journals Division
601 North Morton Street
Bloomington, IN 47404 USA
Order by phone call 1-800-842-6796
Fax orders to 1-812-855-8507
Email: journals@indiana.edu
Order online at: http://iupjournals.org

Best Wishes
to the
Caribbean Writer
on another
literary success!

VIRGIN ISLANDS
COMMUNITY BANK
WE ARE COMMUNITY

Virgin Islands Community Bank is incorporated as
Virgin Islands Community Bank Corp.

Equal
Opportunity
Lender

MEMBER F.D.I.C.

EQUAL HOUSING
LENDER

SUBMISSION GUIDELINES

Submit poems, short stories, personal essays and one-act plays. Only previously unpublished work will be accepted. (If self-published, give details.) Include brief biographical information. Put name, address, telephone number, email address and title of manuscript on separate sheet of paper. Title only on manuscript. Please note that manuscripts will not be returned unless accompanied by a SASE. Only authors of accepted works will be notified. Please mail submissions to:

The Caribbean Writer
University of the Virgin Islands
RR 02, Box 10,000
Kingshill, St. Croix
U. S. Virgin Islands 00850
OR
Email: **submit@thecaribbeanwriter.com**

Prizes Awarded for Volume 17

Berkley Wendell Semple
The Daily News Prize for
poetry

Opal Palmer Adisa
The Canute A. Brodhurst Prize
for short fiction

Michael Winston Bachoo
The Charlotte and Isidor
Paiewonsky Prize for first-
time publication

Willi Chen
The David Hough Literary
Prize for an author residing in
the Caribbean

Winston Nugent
The Marguerite Cobb McKay
Prize for a Virgin Islands author